REACHING FOR PARADISE

REACHING
FOR
PARADISE

*The Playboy Vision
of America*

THOMAS WEYR

Times
BOOKS

Published by TIMES BOOKS, a division
of Quadrangle/The New York Times Book Co., Inc.
Three Park Avenue, New York, N. Y. 10016
Published simultaneously in Canada by
Fitzhenry & Whiteside, Ltd., Toronto
Copyright © 1978 by Thomas Weyr

Library of Congress Cataloging in Publication Data

Weyr, Thomas.
Reaching for paradise.

Includes index.
1. Playboy. I. Title.
PN4900.P5W4   1978   051   78-58170
ISBN 0-8129-0795-7

Manufactured in the United States of America

For Tara and Sascha
Who waited so patiently and so impatiently

Contents

Aviso

THIS is an outsider's book about a social and cultural American phenomenon: *Playboy* magazine and the entertainment conglomerate it spawned, and how they in turn influenced their times and mores. It does not pretend to any intimacy, personal or otherwise, with Hugh Marston Hefner, the owner, or any of his minions; save perhaps for a disputatious, and sometimes irritable, relationship with the editor, Arthur Kretchmer.

The author came to *Playboy* as the virgin to the child—with absolute innocence. Until he tackled this project, *Playboy* lay at the far edge of his horizon and experience. He had heard of the magazine in the fifties, perhaps seen it in a barber shop—a place where a large number of men still profess today to read it—and had a friend who was once offered a job on it, which he turned down. What New York editor in those days would want to live in Chicago?

The first realization that people he actually knew read *Playboy* came in 1963 on his return from four years of reporting in Eastern and Central Europe. His wife discovered that her brother, the general manager of a medical-research company in Virginia, was a subscriber. She was not a prude. As a reporter abroad, she had once posed as a prostitute to get a story. But this was different.

"I thought only truck drivers and bus conductors read it," she said plaintively. "But he has *Playboy* in his house regularly, where his wife and children can see it." She thought for a moment, and then added loyally, "I'm sure he buys it for the articles. The issue I looked at had this very interesting interview with Malcolm X in it and had a lot more information than *Time* or *Newsweek.*" She did not sound convinced.

The author wasn't, either. A short while back, there had been an acrimonious debate with his brother-in-law about John F. Kennedy's sexual habits. They were, the brother-in-law insisted, as pure as the driven snow, and any suggestion of hanky-panky involving the president of the United States was an outrage. "I don't care if you were a reporter in Washington in the fifties or say you knew girls whose bottoms he pinched. Reporters don't know everything. Girls lie." Of course, one knew what such outrage hid. Articles, my foot.

The realization that there were such things as Playboy Clubs dawned in 1964 when the author wrote the early-morning news for a radio network. A colleague appeared early one morning bombed out of his mind, giggling about bunnies, and waving a key in a futile effort to draw suggestive shapes in midair. "Man, the Playboy Club. Woof. Bunnies. It is something else!" He hiccuped and sat vacant-eyed before his typewriter. The author's first association with the Playboy Club, therefore, was writing *four* newscasts that morning instead of two.

The girl was blond, pretty, and fat. The fat was still firm, and she wore her large breasts high. Conversation was a little stiff, as befits old lovers who have not seen each other in some time. It was 1965 on the terrace of the Red Bar at the Hotel Sacher in Vienna. He had courted her in Baroque churches and helped her translate Yeats into German. She was married now, to an Austrian. Her first husband had been American, a genius physicist with a 200 IQ, but quite mad.

"Would you buy me a subscription to *Playboy?*" she asked. "You can't get it here, and Hansjoerg is mad for it."

Now he was outraged. "Aren't yours big enough?"

"Yes," she said evenly. "That's why he likes to look at others. Besides, I like to read it. It's a better link to the America I knew than *The New Yorker.*" She had met her husband at Michigan and had lived in the Midwest.

A year later, he was in Chicago, having, in a burst of greed, abandoned journalism for public relations, to promote the visit of an Austrian minister of finance. In Chicago you could do a lot better with a talking dog who barked. In despair, he called a *Time* correspondent, a friend from cold war days in Vienna and Berlin. The *Time* man could not have cared less about the Austrian minister. He was engaged to marry a *Playboy* cartoon editor, had been to the Playboy mansion, and had met Hefner. "He's an interesting guy and runs a better magazine than people give him credit for." Sure. Sure. Hope you'll be very happy. You *are* coming to this damn press conference? He did not. But the thought that "one of us" took "that magazine" seriously, lingered.

There was other flotsam of information around. The occasional article in *Life, Look,* or the *Saturday Evening Post.* Someone said that Oriana Fallaci had actually interviewed Hefner, that Tom Wolfe had taken him down a peg or two. He does his business on a round bed, you know. No, no, you don't understand—not that—I mean that too, I suppose, but he conducts his business from his bed. And it turns.

Playboy, the book publisher said in the early seventies, has reach. It touches lives. For example, did you know that *Playboy* is very popular in India? Oh, not because of the nudes. They have better erotica. But the ads for consumer goods. It dazzles them. The magazine is passed from hand to hand, almost with reverence. And did you know, he continued, that Hefner's business practices are really very, very conservative? He owns the land underneath the Playboy Club on 59th Street and company expansion is financed internally, not with borrowed money. Everybody borrows these days.

"Sure, I read *Playboy,* " the old man's grandson said on the lawn of a waterfront estate in the Hamptons in the mid-seventies. He poked his finger around in his martini. "I liked it. It had style and a sense of pacing. There was a way of life in it I could identify with. Hip. Now. Not like this, exactly." He gestured at the manicured lawns and the houses on the compound and at the water rocking gently into the shore. "At Princeton, *Playboy* made a splash. It told me what I wanted to know then." Playboy in Scott Fitzgerald country? In East Egg? Preposterous.

The kid was maybe sixteen or seventeen, and he had come to clean up the yard of a country house. Now he stood in the living room and gazed at a huge stack of *Playboy* magazines that teetered perilously on a round and shaky table. "Someday," the kid said with awe in his voice—real awe, no sarcasm—"I'd like a library like that. I bet you do a lot of reading."

A flea market on a Saturday morning in rural New Jersey. Among the blue glass, broken furniture trying, forlornly, to pass as antiques, pots and pans, stacks of old *Playboy*s from the sixties are on sale for 25 cents each. In a magazine warehouse on 19th Street in New York, a 1967 issue retails for $3.50. A junk shop on Columbus Avenue displays old magazines in boxes. *Playboy* cost 25 cents to start, but when the Hispanic owner saw the armful of magazines he had just sold, he raised the price to 35 cents. "That's a lot of womens you got there," he said with a leer.

The only complete set of *Playboy* on the East Coast, from the first issue in December 1953 on, is in the rare book collection of the

Library of Congress. Despite the protective railing, the register that must be signed to gain entry, the careful eye of the congressional retainers, pictures of early Playmates are missing. How had they been spirited through all that security, and why?

It is the same story at the New York Public Library, whose *Playboy* collection only goes back to 1964. The tattered volumes may be read only behind the counters where books are given out. Again there are half a dozen pairs of watchful eyes—and missing pictures.

But no one tore out the text and there, marching across the decades, was an awesome collection of names, the making of any college course in contemporary American literature. Bellow, Mailer, Updike, Cheever, Nabokov, Nelson Algren, Roth, Malamud, Isaac Bashevis Singer. Well, sure, the fiction is always good. Spectorsky saw to that. And then Robie Macauley. He used to edit *Kenyon Review.* Maybe her brother hadn't just been looking at the big knockers.

"And you think the women's magazines aren't sexist?" A literary agent now, she was shouting into the phone at a young client who did not want his prose in *Playboy.* A lot of the younger writers felt that these days, she sighed to herself.

"But it *is* sexist," the writer said defensively. "It shows women as objects, and all that hard sell on consumerism."

"Sure," she said soothingly, "it is sexist. You're right. It exploits women. But what magazine doesn't? You think *Partisan Review* is all that clean? No, it isn't the money. *Playboy* is simply the best showcase for your stories in the country. It's the place that will do you the most good."

The writer remained unconvinced.

"All right, I'll do it," the weary author said after his agent had haggled out a high enough advance with the publisher. "But what makes you think Hefner will see me? His company has had a terrible press lately."

"He'll love it," the publisher said. "No one has taken him seriously before. Besides, New York is full of people who used to work for *Playboy.*"

Hefner both loved the idea and did not love the idea—once he had heard about it. That took a while. Getting to see him took longer. As the author read and later learned, Hefner is more inaccessible than the president of the United States, and proud of it. A passing acquaintance with Kafka's novels helps in understanding the process. So does adult exposure to *The Wizard of Oz.* Ring the bell to *Playboy*'s castle and you are at once under suspicion, on trial, denied entrance, submitted to rigorous questioning. And pressured to confess. What? Ah. Aha!

Until he was fired in the fall of 1977, a man named Lee Gottlieb was the gatekeeper, or, more in tune with the times, the vice-president in charge of public relations. He plays a superb game of Kafka. A grand master. Finally, after four months of stalling, the gates of the Playboy Building in Chicago, the former Colgate-Palmolive Tower, swing open.

The scenery on the tenth-floor editorial office is appropriate: It resembles the set for Robert Wiene's *The Cabinet of Dr. Caligari.* Not surprisingly, Arthur Paul, the art director from the first issue on, graduated from the Chicago Institute of Design at a time when Weimar refugees dominated the staff. Study *Playboy*'s art work, and the influence of German expressionism becomes unmistakable. Paul also likes Michelangelo and Norman Rockwell. "He's putting you on," Hefner will say later. "They are not the greatest artistic influences on his life."

Managing editor Sheldon Wax puffs a contemplative pipe and answers sixty questions in sixty minutes. Few answers are longer than ten words.

Editorial director Arthur Kretchmer is more loquacious—and the first shock. Lean, tall, thick glasses, unruly black hair, a face like Belmondo and a voice like Chivers English marmalade. He could have been at Kronstadt or stormed through the Winter Palace as an extra in Pudovkin's *The Last Days of St. Petersburg.* Jeans, workshirt, boots. Too much uncontrolled passion to be Kafka.

"Who the fuck do you think you are, coming in here with a clipboard and asking questions?"

The Wicked Witch of the East bellowing at the cowardly lion? It helps to do your homework. Nothing soothes the enraged breast of an editorial director quite as readily as someone who picks out the thing he cares for the most. Why, for example, did *Playboy* run a Max Lerner piece in 1966 that advocated admission of Red China to the United Nations? The reputations of brothers-in-law must be upheld. But it is the open sesame to a discussion of politics and social affairs and what role *Playboy* has played in them.

Fire burns in Kretchmer's belly. He cares, cares desperately about almost everything in a decade when few bother to care at all. He believes in the magazine. It is the most important magazine published in America. It disdains seat belts, safety, convention, or caution. "*Playboy* is serious about the right to live life untrammeled."

After that, the journey to Oz took another ten months. Robert Preuss, Hefner's college roommate and the company's business manager and chief operating officer for nearly twenty years, peered suspiciously through air force glasses and revealed only what was already in print, even though he had already been eased out of *Playboy* when the conversation took place.

Richard Rosenzweig, the executive vice-president, tried to charm over a lunch at the Drake in Chicago. The first impression is Sammy Glick, but then it doesn't fit. There is nothing fake in his sincerity and loyalty. Rosenzweig loves Playboy Enterprises, Inc. He believes in the goodness of this corporation as much as Kretchmer seems to disdain all corporations, perhaps even including his own.

Nat Lehrman, newly minted as publisher in 1976, is more circumspect and has a clearer bead on the problems at the publishing end. He had climbed up the editorial ladder at *Playboy* to assistant managing editor, then had become editor and publisher of *Oui, Playboy*'s sister publication. Now he talks knowledgeably about pushing *Playboy* into the 7–11 chains and other convenience stores. "I am going after audiences anywhere I can find them. Magazines have to adapt or die."

For a while, it seemed as if Victor Lownes III would prove to be the good fairy on the Yellow Brick Road. He has known Hefner intimately for twenty years, and he looks the Playboy part. Loose, relaxed, the confidence of family money on him. Lownes runs the clubs, casinos, and hotels. His London gambling operations kept Playboy solvent during the economic crunch of the mid-seventies. He wears expensive jeans with the same elegance he once did Brooks Brothers suits.

Lownes arranges an introduction to Hefner in Chicago. Everything seemed to go swimmingly—but didn't. There were complications that took another six months to resolve. "Heavy" memos from his staff. Letters back and forth. Demands for control over the book. Finally, an interview with Hefner's poised, bright, impressive, and astonishingly pretty daughter, Christie, the heiress-apparent, who gave her stamp of approval, and arranged things with confident dispatch.

At last, on a sunny California afternoon in January, the towers of Oz. They are not readily accessible. You drive east on Sunset Boulevard from the entrance to Bel Air. Charing Cross Road comes up suddenly on the right and plunges over a bump downhill. It is narrow and twisting. Thick foliage climbs up the hills on both sides. The clatter of traffic fades abruptly, as if a soundproof door had slammed shut. The tall lances of a wrought-iron gate appear. Look into the eye of the camera. Identify yourself loudly.

"Just a moment, sir," a voice says from far away.

Silence. Stone vases peek through trees. Terraced green lawns. Pieces of gray are latticed among the leaves.

"Sorry to keep you waiting, sir."

The gates swing open in electronic silence. Weave up a serpentine roadway. The gray mansion swims into view on the left. Tall chimneys, slate roof, battlements, bits of ivy on the walls. A circular fountain sits in a pool rimmed with flagstones and flowerbeds. Holmby Hills. The Playboy Mansion West and the seat of empire. Lines are fluid and move with grace. The house sparkles with the life and personality that only very good buildings have.

Walk through a vaulted hall with carved wooden ceilings and into Hefner's "baronial" living room. It is more splendid than merely baronial, for all of Hefner's love of the word, and has the dimension of formal rooms in Viennese palaces: Schwarzenberg, Kinsky, Pallavicini, Lobkowitz. The library is a small room off the salon. Two windows: one on the courtyard, the other onto a lush green valley. Bookcases flank a fireplace. Leatherbound volumes of *Playboy*. An encyclopedia. A collection of crime stories edited by Ray Russell, Hefner's first editorial hand. Playboy Press paperbacks. Mostly jokes, cartoons, games. Frank Brady's biography, *Hefner*, in hard- and soft-cover. Rollo May's *Love and Will*, with its savage criticism of *Playboy*. A long, brown-gold striped couch under the valley window. Three chocolate-colored club chairs around a coffee table of heavy, dark-stained wood.

Suddenly Hefner glides into the room, as if he had just alighted from a bird. He is smaller and slighter than his public image. Dark blue pajamas, matching robe. A dazzling smile lights up the corners and planes of his face as if it were a chandelier. "Hello, there."

A tape deck with scooter-wheels is mounted on the wall next to the couch. Hefner reached over to a paneled door next to it and reveals a liquor cabinet, glasses, refrigerator. He takes a Pepsi out of the icebox. My God, he *does* drink the stuff. Tapes move, red needles flick in obedience to the sound of voices. Hefner's face is young, shining, vibrant. Edges are blurred, lines softened. Wrinkles barely crack the surface of his skin. He could be thirty. Less. He ages as the afternoon wears on. Suddenly everything about him is pinched and sharp. He looks all of fifty and more. And then his face smoothes into youth again. The picture of Dorian Gray with youth restored over and over by this Shangri-la on the Pacific.

The literary allusions all fit *Playboy* and what it has become. Oscar Wilde's confident and self-possessed elegance was part of *Playboy*'s striving; so was the fairy-tale humor and childish defiance of wicked witches that marked *The Wizard of Oz*. *Playboy* wanted to be known for its elegance, its savoir faire, its wit and disdain of convention. The magazine was very much what Hefner, in his youthful dreams of himself, wanted it to be: the documentation of dreams fulfilled. He was the elegant swordsman stepped down from the epic films of the thirties; an Errol Flynn, a Douglas Fairbanks, Jr., equally adept in drawing rooms and bedrooms; and he was also the righteous crusader, the Jimmy Stewart and Gary Cooper striding down the corridors of power to confront and defy injustice and corruption. And right in the middle of playing the knowing man of the world or the shining idealist, there is the sudden "cut"—and a wink at his pals as if to say, "Get a load of me in this getup."

At the University of Illinois, Hefner had contributed to the humor magazine, *Shaft,* and some of the flavor that marked the early *Playboy* was of a college humor magazine—a little zany, irreverent, and terribly know-it-all, especially about sex. And because it was so knowing about women and how to bed them, it became an organ of rebellion, at times of political rebellion.

In the early fifties, politics had begun to wither. The McCarthy years gave the young this unmistakable message: If you want to prosper and succeed, stay away from politics—especially liberal or left-wing politics. One result was the emergence of sex as a surrogate for politics. Sex became a way of expressing opposition to the status quo; and by embracing the concept of sex as not only a moral good but a moral imperative, *Playboy* offered collegians a chance to express themselves and to oppose their elders, and to do so without endangering future careers. At *Playboy,* you could have your cake and eat it, too.

Earlier than most, Hefner recognized that the cake out there for the eating was larger than it had ever been—and was growing year by year. The United States was entering the promised land; twenty years of unmatched prosperity and affluence—if not for all, then for so many that the rest could be ignored safely. People were making more money than they ever dreamed they would or intended to make. The G.I. Bill flooded campuses with millions of young men who had never expected to go to college and who were the first in their families to do so. They came from homes without reading traditions, and for the most part went to universities bent on the substance of education—and the employment that could be derived from it—and not on cultivating a style of life to go with it.

"Hefner copped the new demographics very well," author David Halberstam says. "Go to an Eastern school and you learn style as well as substance, how to talk and how to read and how to drink wine. That wasn't true in the Midwest. As a result, *Playboy* readers wanted to know about couth things—from wine on up—that had been the provenance of the upper classes and, due to the country's rising educational level, had come into their reach."

Hefner and *Playboy* told people what to do and how to do it well. They were didactic taskmasters. Hefner himself had excelled in design at art school, but not in figure drawing. He knew good design. Simple lines and forms. His graphic vision goes back to Weimar and Dessau, to the instructional masters of the Bauhaus who taught the denizens of the "modern" era how to live their lives by designing houses and furniture, crockery and glasses, parks and playgrounds, pictures and statues. The Bauhaus was the first designer of life-styles. *Playboy* became an enthusiastic disciple.

By the turbulent and affluent sixties, *Playboy* had become an American institution, as typical for its time and place as the *Saturday Evening Post.* Bunnies with their bulging bosoms and pleasantly empty faces reflected a new ritual as accurately as Norman Rockwell's covers did the reality of small-town America. The hard contours and burnt-orange earth tones of Playboy Clubs and "pads" were guidelines to a new elegance and style for millions vaguely dispirited by the neon and plastic garishness of highway and airport. The *Playboy* life-style, which Hefner sold with the unrelenting vigor of the Music Man hitting River City, had become a serious social force and an important factor of commerce. Madison Avenue spotted the magazine's pulling power and became its evangelizer among the shakers and shapers of the consumer society. Hefner's "philosophy" triggered a national debate on the relevance of traditional sexual morality. And in that debate Hefner became, if not the American sexual revolution's Jesus Christ, a role Norman Mailer had preempted, then surely its St. Paul, the didactic popularizer of a tempered hedonism-as-religion.

But it does not take much to push evangelical fervor into paranoia. The world of Franz Kafka was never far off the Playboy stage, and it strode onto those boards in the wake of the Yom Kippur War. Playboy's economics turned sour in the early seventies, and the oil embargo and the energy crisis that followed the 1973 war questioned every premise on which the Playboy life-style rested. It is a high-energy life-style, dependent on electricity and the internal combustion engine. Question it, and the foundation of a $200 million empire is threatened. And questioned it was by the hard realities of the marketplace. Sales plummeted; profits faded; circulation slid. Even worse, Hefner became enmeshed in a federal drug probe. His executive secretary, Bobbie Arnstein, committed suicide. Executive heads rolled. Near-panic gripped the mansions and the Playboy Towers. The brash conglomerate turned into a brooding "Castle" suffused with a desperate seriousness, paranoid, defensive, alive to the enemy all around it, haggard with plots and counterplots.

Yet through all the times of crisis, *Playboy* never lost the giddy quality of Oz or that brave touch of the talkies in the 1930s when Hefner believed that "movies were as real as real life" and "the stuff that dreams are made of." He sold the stuff of dreams as a merchant of dry goods, but he never huckstered them with the unfeeling competence of a Disney, to whose organization Playboy is often—and wrongly, the author thinks—compared. Hefner's dreams were always concrete, affordable, within reach of the masses, limited, even a little narrow. He has in him pieces of both the real wizard with his feet of clay, and of the wizard Dorothy imagines; he is both charlatan and saint, a combination Americans have always found irresistible.

What has marked the growth, decline, and resurgence of Hefner's empire are ambivalence, ambiguity, and contradiction, qualities present in abundance during periods of swift and savage change like the present. Hefner rode the tides of change to wealth and power, but he also helped to channel, civilize, and control change; and not only in matters of sex, the fountainhead of his reputation, but in style, taste, and thought.

This book is about *Playboy* and change. About where and how *Playboy* influenced society and where and how it did not. How it came to be no longer something read secretly or pugnaciously or with shame, or that one would question the well-educated brother's reading. How it made nudity respectable and sex something of a bore—there is, after all, a limit to one's tolerance of sermons, no matter how salacious the text. And finally, how it touched the lives of millions.

It is also about the mutations of empire—the changes in the changer. How Hefner froze at the controls and let his ship buck and heave in the storm before reaching calmer waters. It is about dreams and ambitions achieved, and almost destroyed.

REACHING FOR PARADISE

1

The State of the Art

The most popular men's magazines of the time were the
outdoor-adventure books—*True, Argosy* and the like. They
had a hairy-chested editorial emphasis with articles on
hunting, fishing, chasing the Abominable Snowman over
Tibetan mountaintops. . . . *Esquire* had changed its editorial
emphasis after the war, eliminating most of the lighter
material—the girls, cartoons and humor. So the field was
wide open for the sort of magazine I had in mind . . .

———from Hugh Hefner's interview with *Playboy* in the
twentieth-anniversary issue

In the early 1950s, the world was waiting for Hugh Hefner—or for
someone just like him. The magazine market needed a modern Candide or Don Quixote to fill the gap between the blood and gore of
most men's magazines and the sleazy sex of under-the-counter
books, some wide-eyed youngster for whom life melted on the tongue
like fresh milk and honey, someone wooly-headed enough to take the
risks others dared not take. Sex in conventional men's books was a
tame sidekick to adventure. *Life* and *Look* took care of sexual titillation in the mass market. And *Esquire,* which once had had the
prurience market to itself, was back-pedaling furiously, much to
Hefner's youthful disgust. Its patina of urban sophistication and
naughty sex had first attracted the young Midwesterner to magazines, but the year he worked on it was a bitter disappointment:
Esquire had hitched up its brow and was no longer interested in the

"ogling Eskie" look that had marked the thirties and the war.

Founding editor Arnold Gingrich had returned from a postwar sojourn in Europe determined on "the rescue of *Esquire* from bawditry." The pinup phase, he felt, "had distorted its original character." And although the rescue operation had not been completed when Hefner's brash product first hit the market, it was far enough along to make "the *Playboy* difference" stand out.

But for all the growing disdain of its own sedate sex, *Esquire* had pioneered the genre of magazine Hugh Hefner would lead to such huge popularity—and not only by leaving an empty market space waiting to be filled. During its bawdy period—and the word "bawdy" should be seen in the context of much tamer times—*Esquire* had tilted often with the Post Office, for so long the censorial arm of the U.S. government. In the mid-forties, the magazine had won a significant test case assuring its right of passage through the mails. In the years that followed, the Post Office often ignored the precedents, but won much less often in the courts. It became clear that anyone with the guts to fight unreasonable obscenity charges was likely to prevail.

But for most men's magazines in the early fifties, the Post Office was not much of a problem. They did little subscription business and made their money on newsstand sales, a lesson Hefner never forgot. Nor was sex ever a newsstand come-on then. The kind of yarn that drew readers, says *Seventeen* managing editor Ray Robinson, a men's-book veteran of the fifties, could be summed up in titles like "How I Fought a Polar Bear Underwater off Fire Island and Found God." The magazines, Robinson adds, "were full of blood, guts, and fighting. They didn't pay much attention to women. Women were like bullpen pitchers; doing something, but not called on much."

Robinson earned his spurs in Martin Goodman's Magazine Management Company, which published across the male spectrum: action, adventure, mild sex, and comic books. Its behavior, mannerisms, and peccadilloes were typical for the men's magazine industry in the 1950s. Moreover, Magazine Management trained and fed an extraordinary and successful group of editors and writers who blossomed to prominence in the sixties and seventies. They include Robinson, Bruce Jay Friedman, Mario Puzo, Dick Kaplan of the *Ladies Home Journal,* William Robbins of *Redbook,* James A. Bryans, Bernard Geis, and Don Fine, publisher of Arbor House.

All of them remember their experiences more or less fondly. Though grossly underpaid, they were encouraged to moonlight for other magazines in the chain and were paid $250 for a 5,000-word story. For years World War II was fought over and over on a simple formula of death-defying action and tame sex. In a 1975 *Rolling*

Stone article, Bruce Jay Friedman recalls how he and his writers made up "entirely new bombing raids" and created battles that "had turned the tide against the Axis and brought Hitler to his knees." The master of that particular genre, Friedman notes, was Mario Puzo, "who would create giant mythical armies, lock them in combat in Central Europe and have casualties coming in by the hundreds of thousands."

Puzo himself retains a special affection for his Goodman years. "I earned only a couple of hundred a week, but I boosted my income to as much as $2,000 by writing pieces for $600 each. I created a whole new battle for Berlin, for example. There were only 6,000 casualties on D day, but in my battles there were hundreds of thousands. In a way, I'm prouder of those battle stories than my other writing. They required greater imagination."

Jim Bryans calls Goodman's merchandise "sweaty-armpits men's magazines." Their selling points, he says, were escape, adventure, survival, and fantasy about war, "all purported to be true." For Noah Sarlat, a thirty-year men's-book veteran still with Magazine Management (where he edits tame *Playboy* imitators today), "ours were hair-on-the-chest books, men against nature, the elements, survival, and war stories. We had nine men's books—not as slick as *True,* but aimed at blue-collar workers with high-school diplomas, veterans, and guys still in the service—the Korean War was on then."

A quick look at the 1952 contents tables of *Men,* one of the magazines Sarlat edited, confirms his point: "Deserted Stalin's Red Army—Sensational Adventures of an Ex-Russian GI"; "Shipwrecked in Communist Korea"; "Tug of War Off Pusan—a True Korean Adventure"; "Typhoon—It'll Be a Hell of a Long Time Before the U.S. Navy Forgets Oct. 8, 1945—the Day the China Sea Went Berserk."

Sports were handled in the same, tough, breathless style. "How Gentleman Jim Took John L." was a yarn "as told to Ray Robinson," while a similar feature took off on the battle between Bob Fitzsimmons and Jim Jeffries. Adventure, crime, the outdoors, and some fiction fleshed out the editorial package.

Finally, in each issue of *Men* there was one major sex takeout—part of an endless series on "sin cities" in the United States. "The editors would pick a town, say Houston, San Diego, or San Francisco," Bryans says, "and start the reader off with a walk down such-and-such street where B-girls congregated. It was the most inexplicit sex imaginable. The piece titillated by warning readers to stay away from X Street and its sinful fleshpots. It had a righteous tone about it, a kind of prurient Victorian approach."

In March 1952, for example, *Men* focused on "Frisco—Gateway to Sin." Readers were warned that "not even Frisco's natives believe they'll ever get rid of their hopheads, lushes and prostitutes." In June, *Men* went after "Sin on Top of the World: The Shameful Story of Anchorage, Alaska." In September, *Men* said that "Anything Goes in Fresno" and documented the claim with this caption under a picture of a man walking up some seedy stairs: "Rooming houses do not question girls, who register with several different 'husbands' a night."

Even the sweatiest-armpit books in Goodman's stable ran four or five pages of standard cheesecake every issue. The material was plentiful, since Goodman also owned a couple of pinup magazines, *Eye* and *Foto,* which subsisted on a solid cheesecake diet. Both were more "tame" than "wild" and kept a warier eye on conventional morality than on titillation. Goodman himself made sure of that.

The "art" was brought from the hundreds of photo agencies in mid-Manhattan, but very few of the pictures got past Goodman in their pristine form. The owner, his former editors agree, had a thing about nipples: He was deathly afraid one might show up in print. And he was a virtual Anthony Comstock when it came to even a hint of female genitalia—say, a strand of pubic hair showing beyond the crotch of a bathing suit. Goodman's caution, so extreme in retrospect, had very real roots in the times. The fifties were fearful, and not only because of the tentacles McCarthyism spread into every aspect of American life. A man like Goodman, who had a comic-book emporium as part of his business, was beset by a threatening society on all sides. He had to be careful. He couldn't risk offending community standards, however outlandish.

"There was great fear," Bryans says, "of the government just coming in and saying, 'We'll take your business away and throw you in jail.' "

Every time some small town cracked down on a newsstand for selling what it considered an "obscene" Goodman product, that fear sprang into new flame.

"We used to call Goodman's lawyer 'Settling Sam,' " Bryans remembers. "He'd come in and say, 'Martin, we've got to settle' whenever an obscenity charge came up."

"It was a local censorship problem," Sarlat recalls. "You could run into a crusading D.A., or a little old lady in a supermarket would raise hell with her priest, and the church was off on an antivice rampage to run your magazine out of town."

Features on exotic places in Asia and Africa were the one exception to the non-nipple rule. *Focus* and *Foto* simply followed *National Geographic*'s lead and printed pictures of bare-breasted natives, though never bothering to match the respectable magazine's photographic quality. For people turned off by coarse and grainy pictures, there was always the high gloss and sophistication of *Life,* a much sexier magazine than its P.R. image projected. A summer 1953 cover showed starlet Terry Moore sitting in the California surf, her colored shirt soaked and properly revealing. At times, *Life* even published nudes, and they were less stilted than those in arty photography magazines. *Life* simply had the best photographers around.

By and large, however, nudes were the province of "photography" magazines which dressed the pictures as art. Nymphets with raised arms stood in sylvan glades as morning sunlight poured through treetops and slowly burned the morning mist from some lovely's barely visible nipples. Poses were awkward and stiff—rigid in their determination to keep the male animal quiescent. Some were copies from great art in expectation that a Titian tilt would take the curse off naked flesh.

The fifties did have more explicit sex books than art and cheesecake, though they were hardly comparable to the hardware of the seventies—"feelthy" postcards hot off the *Liberté* or the *Queen Mary* excepted. Typical of the genre were Bob Harrison's *Whisper* and *Titter,* money-makers both, whose proceeds Harrison used to launch *Confidential,* the hottest scandal sheet of the fifties. *Whisper* and *Titter* featured a lot of French underwear, spiked heels, and the occasional whip, but little outright nudity—quite a trick given the depth to which cameras were pushed down a tart's cleavage to reveal acres of leprous flesh. At best—or worst—nipples were seen as shadows.

What made these magazines fit the moral tone of the times so well was their attitude and message: Sex was foul and dirty. It had to be, with those smirking faces and puffy bodies bent into poses designed to match the "provocative" image inexperienced men had of brothels and their inmates. The women shown in such magazines denigrated the act and banned it to the outhouse, where a man beating his meat would feel little joy, but only disgust with himself and for what he was doing. There was such empty sin in those pictures; the bovine faces, the vacuous eyes touched with lazy scorn, the black lips that glowed like scars on pasty complexions. In that world of black-and-white horror, intercourse was the wrath of God personified; men condemned in a circle of Dante's inferno to perpetual coition—or masturbation. The stuff was dirty—good and dirty.

Playboy hit that lineup like a bottle of charged water. Editors at other books gaped unbelievingly at Hefner's daring and insouciance.

For Friedman, "*Playboy* was a quantum leap in the other direction. It changed everything. It was the big-league sex breakthrough."

"*Playboy* had national impact, and people started talking about it right away," says *Seventeen*'s Robinson. "We were interested professionally—and shocked because it was so daring in dealing with the female body," Bryans says.

Like most of his colleagues, Sarlat wondered just how long Hefner could stay out of jail. "I was sure they'd get him on a censorship rap for violating some local ordinance or badger him out of business somehow. We were all impressed by his guts, but mostly we speculated on his future—or his lack of one."

What companies like Magazine Management did do, however, and very quickly, was to launch *Playboy* imitators or to swing some of their existing cheesecake books more sharply into Hefner's wake.

"When *Playboy* made its presence felt, Goodman became very concerned," Bryans remembers, "because he was afraid it might wipe everybody else out. He reacted with *Swank,* but he was chicken about spending money."

Friedman, who was working for Bryans at the time, was pulled off *Focus* to edit *Swank,* but concedes that although the "magazine attempted to be classy and risqué," it failed "to set the world on fire . . . *Playboy* and its legion of imitators in the lit-clit field were beginning to throw their weight around. Risqué was not enough."

Besides, Goodman never did go all the way pictorially.

Hefner, did, or anyway, appeared to. The mix he served up in his first issue in late 1953 was an artful blend of innovation and tried-and-true. He admits that *Playboy* was the "son of *Esquire*" when it first appeared, but he also feels he developed a new product. "The basic premise was new, and you did not find any social sexual values in *Esquire* at all."

Clearly the basic formula was copied from *Esquire:* bawdy jokes, cartoons, risqué humor, quality fiction, fashion. *Playboy*'s centerfold, too, was in the men's-book tradition: girls draped over furniture or on rugs with double-entendre captions. Admittedly, the missing bathing suit did make the difference stand out, but everybody needs at least one gimmick.

That isn't quite fair, of course, but Hefner was more interested in cultivating a garden than in exploring new wildernesses. And, on balance, his genius emerged more fully in the repackaging than in the innovation, though he knew how to give the new wrapping an innovative touch.

Nowhere was this talent more apparent than in the focus of the first issue, the "gimmick" that made Hefner a star: Marilyn Monroe's nude calendar pose.

Hefner had enough experience in the magazine business by then to realize that every issue—but especially a first one—needed a flash of lightning to galvanize public attention. For a while he thought about grouping his magazine around the "3-D" fad that enjoyed a brief vogue in the early fifties. He would include tinted glasses in each issue and the nude could be seen in three dimensions, just as 3-D films could in theaters. He even had some early test shots taken. Then he saw an item in a trade paper about the Monroe calendar. There was a lot of publicity about the nude shots by then. *Life* had even published a stamp-size takeout in a MM cover story, but nobody was reproducing the calendar in full in legitimate publications.

"There were really two Marilyn Monroe calendars," Hefner remembers. "One is sort of a long side-shot, and the other was a seated picture, and we ran that as the first playmate."

What he had found in the newspaper item was the fact that the Baumgarth calendar company in a Chicago suburb owned the rights to the pictures. Hefner tumbled into his creaking Chevy coupe and drove out to Melrose Park. When he returned, he had the rights not only to the Monroe picture but to half a dozen other nude studies as well—and the whole package had cost him $500.

Even by current standards of much greater bodily explicitness and far superior color reproduction, the Monroe picture was sensational. The provocation lay in the sly pose of the body, the mischievous grin, the rich, ruby-red drape that formed the background and lent a Rubens touch to the composition. Monroe had that Rubens feeling to her body, even if the contours had been dieted and exercised into the more angular shape demanded of twentieth-century love Goddesses.

But what heightened the picture's impact was the quality of the persona. Those who looked at the photograph of a pretty girl trying to pick up a few bucks in 1949 to pay the rent, were seeing in 1953–54 a great star who sashayed across the screen promising in every wiggle bedroom delights unseen since Mae West and Jean Harlow. And the dress was off!

There she was, nipples stiff enough to touch, rib cage jutting out over her sucked-in tummy, the great hollow of her belly button, the curve of flesh that hinted at the paradise of pubic hair, a dark shadow of hidden bliss. One eye was buried in her arm; the other winked an invitation. White teeth and red lips formed a smile that might coo come hither—or anything imagination could concoct.

Could text add anything to such a picture beyond a meaningless leer? Hefner's prose did. He was good at counterpunching myth, at taking face-value acceptance and rearranging the pieces so that old information sounded new, fresh, vital, important. In this case, Hefner was out to challenge a reader's perception, to debunk the star's halo—a little, anyway—and to impart the secrets he knew.

Monroe's figure was not the key to her mystique, he wrote. Other women had better bodies, though he was not, of course, disparaging her 37-inch bust, just pointing out that other women had more imposing measurements. The secret lay in the mythology she had become, her enshrinement in Hollywood's pantheon of the gods, "as natural sex personified." And how had she gotten there? Well, Hefner had a few ideas:

"What makes Marilyn the undisputed love Goddess of this particular generation? Publicity is the most obvious answer. Nobody climbs to stardom without a healthy boost from the rear by a Grade-A publicity man. In this case there were two—Harry Brandon and Ray Craft . . ."

Never mind that this was fan-book material available on every newsstand. In Hefner's hands, no matter how pompous the prose, it radiated the authority of deep conviction; anything he touched did. And because he believed in the freshness and originality of what he said, he made others into believers. His was the sincerity that makes converts.

He also had the packager's eye for the wrappings that would suit the nude best and the trader's instinct for buying well, cheaply. The editorial content of the first issue cost only $2,000—partly because publishers would not sell him the Hemingway, O'Hara, and Thurber stories he wanted.

So he dug into the *Decameron* to find the first of his "ribald classics," turned to Ambrose Bierce and A. Conan Doyle for stories, assembled a page of jokes, got a piece on the high cost of alimony (illustrated with pictures of old friend and first *Playboy* factotum, Eldon Sellers, who looked the part of a hapless male victim), added a football story, with free pictures supplied by the University of Illinois Athletic Office, a food piece about rice and chicken, complete with warning that it was *hot* and advice to drink ice-cold beer, a music feature that focused on the Dorsey brothers and wondered whether they would bring back the swing era, and a publicity hand-out about "Desk Design for the Modern Office."

"VIP on Sex," a cartoon feature, and a conventional layout of pretty girls added visual content. A "Men's Shop" column flogged leisure products with little initial success, but the idea of including one showed Hefner's intuitive grasp of magazines as merchandisers and mail-order department stores. Eventually he sold millions in *Playboy* products that way.

As for the overall conception of the magazine, Hefner laid it out in a statement of purpose and intent at the front of the book:

Playboy would be a magazine for any man between eighteen and eighty, but was not designed for family consumption. And, Hefner pleaded, should "somebody's sister, wife or mother-in-law" have picked it up by mistake, would she please pass it on to the man in her life and return to the *Ladies Home Companion*. *Playboy*'s content, he promised, would "form a pleasure primer styled for the masculine taste."

Next, Hefner knocked other men's magazines for "thrashing through thorny thickets or splashing about in fast-flowing streams," pursuits he was willing to discuss on occasions, but not often. Instead, "we plan spending most of our time inside." Hefner was specific on just how:

"We like our apartment. We enjoy mixing up cocktails and an hors d'oeuvre or two, putting a little mood music on the phonograph and inviting in a female acquaintance for a quiet discussion on Picasso, Nietzsche, jazz, sex."

Art, philosophy, music, and love—or a 1950s version of a loaf of bread, a jug of wine, and thou beside me singing in the (tamed) wilderness. The paragraph says a lot about Hefner and his striving for *Playboy*. He has been kissed by the muse. He knows that Aphrodite without Athena means sweaty bodies between soggy sheets. He is not a sly pornographer. Seduction, he knows, is as much a matter of mind as of body.

(Years later, he is embarrassed enough by his sentiments to call them "cliché symbols"—when he thinks the questioning about them is hostile—but to recoup, when he realizes that it is not, by claiming them as "touchstones of universal enough significance to say more than they were really saying." Sex by itself was never enough, he adds. "The whole idea behind *Playboy* was to put the two parts back together again—mind and body—that have been in conflict so long in our society. Sex, after all, is more a social than a physical experience.")

But a humanistic approach alone did not suffice: "We believe, too, that we are filling a publishing need only slightly less important than one just taken care of by the Kinsey Report," Hefner continued his opening statement.

The Kinsey Report marked the beginning of scientific probing into the sexual process, a probing based on statistical method more than on Freudian intuitive insight. Hefner recognized Kinsey as the incontrovertible word of the new God based on the new holy writ—demonstrable evidence. Kinsey would add a dash of scientific truth to the *Playboy* mix.

Next, Hefner showed a shimmer of social conscience: "Affairs of state will be out of our province. We don't expect to solve any world problems or prove any great moral truths. If we are able to give the American male a few extra laughs and a little diversion from the anxieties of the atomic age, we'll feel we've justified our existence."

Eventually, however, "affairs of state" did become a *Playboy* province that reached from ecology to Vietnam. Religion, the greatest moral truth, was a dominant sector of nonfiction for nearly a decade. And "the anxieties of the atomic age" were midwife to *Playboy*'s birth and nurse to its growth. As for "a few extra laughs and a little diversion," why, they were just what a generation grown up under the mushroom cloud and Senator McCarthy's cudgel needed.

That first issue was in near-perfect tune with the times. Hefner touched all the bases, no matter how crudely, and he had crafted an editorial package with real sales appeal that would prove infinitely expandable and adaptable. For the better part of twenty years, Hefner had a sure instinct of what to add, when, and why.

How had he put the package together? Why did it work? How much of his success was due to blind luck and to good timing? Of being the right man at the right place with the right idea—as he himself describes it? Where had he gotten the unvarnished chutzpah of starting a magazine on such a shoestring in the first place?

Luck, timing, and ignorance certainly played their part. So did the state of the magazine art and the state of the nation. And finally, so did Hefner himself: his determination, his personality, the driving hard work he put into his own business, his dream of the good life. He was Horatio Alger, sculpted by fate and genes into an American legend.

Take the legend first. It has gone through the hands of good public-relations men, bold promoters, clever writers. Mostly, the story became legend because it was simple, straightforward, attractive, believable, popular. People wanted to believe that it could still happen. And, stripped of the more outrageous flackery, much of it was true.

There he was twenty-seven years old, crew-cut, married, the father of one, upwardly mobile, a job-hopper, fairly well educated, out to start a magazine on nothing flat. Stock publicity pictures show an eager-faced youngster in a checked sports shirt open at the neck, poised over a typewriter set up on a card table, with a pot of glue and stacks of paper behind it. The captions say he is laying out the first issue in the kitchen of his South Harper Street apartment on Chicago's South Side. He was making $120 a week working as circulation manager for a magazine and his initial stake was $600—a $200 bank loan, plus another $400 from the loan company down the street, with his furniture up for collateral.

Hefner says in his *Playboy* interview that he raised another $3,000 in $50 and $100 bits from friends, acquaintances, and relatives, either as loans or as stock. Other *Playboy* publicity puts the initial capital as high as $12,000. It was a private deal. Who is ever to know? Take your pick. Certainly, $3,000 makes for a better story. In any event, the money wasn't even a shoestring—just enough to pay for stationery, postage, and make debts on. Stationery, Hefner says, was important. A letterhead lent him and his unborn magazine instant life. And he was a man alone.

His wife, Millie, helped. She shared his concerns and his hopes and took part in making what decisions had to be made. Eldon Sellers, an old friend, hung around and ran errands. His parents helped a little; so did the contacts Hefner had made in the half a dozen jobs he had held since graduating from the University of Illinois in 1949. He juggled his job schedule to find time for the needed coming and going, the meetings, the cajoling.

He wrote letters to wholesalers, distributors, retailers, potential investors and contributors, syndicates, publishers, agents, owners of rights to editorial matter. The letters were flashy and self-confident in tone, larded with that special intimacy for strangers that is so much the stock-in-trade of mail order solicitation. Hefner had made a living writing mail-promotion pieces, and he had the style in his fingertips. Results showed it. Orders began to trickle in for the as-yet-unedited, un-laid-out, and unprinted publications. Perhaps the tentative title—*Stag Party*—helped. Everybody had his own vision of what went on at them. There was enough interest, anyway, for Hefner to look for a printer who would extend credit and to move his personal transportation from the collapsing Chevy to an orange-and-cream-colored Studebaker sedan.

Where Hefner felt that his fledgling magazine was weakest, was, paradoxically, an area of his own strength—visual content. He was sure enough about the copy, promotion, and circulation, but the artwork he picked up on his rounds lacked the style and vitality he wanted. He prized good design, and from childhood on had been as interested in drawing and painting as in writing. He had submitted cartoon strips (unsuccessfully) to newspaper syndicates, published a self-illustrated book on Chicago, attended an anatomy course at the Chicago Art Institute. But the bargain basement he rifled so successfully for editorial material did not produce corresponding visual quality.

He discussed the problem with an *Esquire* writer who had stayed behind when the magazine left Chicago. Norman Sklarawitz had a friend who ran a design studio on the Loop where he did free-lance work for such major accounts as Scott Foresman and the Marshall Field stores. Why didn't Hefner drop in and see him? Hefner decided to try it. There was a story he wanted illustrated. Perhaps Arthur Paul was the man to do it. He showed up, seedy-looking, unshaven, heels worn down, a far image from a successful magazine publisher. The pictures Paul had on the walls of his studio impressed him. He asked if it was Paul's own or work he admired. Paul said it was his own. They began to talk about *Stag Party*—and quickly found they had many ideas about magazine design in common.

"It was a strange time for magazines then," Paul mused twenty-odd years later. "There was a tremendous look-alike quality that disturbed me. Illustrations were all the same, which was understandable since they all came out of that tight New York community. A good illustrator would go into one building and see four or five art directors. They'd all agree to use his stuff, and it would appear in several magazines at the same time. Also, none of it was very personal.

"I wanted to identify with a fresh feeling in design and do exciting illustrations. People thought my things were exciting but wouldn't buy them because they feared the decision makers wouldn't. That's what really prompted me to go along with Hefner. I didn't expect *Stag Party* to get off the ground, but it was a way of implementing some of my ideas. I talked it over with my wife. She was pregnant. She knew I'd get all involved with the project if I agreed to do it. My business was growing. So I had to do it as a free-lance situation. That was all right with Hefner. He'd bring material in, get artwork, which I tried to change, or do some myself."

Paul was dubious about *Stag Party* as a title, and he was not alone. But Hefner liked it and would have stuck with it had he not received a letter from lawyers representing a New York men's magazine entitled *Stag* (part of the Magazine Management chain), asking that he cease and desist. The first issue of the magazine had been laid out by then, the Monroe color transparencies put in place, agreement reached with a printer, arrangement for distribution made. Clearly, a crisis. After some desperate brainstorming at the South Harper Street apartment, somebody came up with the name *Playboy*. In his *Playboy* interview, Hefner takes credit for finding the name, but in his biography of Hefner, Frank Brady awards the laurel to Eldon Sellers. Whatever, they all pounced on the name as perfect, and up on the cover it went. Art Paul returned to his studio and doodled the rabbit logo on a sheet of paper.

The print run of that first, undated issue—Hefner wasn't sure there ever would be a second one, and he figured that dateless he could leave the magazine linger on newsstands—totaled 70,000 copies. Hefner and his friends waited nervously at the printers for the first copies off the presses. It was late October 1953. The magazine went on sale in December and sold 53,000 copies at 50 cents each —literally a success beyond Hefner's wildest dreams.

"It had a graphic touch and a sense of pacing," Paul says of that first issue. "I wanted the cover to stand out. Other magazines had a face and a lot of type. I was looking for something that would really be distinctive as a circulation booster. And that issue didn't look like any other magazine. We had a small logo of red in black and white, a Marilyn Monroe picture (big smile, left arm raised, body sheathed in a plunging black dress) and a VIP drawing. The rest of the cover was white. It was a visual way of showing content. The look was crude, but gave it the air of a college humor magazine, and I think that had a lot to do with people picking it up."

As the sales figures came in, Hefner was back at the kitchen table laying out the January issue, dated this time, with humor by Max Shulman, another Conan Doyle story, the first "Dear Playboy" letters, and several Milton Caniff cartoon panels from "Male Call," his World War II strip drawn for GI consumption and heavy on wasp waists and bulging bosoms. Hefner and *Playboy* were on their way to fame, success, fortune, and all the other cookies of the American dream.

So much for the legend. What about the man behind it? The real Hugh Hefner has been asked to stand up so often, he may no longer be able to. Next to Richard Nixon, he is probably the most over-analyzed public figure in America. "What's Hef really like" was for years a favored parlor game, and one Hefner lent his considerable skills to promote. When some of the answers turned nasty (he's queer; he doesn't like women; he isn't a Playboy; his life-style is a joke), Hefner pleaded not guilty, and would you guys knock it off, please? But they didn't, and the figure who emerged from all the scrutiny was too distorted by flackery and fakery, ridicule and self-adulation, to ever allow an honest and true portrait. Too many layers of paints—Hefner's and others'—cover the original for anyone to scrape them off. The following sketch doesn't try; at best it is a line drawing of Hefner's background and of his development into the "editor-publisher" persona he prizes so highly. It is told mostly in his own words.

Hugh Marston Hefner was born in Chicago on April 9, 1926, the son of Glenn and Grace Hefner. He grew up relatively prosperous and knew poverty only secondhand ("my best friend in grade school was poor"). His father, an accountant, worked for a large firm, owned a house and a car, and was not savaged by the Depression. Home life was warm, close, optimistic, strict enough to be shadowed by the puritan pieties the Hefners brought from their native Nebraska, but not to be oppressed by it. Swearing, smoking, and drinking were proscribed, but the ban did not rouse "Hef" to violent rebellion. He still doesn't swear with the ease that is the communications-business norm, drinks sparingly, if at all, and took up a pipe in his thirties to give his hands something to do during TV performances. (He also hoped the pipe would cut into his wild consumption of Pepsis, which have ruined his teeth, but it didn't.) He remembers his childhood with great affection and little rancor, and sounds dispassionate about himself during the bouts of self-analysis interviewers inevitably force him to undergo.

"I've had very strong, very idealistic, very democratically rooted values from a very early age on. I got them from my parents. My attitudes on our traditional values and social ideals are obviously rooted in the home because I had a strong Methodist upbringing and accepted the best of it and very much rejected some of the less human parts of it. My folks were very typical of their generation. They believed in the basic American dream of the Horatio Alger type. I never doubted that I could earn a good living. I felt that I would probably be as successful as my father had been, and more so. But the mini-battles I fought on the playground are not so unrelated to the stuff that happened in later years. It's very clear to me, looking back, that the boy was father to the man. I can really see the roots and the progression of an awful lot of what I am today."

Later, as if to make the point, he asked, "Ever hear of the bunny blanket? Well, when I was very young, about six, I had my only serious illness, a mastoid operation. When I got out of the hospital, I was promised my first dog. I'd had a favorite blanket, as kids have, with little rabbits all over it, and it was called my bunny blanket. So when I got my dog, which was then the most cherished thing I could possess, I naturally gave the dog the blanket. The dog was a very handsome wire-haired fox terrier, a show dog, which we got for a very good price. It died within a week. Now, when it died, the blanket had to be burned. That was the end of the bunny blanket. So the kid who lost the bunny blanket got the bunnies."

Hefner chuckled. It was clearly a practiced story.

"I've been editing and publishing all my life—literally ever since I was a very small boy. I created my first newspaper when I was nine or ten. In seventh grade I started a newspaper that turned into the official school newspaper. In the 1950s my wife was a substitute teacher in that school, and it was still going then and maybe is today. I used to do cartoons and little comic strips. When I wrote stories, I bound and illustrated them. In other words, there was the editing and publishing phenomenon going on back then.

"As a little kid, I was interested in mystery stories, the occult, hypnosis, ESP. The books I read for the most part were Poe, H. G. Wells, Conan Doyle, Sax Rohmer's Dr. Fu Manchu series. My first club wasn't the Playboy Club. I was a big organizer of clubs as a kid.

There were some gang clubs. We were all big horror fans, so I had something called 'The Shudder Club,' with little buttons and insignia and a little magazine. All that set up my interest in psychology—that and the fact that I was always the one other kids came to in terms of whatever schoolboys' counterparts of psychological problems are.

"Film had a tremendous impact on me growing up. I'm probably the most McLuhanesque editor and publisher around today, and was before the term had any meaning. In many ways, the motion picture was as real as life in the 1930s—the stuff that dreams are made of. (There is no contradiction since Hefner always made reality conform to his dreams.) An awful lot of what I'm all about and what *Playboy* is all about come from film, especially the Capra stuff: *Mr. Smith Goes to Washington, Meet John Doe,* and *Mr. Deeds Goes to Town.* What I liked about them was the idea of one man alone."

Hefner enjoyed high school, coming into his own in his last two years, a period he counts among the happiest in his life, filled with extracurricular activities, dating, a little petting, a passable academic record. "I was thought of as a good student but was not a member of the honor society. Courses I liked very much I did well in. In others I didn't do well at all."

Movies and magazines were his major interests, but he was also into "a broad spectrum of the creative and performing arts that ran from songwriting to playwriting. I took part in a radio workshop and produced my first movie when I was sixteen—a real epic." He read *Time* from the mid-thirties on and pounced on *Life* as soon as he learned that Henry Luce "was going to put out a picture magazine."

Hefner graduated from high school in February 1944 and joined the army at once rather than waiting for the draft on his eighteenth birthday. He spent two bored and resentful years as an army clerk. Time hung heavy, and he used it to deepen his love affair with magazines, regularly reading the newsweeklies, *Life, Look, Esquire, True, Park East.* "I was familiar with almost everything and intrigued by the phenomenon of magazine publishing, by the way they were put together and printed, by graphics and layout, more with the editing-publishing implications than with the pure writing."

Hefner was discharged in the spring of 1946, too late to start college until fall. He joined the 52-20 club, the government program that paid unemployed veterans $20 a week for a year, and spent the waiting months "trying to get going as a cartoonist" (which prompted attendance at the Art Institute anatomy course where he found that "I was lousy at drawing and very good at design"). He denies feeling adrift, as some writings about him contend. "I knew I wanted to go to college and felt very much as if I were behind. Everybody had lost a couple of years."

What sharpened his own sense of a late start was the advantage he felt his girlfriend, Millie Williams, had won by starting out at the University of Illinois a year ahead of him. They began going steady in high school and corresponded while he was in the army. And he picked the University of Illinois largely to be with her—and to catch up with her.

He decided on a major in psychology and a minor in creative writing and art rather than on journalism because "I felt that the mechanics of journalism would be less important to me" and because he wanted to take advantage of "a special school they had at Illinois for veterans that offered a much broader curriculum. You could pick courses from various schools, and that's what I did. In retrospect, it was very much the right decision."

But he was less happy in college than he had been in high school. "There were a lot of insecurities from the lost two years. I was very much afraid I wasn't going to cut it, so I studied." He went summers and doubled up on courses, and "did extremely well, made freshmen honors, etc. Toward the end, it began to drop off as my interests went elsewhere. But overall, my classwork in college was very good."

The course he enjoyed most was neither in social psychology, his major area (though he read Freud, he felt social psychology would be more helpful in a magazine career), nor in art, but in creative writing. The course was a one-shot affair, taught by an Illinois alumnus named Samuel Raphaelson who wrote *The Jazz Singer* and several other screenplays, including *Skylark* and *Accent on Youth.* Hefner seems to have been as much attracted by the man's fame— a first bout of Hefner's habitual stargazing—as by the substance of what he taught.

He was something of a Joe College, hooked on football and girls as much if not more than on his courses or the serious issues of the day. "Football intrigued me," he admits. "We had sensational teams while I was at Illinois." The pressure-cooker atmosphere on postwar campuses, however, with hordes of bright young men scrambling for an education and the better life it promised, forced a concentration on self.

"I was concerned with what was going to happen to Hugh Hefner, with getting through college, and finding out what I was going to make of my life."

Politics and international affairs did not intrude much. He knew Henry Wallace was mounting an independent run for the presidency in 1948 but did not care enough to register to vote in that election. Still, Hefner claims to have been issue-oriented, interested in social problems, aware, caring. He had encountered racial prejudice in the army first and later at Urbana, where restaurants were still segregated in the 1940s. And he refused to join a fraternity because he disliked their exclusionary attitudes. (Yet he made *Playboy* a hero of frat row.)

Like most veterans, Hefner raced through college and panted to his B.A. in February 1949, a bare semester behind Millie, to whom he was now engaged, and whom he married that June, shortly after landing a job in the personnel department of the Chicago Carton Company for $45 a week. Early 1949 was not a good time to face life beyond school. Jobs were hard to get. "I couldn't get anything in an advertising agency or on a newspaper or magazine, and I was intrigued that they were in printing, even though what they printed was cartons. And personnel was vaguely related to psychology."

He worked at the carton company until September 1949, when he quit in disgust and decided to become a free-lance cartoonist. "I did two cartoon comic strips. One was called 'Fred Frat,' which was a humorous college-adventure kind of thing. The other was 'Gene Phantos, Psycho-Investigator,' an adventure strip that featured a combined psychiatrist and private investigator. I also did a lot of one-panel cartoons that I tried to sell with little success."

Discouraged by his failure to move the "real" world, Hefner enrolled at Northwestern in January 1950 for graduate work in sociology. "Going back to school was an escape. Okay, if I can't do what I want to do out here in the real world, I'll go back to the halls of ivy, and write or whatever on the side."

Millie was teaching school, and both families chipped in enough to assure financial survival. But Hefner's second academic career ended in June 1950, when he found a copywriting job with Carson-Pirie-Scott, an old-line Chicago department store. Academe, too, he felt, was pointless. Six months later, he quit to work for an advertising agency, a job that lasted five weeks. Then a $60-a-week job at *Esquire* beckoned. He spent all of 1951 writing mail-order subscription pitches, both so-called "cold mailings" for new subscriptions and renewal letters. At the end of the year, *Esquire* moved what was still left of its operations in Chicago to New York and offered to take Hefner along at $80 a week. He held out for $85 and was refused, being told, in the bargain, that he was not a good company man.

After *Playboy* was established, Victor Lownes, who began his *Playboy* career as promotion manager, pounced on the story and quickly embellished it into the legend that *Esquire* could have saved itself *Playboy*'s formidable competition for a lousy five bucks a week. But the $5 ploy, in fact, was more of a ruse to stay in Chicago than to get more money in New York. Hefner didn't want to leave the Midwest, and neither did Millie. Chicago was home, familiar, comfortable.

So Hefner found himself an $80-a-week job anyway, and one, moreover, that helped broaden his magazine know-how: He learned newsstand operations for Publishers Development Corporation, a multimagazine publisher. "PDC had an art photography book, an outright nudist magazine, a men's mag called *Modern Man* which was rather like a poor-grade *True* or *Argosy,* with a few nudes handled pretty much like in the art books, a junior arts and activities magazine aimed at grade-school children, and a couple of trade books."

The $80 a week wasn't bad money for a twenty-five-year-old liberal arts graduate in the communications business then. But Millie made more teaching school, and Hefner's secretary at *Esquire* earned more than he did. Hefner accepted both as white-collar facts of life. "I think it was rather expected that wives worked at the beginning of a marriage when there weren't any children. When you went to college, you started out in your chosen white-collar job lower economically than if you went right out of high school into a blue-collar job." And the Hefners weren't badly off. In June 1952 they moved into their five-room apartment on South Harper Street, fixed it up into a showcase written up in a local Sunday supplement, and got ready for the baby Millie expected in November.

Soon after Christie Hefner was born, her father switched jobs. Millie had, of course, stopped teaching, and the young family needed more money. Hefner got an offer of $120 a week to become circulation promotion manager for *Children's Activities*—a magazine that did just what its title said it did. Wife, child, home, job. Hefner seemed frozen into a conventional bourgeois existence, and one, he realized, he had never wanted. Two quotes that had been his teen-age "karmas" returned to haunt him: Polonius's advice to Laertes, "to thine own self be true," and Robert Browning's "one's reach should always exceed one's grasp." He worried that he was living up to neither. He didn't like working for someone else. But his efforts as a free-lance cartoonist had produced nothing, and though his cartoon book about Chicago, *That Toddlin' Town,* had been a modest success, it had not established him either. He was pushing twenty-seven. If he wanted to strike out on his own, it was now or never.

And why not a magazine of his own? He had dreamed about it long enough. He had amassed the experience—mail order and newsstand, circulation and promotion, cartoons, editorial content—so, really, why not? The Korean War was winding down. With Eisenhower's election, a new optimism had gripped the country. The economy still glowed with ruddy health, despite fears of a post-Korea downturn. The fifties were taking on a character and personality of their own, shucking the ballast of the thirties and forties.

Untouched and uninvolved by Depression, war, or ideological division, this would be the decade of Hefner's flowering. Intuitively, he understood the new mood, the turning inward that followed the heady experience of total victory and unlimited power.

2

"Playboy's" Fifties

"**I** picked up the first issue in December '53 or January '54. It was a strange-looking thing, printed on this funny paper, but I figured I could unload a few trunkies on this guy from the file. I was a free-lance writer then, though for a couple of months I'd had a job on the Walgreen Drug Store Chain house organ. I'd sold a couple of things, including a piece to *Esquire.* The address was on the masthead, sixty-something South Harper Street. I thought it was an office building, not an apartment.. At home I hustled up a few rejects, put them in an envelope with a note that I had sold a piece to *Esquire,* and sent it in. I wanted to make a couple of bucks and thought the magazine would last just long enough to buy my stories."

Ray Russell was twenty-eight years old then. A born-and-bred Chicagoan, he had left his home town only once, for military service, and then "gravitated to writing by default" after trying a musical conservatory and the Goodman Drama School.

"Anyway, a couple of weeks later—I had begun to wonder why I hadn't heard, I'd included a stamped, self-addressed envelope—Hefner called and asked to see me. We made a date to meet at a bar in the Loop, and he offered me a job. I told him *Playboy* was shaky and Walgreen had been around for fifty years, and would be for another fifty. Hefner said yes, he understood that, but that *Playboy* would catch on. I thought, 'Well, so what if I do work there for only six months or a year and the magazine folds'—it would still be better than what I had. A house organ just wasn't the same thing as a magazine which would give me real editorial experience. I didn't even know what a paste-up was. When Hefner asked me how much

I was getting at Walgreen, I said $100 a week. Actually, I was making only $90 and supporting a wife and kid on that. But he said, 'I'll match it.' I went to work two weeks later as his first editor. You know, he never did buy those stories. I don't think he was that taken with them, but saw something in terms of style so that he wanted me to be his right-hand man."

Hefner concurs. He didn't like the stories, didn't think they were suitable for his magazine. But he liked Russell's way with words. So he called and arranged the interview. It was typical for Hefner's hiring practices during the fifties. The staff was a lot of picked-up pieces.

About the time Hefner got Russell, Art Paul decided to cut loose from his design studio and come to work full-time for *Playboy*. Eldon Sellers, something of a shadowy figure in the magazine's history, hung around as a general assistant for everything. It would prove an infinitely expandable nucleus. *Playboy* was doing well by any standards—fabulously by Hefner's own. He had rated chances for a second issue a toss-up at best. But by Vol. 1, No. 3, he saw enough money coming in to assure continued publication and faced too much work to keep laying out the magazine on a card table at home. Christie was growing, and *Playboy*'s clutter disrupted an already uneasy home life. So Hefner went to look for an office. He found one in a graystone building at 11 East Superior Street, a couple of blocks west of Michigan Avenue. It was a four-room, top-floor apartment.

It was a strange house for an office and doubly so for a magazine like *Playboy*. The street has kept its residential look for all the commerce that has penetrated the block. Trees line the sidewalks. The neighborhood looks lived in. A food market squats on the corner of East Superior and North State. On Chicago Avenue, to the north, a YMCA sign blinks dubious greetings across a parking lot and a playground. Holy Name Cathedral, directly across the street from the new *Playboy* office, must have frowned disapprovingly.

A hideous building of nubby yellow stone, the church reflects the vulgar pomp and circumstance of Grant's gilded age, when it was built in the eclectic, neo-Gothic style so popular in the 1870s. It has the obligatory rose window copied from Chartres, a slim tower, some Romanesque elements. More symbol of power and money than grace or love, certainly more Protestant than Catholic, the cathedral broods over the street without striking a spark of joy. However subliminally, the church must have reminded Hefner of his childhood Methodist heritage.

Nor was the Catholic bastion the only sign of a frowning God. The Salvation Army had its headquarters next door to the *Playboy* office; the diocesan family court was down a couple of houses. A convent and the cathedral's chancery were nearby; so were the national offices of a Methodist publishing house. And St. James's Episcopal Cathedral was two blocks away on North Wabash Avenue.

Sex, however, was not a novelty for Chicago's ecclesiastic compound. It had lived cheek-by-jowl with tenderloin for years. The nightclubs along Rush Street and the squads of hookers on that turf had long been an honored tradition. But that was comfortable vice, sequestered, salvageable, a contained example of sinning—not sin in the mass media, such as Hefner committed to print every month.

What added to the site's incongruity was the touch of American Gothic. East Superior Street could have modeled one of Hopper's cityscapes: the harsh lines of the graystones; the alley in back with its ducked row of houses and parking spaces; the fading grace of the French windows; the blistered and peeling gray paint offset by a mottled white trim on windows and below the roof line.

Yet the location symbolized much of what *Playboy* would become. It cracked the bourgeois facade without breaking it. The church would play a large role in the magazine's development and growth. The magazine was American urban. It responded to the challenge of the eye and to the graphic vision. Nevertheless, at the core, *Playboy* remained as conservative as the street on which it grew up.

Those who took part in the growing-up process were neophytes, and that, too, fits the Horatio Alger image. Hefner made it on his own and in his own way.

"Both of us were amateurs as magazine editors," Russell says of himself and Hefner. "We were feeling our way. Paul was, too. He'd never art-directed a magazine before. We were learning while earning, and learning from our mistakes. If we had a concept for the magazine, it was amorphous and became more clearly focused only as we went along."

But they talked concept and future directions in endless bull sessions that were so much part of their working day.

"We did spend a lot of time discussing things," Paul remembers. "Hefner had a keen sense of graphics because he was a cartoonist, though not a very good draftsman, and that sense was very supportive for my work. He could accept me and my feeling for design. He listened to what I said about the visual approach to magazines. And he taught me about editorial work, what it means to an editor. I thought his approach was brilliant. We disagreed a lot, and gave in to each other many times, and talked far into the night. We learned a great deal from each other. It was a good learning process. I didn't think more than one issue ahead."

Russell concurs: "Ours was an issue-to-issue approach."

Hefner doesn't disagree exactly, but he argues, and with some cogency, that "all the basic elements were there. I knew what I wanted to produce conceptually." The execution, however, as Hefner admits readily, left something to be desired. "The book was largely reprint material and pictorial features brought from Graphic House and the calendar company and from other big picture houses. It was pickup stuff. We didn't have any photographers or a real staff. It was close to a year before we were shooting our own layouts."

Still, even within such narrow confines, Hefner's dogged pursuit of quality began to show through. He found a story by Erskine Caldwell he could afford and printed it in the February 1954 issue. It would be the first of many Caldwell appearances. His earthy southern sexuality quickly became a reader favorite. In June, *Playboy* landed Somerset Maugham; in July, Thorne Smith; in August, Robert Ruark. Sex, class, humor, adventure. The categories all fitted neatly.

Russell quickly carried the heavy in-house writing load. He contributed fiction and nonfiction, and he and Hefner wrote fillers, picture captions, service features, the party jokes. They dug through the public domain for other material, developed the ribald classic feature (still a *Playboy* staple today), and scrounged around for cheap second-serial rights to famous names.

The Playmates, curiously enough, lagged behind the rest of the content. After Marilyn Monroe, it was downhill for months. Miss April, for example, was a horror: fat thighs, frizzy hair, mashed-in face. At least Miss July was not repulsive. She had good legs, and her body, tightly stretched, reclined on a tigerskin rug. Playmates that first year often resembled their sisters from the girlie magazines Hefner was trying to escape. It could hardly be otherwise with pictures for *Playboy* and *Art Photography* coming from the same sources. M. J. Sobran, a regular contributor to *National Review,* took them apart in a 1974 article on *Playboy:*

"Many in those early days," he wrote, "had a rather self-conscious fallen look . . . rather like the girls in other girlie mags, like *Rogue* and *Dude.* You know the pose: breast thrust forth, tummy sucked in, legs coyly crossed—and the face, oh the face! What it lacked in beauty, it made up in ardor and mascara. Come hither, reader, it said —chin up, mouth open, tongue between bared teeth, eyes half open but gazing right at you mister, and yes it said yes—though she looked like a girl, who off camera, chewed gum and said yeah . . ."

All right. They were feeling their way. So some of the girls were dogs, but not all of them. And readers loved them, dogs or not. They loved everything about *Playboy* and told the magazine so in an astonishing outpouring of mail. Rapport was immediate, kinetic, attesting to the deepest kind of involvement. Letters were filled with suggestions for improvement, everything from book reviews to a fashion page, and with gratitude for *Playboy*'s having breached the "guns and wild-game-hunt" syndrome of other men's magazines.

But why the empathy and identification, and why did it happen so quickly?

Hefner's answer is anything but modest: "Because there, for the first time in print, they found expressed what they believed in and weren't finding anywhere else. No other publication was expressing that point of view which was the same as you'd get discussing these things (like sex, like life-styles) in a college dorm. There was still that safe, tut-tut attitude about sex going on in other books. Here was a magazine that saw life as a celebration without being too self-conscious or too patronizing about it. And when it arrived, it was very fresh, though it was obviously put together with Scotch tape and paper clips. Look at those first issues, and it is very hard to believe that this is going to be the magazine with the greatest impact on our society over the next twenty years. But the audience reaction was so immediate that it had to be something beyond what we were then delivering because we were not delivering the magazine that elicited the response. Readers responded to the *concept* of the book that was so on target and so right for the times. Even our growing pains helped the empathy. And it was such an open book, so unembarrassed, so unabashed in saying, 'Here we are and here's what we're doing.' "

But growing pains did not hurt much. Hefner tackled things as they came up, grabbed opportunities where he found them, made do with what he had, added to the staff as the need arose and the cash became available. But there was, through all the early scrambling and chaos, a clear line in his approach. And when he was done, the pieces fitted.

Hefner and Paul put their names on the masthead in the second issue. Russell's went up as associate editor in April. Thomas Mario began a twenty-year association as food-and-drink editor that spring with a tome on oysters that already bore his trademark of cloying titles ("Oyster Stew for a Quartet of Playboys") and deep-fried prose. Paul went looking for an assistant, now that Hefner had one, and found Joseph Paczek, who was doing layouts at the Berton-Brown advertising agency. Paczek went on the payroll at $70 a week and twenty-three years later was still there.

Office help, too, was needed, and, sensibly, Hefner went looking for someone with experience and a steady hand, not a pretty bubble-head. Marge Pitner had a bookkeeping background and became something of a Girl Friday. She typed manuscripts for the printer, handled what little advertising there was, answered subscription letters (a coupon had been included from the second issue on, and a trickle of orders came in), and moved general traffic.

"I guess it was important to have someone in the office when the others were out who could handle herself," she says of the early days.

Curiously, she did not type many letters for Hefner. He wrote and typed his own "of any consequence." Ms. Pitner is still with the company, far removed from the center, she says, working on employee profit-sharing and payroll liaison.

That summer Hefner hired a second secretary, Pat Pappas, to round out his first year's staff. (Ms. Pappas is still with *Playboy* as administrative editor.)

Office life seems to have been spartan as befits so small a staff. Everybody helped out with the chores. Hefner and Russell would cart the office copies of the magazine, which the printer had left at the front door in the morning, up three flights of stairs. "I always got winded," Russell remembers. "Art Paul refused outright to handle them and said he hadn't been hired as a manual laborer. I never had the guts to do that, so Hef and I broke our backs carrying the stuff up." Subscriptions were sent out by first-class mail. Marge Pitner weighed copies on Hefner's bathroom scale, which the publisher had lugged from home to the office. That, however, was not the scale's primary purpose. Within a very few months, Hefner more or less lived at 11 East Superior Street and kept the essentials of everyday living in an office that retained its apartment character. There was little sense of permanence, of course. Russell, for one, always expected the next issue to be the last. But Hefner paid his bills and met his payroll and had necessary access to credit—all events that filled him with some wonder, but which he took in his stride nevertheless.

At the end of the first year, circulation topped 100,000. *Playboy* was selling on newsstands across the country for 50 cents a copy. *Time* and *Newsweek* had given the new publication write-ups; so had professional writers' magazines. Authors and cartoonists smelled a new market. In Chicago, at least, *Playboy* was becoming established with local talent. Lines had been put out to photographers, writers, cartoonists, and illustrators. The magazine still had an acceptance problem with publishers, agents, record companies, films, and others, especially in New York, and that would linger until the rates it paid went up. It was a long time, for example, before publishers sent *Playboy* bound galleys for reviews. But there were chinks in New York's armor. Russell found people doing criticism for other magazines who were willing to supply reviews ahead of time so that *Playboy* was not hopelessly behind the new releases.

By Christmas 1954, *Playboy* had come a long way. As Hefner says, the concept had outrun the delivered package, but readers did not mind waiting. And anyway, they were having too good a time with what was on the plate. The future glowed brightly, even for the reluctant Russell, who still nursed his doubts about the magazine's ability to survive. Hefner felt good enough to celebrate and took the staff to the Charmette Coffee Shop on the corner of Chicago and Michigan Avenues, a few blocks from the office, for a Christmas party. In his *Playboy* interview, Hefner gives the episode short and almost sarcastic shrift:

"On our first anniversary, I remember, the employees of the company—seven of us by that time—celebrated in a booth at a local sandwich shop. I knew we were in business to stay, so I picked up the check."

In addition to Hefner and his "sextet"—Paul, Russell, Sellers, Paczek, Pitner, and Pappas—one other figure loomed large in *Playboy*'s progress, and he was not then a member of the staff. He was Victor Lownes III, and next to Hefner himself, he has exercised the largest sustained influence on the corporate Playboy and its development. In the seventies, his gambling operations in Britain kept the company solvent and have now replaced the magazine as the major corporate money-maker.

Lownes' relationship with Hefner differs from all others the editor-publisher developed over the years. It was personal first, professional second, and was tinged from the beginning by a curious father-son character—curious because it shifted from one to the other over the years and particular situations. Lownes was born with many of the things Hefner aspired to, and later Lownes would copy much of the life-style Hefner's millions allowed him to acquire. For many, Lownes was the dark side of Hefner's moon.

Legends cling to Lownes like brambles: He is a demon adept at cracking female hearts like glass; fear and terror stalk the offices of those who work for him; he built an empire in England to outshine Hefner's; his life is a cesspool of vice, so depraved that to mention his excesses in print is to invite the laws of libel.

Whatever the truth, the charcoal that blackens his reputation hides a man of charm, wit, and grace, who drops names with discretion, and comes across as so serenely self-confident that he has no need to nurse, or exhibit, a clearly massive ego. More than anyone else in Hefner's early years, Lownes seems to have been a role model. His ease with people, his instinctive good manners, the cold eye he can use with devastating effect to freeze people he dislikes, his stage and television presence, they all were qualities Hefner did not possess and had to learn, often painfully.

They met at a party Lownes threw at his Wells Street bachelor pad for comedian Jonathan Winters in early 1954. Recently separated from his wife, the then twenty-five-year-old Lownes was dating Mary Ann LaJoie, a Merrill Abbot dancer at the Palmer House, and had begun to meet "a lot of celebrities." He had dabbled some in show business, having arranged a Mabel Mercer concert in Chicago the previous winter. And he had posed for a photographer friend, Mike Shea, who shot a layout on a new United Airlines executive flight which *Playboy* was running. Lownes had posed as an executive aboard.

"Mike asked whether he could bring the guy who published the magazine, and I said 'Sure.' I'd never seen a copy, except once on a newsstand. I sort of picked it up and put it back because I felt the content was pretty strong stuff. I'm a chap who finds it embarrassing to buy athlete's-foot powder."

Hefner came with a date and the photographer. During the party, Lownes played tapes of the Mercer concert. The sound intrigued the publisher. He knew that the singer was the darling of New York sophisticates, and he loved what she did with Cole Porter tunes. Would Lownes write an article about Mabel Mercer for *Playboy?* He would. Next, Hefner asked Lownes for a piece on Jonathan Winters and published that. Then Lownes did a third piece, but does not remember what it was about.

"One day I was in the office and looked on Hefner's desk. I spotted a memo from Ray Russell that said my piece was really rubbish and that *Playboy* had to start using pros, not friendly amateurs. I was hurt, but Hefner said coldly, 'That's what you get for reading other people's mail,' and the subject of my contributions never came up again."

But Hefner was not about to let his new friend go, and he found other ways to wrap him into his fledgling operation. Lownes had been a Chesterfield representative at the University of Chicago—the cigarette company had them nationwide to push its products on campus—and wondered whether *Playboy* could not be promoted the same way. From the beginning, collegians had been its readiest audience. And proof of campus acceptance could build a solid foundation for future advertising. Wisely, Hefner had not bothered with ads in the beginning, figuring he could sell space only to body-builders and truss makers, who would neither shine up his image nor enrich his coffers. A college bureau, Hefner and Lownes figured, would institutionalize *Playboy*'s campus acceptance, especially if the reps moved not only subscriptions but *Playboy* products as well. That, in turn, would draw the ad agencies like honey.

But the talk was not translated into action until mid–1955 when Lownes quit his job because he had lost his deferment as married man and father and expected to be drafted. Hefner suggested that while he was waiting to be called, he join *Playboy* full time and set up the college bureau. Lownes agreed and soon after was able to wangle a three-month deferment—he had met a girl at a farewell party who, by one of those far-out strokes of accident and fortune, happened to work for the head of Lownes' draft board. When his deferment expired, men twenty-six and over were no longer called up.

The college bureau and the promotional activities associated with it suited Lownes and his talents perfectly, and it was just the right slot for his burgeoning friendship with Hefner. In it, he was more of a complement than a challenge to *Playboy*'s owner, and thus Hefner could indulge the attraction without fearing the competition. Much of Lownes' attraction is summed up in a paragraph in Hefner's *Playboy* interview:

"I remember, in the days prior to *Playboy,* walking the streets of Chicago late at night, looking at the lights of the high-rise apartment buildings and very much wanting to be part of the 'good life' I thought the people in those buildings must be leading. . . . I wanted to be where it was happening—whatever 'it' was."

Lownes did not have to wonder what the "it" was. He knew. His family had money and connections, and he understood the value of both early on—beginning with a dollar his grandparents gave him as a little boy in New York when he visited their apartment at the Sherry-Netherland. He could only buy staples and gummed reinforcers with it because he was not allowed to cross the street and a stationery was the only store on the block.

Born in Buffalo, New York, in 1928, he grew up in Florida, where his father was a prosperous contractor, "hip for his time," Lownes says, because he read *Time* every week. The relationship was difficult, and young Lownes was soon shipped off to military school in New Mexico, where he roomed with Nicky Hilton and deepened his knowledge of the champagne life. Fed up with military school, he grabbed at an opportunity to enroll at the University of Chicago at sixteen under Chancellor Robert Hutchins' innovative admissions policy for gifted students not yet out of high school.

Again, familial connections smoothed his way. He stayed for a while in a mansion on Lake Shore Drive owned by the family of a "disbarred monkey-gland doctor"—yet another view of moneyed society—and was quickly taken in hand in matters of style and dress. He was rushed down to Brooks Brothers, told what to buy and how to select it, and generally "filled full of the sophisticated chic of the times and a desire to be with it."

The year was 1944, and he indulged "the desire to be with it" for the seven years he spent at the University of Chicago. He had not meant to stay that long, but in 1946, barely eighteen, he married "the most attractive girl on campus." Both families had money and indulged the young couple with adequate allowances, enough to live well, run a car, and eventually to have two children. Whenever funds ran low, Lownes took odd jobs, mostly in the promotion field— flogging a black-and-tan nightclub or a bartender who took orders in rhyme—and once put in a stint as classified ad manager for *Dog World* magazine.

When he finally left school, Lownes had enough credits for two B.A.s, mostly in political science, economics, and business administration. Again the family stepped in, and Lownes took a job in the Chicago office of a company owned by his grandfather. Within two years, he managed the office "thanks to my skill and my connections." But then he opted out of the American dream and separated from his wife. "The future looked bleak. I was trapped in a dull job and building a house in the suburbs. 'Jesus,' I said to myself, 'that's a terrible way to spend the next fifty years.' "

Once at *Playboy* and liberated from the draft, Lownes knew he would not have to do that. He threw his prodigious energies into building up *Playboy*'s college market. Campus receptivity was a given—the volume of mail alone attested to that. Collegians threw *Playboy* parties from Cornell to Stanford and bombarded *Playboy* with requests for Playmates as prom queens. When ivied Dartmouth carved an ice bunny for its winter carnival, the wire photo made papers coast-to-coast.

Lownes got hold of a list of campus Chesterfield representatives and pitched them to work for *Playboy* in return for free subscriptions. The ploy worked better than money could have. Soon Lownes had reps on 300 campuses. Playboy products, too, sold briskly. Ceramic cufflinks emblazoned with the rabbit logo were status symbols collegians wore to flaunt their loyalty to the magazine and to thumb their noses at society. You couldn't beat that for brand identification.

Inevitably, advertising agencies showed interest. But instead of embracing their advances, Lownes and Hefner decided on a more subtle strategy. They established strict standards for advertising respectability—as strict as the *New Yorker*'s and stricter than *Playboy*'s standards are today. Ads in "bad taste" were out. On Madison Avenue, *Playboy* would travel first class or not at all. Lownes put that message across on the advertising luncheon circuit where he was soon a desired speaker since he always decorated the podium with a Playmate. "We had no advertising at all," Lownes grins today, "but boy, did I talk tough."

The talk paid off. Soon agencies were clamoring to buy. "It got to the point where we used to say that we had a closetful of ten-foot poles—from people who said they'd never touch *Playboy* with a ten-foot pole." Apparel broke ranks first, and was quickly onto so good a thing that others followed. By the time an ad ran, the rate card was based on only half the circulation advertisers actually received. Circulation growth was that rapid. And rates were low, too: $650 for a black-and-white page, $1,075 for a four-color ad.

By the time advertising became a serious *Playboy* factor, Hefner had put together most of the other elements he needed to keep up with his own runaway growth. In March 1955 he got some idea of just how explosive others viewed *Playboy*'s expansion when a Chicago syndicate offered to buy him out for $1 million. The offer occupies a dim corner in Hefner's memory, and he says he never for a moment considered taking it. "I wasn't interested in the money," he contends with obvious sincerity. He didn't have to be. *Playboy*'s bank account had swelled to $250,000. The magazine rented more space at 11 East Superior Street and eventually spilled into other buildings nearby to handle the overflow.

More staff was added, still in picked-up pieces but with the overall design clearly in mind, and new staffers, whatever their background, bent to its needs.

Anson "Smokey" Mount was a "good ole boy" from Tennessee recovering from Korean War wounds in a Chicago veterans' hospital, studying for an M.A., driving a cab, and writing short stories. He submitted two to *Playboy*. Hefner bought one for $500 and a second for $1,000. (Rates had gone up after Russell irritably told Hefner to stop bugging him about stories *Esquire* had and *Playboy* didn't unless he was prepared to pay competitive rates, which Hefner proceeded to do.) A third contribution didn't come up. Hefner offered Mount a job at $75 a week as Lownes' assistant. Mount says —only half-facetiously—that Hefner was trying to save money. Mount stayed almost twenty years, becoming a *Playboy* fixture and something of a star by bringing religion and football into the magazine, before he was fired in the fiscal crisis that shook the empire in 1974.

In June 1955 Hefner hired another contributor, Jack J. Kessie, who had written several fashion pieces, as an assistant editor at $100 a week. A tall, shaggy, good-looking man who wore his sartorial elegance with ease, Kessie had some of Lownes' qualities in matters of taste and style, and they were qualities Hefner found attractive. Both Lownes and Kessie are scathing about Hefner's clothes, especially his zany insistence on white socks and padded suits. The boss, Kessie insists, never heard of Brooks Brothers. (It is a charge Hefner denies. "There is no truth to that whatsoever," he says earnestly,` firmly, and sincerely.)

Kessie shared the in-house writing load with Russell, freeing him to do more fiction, his forte, and to craft some articles. "I did clothes (under the pseudonym of Blake Rutherford), filler material, Up Front, Playboy After Hours," Kessie says. "I stole anecdotes from newspapers and magazines. They still do that. We paid very little for outside work and used a lot of reprints. There was very little good nonfiction. Mostly we did bawdy stories along the lines of 'My First Experience at a Stag Film.' And let me tell you, that was risqué in those days. Hefner used to tell us that he had the book done for his satisfaction and that if he liked it others would, too. That magazine was written and edited for Hugh M. Hefner."

In the spring of 1955, Hefner decided that he needed a production manager. Again he turned to his *Esquire* connection. *Esquire* had kept a production team in Chicago, of which John Mastro was a member. Mastro had known Hefner casually, but the two men were not friends.

"I was doing direct mail when Hefner approached me. He offered me $25 a week more than I was making, and that upped me, let's see, to $150 a week. When I started, Hefner put me in a second-floor bedroom, screwed in a brighter bulb, and shoved two desks inside. I left a nice office at *Esquire* and ended up in a bedroom facing an alley. It was a letdown, but it passed."

Hefner kept close tabs on his new team member. From the beginning, he was determined that *Playboy* have as high quality a look as he could afford. "He's kind of a perfectionist," Mastro, still with the magazine, says, "tough and demanding. There was nothing he didn't look at, and he knew what he wanted. The question for us—production was me and a girl, then—was whether we could achieve that. We were determined not to turn out a cheap book. Quality takes some of the shock off nudity."

Editorial, art, promotion, production. There was even a business manager on the masthead. Philip Miller, however, worried as much about paper clips and frayed typewriter ribbons as he did about cash flow and billing. Everybody doubled and tripled workloads in the early years. What couldn't be done in-house was farmed out. Hefner's father did the books for the first few issues, but then Hefner went to his college roommate, Robert Preuss, who ran his own CPA firm.

"We had kept in touch after college through our wives," Preuss remembers. "So Hefner became a client. First I handled his accounts, then we became his auditors, and in 1958 he said, 'Why not sell out and come in with me full time?' "

Toward the end of *Playboy*'s second year, the magazine was beginning to deliver a product to match the concept, and the concept was beginning to lose some of its original amorphous quality. How far the process had gone, however, and just how deliberate its execution had been remains the subject of some controversy among the original staffers. This is how Lownes and Russell saw the picture:

"Hefner stoked the rebellion against the idea that pleasure automatically equates evil," Lownes says. "According to Hefner's gospel, this was not necessarily so. The Puritan ethic had to equate anything but work with evil. We felt that America had outgrown that attitude and reached a stage where everybody could enjoy a life and a philosophy that didn't condemn pleasure as such."

More and more young men, Lownes believes, shared that feeling in the mid-fifties and rebelled against convention in much the same fashion he and Hefner had. Pressure for early marriage was intense. The institution was a wall against sexual fury running amok and it kept "the family escutcheon from being soiled." Boys who did not know themselves well married girls they did not really know at all. People were locked young into treadmill existences and urged to stay in the mainstream—or else. Yet for all the conformity that marked the fifties, taboos against accumulation of material wealth were falling. The contradiction between the virtue of possessions and the evil of enjoying them simply could not endure.

Nor could the barriers against sexual pleasure survive. Sex, for good or ill, was becoming a part of materialism. With the pill just across the horizon and other birth-control methods much more widely available, moralizers could not paint the dangers of intercourse in such garish colors. Sex per se did not harm, and the rationale for sexual guilt began to wilt even in the broad middle classes.

Russell, on the other hand, sees development of the *Playboy* message much more prosaically. It was something, he contends, that happened more by accident than design.

"Looking back, you can create hindsights and say, 'Yes, long ago I realized where the magazine was going.' But that would be an invention. A lot of it was good luck, random chance, being carried on the tides of the times, rather than being the leader of the times. It was a matter of being the right kind of magazine able to take advantage of a rising economy more than any degree of conscious planning."

Much of the early bravado, Russell feels, was just big talk. "Hefner was a canny, shrewd businessman interested in survival—and I certainly can't fault him for that—but he wasn't a crusader. He carefully toed the line of acceptability. Those wars against censorship you hear about weren't quite as brave as they are painted. Hefner took great pains not to tangle with the Post Office, the Catholic church, and other pressure groups.

"Text was edited to be sexually less explicit. I had a discussion with Hefner about the word 'ass' in a story I was editing. We debated it and Hefner said, 'no, we can't use that—make it "rump" or "butt." ' ("I have no memory of that," Hefner shrugs, "but I would think it more likely the other way around. Rump sounds so unromantic.") I was instructed to bowdlerize excerpts from classics by Boccaccio and Balzac. I remember one story from the *Decameron,* involving an amorous young priest. Hefner had me change him to a young student, to keep the Church off our neck."

Yet the risk of offending the powers that be had to be taken. Sex sold magazines. They all knew that. "We could have all the Nabokovs in the world and the best articles on correct attire without attracting readers. They bought the magazine for the girls. We couldn't take sex out. The magazine would die like a dog. So there had to be enough sex for the guy to buy it, but not enough to get you into trouble. Showing a nipple could get you into trouble. The Marilyn Monroe picture in the first issue was a nipple shot, but you didn't see nipples very often after that," Russell says.

In fairness to Hefner, he did not duck all confrontation with society's censors. Instead, he tried to narrow the turf on which he met them. Perhaps that was less than heroic, but Hefner did not, in the beginning, lay claim to a hero's mantle. He wanted to survive, so he tried to fight only those battles he could not avoid and had a fair chance of winning. Inevitably, the Post Office was the first challenge.

In the decade that followed the Post Office's loss of the *Esquire* case, it had continued to exercise censorial functions, but on a much more hit-or-miss basis than before. Though it often lost in court, the Post Office could and did cause trouble. Each new magazine that risked its ire had to grapple with the threat of censorship, and *Playboy* was no exception. When it first applied for the cheaper second-class mailing privilege, the Post Office stalled. Then, when *Playboy,* the staff drowned in more work than it could handle, skipped an issue early in 1955, the Post Office went to the fine print in the law that required regular publication. Hefner's second-class application was refused because the magazine was not published regularly. Undaunted, Hefner applied again, and the Post Office stalled once more. Finally it conceded that the content was offensive. Hefner went to court and won. Pending second-class privileges were awarded in November 1955, a year after he had first applied, and were made permanent six months later. High time, too, for the subscription business had grown far too large for Marge Pitner to handle, let alone for Hefner and Russell to drag copies upstairs. That September, Hefner promoted Russell to executive editor and Kessie to associate editor. There was room for staff growth—and for deep thought on how to get a sharper bead on the audience *Playboy* served. Who was the reader, anyway?

"For the most part, we appealed to the urban young man, not the rural young man or the middle-aged urban male," Russell says. "Generally, our guy had some college. He was interested in getting on in the world—in business, in a large corporation, as a lawyer. He was someone on the way up who wanted to know how to live well, how to order the right wines, what car to drive, what books to read. He liked a good short story and a cartoon. He was very heterosexual. We aimed at the button-down, striped-tie guy. Readers guided us in a kind of ESP way about what they wanted. It's a mistake to think we sat down with a slide rule to develop this magazine on an a-b-c basis. We just happened to find things that went over big without being rigid or codified. Remember that we were young men very much like our readers—educated, but not overeducated, hip, fond of money and material things like snazzy cars, plush apartments, and dressing well. We liked that. We did not manufacture a phony image. It was sincere. Not all of us were swingers, but we believed in the complete package, just as our readers did. We were speaking to a group like ourselves, and we spoke the same language."

But as the months passed and the magazine continued to grow, both Hefner and Russell felt that the amorphous shape of the same language was not enough. *Playboy* needed a sharper self-definition, one that could come to terms with the negative connotations in the magazine's name.

"We liked the title well enough, but we also felt that *Playboy* had a 1920s F. Scott Fitzgerald sound to it, a ne'er-do-well, a wastrel. I used to write the subscription pitches, and in early 1956, Hefner and I decided we should use one of them to decontaminate the name 'Playboy' and give it more respectability. We wanted to get over the Tommy Manville image, stress good breeding, fine wines, theater, and," Russell added irreverently, "all that shit. In doing that, we sort of firmed up the *Playboy* concept by being forced to think what the word meant to us. I ended up writing a capsulated concept of the magazine, a kind of *Playboy* platform."

Since Hefner, too, takes credit for the blurb and has used it as an early self-definition, the sales pitch merits close scrutiny. Published on the inside back cover of the April 1956 issue, it said:

What is a Playboy? Is he simply a wastrel, a ne'er-do-well, a fashionable bum? Far from it: He can be a sharp-minded young business executive, a worker in the arts, a university professor, an architect or engineer. He can be many things, provided he possesses a certain point of view. He must see life not as a vale of tears, but as a happy time, he must take joy in his work, without regarding it as the end all of living; he must be an alert man, an aware man, a man of taste, a man sensitive to pleasure, a man who—without acquiring the stigma of voluptuary or dilettante—can live life to the hilt. This is the sort of man we mean when we use the word playboy. Does the description fit you? If so, we imagine you will agree that *Playboy* belongs in your life. And we suggest you enter your subscription at the first opportunity.

An order blank followed the lofty words: $13 for a three-year subscription, $10 for two years, and $6 for one year.

When the statement appeared, *Playboy* was selling better than 500,000 copies a month. Hefner wondered how much further he could take it by himself, and more importantly, whether the magazine was really saying what he wanted it to say. Paying higher rates helped, of course, but money alone would not give *Playboy* instant quality. And Hefner wanted the quality to match his aspirations of the good life as he imagined it was lived in the Chicago high-rises. He had not yet managed to crack that world. Pub crawling with Lownes and Sellers was all right, picking up girls was fun, but there was more to his ambition than that. And it was all tied up with *Playboy.* He needed and wanted a smooth professional to run his magazine, one with certified credentials. He picked Auguste Comte Spectorsky.

"I don't remember exactly how he was brought to my attention. My frame of reference was *Park East,* which he had edited and with which I was familiar before I was familiar with him, and *The Exurbanites.* That and his general background. He'd worked for the *New Yorker* and also edited *Living for Young Homemakers.* By the time he joined us he was working for that NBC afternoon show, 'The Home Show.' I was looking for someone who had good editorial credentials and ideally came from the East. As a bunch of not-quite-dry-behind-the-ears upstarts from the Midwest, we did have to deal with a certain New York prejudice that has never quite gone away, and it seemed to me that if we could find a fellow who, in addition to everything else, had good ties and credentials in the East, he would serve us well. Spec was tailor-made. It was a very happy marriage from the beginning."

The sentiment is pious, as befits the dead, and not everyone who knew Spectorsky alive has been as kind. Moreover, even if the marriage was not all that happy, Hefner had chosen well. Spectorsky had what Hefner wanted then: experience and sophistication, and, most important, he was willing to take them to Chicago and to *Playboy* at a time when few others would. Whatever his motives, he was a pioneer. (Let the Promised Land remain the island in the East River he had left behind him.)

Spectorsky's career before *Playboy* was mottled, at best. He had something of a reputation as a man of letters in New York, but it was flawed and pockmarked with failures. Both *Park East* and *Living for Young Homemakers* (whose managing editor he was) died under him. He wrote too much and published too indiscriminately, running a bizarre gamut from *The New York Times Book Review* to Goodman's *Swank* (where Bruce Jay Friedman commissioned a piece on girl pinching and turned down three drafts before paying Spectorsky half the agreed-on sum as a kill fee). There were rumors in New York that he had not written the best-selling *Exurbanites*, and, to boot, had stolen the idea from a *Life* researcher.

But Spec was born in Paris (1910) and spoke passable French. He had done graduate work in physics at Columbia before abandoning science for journalism and literature. His job credits included a stint at the *New Yorker*, as story editor for 20th Century-Fox, and as editor of the only out-of-New York newspaper literary supplement up to that time to win national recognition, that of the *Chicago Sun*. He had broad contacts in the communications and literary world of New York. And no matter who wrote *The Exurbanites*, the book did illuminate the changing social patterns that affluence brought to the 1950s, and the culture shock that flowed from the invasion of bucolic Fairfax County. It was a social document, and it remains a landmark for students of the period.

Having settled on Spectorsky as the most likely candidate, Hefner got in touch with him in New York. According to Frank Brady's biography, *Hefner*, this is what happened:

> Spectorsky was at home, having a drink when the phone rang. "My name is Hugh Hefner," said the voice at the other end. "Have you ever heard of me?"
>
> "No," said Spectorsky.
>
> "Have you ever heard of *Playboy* magazine?" asked Hefner.
>
> "No."
>
> "Well, may I ask you another question? Are you irrevocably wedded to television?"
>
> "I'm not irrevocably wedded to anything," replied Spectorsky, perhaps thinking of his three previous marriages.
>
> "Good," said Hefner. "I'll be in New York tomorrow to see you."

It makes for a good if unlikely story. By 1956 most people in New York publishing had heard of *Playboy* and of Hefner. Asked if Brady's story was true, Hefner replied hesitantly, "I don't think so. I don't know. But it's difficult for me to believe that Spec never heard of *Playboy*. Later he introduced me in New York as the new Harold Ross." It is a judgment that people who knew Spectorsky in New York in the 1950s—like Doubleday's long-time editor-in-chief, Ken McCormick—share. McCormick maintains that Spectorsky was much too sharp and savvy about the ways of publishing to have missed *Playboy*'s arrival.

Spectorsky seems to have agonized some about accepting Hefner's offer. It was certainly tempting enough: $750 a week, stock options, a hefty expense account. But it did mean Chicago and opting out of Manhattan's literary world. On the other hand an afternoon TV program wasn't much of a challenge. There were legal problems surrounding his last divorce. He was preparing to marry for a fourth time. (His intended was Theo Fredericks, then Doubleday's subsidiary-rights director.) That would take money.

According to Walter Goodman, who became *Playboy*'s first articles editor in 1960, Spectorsky once volunteered the story that he had called Lionel Trilling for advice. "He told Trilling that he was concerned about taking this job in Chicago with *Playboy* and with Hefner, and would Trilling think he was selling out if he did," Goodman remembers. "And Trilling apparently replied, 'You have nothing to sell out.' Now, why a man would tell that story against himself, I don't know, except that he was conscious of his position out there and often talked of the creature comforts he had gained by coming to Chicago."

If nothing else, Trilling's putdown must have made the decision to leave New York easier. It would certainly account for Spectorsky's fierce desire to return only in triumph, and the love-hate he felt for Manhattan in his later years. Both feelings dovetailed with Hefner's own and must have given their early years at least some common basis.

On a Saturday in the spring of 1956, Spectorsky flew to Chicago for an initial look. Kessie was working that day, "making points, I guess," and was the first to meet the future editorial director. He regarded him with some awe and wondered uneasily what the two men were up to, closeted so long in Hefner's office. It would not be the only meeting.

Negotiations were long and complex. Spectorsky wanted a deal not only for himself but for Theo Fredericks, shrewdly figuring that she would be too bored in Chicago to survive without a job. She began her *Playboy* career in charge of reader services and soon advanced to personnel director, a post in which she devised complicated tests for job applicants and trained bunny mothers in the art of manners. Her name left *Playboy*'s masthead in late 1973, twenty months after Spectorsky's death.

When all details had been ironed out, Hefner made the formal announcement to his still-small staff: Spectorsky would be in overall charge of the magazine.

"Everybody was wary," Kessie recalls. "We didn't know what to expect from this Easterner who spoke French. This was the big time, and we were scared."

"Hefner hired him because we needed an experienced guy who could make up for our amateurish errors and bring New York know-how to us hicks way out west in Chicago," Russell, who at the beginning was more angry than scared, remembers. "I kind of resented him at first. I was afraid he'd get between me and Hefner, but that didn't happen. And I warmed up to him right away. He knew his stuff. I learned from him. Hef was right. We needed this guy. We got along fine until he died. I loved him."

So did Kessie. "Spec was a very gentle man, loaded with tact, wouldn't hurt a person for anything, plus all that intelligence piled on."

Paul and Lownes appear to have gotten along less well with Spectorsky. Both operated from different power centers. Abrasion and conflict were inevitable. It is difficult to plumb the depth of that feeling twenty years later. But, for the record, both men say only nice things about him today, and Lownes' appreciation of Spectorsky's talent sounds sincere.

Hefner's relationships with Spectorsky is much harder to assess. As the owner, Hefner quickly asserted his overall mastery, which led to a state of permanent tension between them. Spectorsky's feelings seem to have bounced between loathing and affection, while Hefner simply did not feel that strongly about his top editorial hand, though what he did feel was often ambiguous:

"I think there was mutual respect. I had a lot of respect for him. I think we got on very well. I do think there was a period in which . . ." Hefner broke off in mid-sentence, something he does often, and began again. "You see, Spec went through a period of rather extended ill health and"—Hefner paused again—"and, so I do think there was a period in which . . ." Another pause. The sentences do not come easily now; perhaps his feelings pain him, or he has not clarified them of late. "I, you know, may have been insensitive, you know, in the relationship, etc., as we were trying to build things in the early sixties, and also a period in which . . ." Another long pause for thought without distraction of pipe or Pepsi that so often mark breaks in the continuity of his conversation. Hefner is striving for clarity and honesty and care. "You can get caught up in trying to do a thing very well and . . ." Yet another pause. "No one can really do a thing very well if they don't have a certain perfectionist quality about them, attention to detail, and that can be a little rough on anybody who is the guy that has to do it."

Past that break, Hefner talks more easily. He has been harsher on Spectorsky before and does not want to appear in print once again as the hardhearted villain. (Which he is not. He did keep many of his early employees on the payroll longer than others would have, given the magazine's growth and requirements and the talents involved. Moreover, most of those who left, left well-off.) But then he cannot keep his chief gripe to himself. Spectorsky was a fine editor but never an effective associate publisher. In fact, Hefner complains, he never cared about the other aspects of the magazine—not about circulation or advertising or anything—and he should have.

Spectorsky himself has said on the record that he considered his relationship with Hefner the most important of his adult life. Hefner goes further and quotes Theo Fredericks as telling him that Spectorsky saw their relationship as that of father and son, with Hefner father to a man sixteen years his senior. And some of Spectorsky's petulance about his boss does bring that out. Take this assessment from Ray Russell:

"I think he regarded him with a strange mixture of grudging respect for Hef's best qualities and withering contempt for his worst. During the period of Hef's long, reclusive hibernations, Spec would call him such uncomplimentary names as 'Godzilla of Sleepy Hollow' and would refer to the mansion as the 'bunker,' with obvious Hitlerian connotations. I think he considered Hef to be in a permanent condition of bad taste. Spectorsky, a very elegant man and a lover of Mozart, probably couuldn't help finding much of Hefner's personality, life-style, and taste, to be unspeakably coarse."

Initially, Spectorsky's arrival did not have major impact. He did suggest to Hefner that he change the name of the magazine, a suggestion refused out of hand. For the rest, Spectorsky moved gingerly to establish his power and his influence. Life at 11 East Superior Street became a little more sophisticated than it had been, but the tenor did not change much. Social and personal relationships among a staff that remained small through the fifties were both close and distant. Office life was informal and relaxed, but friendships rarely extended into off-hours.

"The ambience was warm, unstructured, and unstratified," Russell says. "If I needed something—say, a signature on a check—I went up to his office and shouted, 'Hey, Hef, I need this.' There was a lot of interplay, in a business sense, among all the people running in and out of each others' offices. My memories are warm and pleasant. Working for *Playboy* was a lot of fun."

But it was not, as Russell and others stress, one long, boozy party, an impression Hefner tried to foster later with new employees (especially when the *Show Business Illustrated* crew arrived from New York in 1961). "We worked hard and well," Russell says. "There was a lot of interchange of ideas, some shouting, and occasionally we'd get red in the face to make our points. Nobody expected to have any nude girls running down the corridors, and there weren't."

"We did well with a small group of people," Lownes remembers. "The atmosphere was exciting, manic, dedicated. We worked long hours and lived according to the Puritan ethic. The idea that work is a pleasure and a virtue was expressed in our working pattern. Hefner and I started our day at eleven in the morning and finished at three A.M."

That didn't leave much time for normal office socializing. Hefner seldom went to lunch with his staff or out for an after-work drink. From the beginning, he kept his social life, of which Lownes and Sellers were a part, divorced from his work.

"Oh, we made token visits to each others' homes and apartments," Russell recalls. "Sometimes Hefner came over, but we all had our own friends."

Production chief Mastro liked that setup just fine. "I never saw much of the social thing. There should be that division. As it was, we were more of a family than an office. We practically sat in each other's laps. The social thing had to be held at a distance. He'd take a dozen of us to the Red Robin for a Christmas party and give us a bonus. I don't think you should ever get too close to anyone who can chew you out so that he can't if you fall on your ass. And Hef could chew ass."

Kessie remembers a pattern of lunches with Spectorsky, Theo Fredericks, and Russell. He clearly adored Spectorsky and basked in his reflected glory. Some who knew the two contend that Spectorsky treated Kessie as badly as Hefner treated him, often insulting and humiliating his subordinate. If so, Kessie has put that out of his mind. His memory of Spectorsky is unsullied, perhaps because he was named managing editor in 1960 when Russell quit, either because "I wanted to do other things," or, as some maintain, because he felt the magazine had peaked.

The social and political tides of the fifties, what there were of them beyond McCarthyism and the cold war, did not touch the early *Playboy*. Editors were generally liberal, voted Democratic, loved Adlai Stevenson, despised McCarthy, and pitied those destroyed by him. "We considered McCarthy an asshole," Lownes says. "The rumors of his drinking had spread. And once you knew that, he didn't seem such a large threat."

For most of the staff the fact of *Playboy*'s existence was revolutionary enough.

"According to one school of thought, *Playboy* was a crusading journal," Russell says, "waging war against censorship and leading the vanguard of the sexual revolution. Sure, all of us who held top posts during the formative years would like to think we were bold iconoclasts and shapers of public opinion—but it simply isn't true. We were not seriously involved in the larger scene. Our leanings were more left than right, but only in a vague, general way. Remember, we were very young. Nobody was an active, card-carrying liberal, or an intellectual. I define an intellectual as someone who derives pleasure from intellectual things, and Hefner was not that kind of man. Intelligent and bright, yes, he didn't miss much, but intellectual would be the last word I'd choose to describe him."

Kessie says much the same thing about *Playboy*'s interests in the early years. "Hefner knew who Ike was. The rest of the gang was more interested. We were aware of the cold war. Like most pseudo-left intellectuals, it was anybody but Ike with us. We tried not to operate in a social-political vacuum, but sometimes we did. Russell, Spec, and I wanted more literature and less tits and ass. But Hefner held us off. He said that tits and ass tastefully done sold the magazine. Add all the Bertrand Russells you want, and they won't sell one extra copy. We snuck in a good article here and a lofty piece of fiction there, anyway. Hef never read any issue cover-to-cover—captions sometimes, girls, cartoons, party jokes. Spec finally brought him round that there were other things, and starting in 1957 and 1958, we began to make the breakthrough . . ."

For most of 1956, Spectorsky felt his way, learning the *Playboy* routine and the capabilities of his staff. He produced no sudden revolution or rush into higher quality. He wooed editors and agents he knew in New York, brought Hefner along on some trips, sounded out possible staffers, watched in some amazement at the young magazine's continued explosive growth. Circulation had pushed past 600,-000, and was closing fast on the twenty-four-year-old *Esquire*'s. That fall it was 90,000 copies behind; within a year, *Playboy* had passed *Esquire*. *Time* reported that *Playboy*'s pretax profit in its 1956 fiscal year amounted to $750,000.

There was also the move from 11 East Superior Street to 232 East Ohio Street to supervise and take part in. Hefner's operation had long since engulfed the whole graystone and spilled into several other buildings. The need for more space was pressing. The new quarters provided that, but lacked the visual charm and religious intrusion of East Superior Street. It is a grim building still, a four-story red-brick structure with gray concrete trim, not unlike a factory loft. Today East Ohio Street has been greatly rebuilt and gleams with new glass sheaths and a Holiday Inn. But there is enough grime of old Chicago left—the Commercial Mart across a parking lot, a few narrow-bosomed houses, a garage—to give some idea of the mid-fifties scene.

Hefner invested around $500,000 in doing the offices over. Most of the money went inside. Not a dollar seems to have been spent on the facade, which still glowers unblinking in the harsh Chicago sunlight. Swinging glass doors topped by a full-width glass pane with PLAYBOY emblazoned above the house number and the ubiquitous rabbit above the name was the only visible touch of glamour.

The move, coupled with internal growth, made the need for new staff more urgent. Neither Hefner nor Spectorsky were in any great hurry, and Spectorsky particularly kept the editorial side lean and hungry. But some things had to be done, for example the hiring of a new picture editor to take some of the load off Art Paul, and to coordinate *Playboy*'s expanding in-house photo division.

On one scouting expedition to Manhattan, Hefner and Spectorsky first encountered the later common "New York syndrome." People were eager to work for *Playboy*—the pay was attractive and the package was, too—but live in Chicago? Hot in summer, cold in winter, no theater, no congenial bars or decent French restaurants, no other magazine editors to talk to. Ugh.

Mark Strage, the picture editor of *Pageant,* (a digest-size general book with strong male orientations widely praised for its innovative style) was approached. A Harbin-born White Russian who spoke French, Italian, and Russian and possessed the patina of worldly sophistication, Strage must have appealed, for different reasons, to both Hefner and Spectorsky.

"Hefner invited me to the Waldorf to talk about the job. Spectorsky was drinking triple martinis, I had scotch, and Hefner Pepsi. I had heard of *Playboy,* of course, both from our own circulation people and from the photographers I dealt with. Hefner offered me the job as picture editor and said, 'I'm not sure what you're making, but I'll give you seventy-five percent more.' I was earning $125 a week then, so money wasn't the problem—Chicago was. I explained that all the photographers were in New York. That really set Hefner off. He said, 'Listen, if I had started this magazine in New York, I'd never have succeeded. In Chicago I'm a big fish in a small pond. I can get the best talent there is.' Spectorsky just said, 'I live ten minutes from my yacht club.' "

As he listened, Strage was desperately trying to think of a way to land this exotic fish without leaving Manhattan. Then Hefner asked how he would go about getting pictures from the latest Floyd Patterson fight. That was easy. Strage picked up the phone, called a photographer he knew who covered Patterson's fights, and asked him to bring pictures over right away. Twenty minutes later, Hefner and Spectorsky pored over two boxes full. Hefner liked them and eventually ran several.

"That's what I mean about working out of New York," Strage said piously. "I couldn't do that in Chicago."

The ploy didn't work. Hefner and Spectorsky insisted on Chicago. They finally settled on Vincent J. Tajari, a former editor of *Art Photography*. Tajari spent the next fifteen years at *Playboy,* building a stable of photographers to rival *Life,* and equipping *Playboy* with excellent technical facilities.

But *Playboy* did need a New York presence, and toward the end of 1956, Spectorsky got one; Ken Purdy, identified by the magazine as "illustrious ex-skipper of *True* and *Argosy,* free-lance fictioneer of note and sports car buff." Purdy stayed with Playboy till his death in the 1970s, contributing fiction and a stream of articles on the automobile and its mythology. Next, Leonard Feather came aboard as jazz editor, and Nathan Mandelbaum as fashion director (thus relieving Kessie-Rutherford and freeing him for other duties). Feather was the author of a jazz encyclopedia and had worked for *Downbeat* and *Metronome,* Mandelbaum had Hearst and Condé Nast credits.

Spectorsky and Hefner put their commitment to quality in print in the Playbill—the up-front section of the magazine—in the January 1957 issue:

"We here highly resolve to give our readers even better fiction, cartoons, articles, photo features, humor, coverage of fashion, food and drink, better everything in 1957."

It was the prologue of Kessie's qualitative breakthrough. That issue ran a Ray Bradbury story about a man obsessed with Picasso and used Picasso as an illustrator, printing material never published in an American magazine before. In the same issue, *Playboy* announced establishment of a $1,000 fiction award with novelist Herbert Gold as the first recipient. (He should have been. Gold had started writing for *Playboy* in 1954, when he picked up a copy in Haiti and thought it the perfect market for his bawdy stories about a disc jockey that none of the other magazines would buy. Rather than using his agent, the prestigious James Oliver Brown, Gold sent the story directly to Chicago, where it was bought promptly. Brown came around quickly, too, and together, Gold and Brown gave *Playboy* a first taste of true literary patina.)

February brought a Budd Schulberg novelette, clearly autobiographical, about growing up in Hollywood. In March, John Lardner looked at the boxing year ahead. The reprint and public-domain stories, the sports and other handouts, were pretty much gone from *Playboy*'s pages—as they should have been, given the rates Hefner was paying, considerably higher "than any other magazine in the men's field," as the editor-publisher announced proudly.

In May 1957, the *Herald Tribune*'s TV critic, John Crosby, wrote perceptively and wittily about the new medium's problems with sex and advertising. The article, "It's Like This With TV," was, in effect, one of the early pieces of social commentary published in *Playboy*. Crosby's point: So far, TV had been unable to use sex for entertainment, the way theater, burlesque, circus, and film had, because Madison Avenue was basically antisexual. Women are supposed to sell by focusing attention on the product, not their bodies. For example, they should sell toasters, "specifically . . . Westrolux Auto-Magnetic Super Triotic Toast-mistress, the 1957 model, not last year's. In every toaster ad you ever saw, the girl is a symbol of domesticity. When you're selling . . . toastmistresses, sex is positively a hindrance. If a man's mind gets running along certain channels he's not likely to care whether the toast is burned . . ." Betty Furness, Crosby argued, sold refrigerators so much to the ad agencies' liking because she could switch off her sex appeal almost at will. For 1957 this was raw stuff, and few other popular magazines would have given Crosby space for making sex the focus of media analysis and advertising criticism.

Mort Sahl's political humor was analyzed in June. Gerald Kersh and Harvey Swados contributed fiction in July. Nelson Algren published a story about a drug-addicted whore and her pimp and why and how he deserted her. In the tradition of *The Man With the Golden Arm,* the style is sharp, biting, and personal. If this was out of Algren's bottom drawer, as many contend most of his *Playboy* contributions were, he kept good shirts there.

Leonard Feather submitted an early piece on rock and roll, and here *Playboy* hewed to the conservative side, as befitted its growing role as temple to the jazz muse. The article was knowledgeable enough but lacked projective thrust about r and r's impact on pop music—though it appeared a couple of years after Alan Freed made rock and roll a national phenomenon on the stage of New York movie houses. Already, one salient feature of *Playboy* nonfiction was apparent: meticulous information. Example:

Much of the music played is harmonically simple, based on such dyed-in-the-wool chord textures as "I Got Rhythm" and the 12-bar blues, but performed with few of the subtle nuances through which modern jazzmen can sublimate them. What [Count] Basie lacked, what Sam Taylor had, was the pile-driving rhythm, the sledgehammer accent on the second and fourth beat of the bar, that is administered to rock 'n roll addicts as shock therapy.

Feather's conclusions are predictably scornful:

Rock 'n roll may have the same roots as jazz, but it is, for the most part, a bastardized, commercialized, debased version of it. Its main appeal is to adolescent rebellion and insecurity. Rock 'n roll shares a common beginning with jazz but it has evolved no further than a primitive, gibbering ape.

It took *Playboy* more than fifteen years after that to overcome its antipathy to rock. Throughout the sixties, while jazz was dying across the country, Hefner stuck to jazz polls, gave prizes to jazz artists, and willed the music alive in his magazine's pages. Paradoxically, *Playboy* was again late when the jazz revival of the mid-seventies surprised the music world.

The early stirrings of the Eisenhower era's only genuine literary movement—the beats—were also recorded in *Playboy,* but again it was neither first nor particularly bold. Sometime in 1957 New York agent Sterling Lord (agents were the first to break the wobbly ranks of *Playboy* holdouts) sent Russell a story by one John H. Kerouac. Russell read it, liked it, bought it, put a new title—"The Rambling, Rumbling Blues"—on the story, and scheduled publication some months ahead. "Then, wham, he suddenly hit it big as Jack Kerouac, and in the magazine the story went," Russell remembers. As fast, anyway, as scheduling permitted—January 1958. (Meanwhile, *Playboy* managed to squeeze a brief discussion of *On the Road* in the November 1957 "After Hours" section.) The introduction to "Rambling, Rumbling Blues" leaned heavily on the success of *On the Road.* The novel, *Playboy* said, had been widely hailed as "a literary sensation." It quoted *The New York Times* as having called publication "an historic occasion" and other reviewers as comparing Kerouac to Whitman, Wolfe, Twain, and Hemingway.

Nevertheless, *Playboy* wasn't really sure if it liked the beats, or if it ought to. The ambivalence showed in the handling of editorial material. Publication of Kerouac's story was followed the next month with a three-part dissection of the beat mystique written by Herbert Gold, Sam Boal, and Noel Clad. The in-house written introductory material tried for fairness and balance but couldn't sustain it for long. "We'll wager your eyes will linger over this month's leading feature, the Beat Mystique," the Playbill began in *Playboy*'s own version of "backwards roll the sentences till reels the mind"

Time-style, "which dips into the deep-freeze of coolsville and comes up with a penetrating and peppy triple-decker report on the off-beat generation." Subheads announced "aspects of the new nihilism—frozen faced, far out, devoid of normal meanings," while the actual introduction above the package called the Beat Generation "an apt coinage to characterize the angry, roving youngsters whom writers like Kerouac have caught in print . . . beat is a national phenomenon which knows no barriers of age—or economic or social status. From the dope-addicted frigid cat to the baby-faced imitator wishfully thinking he were vicious, the beat attitude infiltrates all levels of our society . . ."

Gold, at least, left no doubt about his feelings. He didn't like the beats and what they stood for, and said so cogently, succinctly, and simply. He objected to their lack of manners, coarse language, and inability to feel. Gold embedded his polemic in descriptive fact (something Spectorsky always required, often at exhaustive and tedious length) and social context. And his conclusions are skillfully drawn and often perceptive:

"The drug-taking hipster is not a sexual anarchist; he is a sexual zero, and heroin is his mama, papa, and someone in bed." And: "He stammers because something is missing, a vital part, the central works. His soul, sense of meaning, individual dignity (call it how you like) has been excised as unnecessary by a civilization very often producing without good purpose. He feels that love is not love, work is not work, even protest is not protest anymore. On the consumer's assembly line, in the leisure-time sweatshop, he pieceworks that worst of all products of anxiety—boredom."

Curiously, what is missing in Gold's piece is a sense of beat history—curiously because Gold had been at Columbia in the 1940s when the beat movement first took shape. "I knew Allen [Ginsberg]," Gold said in the mid-seventies, "and liked him and did not want to mention him negatively, so I didn't mention him at all. Remember that all this happened before things like Mailer's *Advertisements for Myself* and at the time it seemed to me a kind of vulgar self-promotion among the prominent beats. I guess I was pretty hard on them. Kerouac reads like a parody now. Maybe cooking Jell-O on an open fire, which was Kerouac's main erotic kick, was fresh at one time, but when the flower children came, the originality disappeared."

Sam Boal went to a beat party in New York, Noel Clad to one in San Francisco. Both came back with good reportage—or fair fiction—new journalism, in fact, about people one dared not risk naming yet. (*Confidential* was in trouble, Tom Wolfe still in school.) Both articles made the same point: Beat parties were weird, different, and those who pretended to have a good time at them didn't know what a good time was. All those drugs and jug wines. I mean weird.

Playboy and the beats are significant on a number of levels. For one thing, the three articles and the Kerouac story served both editorial and reader needs. *Playboy* was now on record as having displayed and confronted the movement. It had given readers as much or more information on the beats than they would find in *Time* or *Newsweek,* and the magazine had provided a point of view. Readers could discourse knowledgeably about the subject at parties, even give beat parties themselves, and they had been exposed to another alternative life-style (though at the time the term itself had little currency).

For another, it forced Hefner, Russell, and Kessie to join Spectorsky in defining the magazine's attitude to a new phenomenon. That required more rigorously intellectual discipline than the editors were then used to, and certainly more than the early attempts at self-definition Russell and Hefner had undertaken. Most important, *Playboy* had to deal with an ambiguous reality.

"We liked the sort of freedom they espoused," Russell muses, "the liberated atmosphere, the artistic expression in poetry and prose. We were in favor of any kind of sexual liberation, as long as it was heterosexual lib. All that was positive. But we also felt there was a lot in it counter to what we promoted in *Playboy.* The sandaled, dirty feet, unwashed aspects of the beats ran against the grain of the well-groomed, button-down, Aqua Velva look our reader wanted. The antiestablishment attitude, lack of material ambition, or desire to get ahead, which typified the beats, was not what *Playboy* was all about. We were telling people how to make out, not just with girls, but in business and in their jobs. We thought readers getting a bigger car or a bigger apartment was great. There was a lot about the beats we liked and a lot that was not part of our orbit or our world."

Hefner is equally ambiguous: "Our general attitude was that they were an interesting phenomenon and that by and large we were quite sympathetic to them. But they weren't us. The beats didn't fit the particular life-style we were describing in the magazine, or any variation on the life-style. They were on the periphery, commenting on other aspects of society. So we were apt to give them a shot one time and a compliment at another."

Kerouac made three more appearances in *Playboy*—two as a writer, one as a corpse. In the seventies, John C. Holmes (whose novel *Go* was the beat *roman à clef*) wrote very movingly about Kerouac's boozy, lonely later life, his agonizing death, and his dreary, unutterably sad, and lonely funeral. When Kerouac died, nobody else gave much of a damn. That *Playboy* did is characteristic and in keeping with a magazine that is, in many ways, a logbook of American popular culture.

Certainly, Kerouac's second *Playboy* piece fits that mood. It was an essay on the origins of the beat movement which *Playboy* asked him to write from a speech he had given at Hunter College in New York in the late fifties and which the magazine printed in mid–1959. The article is hardly a critical evaluation—Kerouac was not capable of that—but it is an eloquent plea to take the beats seriously, to see the movement as rooted in American music, American language, and American popular culture, from the first *King Kong* and Jiggs and Maggie to Bobby Thomson's 1951 home run that gave the Giants a pennant.

Kerouac's last piece in *Playboy* was a short story about the origins of Dean Moriarty, the hero of *On the Road,* printed in December 1959. It is already heavily nostalgic for what beat had been, for roots and origins, for the time before fame and the disillusionment that followed. For *Playboy* to run it was also in character. There is a strong nostalgic strain in the magazine, as there is in Hefner himself, who even today, despite the wealth and the girls and the constant expression of how great life is now, hankers for the thirties and the forties, for the films of his childhood, for the Andrews Sisters.

By the time *Playboy* was five years old, Spectorsky had put his stamp firmly on the magazine—alongside Hefner's own. The original formula had not been changed, only expanded. Remorselessly, the brand names of literary and journalistic quality marched side by side with nudity, service features, and dreadful trivia. Blake Rutherford and the ever-changing fashion directors (Mandelbaum had not lasted long) lectured on sartorial elegance. Russell wrote glib humor and satire. Girls were on parade in full color, sometimes nippled, sometimes merely exposing acres of mammary glands. Thomas Mario punned and alliterated his way through food and drink, ("a bracing batch of tinkly, tasty, frosty coolers, cunningly concocted for the exclusive dogday delight of *Playboy* readers and their fetching friends," he wrote in July 1957).

But John Keats won the first nonfiction award in 1958 with a probing look at the auto industry, "Eros and Unreason in Detroit." John Steinbeck gave *Playboy* a novelette. J. P. Donleavy showed up six months after *The Ginger Man* assured him fame and reputation. Philip Wylie did his number on Mom with spleen and acid. Ben Hecht, Marion Hargrove (many Playboy readers then still remembered *See Here, Private Hargrove),* Jules Feiffer, and P. G. Wodehouse lent their style and wit. William Iversen's "The Pious Pornographers" took apart the women's magazines and their sly attitude toward sex. The piece, it was widely agreed, made a cast-iron case that the chaste *Ladies Home Journal* and her sisters in virtue were as much by sex possessed as the nuns of Loudon.

Nevertheless, Hefner was not yet comfortable with the serious strain in his magazine. So when in August 1959 *Playboy* ran its first truly political article—a Ralph Ginzburg (later publisher of *Eros* and *Moneysworth*) polemic against the hold of old men on the American political system entitled "The Cult of the Aged Leader"—Hefner felt constrained to print an embarrassed introduction justifying its publication:

> The knitted brow is not a common sight around *Playboy*. While not insensitive to the world's woes, we usually worry about them after office hours. . . . Once in a while, though, our happy editorial forehead creases over a problem that seems uniquely close to our . . . interests. The sick sex in the "blameless" ladies' magazines was one such brow corrugator. . . . Now the topic of our concern is the advanced age of the men who run our country . . .

The subject matter, of course, was perfect for *Playboy*'s under-thirty audience. The fifties were drawing to a close. The impatience that heralded the sixties was beginning to poke through the placid surface of the Eisenhower years. The accent was on youth in all areas of American life save government. Both political parties paid it heed the next year when they nominated candidates in their mid-forties. Spectorsky's editorial hand that picked the Ginzburg project had a sure sense for the future.

The article itself, though, is badly flawed, at times savage in its judgment, at others ludicrous in its assumptions and conclusions. The expository parts—as is still so often the case with *Playboy*'s nonfiction—are clearly the best. Ginzburg builds a carefully documented case. Business retires executives at sixty-five. From the halls of academe to corporate boardrooms, men in their early forties or younger were assuming top positions. Princeton had just named a new president of thirty-nine, MIT one of forty-four. GE's head had retired at fifty-nine to make room for a man of forty. Eisenhower, in contrast, was sixty-eight, and young for the political power game. House Speaker Sam Rayburn was seventy-seven, and GOP leader Joe Martin wasn't much younger. Rhode Island's Senator Theodore Green, the just-retired chairman of the Foreign Relations Committee, was ninety.

In politics, Ginzburg argued, age built a barrier to youth and did so to the nation's detriment. He urged breaking the Capitol Hill barons' power and picking new committee chairmen on the basis of merit and ability, not seniority. The idea wasn't new then, but took fifteen years to implement. A second proposal to keep the wisdom of the aged and ousted by putting them into honorary Senate seats has been varied over the years but never put into practice.

So far, so good. But Ginzburg steps onto thin ice—and predictably falls through it—when he begins to jiggle with historical and political fact and interpretation. Thus in 1940 Churchill is young because he is only sixty-five while Chamberlain is old because he is seventy-one; not, note, that Churchill is a young sixty-five and Chamberlain an old seventy-one and that the relationship was as true thirty years before. Ginzburg accepts de Gaulle's vigor at sixty-eight, but says it is a fluke. Konrad Adenauer is dotty at eighty-two, all the evidence of Adenauer's wit and flair to the contrary. The Soviet leadership, Ginzburg maintains, is young compared to our own. True, Khrushchev is sixty-four, but the second most powerful man in Russia is only forty-nine. He is, Ginzburg writes poker-faced, Foreign Minister Andrei Gromyko. The statement is mind-boggling in its political innocence, given Gromyko's lack of a political base and lifelong technocratic status.

At best, therefore, the piece is uneven. And it does illustrate *Playboy*'s consistent failure to understand foreign affairs, down to only rarely (Max Lerner, John Kenneth Galbraith, Arnold Toynbee) printing writers and thinkers who do. But for all that, publication documented Hefner and Spectorsky's desire to be taken seriously, and to risk the criticism such seriousness invites. Several months later, in October, *Playboy* took up an even graver matter and devoted its first editorial to the subject—the dangers of radioactive fallout and what readers should do about it. Entitled "The Contaminators, A Statement by the Editors of *Playboy*," it was an impassioned and reasoned plea for ending nuclear testing, and a warning about the dangers of strontium 90.

This is how Ray Russell remembers the story:

"It was one of the first (if not the first), antipollution editorials in a popular magazine. It was my baby right from the start, and I had to put up an eloquent battle for it at an editorial meeting. I was met by total opposition at first from Hef, Spec, Kessie, et al: No, we're an entertainment magazine; it's too serious; too controversial; too downbeat, etc. But I pleaded my case pretty well (hinting that controversy could stimulate circulation), and finally Hef gave me the green light. I drafted the piece, with research assistance from other staffers, and it was published as an unsigned editorial statement about the dangers of strontium 90 (which was the big pollution scare back then)."

Russell began his editorial dramatically:

A conspiracy of silence exists on a subject of such urgency that it can, without
extravagance, be called the most important issue of our time. It is the release
into our atmosphere, by nuclear fission, of strontium 90, a man-made radioactive element. Radioactivity is, among other things, a proven cause of leukemia,
a cancer-like condition in which the marrow of the bones forms excessive
quantities of white blood cells, with death the result . . .

   This, you may now be saying to yourself, is an odd message to be appearing
in a magazine dedicated, as *Playboy* is, to life's good things, to the joy and
fun to be found in the world: but these good things, this joy and fun will cease
to exist if life itself ceases to exist. And that is precisely what may happen.
. . . It is . . . time for action . . . writing to our Congressmen, demanding quick
investigation; writing to our newspapers, demanding complete coverage. And
doing it today, for tomorrow may be—literally—too late.

In the editorial, Russell did two things to light up *Playboy*'s future:
He cemented the magazine's tradition of presenting complex information simply, and he justified the case for *Playboy* the concerned
citizen, a mantle the magazine would wear with great aplomb
throughout the 1960s. The justification this time came in the huge
volume of mail the editorial elicited. Nearly everybody prominent in
the ban-the-bomb movement wrote approving letters—Bertrand
Russell, Harold C. Urey (a Nobel chemist), S. I. Hayakawa, Hubert
Humphrey, Norman Thomas, David Riesman, to cite a few. Clearly,
all of them began to sense *Playboy*'s reach, especially on the campuses which were slowly awakening from the political torpor of the
McCarthy era.
   Russell needed all the support he could get. The unease Hefner
and others felt about the editorial was heightened by "a negative
reaction from a local Republican politician who happened to be a
friend of Vic Lownes. Vic—who seldom lost an opportunity to make
the editorial department look bad—gleefully reported this man's
displeasure to Hef, who sent me a rather gloomy memo, wondering
if we had done the right thing." The volume and quality of the mail,
Russell says, helped make his point—"and raised Hef's estimation
of me by several degrees."
   Clearly, *Playboy* was successful enough then to risk a course-
correction toward higher quality. That October issue ran a knowledgeable and perceptive piece on investing in the stock market. It
explained the market's operations in terms a simpleton could understand, yet included information sophisticated enough to be a real
help to fledgling investors.
   Thus, as the fifties drew to a close, *Playboy* was already much
more than a men's magazine or an "entertainment for men" package
only. It had begun to stake out a more ambitious terrain, and the

magazine's influence was seeping across the entire spectrum of American society. Like it or not, Playboy demanded to be taken seriously, and had reached a level of quality where it soon would be, often to its sorrow. In the halls of academe, in the Churches, in editorial offices, even in the halls of Congress, its bite was being felt —and the first knives were being sharpened.

3

The Tastemakers

For all the "corrugated brows" that appeared in *Playboy* in the 1950s, it was first and foremost a service magazine that propagated a distinctive life-style, one often in conflict with the mores of the decade but just as often a proselytizer for its values. Paradoxically, the very rigidities of the early *Playboy* life-style helped pave the way for the "alternate" forms that would mark the sixties. There had to be standards to rebel against. *Playboy* helped set them up, and then opposed them.

In the beginning, *Playboy* was the most didactic of taskmasters. It told readers what to wear, eat, drink, read, and drive, how to furnish their homes and listen to music, which nightclubs, restaurants, plays, and films to attend, what equipment to own and—endlessly—about bringing nubile women to bed. It also told them how to play, to play with toys.

Toys are one of the things *Playboy* is all about. Adult toys. How to acquire them, how to use them.

"Hefner helped the world discover toys," editor Arthur Kretchmer says. "I mean, that's one of the most critical things about him —that he said, 'Play, it's okay to play.' Our particular obsession with possessions is a reflection of that. Listen, I like toys. I was born of socialist grandparents and am as somber a Jewish intellectual as you can be, and I like my toys. I don't like a life that is colorless and bare. It's more fun to drive around in my four-year-old Fiat 128 than it is to drive around in a big Cadillac. I own a very good stereo system. I don't know how anybody can live without a very good stereo system. You should kill for a very good stereo system. And we

55

celebrate that. There are certain things one wants to indulge in. We are about indulgence and celebration of frivolity more than we are about envy and greed.

"Hefner's central message, which nobody got at first, was 'Celebrate your life. Free it up. Your sexuality can be as good as anybody else's if you take the inhibitions out, if you don't destroy yourself internally.' We try to show things that are attainable but special—possible but special. Part of our package is to say there are things that are qualitatively better, that are desirable, that there is a world of objects and toys out there. We don't tell the guy how to get these things, but say, 'Hey, these are things that are nice to have, that are fun to have, or, sometimes, that it's not nice to have.' "

Hefner first articulated that vision of himself in the June 1957 Playbill, the up-front summary introduction to each month's issue. The picture showed a young man standing at the bottom of a staircase, a smiling blonde punching an elevator button behind him, swinging glass doors emblazoned with "Playboy" and the bunny logo, a couple of parked cars in the street outside. Hefner wore a dark suit, striped tie, button-down shirt and crew-cut. One hand on the railing, the other shoved casually into a trouser pocket, the image is one of unflappable cool. The story accompanying the picture said:

> His dress is conservative and casual. He always wears loafers. . . . There is an electronic entertainment wall in his office, very much like the one featured in *Playboy*'s Penthouse apartment (published in the September 1956 issue) that includes hi-fi, AM-FM radio, tape and television, and will store up to 2000 LPs. Brubeck, Kenton or Sinatra is usually on the turntable when Hefner is working.
>
> He is essentially an indoor man, though he discovered the pleasures of the ski slope last winter. He likes jazz, foreign films, Ivy League clothes, gin and tonic and pretty girls—the same sort of things that *Playboy* readers like—and his approach to life is as fresh, sophisticated and yet admittedly sentimental as is the magazine.

The self-portrait—Hefner had written his own text—neatly wraps up his approach to style, taste, and play. Hefner had strong opinions about them and realized early that they were as integral a part of his magazine package as sex. The 1950s needed a guidebook to the good things, to the toys of life. Affluence was spreading, the economy expanding into twenty years of uninterrupted growth. Campuses were crowded with young men who had never expected to go to college. Even the Ivy League was accommodating sons of high school dropouts. The sheepskin was a meal ticket, not a certificate of learning. The "right thing" was found off campus—in *Playboy,* for example.

Service features were an integral part of the book from Vol. I, No. 1. Hefner worried about food, drink, and fashion and made them regular editorial staples. *Playboy* covered jazz, automobiles, and hi-fi equipment, and soon was into architecture and home furnishings. And it treated them all with the absolute conviction of the Ten Commandments. Hefner is a didactic and opinionated man; Spectorsky, if anything, was more so. Authority permeates the magazine. All the upwardly mobile had to do, the magazine suggested at every level, from the explicit to the subliminal, was follow its advice.

Hefner does not like to be reminded of that phase in his development. He views *Playboy* as an open book that always championed alternate ways of living, and he will admit only to an "instructional" bent in the fifties. Trying to reconcile a dilemma he did not wish to admit existed, he said:

"It was intended as a book of service that points the way and supplies some charts as it were for a new world or jungle that you know a young man is just arriving at. *Playboy* is most concerned with that period of self-discovery when men establish their identity. We were trying to communicate in a way that supplied a certain authority, so there is a certain amount of that instructional-guide aspect in the food pieces and the rest. But we weren't talking down to the reader. There was no snobbism to keep him outside. I mean all the implications of a manual of living the good life would be to make a person feel at ease, so he'd know what to look for, and feel confident that he was properly outfitted."

For its first dozen years or so, *Playboy* left no doubt in the reader's mind about how he should be outfitted. In matters of fashion, there was little alternate anything. Once Lownes and Kessie had converted Hefner to the Ivy look, he remained hooked, for all the styles that came and went, on "the kind of thing men like Fred Astaire and Cary Grant and some other extremely well-dressed men have continued to wear no matter what else was in fashion. So there is a traditional part to our view."

First Kessie, alias Blake Rutherford, and after him Robert Green, laid down the sartorial law with firm hand. Rutherford, especially, brooked no deviation from the norm. For years he played an unforgiving Jeeves to the American Bertie Woosters who bought *Playboy.* Being American, these Berties had never felt guilt about argyle socks. They had never known any better. So Blake Rutherford's Jeeves had to make them feel guilty by explaining that there was such a thing as bad taste.

(Perhaps Jeeves's creator, P. G. Wodehouse, helped. *Playboy* began printing his stories regularly in the fifties, though Hefner was never a devotee of the Wodehouse cult and thinks that either Spectorsky or Russell brought him into the book. For all the incongruity of the real Bertie Wooster running among the bunnies, the fit was a good one. There is a link, however faint, between Wooster's world and Hefner's, despite the former's asexuality—or perhaps because of it.)

Blake Rutherford was nothing if not definitive in his exposition of bad taste and how to avoid it. His fashion directives were clear. Take Blake on "Ivy in Action" as he chastises "so many right-thinking guys" perfectly clothed in business suits in the office but gone ape at the beach or on the tennis courts. "The moment they're liberated from the suit-and-tie ritual, it seems their sense of Ivy-bred style takes a nose dive, and they emerge from the clubhouse or locker room in a get-up that would embarrass Lord Invader [a popular calypso singer of the 1950s]. . . . These peacock-clad clods . . . are actually competing with women to see who can look prettier." And wearing "gruesome garbage" like "Old Testament sandals, ballet-dancer shirts that tie north of the navel, too-short swim trunks laced and latticed up the side, etc.—all of which you'll want to forget." Get it, you peacock-clad clod? Then drop it. Instead, buy India Madras swim trunks with a fly front, a red-white button-front check shirt from Hathaway, and a Raffia flat-top cap. The trunks are a great improvement over "balloon-bottomed boxer shorts." For tennis, Rutherford counsels white shorts and sneakers with a red Lacoste shirt and a white sweater for after the game. Boating requires "sun tan" slacks, light but tough enough to protect from sun and spray, marine-blue sweatshirts and zip-up jackets. For drinks and dinner at the yacht club, "you'll want to change" into a navy-blue blazer with brass buttons, gray, white, or, daringly, "Regatta stripes" slacks "and a checked button-down shirt." As for golf, ask your club whether the more comfortable shorts are allowed, and then ask yourself whether you look good in them—"not everyone, by a long shot does." If you do "you'll especially want to team up with a pair of olive-green poplin shorts by Corbin, pleatless, with belt in the back." Add long socks that really stay up, long-sleeve shirt to avoid sunburn, a small brim cap. "Your golf shoes should be the best you can afford, sturdy ones of stout calf kept well polished."

Evening clothes anyone? "Formal Forecast: The Return to Black," Rutherford-Kessie's headline states. "Dinner jackets and tailcoats are fashionably stark after dark," the subhead says. Rutherford disparages the "gaudier evening plumage" of seasons past in favor of black. "Now we said black. Not midnight blue, not maroon, not burnt ochre. Just black. Black looks and feels right . . . so leave your rainbow-hued jackets to the funny-type entertainers on TV. You can distinguish yourself in other ways." Like cut, natural tailoring, no padded shoulders, tapered trousers, "uncompressed body lines." Could Jeeves have said it better or with more authority? And he didn't give Bertie any "form chart for formal wear" either.

What about shoes? Rutherford has "fashion afoot" and "the news in shoes: for leisure, business and evening wear." Here Jeeves might have balked. Rutherford ordains that the stodgy British brogans—"heavy, solid, and frequently stolid in appearance" are out, "conservative continental styling" is in. British shoes, he explains, reflect a climate "rather more grim than our own." Besides, how many Playboys are going to "spend much time tramping through furze and gorse." Result? "All but a few die-hards will abandon the heavy wing-tip shoe and the brutal blucher done up in cordovan or thick calfskin and about as hefty as a football shoe." But watch out for gimmicks, gaudy buckles, and the like "when these tasteless and pointless innovations flash out . . . you stroll right on by." And keep those shoes looking first-rate. Don't wear the same shoe two days running, "drop them off at the cobbler's" whenever heels are even slightly worn down, "and have the shoeshine boy drop by your office daily."

It is easy to poke fun at such dictums, but Kessie writes clearly and simply, and there is no nonsense about alternate anything. The right stuff is right here. Do it. Don't be a clod or one of those buffoons on TV. Know what you're wearing and why. White shirts in the evening. Period. Striped shirts during the day. (*Playboy* wryly changed on that one a decade later when a reader with a long memory asked what happened to the no-stripes-after-dark rule? Forget it, *Playboy* grinned. We change. The world does. You can wear striped shirts in the evening. I mean, you still wear regular shirts?)

The world of pseudo-Wodehouse entered *Playboy* fashions most forcefully, however, during Frederic Birmingham's brief tenure as fashion director. Consider, if you will, his piece on "Spring House Party" in May 1958:

Of all the delightfully romantic social occasions invented by man, none has the glamorous excitement of the weekend house-party in the country. These delicious convocations—big enough for the rovingest eye and intimate enough for delectable dalliances—share the traditional glamor of an ocean cruise and offer much more, too. There's the same gaiety and conviviality of "social" rooms and lounges that one finds on shipboard, but at the weekend house-party the group is smaller and hand-picked by the host instead of by anonymous travel agents; the private goings-on in staterooms are matched by the

cozier room-to-room visiting; and the comparative shortness of the precious
weekend hours more quickly dissipates the chillier barriers. Everyone's bent
on fun, and there's a conspiratorial air of promise from the moment the guests
foregather.

Country weekends, Fred Birmingham opines, are a recent development in the United States, at least the elegant variety. No more
arriving at the country cousin's house and doffing collar and jacket,
rolling up one's sleeves, and there one was. Now it requires careful
packing and judicious choice of wardrobe.

"In selecting a weekend wardrobe, don't stint: better to be over-
supplied with the right duds for the variety of occasions that might
arise, than to make like a world wanderer who must travel light."
And Birmingham does not stint with suggestions: Blue blazer with
brass buttons or striped Dacron jacket with matching trousers for
cocktails, a silk dinner jacket, or, for those less formally inclined "a
smoke-blue jacket of light cotton-worsted mix, fine for small hours
and small talk" with a $39.50 price tag. (Ah, those prices. That's the
true nostalgia of reading back issues of consumer magazines.) Black,
leather-soled shoes (wear them when you arrive) and rubber-soled
models for more rugged outdoor activity. Travel in a suit. Don't take
tweeds. Too hot for train or car. Drape a light, water-repellent
topcoat over one arm. Wear a hat. Check for sunglasses, "leather-
palmed string gloves for top-down driving, windproof lighter, pipe
and pouch." Leave a house gift. Liquor is best. But not your regular
brand. Something more exotic your host won't feel obligated to open
in your presence: a good bottle of wine, a fine brandy or liqueur. Oh,
and watch out that the splendid view of the garden you had from
your window really was your window—not hers. After all, this is
Playboy.

Robert L. Green's arrival as fashion director in 1959 widened
Playboy's horizon. Green is a recognized authority in the fashion
world, and while he was no less didactic than Kessie, his tastes were
broader. *Playboy* paid attention to the surge of Italian fashion in the
fifties and the slide of London's Savile Row. Green followed developments in fabric manufacture, such as the tropical worsteds English
and Scots cloth makers had developed especially for the American
market. And he charted the dash and color President Kennedy
brought to male attire. But overall, Green gave ground only slowly.
He was less conservative than Hefner or Kessie, liked bolder colors
and stripes, greater innovation in cut and fit, but the difference was
one of degree, not of kind.

Playboy did not really react to radically changing fashions until

1968, when Bill Blass showed his first line of men's clothing in the magazine. Then the fashion pages began to explode. Bold blues and browns, flared jackets, stark blacks were dominant. Edwardian jackets made of red brocade and parrot yellow cloth proliferated; green suits with shocking pink shirts; slacks in solid reds and greens, and with floral patterns.

Despite Spectorsky's distaste for the peacock look, *Playboy* was soon awash with gaudy color and far-out design. Men's wear had been one of the magazine's earliest advertisers, and as the fashion revolution spread, manufacturers applauded and bought space. In Chicago, Spectorsky and his editors began to lose control. They abandoned the graphics that had illustrated fashion pieces and shown up details so well, and used photography. And women. Suddenly nudity was all over the fashion pages, and clothes per se made little sense. For a while in the mid-seventies, fashion was just another sex feature.

"Chicago is not a fashion town," says current fashion editor David Platt, "and our editors weren't the first to see the kind of changes that took place. There was a deathly fear that our fashion pages look faggoty. A girl admiring a guy gives added security. They saw kids in jeans, but it took a long time for the office to change. Spec was the grand old man, and he was very nervous about all that."

By 1973 fear of faggotry had driven *Playboy*'s fashion pages into S-M and bondage. Fashion became far out—much further out than straight sex features. A nude ballet of leather, for example, was entitled "The Skin Game," and the text spelled out the message for the dense: "Luxurious, sensuous leather—if it were any more erotic, it would be arrested." Another fashion feature focused on a magician turning caged women into tigers. In a third, nudes are tied with belts to slabs of glistening white plastic. Clearly high-fashion models, the girls are not as pneumatic as the *Playboy* norm, and the touch of cruelty emerges with a sharper edge.

The photography, too, became harsher and more strident. Black lace and garters are slashed with crimson stockings and red shoes. There is a touch of Weimar in the pictures—Berlin in the twenties and the shadow of Dietrich—but all seen in color and through the lenses of Andy Warhol, The Factory, Viva, and the high rock culture exemplified by Bianca Jagger. Men's ties are used as ropes to truss girls. The connection to clothes is more and more tenuous. Women's fashions smother those of men. They are startling, dramatic, and inventive. The feature takes on a life of its own, apart from the rest of the magazine. It is skinnier and more intense. Dirtier, too. Given to the fetish. One spread on shoes shows our macho hero treading his white boot on my lady fair's pubic hair while she humbly ties his laces. It is a far cry from Kessie's firm direction of the fifties, when decorum and good taste still ruled.

What happened to fashion in the mid-seventies was the same thing that happened to many other parts of the magazine—the impact of raunchier competitors like *Penthouse* and the need to do something about them. Since editors weren't too sure what they should do, the whole book was "heated up," and fashions were a natural area to which more sex could be added. In the process, the fashion features provided little guidance or service. Hefner admits that the illustrations had taken over and "become more sexual graphics than service features, and then you've lost the point."

Playboy has been trying to get it back in recent years with but mixed success. The years on the frontiers of fashion's avant-garde have blurred its vision. Unlike other sections, clothes have never made it back to basics.

Food and drink, however, never left home. Features on them were always pretentious and rarely practical. The focus was on the eye. In *Playboy*, food and drink had to look good. Taste was a bonus. The tone was set by Thomas Mario, *Playboy*'s food and drink editor for twenty years, who sent in a piece over the transom in early 1954 entitled "Oyster Stew for a Quartet of Playboys."

"I thought maybe he could give us a monthly food article," Russell remembers. "He was a headwaiter at a men's club on Long Island. His stuff was funny, with titles like 'The Face in the Aspic' or 'The Curry With the Singe on Top' or 'The Life of Spice.' I was too scared to change the prose of his first piece. What did we know about oysters?"

Russell never met Mario. Hefner doesn't remember ever meeting him; neither does Kretchmer. Magazine and cook parted company in the mid-seventies because, Kretchmer says, "Tom's stuff was a little too complex. It required too much time. The life-style Tom represented is passé."

But until *Playboy* grew too big for Mario's britches, he lectured on food and drink, month in and month out. The quality of both may have varied, but the quality of the prose rarely did, whether it was his own or that of a rewrite man. It was awful, punning, coy, alliterative, ultimately maddening. A piece on the clam was called "Happy as a Clam" and described as "a mischievous mollusk's piquant personality on the land, on the sea, on the table." Mario begins a tome on casseroles with "of all feasts, a casserole is the most moveable" and one on soul food with "any chef who's captain of his soul food must know his spices and face the rewarding fire of cayenne and Tabasco sauce."

When he wasn't alliterating, Mario could be every bit as didactic as Kessie. His instructions for making drinks properly:

> Don't use inferior liquor . . . its lousiness . . . particularly bad whiskey, seems . . . intensified in a tall drink. You should seek a standard brand of liquor that is mellow, smooth and pleasing whether taken straight or mixed. Be equally meticulous about all the other makin's . . . insist on fresh lemon juice squeezed at the last possible moment . . . use the best brand of carbonated water . . . serve splits . . . add just before drinks are delivered . . . pour it against the side of the tilted glass. Be sure . . . [it] is ice cold . . . Plain tap water, if you must use it, must be clear and clean . . ."

After Mario faded from the magazine in the early seventies—though his name remained on the masthead through 1977—emphasis shifted from food and its appearance to occasionally useful features on how singles could cook simply, and to the looks of drinks. The more exotic the drinks, the better *Playboy* liked them. The metamorphosis was similar to fashion. Service gave way to sex. The lavish cocktail concoctions out of the 1930s, with their garnishes of fruit and sprigs of green, seemed to fit better into 1970s girl pictorials than gin and white wine. Suddenly *Playboy*'s watering holes crawled with lady barflies in slinky dresses with plunging necklines.

Hefner admits to a lack of interest in food and drink. His tastes are anything but sophisticated, though he operates a restaurant kitchen in his Los Angeles mansion, and has a first-rate chef to manage it. His own tastes run to club sandwiches and fried chicken.

The visual arts are something else, however. Fashion was more a natural outgrowth of Hefner's interest in other visual matters than any primary motivation. He still talks knowledgeably about architecture, design, painting, interior decoration, color, furnishings, simplicity of line, the charm of fussy buildings, and cluttered rooms.

"When I came out of college, my tastes were very contemporary and that held in terms of my own apartment. It was a Mies and Wright kind of architecture and the Knoll–Herman Miller style of furnishings that most appealed to me. And you will find those tastes reflected in most of our early design pieces. They were simple, clean, and contemporary. I'm very fond of earth tones, burnt orange. You'll find them all around you in all the clubs. Where those tastes came from, I'm not sure, because they were mostly formed in my college years and in the years before *Playboy.* My family really has no interest in art or sense of design at all. It is difficult to know how one develops taste. I have a very strong graphic-design sense. Of all the art courses I took at Illinois, the only one I excelled in was design.

That was a straight A. But when it got to anatomy and object art, it was not so good."

Hefner's interests in design and architecture were often reflected in early issues of the magazine. Designs for offices, apartments, and houses were published regularly, and sometimes actually built. The entertainment wall in his East Ohio Street office had been, as the Playbill noted, part of the Penthouse Apartment feature published in 1956, the single most popular spread of the 1950s. Spectorsky later suggested a "kitchenless kitchen" feature which Hefner had built as part of the set for his first Playboy TV series in 1959. "The circular bed was originally an editorial feature, and it became my bed."

A lavish bachelor country weekend house was designed for a 1959 issue because, *Playboy* argued, there weren't any on the market tailored specifically for the wealthy urban bachelor's needs. The place was spectacular, all sliding glass walls, patios, flowing open spaces that melded outdoor and in to make living room and pool area one. A free-standing fireplace-hearth dominated the living room. The feature was the first of many houses *Playboy*'s "modern living" editors found from one end of the country to the other, had splendidly photographed, and wrote up complete with floor plans.

One of the most striking, however, was a design Hefner had made for his own use, and that wound up in *Playboy* as a discard.

"I was going to build a town house on the Near North Side on a very narrow piece of land," Hefner remembers. "It was to be a multilevel structure built around a swimming pool." Cost projections were prohibitive, and while he pondered them, Hefner also looked at other available houses. One of them was a handsome brick town house on North State Parkway.

"The family that owned it was involved in a divorce case, and the wife wanted to sell it. I had never been inside and had no idea that a house of that scale and grandeur existed in Chicago. I walked through the main room and down to what was then an extended garage basement. I realized I could do the pool right there, and that for a little more money than the town house would cost could have the whole mansion."

Having decided to buy the mansion the day he saw it, Hefner proceeded to turn plans for the town house into a *Playboy* feature. Too bad no one ever built it because it was a well-designed, innovative structure, very much out of the 1930s, yet carefully integrated into the brownstones that surrounded the lot. But even in 1961 the project would have cost a half million, and in the late seventies it was clearly out of sight.

Moreover, Hefner would no longer have built it. Over the years his tastes changed. His faith in the *machine à vivre* of the late forties and early fifties has ebbed. In furnishing the Chicago mansion, he had already begun to experiment with mixing traditional and modern, a mix he concedes today did not work as well as he had hoped. The Los Angeles mansion shows a much more traditional strain.

"One typically does get more traditional as one grows older," Hefner says. "I have an appreciation for the filigree today that I did not have as a young man. The simplicity of Mies has a sterility to it. An entire city that was nothing more than skeletons would be very sterile. A lot of junk passed for good design when I was young just because it was simple, and simplicity was the natural thing."

Sports cars and jazz were two other *Playboy* staples, which buffs followed with near-religious devotion. Debates over the virtues of MGs, Jaguar XKEs, Porsches, and Corvettes raged fiercely, but none so fierce as the one over Ford's T-Bird. It was not, hundreds of readers argued over many months, a true sports car, and how could *Playboy*'s Ken Purdy even class it as a sports car? Passions ran deep, and the Playboy who wrote that his only interests were sports cars and Playmates put first things first.

Playboy's real hero in the 1950s was the Marquis de Portago, the Spanish Grand Prix driver who died in flames near the end of the Mille Miglia race in 1957. Ken Purdy's tribute, "The Life and Death of a Spanish Grandee," was one of the most popular articles *Playboy* ever ran. In the placid Eisenhower years, Portago had everything thousands of Playboys really lusted for: drama, high adventure, wealth, the love of beautiful women, and of one woman, his wife, superb competence at everything, a profession he loved, and those glorious cars.

Jazz was and is Hefner's preferred sound. *Playboy* stuck to jazz through rock and became something of a jazz museum. Hefner admits he shifted late to rock and that his tardiness was an editorial mistake. But he is a man of strong convictions, and his tastes change slowly. Before they did, *Playboy* published a string of knowledgeable jazz articles, mostly by Nat Hentoff, that gave *Playboy* the flavor of a music magazine. The flavor was heightened by the innovative coverage of sound technology. The magazine always stayed on top of breaking hi-fi news and was among the first to explain transistor technology, well before it had won widespread manufacturers' acceptance.

Regular coverage of the arts is largely staff written and often seemed more a duty than a pleasure. There is no common denominator, no point of view—only *Playboy*'s obsessive desire to be informative without being condescending. Editors put their arms around readers to lead them gently through the jungles of high and low culture. Reviews tend to be nicer than those published in other books. Critical savagery is not Hefner's style.

"We have tended to be supportive of the arts and paid more attention to things we like and can recommend than putting things down. Granted, putdowns can make for more readable reviews. But *Playboy*'s positive and loving approach to life holds for reviews, too. A guy like John Simon, you get the feeling sometimes he doesn't like movies. If you took reviews in, say, *Time* and *Playboy,* you'd find we have done more favorable reviews of the same film. We serve as a tour guide. . . ."

That's not a bad summary of *Playboy*'s role as an American tastemaker. The magazine covers all the bases, still, though not as didactically as in the past. Since it is less critical than other publications, its opinions often lack bite, while service areas remain too smothered in nudity to deliver all the promised service. But for all that, *Playboy* never lost its role as catalog of life-styles and tastes. If you wanted to live the good life and didn't really know how, *Playboy* told you. It still does. And not only in the magazines, but through its products—everything from martini pitchers to playing cards— and in the clubs.

4

The Myth Takes Flesh

"**N**EW YORK'S New Playboy Club Needs Bunnies," the headline above the small help-wanted ad in *The New York Times* of January 13, 1976, said. The brief text explained that "the money's good, the work exciting, the opportunities for travel, excellent. It's a sophisticated world—and it's yours if you qualify to be a Playboy Bunny. Interested? Then bring your swimsuit or leotard and a pair of three-inch heels to the St. Moritz between 1 and 9 P.M., January 14, 15, 16, and 17."

Two years had passed since the club on 59th Street had closed its door for a $3 million face-lift. For a company earning $20 million a year in pretax profits, that seemed affordable, even if it was double the original renovation estimate. But since the club's closing, Playboy earnings had slid down a greased pole. Only a strong first quarter had kept the company in the black in 1975, and at that, net profits were a meager $1 million. Even worse, the club-hotel division had lost more money than any other part of Hugh Hefner's $200 million entertainment conglomerate.

The clubs, it was said, were passé, relics left over from the 1950s, even though the first one had opened in 1960. They were not relevant to the seventies and hadn't been for years.

"You are dealing with spicy respectability in the clubs," said Robert Gutwillig, a former New York book publisher who in five years with Playboy scooted from heading a nonexistent book division to marketing vice-president before he was forced out of the company. "All they have there now is a bunch of salesmen talking to each other. The sexual revolution swept right past the clubs. When Hefner started them, no one was picking up girls in singles bars. In terms of sexual titillation, the clubs are ancillary to what is readily available."

As for the bunnies and Hefner's look-but-don't-touch policy, they, too, were no longer in demand. Who wanted to look? Who still wanted to be a bunny? Well, a mob of 2,500 girls. That's how many applied for the 120 positions open in the New York club. The small ad brought not only a horde of applicants, but more media space—and mostly favorable space—than Playboy had won in a long, long time.

Reporters crowded the girls. Local TV stations smeared the bunny parade on the evening news. Everybody in town ran feature stories. Feminists asked "tough" questions about the girls being "sexual objects." But it was a recession winter and most of the would-be bunnies, eager to make $200 to $500 a week, gaped uncomprehendingly at reporters with jobs who asked the unemployed about working.

Six weeks later, *Times* reporter Judy Klemesrud did a follow-up story "All Right, Bunnies—Forward, Hop." She spent a day watching about a hundred women go through their last training paces. A middle-aged redhead had been brought in from Chicago to supervise the bunny training program, and experienced bunnies had been flown in from other cities to make sure that the new hands learned how to do the bunny dip properly and knew their Bunny Training Manual. Should a customer ask for a Presbyterian, for example, the bunnies would know at once that he was not interested in religion but in a mix of soda, ginger ale, and bourbon.

About 10 percent of the girls were black, Klemesrud reported, and there were complaints about an unbalanced racial mix. The bunny roster included actresses, models, secretaries, bank tellers, a coloratura soprano, and a former bunny active in the bunny union at the New York club before its closing. Again, questions about women's lib, but they were dismissed out of hand. "We're exploiting men, they're not exploiting us," one explained. "You're one up on women's lib because you can step out of the costume and go home with all that money," another said.

Still, the *Times* had the last word, and Klemesrud's closing paragraph summed up much of the prevalent attitudes about bunnies in 1976:

> Toward the end of the day's training session, as the Bunnies marched round and round with their heavy trays held high . . . they spontaneously began whistling the theme song from . . . 'Bridge on the River Kwai' . . . Somehow, the song seemed appropriate.

On March 8, 1976, Hefner took a full-page ad in *The New York Times* to extol the marvels of his renovated showcase. Keyholders —those who had paid $25 for their plastic card—were invited to "Come to the Cabaret" and see David Steinberg and Lainie Kazan. Bill Cosby would start his stint on Saturday night. The former chef of The Four Seasons presided in the kitchen of the VIP room restaurant. The ad featured a picture of Hefner and a story that he had given Mayor Abe Beame a key to the club, and that Beame had responded with a certificate of appreciation. It was the least the mayor could do, given Hefner's $3 million investment in the financially strapped city and his large contribution to the Police Athletic League.

On official opening night, a salesman—salesmen are as much of a club myth as bunnies—said, "They're making a mistake giving you such a big glass. It makes you think you're being shortchanged and only getting half a drink when you're not."

The remark holds for what the clubs have become: more promise and less delivery. The charge is not fair because Playboy never overpromised. But passing years and changing mores raised expectations. Customers wanted more than just looking at sex and stayed away in the same droves that had once attended.

Much of the blame has to be Hefner's. He never bothered changing the concept behind the clubs. All the $3 million bought him in New York was a done-over version of what he had in the first place. There was a spacious lobby guarded by a bunny in a poison-green bodice. A booth next to the cloakroom hawked Playboy wares, a feature of all clubs. Stained wood and uncut stone covered the walls. Muted browns, ochres, and the all-pervasive burnt orange were everywhere —Hefner's beloved earth tones. Curved stairs lead gently into the Playmate bar. Club chairs. Tables. Electronic games. A heavy, solid bar with mirrors behind it and a galaxy of blown-up *Playboy* transparencies as decorations for the bottles. A hot-dog stand at one end with an open umbrella over it. Two men barkeeps in brown vests behind the bar, and bunnies passing through the cigarette smoke, hopping from table to table taking orders like so many butterflies.

A circular floor disco surrounded by tables stands half a flight up and behind the lobby. At night you can barely hear yourself talk in the bar. The disco sound drowns everything. On the left, elevators wait to whisk customers upstairs to the Penthouse for entertainment and to the VIP room for gourmet food. The layout is standard for all clubs. The VIP rooms are blue indigo and crystal. Wineglasses resemble vases. Cloth napkins gleam. At best, the gourmet food is mediocre.

But the clubs were the first extension of the *Playboy* life-style, the first attempt to move it off the printed page into a three-dimensional world. For the better part of a decade, the clubs were so successful and made so much money that Playboy moved from them into a host of other businesses—hotels, resorts, films, records, a limousine service, movie theaters, real estate, a modeling agency. In the process, what had been a small company in 1959 with sales of $5.5 million and net earnings of $20,000 had in the 1970s grown into a giant corporation with 5,000 employees, sales of almost $200 million, and net earnings that regularly topped $10 million annually.

By 1972 Playboy was a packager of life-styles and was becoming a major force in the nation's leisure industry that might well dictate discretionary spending patterns for millions of affluent young men. Their affluence, Hefner and his executives believed, was a given on which long-range planning decisions could be made confidently and rationally. Indeed, preparations for Playboy's version of *Brave New World* were already under way. Executive Vice-President and Chief Operating Officer Robert Preuss explained corporate thinking to writer J. Anthony Lukas for a 1972 *New York Times Magazine* article this way:

> A man gets up in his Playboy town house at Lake Geneva [one of the resorts], calls a Playboy limousine to take him to the airport where he gets in a Playboy chartered plane, flies to New York, takes a Playboy limousine to a Playboy hotel in midtown Manhattan, changes into his Playboy suit, takes a Playboy ferry to a Playboy convention center on Randall's Island for his business meeting, that night goes to a Playboy restaurant and then to a Playboy theater where he sees a Playboy movie. That's the Playboy environment. And while we don't have all those things yet, we have many of them and we're exploring the rest.

That was much more than merely shaping magazine readers' tastes in clothes, food, entertainment, and the arts. It was creating appetites and fulfilling them, grasping for a growing slice of the economic pie. It was a grasp, however, that would finally exceed Playboy's reach.

Like so much that followed, Playboy stumbled into the club business almost by accident. Hefner and Lownes worked late hours, and when they hit the street at two or three A.M., there weren't too many places left open. Often, drinking at neighborhood bars—there was one right behind the Playboy offices on East Ohio Street, where a museum of contemporary crafts now stands—they would talk of having a club of their own where they could hang out undisturbed any time they felt like it. Lownes had even done some promotional work for a friend named Arnold Morton who owned a private key club, Walton's Walk, which Lownes and Hefner frequented.

In early 1959 they began to take their idle talk about a club more seriously. *Playboy* ran a feature on the Gaslight Clubs—exclusive eateries in several major cities that featured skimpily dressed waitresses, good food, and an expansive ambience. The *Playboy* article drew 3,000 letters asking how one went about joining a Gaslight Club. "That volume of mail told us we had an audience for a club of our own," Lownes says.

But for most of that year they put the club idea on a back burner. Hefner was tinkering with a syndicated TV show that would polish *Playboy*'s image with the public and with advertisers, and he wanted to stage a huge jazz concert to coincide with a city-sponsored festival of the Americas. Not only would the concert give *Playboy* more exposure, it would also anchor the magazine's role as a music publication more firmly in the public's mind.

Lownes hired the Chicago editor of *Downbeat,* a music buff named Don Gold, to help line up talent. Gold agreed provided he was promised a job with *Playboy* after the concert. He was, and buckled down to lining up the best the jazz world had to offer. Talent, however, would prove the least of Hefner's problems. It was the first time he had gone "public" in a serious way in his home town—and the first time he had offered an inviting target to his enemies. He had made more of them than he apparently realized, despite the years spent across the street from the seat of the city's canonical power.

All through his rise to fame and fortune, Hefner was never perceived as a Chicago personality. "Chicago is a neighborhood town," columnist Mike Royko explains, "and Hefner is not a neighborhood guy." People, Royko believes, do not identify with those who hang out on Astor Street on the Near North Side. Chicago is also a Catholic town, more drawn to home and hearth than to the gaudy extravagance of the "good life." The concert was an occasion to make Hefner pay for his sins.

"We'd made the deal for use of Soldiers Field with Jack Riley, a city official," Lownes remembers, "but the church drove us out. I was very indignant. So was the press. One paper even ran a headline, 'One-eyed Jack Is Wild'—Riley had only one eye, you see—and some suggested I denounce Riley for being so responsive to the church."

But there was little time for playing scapegoat. The contracts with musicians were signed, the money committed. Hefner and Lownes had to find another location. "I got hold of the guy who ran Chicago Stadium [a much smaller arena], Arthur Wirtz, and made a deal with him."

The concert was staged on August 7, 8, 9, 1959, and though

Hefner lost money, the dispute with the city earned him and his concert nationwide coverage and made the undertaking a public relations success and an artistic triumph. It also speeded Playboy's entry into the club field.

"Wirtz was so impressed by our success, he asked if we wanted to rent a club he had called The Colony on East Walton Street. He made a terrific deal with us where we paid a percentage on gross revenues and he cleaned up," Lownes says.

Lownes and Hefner took in their friend Arnold Morton as partner to give their new venture needed professional experience. Morton had extensive connections. His family had been in the food and entertainment business for years, and his father, Morton C. Morton, still ran Morton's Restaurant near the University of Chicago. Morton père was even a *Playboy* advertiser. His ads touted the "Mortoni," a concoction made of two fifths gin, one ounce of vermouth and a peeled Bermuda onion.

Despite the pressures of the TV show, the trio opened the first Playboy Club at 116 East Walton Street on February 1, 1960. "There were lines around the block for weeks," Morton remembers. Success was almost instantaneous, largely due to the magazine's drawing power. Returns on mail-order solicitations, inviting people to join at $25 each, were "incredible," Lownes says. He makes no bones about basing the club formula "squarely on that developed in the Gaslight Clubs."

"We had started thinking about girls for the clubs, too. Hefner's idea was to put Playmates in nighties as the feature attraction. I was going out with a Latvian girl I had met on the TV show. Ilsa came up with the idea of having the girls dressed up as bunnies. We discussed it. But for *Playboy*, the bunny was a male image, so Hefner dismissed the idea. It didn't seem to make sense for us. But Ilsa said we were making a big mistake in not going with the bunny costumes. They would be so cute and sexy. And the outside world didn't make the male-female bunny distinction we did. Ilsa's mother was a seamstress, and she offered to run up a costume to show us."

Lownes went back to Hefner and talked to him about the bunnies again. Now Hefner agreed to try. "We had one made up. It looked like a one-piece bathing suit. It didn't have a collar, cuffs, or a bowtie. A club customer suggested that later."

The debate over the bunny costume, specifically who should get the credit for thinking it up, later contributed to a rift between Lownes and Hefner. Lownes admits it was not his original idea "but I campaign-managed it," an assertion that annoyed the Playboy chieftain and did not make relations easier.

But for the next couple of years, as the company careened through such diverse projects as the TV show and the new magazine, *Show Business Illustrated,* the differences remained muted. The two men were clearly onto a good thing with the Chicago club and expansion into other cities.

"Hef, Lownes, and I got together on an exciting commercial package," Arnold Morton remembers, "a new market product. It was exciting and fun, and I learned that quality also has a mass appeal."

The greatest mass and quality in the country were to be had in New York, and soon Playboy was planning its move to Gotham. Lownes found a six-story building near the Sherry-Netherland that housed some offices and an art gallery. He began a massive and expensive renovation. A *Playboy* advertising and a mailing blitz boosted key sales in the New York area to more than 60,000. Morton got busy about the liquor license. He did not anticipate much trouble. As early as the spring of 1960, he had been approached about it. Someone suggested to him that the State Liquor Authority in New York would issue one for $50,000. That seemed steep, but Morton knew New York prices were higher, and he realized that for some people *Playboy* still had an unsavory reputation.

Months passed, and the New York club still had not been granted a license. The complications, it soon turned out, were of a shakedown nature. The SLA wanted more money, another $100,000 to be exact, and the threads of corruption led all the way to the chairman of the New York Republican party, L. Judson Morehouse.

"Morehouse was holding us up," Lownes says. "Sure, we could have blown the whistle on him. But to whom? If we screamed extortion and bribery, the SLA would just shrug that we're saying that because they wouldn't issue a license to an immoral magazine."

Playboy paid and the New York club opened its doors, with a license, on December 15, 1962. Then Hefner, Lownes, and Morton went to Frank Hogan the New York District Attorney. A grand jury was called. The Playboy executives testified. Eventually the scandal broke and ended Morehouse's political career. The prosecutors were properly grateful to Playboy. Even Governor Rockefeller thanked Hefner and Co. for having the courage to come forward and fight extortion, and he promised that the state would not retaliate.

But it is hard to keep an offended bureaucracy in line. The club was denied a cabaret license under a New York law against "girls mingling" with customers and possibly encouraging prostitution. The strict rules Lownes and Hefner had imposed on bunny behavior cut no ice. Eventually Playboy took the case to court and won. In the meantime, it was allowed to hire live musicians but not live comedians or other entertainers.

The publicity surrounding the case was enormous, especially after

Morehouse and New York State's GOP establishment became involved. But these were the kind of headlines Playboy could have
done without. The situation was much more ambiguous than the fuss
over the Chicago jazz concert where lines had been drawn sharply.
After all, Playboy had paid the money for the license, and the nightclub business was notorious for corruption and underworld influence. And if the case did anything, it hardened Lownes and Hefner's
resolve to stick to the tight rules laid down for the clubs and for the
bunnies who worked in them. Should the thought of adding discreet
brothels to the clubs have ever entered their minds, that case
scotched it.

Despite growth and success of the clubs and the magazine, the
magnetic and mercurial Lownes became restless. "I began to feel I
was on another treadmill, that I was being trapped by my own
success. I became annoyed with the direction the company was
taking. People were making waves. There was too much bureaucratic
overhead. Hefner had employed his brother. I wanted to broaden my
horizons. Sure, they seemed endless what with our opening new
clubs and hiring talent to perform in them, and the promotional
work I was doing for the magazine. But it all seemed the same. I was
dissatisfied."

In July 1962 Lownes left Playboy over what he calls "some petty
thing. I was taken to task for criticizing someone in the club rather
than sending a memo." He moved to New York and opened a
promotional firm with Playboy as a major client. The split was not
complete, for Lownes remained president of the New York Club and
was up to his eyeballs in the license fight. But the Lownes-Hefner
team that had worked so well for eight years had broken up and there
were some who wondered how well Hefner would fare without
Lownes.

The split, which did not affect their personal friendship, proved to
be temporary. Still restless in New York, Lownes decided to move
to Europe and convinced Hefner that "swinging" London offered
new opportunities for growth. Specifically, he wanted to open a
Playboy club with gaming operations. Hefner was enthusiastic, and
in December 1963 Lownes set out to remake the Old World in the
bunny image. It took two-and-a-half years to cut through the English
legal jungle, but in the summer of 1966, everything was in place, and
Lownes opened the London Playboy Club. English bunnies—as
busty if not bustier than their American counterparts and trained by
U.S. bunnies—served patrons drinks and food and made for the most
fetching croupiers of any casino in Europe. And when the financial
storms broke over the Playboy empire in the mid–1970s, it was

Lownes's English operations that kept the company in the black, however precariously.

By mid–1966, the club operation was all roses. Half a million keyholders frequented fifteen clubs from New York to Los Angeles. London was about to open at a cost of $4 million. A resort complex was under construction at Lake Geneva, Wisconsin, within easy driving distance of both the Chicago and Milwaukee metropolitan areas. In its June 25 issue, *Business Week* took stock of what was happening in an "industries" piece, titled "Playboy Holds Key to Nightclub Success." The subhead summed up Playboy's achievement:

"By mass merchandising a champagne atmosphere at beer price, Playboy Clubs have built a profitable chain of 15 nightclubs. Now it's starting to build resort hotels."

Hefner's innovation lay in mass-marketing, *Business Week* said. "The chain of Playboy Clubs is a middle-class phenomenon not unlike the supermarket, and it has been successful for many of the same reasons: low prices, good value for the money, a reassuring uniformity of layout and product, and tight control of quality and operations from a central headquarters."

The stock market had lunged for a magic 1,000 on the Dow Jones Industrials that year, and the roaring affluence of many had driven most nightclubs beyond middle-class reach. A night out for two at the Playboy Club could still be had for less than $20, *Business Week* reported, $6 less than in most other clubs, and a lot less than the cost in an ordinary New York City nightclub.

In addition to the income they generated, Playboy keys had a major advantage for mid-sixties management: They were a credit instrument that virtually eliminated cash transactions—and the petty pilfering by employees that is "a nightmare for most club operators." Wholesale purchase of entertainment packages also kept down costs and boosted profits, the magazine reported.

Playboy buys entertainment on a wholesale basis to fill the four rooms in the standard layout of each club where some kind of instrumental or vocal diversion is offered. Sixty acts and nearly three dozen trios are employed each week. Waving the carrot of steady work [Playboy] can lure good entertainers at minimum cost. Often the acts are unknown when they are first booked, but Playboy also books big names. Star or not, Playboy's top price is $1,000 a week, a third of what even a middling attraction can make in Las Vegas. Playboy can get away with lower pay . . . because [it] can offer an entertainer close to a year of solid work. Exposure on a national circuit, and steady employment, are powerful persuaders.

The clubs charged a flat $1.50 for drinks and $1.50 for full meals. They took a beating on food where costs took up an astronomic 51 percent, *Business Week* said, but made it up on drinks where costs averaged 16 percent of bar revenue compared to customary nightclub costs of 25 percent. Flat costs had the advantage of reducing billing errors and overall billing expenses.

But for all the laudatory comment on the clubs' streamlined operations and business methods, *Business Week* was at a loss to explain their spectacular success in the short six years they had been open. It quoted Hefner as believing the clubs were the waves of the entertainment future, and crediting their success to "our ability to provide something you can't get on TV or in your home." The "something," the magazine explained a bit lamely, was probably the exclusiveness "that Playboy carefully cultivates," a statement it took back in the next sentence by quoting "one critic" as saying that "it's a sociopsychological thing that really doesn't exist. You can hardly be exclusive in a membership of a half-million."

Long-range, all that would be true enough, but for the mid and late sixties, the cachet of belonging to something special lingered, even though it was already apparent then that the clubs did not address the same audience as the magazine—that there was, in fact, relatively little overlap. But since both clubs and magazine were a smashing success, no one in the company bothered thinking about the future implications of serving two distinct clienteles. Long-range planning had little room in a corporation growing too fast for anyone to stay on top even of breaking developments.

For the rest of the decade, the clubs prospered. The bunnies became an American cult—laughed at by some, admired by others, ignored by few. The media picked up quickly on them, and most of the time Playboy was happy to oblige with free cheesecake, as long as the sign of the Playboy Clubs was part of the picture. Feature stories about bunnies proliferated. More and more men wondered whether rules about dating them really were as strict as Hefner and Lownes contended—and crowded the clubs to find out for themselves. Interest grew so great that a couple of magazines tried—and failed—to sneak women reporters into the clubs to work as bunnies and come out with the real scoop.

Late in 1962 the idea was tossed around in the offices of Huntington Hartford's *Show* magazine by a stunning apprentice writer and two shell-shocked veterans of a Hefner magazine venture—Frank Gibney and Marvin Barrett. They had returned to New York less than enchanted with Playboy's way of doing things. The writer was Gloria Steinem who had written a few casual pieces for *Show* and done some research.

"It wasn't spite," Gibney says. "We weren't trying to zing the guy. I basically thought that Hughie was funny, and he was an object of public comment. Besides, I always felt the clubs and the bunnies were a distortion of humanity, a calculated playing-up to the worst instincts of two-bit voyeurism."

For *Show,* a serious magazine of the arts which featured regular criticism by Arthur Schlesinger and Norman Podhoretz, the bunny story would be "a great leavener," not to mention a circulation booster.

If any woman writer could pull this one off, it was la Steinem. As *Show* wrote on top of the first of a two-part series, *"Show* chose a writer who combines the hidden qualities of a Phi Beta Kappa, magna cum laude graduate of Smith College with more obvious ones of an ex-dancer and beauty queen." Steinem's pieces ran in the May and June issues of 1963 in the form of a diary beginning on January 24th, 1963, just six weeks after the New York Club had opened, to February 22.

The exposé has become something of a classic, and it first made Steinem's reputation as a writer and a reporter. In true muckraking fashion, it ripped the smiling, heavily-made-up mask from the bunny's glamorous face and revealed the tawdry despair that lurked below. Bunnies worked till they dropped, made a lot less money than they were promised, were at the mercy of busboys, and suffered under a set of rules that might make Capuchin monks rebel. Costumes were purposely too tight so that they left work every night with red welts and bruises all over their bodies. Most bunnies stuffed their bosoms with everything from garbage bags and Kleenex to sweat socks and Kotex to appear larger. Employees barely had time to eat, and company food consisted mostly of stew, except for fish once a week. Men pawed them constantly, offered them hotel keys, large sums of money to work private parties, and bellowed like water buffalos in heat when they were refused. But bunnies were fair game for "number-one" keyholders—allegedly top media people, key Playboy Club executives "and a few other VIPs." The girls were not required to accept invitations from the number-ones but often got into trouble with the "Room Directors"—described as Hefner's Simon Legrees—if they didn't. And, of course, there was an open invitation to attend parties at Victor Lownes' apartment—without dates. In short, Steinem found little glamour, much drudgery, and exploitation. Some people contend that her conversion to militant feminist was born of that experience.

Curiously, Hefner is neither angry nor outraged about Steinem's coup—just a little bored. It was, he said briskly, "much ado about nothing and the beginning of her career. She wanted to cut us up, but there wasn't much to write about or to put down. I'm sure most readers were disappointed. People expected to get hot stories, and there weren't any hot stories. Nothing was exposed."

One reason for his tranquil memory might have been the ultimate effect of the Steinem pieces. Sure, the clubs got some bad publicity —among the highbrows who read *Show* and wouldn't be caught dead in a Playboy Club anyway. Those who read about Steinem's experiences in press accounts had their appetite whetted and swelled the lines waiting outside in the snow trying to get in. Why, Steinem had confirmed that bunnies were not that invulnerable. *Somebody* got to them!

Besides, Steinem could be balanced off by Norman Mailer, who had spent time in the Playboy Club around five in the afternoon on the day of the first Patterson-Liston fight, and whose writing about that experience in his "Ten Thousand Words a Minute" (part of his book *The Presidential Papers*) lent the clubs a literary and symbolic cachet they could have won from few other public personalities.

> As the fight approached, [columnist Pete] Hamill and I had been growing nervous in a pleasant way, we were feeling that mixture of apprehension and anticipation which is one of the large pleasures of going to a big fight. Time slows down, the senses become keyed, one's nose for magic is acute.
>
> Such a mood had been building in each of us over the afternoon. About five we had gone to the Playboy Club with Gene Courtney of the *Philadelphia Inquirer,* and it had looked about the way one thought it would look. It was full of corporation executives, and after cancer gulch, the colors were lush, plum colors, velvet reds with the blood removed, a dash of cream, the flesh-orange and strawberry wine of a peach melba. Dutch chocolate colors, champagne colors, the beige of an onion in white wine sauce. The bunnies went by in their costumes, electric-blue silk, kelly-green, flame-pink, pinups from a magazine, faces painted into sweetmeats, flower tops, tame lynx, piggie, poodle, a queen or two from a beauty contest. They wore a Gay-Nineties rig which exaggerated their hips, bound their waist in a ceinture and lifted them into a phallic brassiere—each breast looked like the big bullet on the front bumper of a Cadillac. Long black stockings, long long stockings, up almost to the waist on each side, and to the back, on the curve of the can, as if ejected tenderly from the body, was the puff of chastity, a little white ball of a bunny's tail which bobbled as they walked. We were in bossland.
>
> "We drank, standing at the bar, talking about fights and fighters. . . .

The writers started talking about that night's fight. Courtney thought Liston would win; Mailer favored Patterson. Courtney produced a Playboy lighter with a bunny on it. They began to spin it. If one ear pointed to Mailer, Patterson was knocked down; if it pointed at Courtney, Liston hit the deck. Two ears at either one meant a knockout. Mailer had earlier picked Patterson in six, and, dutifully, the lighter pointed two rabbit ears at Courtney on the sixth spin. It had also correctly reflected Mailer's prediction on knockdown and rounds. "The cigarette lighter had given me a perfect fight."

"Well, the Playboy Club was the place for magic, and this mood of expectation, of omen and portent, stayed with us."

Liston flattened Patterson in one round. If the Playboy Club was magic, the magic surely did not hold outside the premises, not after the mid-sixties anyway when storm warnings had begun to fly in the world around them.

For even as *Business Week* confirmed the clubs' commercial success, and the opening of the London Club—with "tout everybody" there from the Earl of Suffolk and the Marquis of Tavistock, Rudolf Nureyev, and Lee Radziwill to Woody Allen, Julie Christie, Rex Harrison, Jean-Paul Belmondo, Vanessa Redgrave, and Henry Luce III—reinforced the magic of international glamour that clung to them, a subtle cancer had begun to spread through their vitals: the urban crisis.

It was not a new crisis. American cities had been left to decay for decades. But the promise of the sixties, symbolized by President Kennedy's visionary rhetoric, raised new questions and doubts about the quality of urban life. If the country was moving again, if things were getting better in so many other places, people in blighted ghettos and crumbling inner cities wondered, why are they so much worse where we live? They asked the question first in Harlem in 1964, and with much greater emphasis in Watts a year later. Riots and street demonstrations swept city after city. Newark and Detroit burned. Johnson called out the troops.

The middle-class exodus into suburbia, a more or less orderly retreat stretched over the past two decades, became a panicked rout. Those who remained hid in their homes behind triple locks and electronic surveillance gear, adding to the ebb of people from the entertainment centers of cities, as every color television bound yet more millions to set and living room. Core cities became ghost towns at night. Faster than anyone might have anticipated, the neighborhoods in which most Playboy Clubs were located deteriorated beyond real hope of repair. The Los Angeles Club, built on the once-glamorous Sunset Strip, found itself, as the seventies began, surrounded by honky-tonk strip joints frequented by young runaways. Indeed, so bad had the neighborhood become that the club was moved, at great expense, to the posher surroundings of Century City. The old neighborhood hardly sported an atmosphere likely to attract sophisticated Playboys, let alone the staid middle-aged and middle-class crowd that had been the rockbed base of the clubs from the beginning.

Thus, as the sixties ended, the wild success the clubs had enjoyed in their brief heyday was over also. Perhaps everything had been too explosive to last. Within a seven-year period Playboy had opened seventeen clubs, fifteen in the United States, one in Montreal, and the London Club. Baltimore, St. Louis, and Boston were franchise operations; the rest were managed by wholly owned subsidiaries of the parent company. Then, abruptly, with the opening of the Denver Club, expansion ceased. Coincidentally, 1967 was the year of Detroit and Newark, the year the depth of the urban crisis really hit. By 1971, when the company went public, failure to open new clubs, the underwriters noted, had eaten into sale of new keys, an important source of revenue.

There were other problems. The "socio-psychological thing" *Business Week*'s critic had noted in 1966 began to work against Playboy. The clubs were no longer perceived as chic and sophisticated. Businessmen who once frequented them regularly no longer did. As sexual barriers fell, there was titillation to be had elsewhere at the same price. Topless luncheon places opened in major cities, from New York to San Francisco. What had seemed daring ten years before, was tame now.

Morton says he began to have his own doubts about the continued validity of the club concept around 1969 or 1970, a couple of years before he left the company.

"The audience was becoming more and more mid-American. The more sophisticated kids weren't coming in. We settled for mediocrity. Hefner now has the greatest blue-collar clubs of the Western world. He's hung up on entertainment, and I don't think young people want to be entertained. They don't want to be shushed by the stand-up comics. They want to be loose and informal. The clubs are stiff and formal. You are told to sit down. The product should have been upgraded a long time ago. The design of the places makes people feel down. They all look as if a cookie cutter took over.

"I was responsible for a lot of things that went wrong. But when I realized that things had to change, there was no way I could get Hef and his community of cronies to understand. There was always too much emphasis on bunnies. They ran the clubs as much as the managers did and could always get to Hefner. Hef thinks the only worthwhile things about the clubs are the bunnies. He just won't let go of them."

But at corporate headquarters in Chicago, few people bothered about the failing clubs. Preuss and other executives, looking for something to do with all that extra cash, had persuaded Hefner to move full tilt into hotels and resorts. Again, the company had stumbled into the business by accident. Back in January 1964, Playboy had picked up a 200-room resort hotel in Ocho Rios, Jamaica, on ten acres of beachfront. The cost had been around $2.5 million. Profits looked good from the start, and two years later, Hefner was deep in plans for a second resort on a 1,350-acre spread at Lake Geneva, Wisconsin. It opened for business in May 1968, and both hotels did so well that Playboy decided to expand further.

"I only wish Jamaica had flopped," Lownes laughed ruefully in the summer of 1976, a year after he had agreed to spend part of his time in Chicago to rescue the then desperately troubled club-hotel division. "If Jamaica had flopped, they wouldn't have made all those other big mistakes."

There were three of them, made in rapid succession in 1969–70. The first and biggest was a follow-up to Lake Geneva—an even gaudier resort built on 567 acres in the Vernon Valley of New Jersey, fifty miles from New York. Next Playboy bought hotels in Miami Beach and Chicago. The hotels lost money, painful but bearable. But for many years, Great Gorge, the New Jersey resort, was a financial disaster.

Nobody who is still at Playboy is quite sure why the company bought the Miami hotel. True, terms were favorable—very little down and a twenty-year 7 percent mortgage for the remaining $12.5 million—and the Miami Playboy Club had always been profitable. But in 1970 Miami Beach had been badly overbuilt, and the hotel (renamed the Playboy Plaza) had suffered "substantial" operating losses from the day the Hilton chain opened it in 1967. Ex-marketing head Gutwillig thinks the favorable purchase terms "should have been the tip-off that it was a bummer."

Nevertheless, Playboy invested $1.5 million in renovating a new hotel to give it the bunny look. It was money down the drain. Miami Beach was not Playboy territory. The customer was different. He tended to middle age and to bringing his wife. For that combination bunnies were a turn-off. The message from Florida was clear and chilling: The rabbit was no magic talisman that turned everything it touched to gold. The company lost $6 million, finally unloaded the hotel in 1974 at book value: $13.5 million.

The Playboy Towers Hotel in Chicago was acquired even more haphazardly. In 1967 Hefner decided that East Ohio Street no longer suited his purposes and leased one of Chicago's most prestigious office towers, the thirty-seven-story Palmolive Building in the heart of the city's "Gold Coast." Next door to the renamed Playboy Building stood an aging and creaking hotel, the Knickerbocker, that could

only look enviously at its more glamorous neighborhood competition
—the tony Drake across the street, for example. The Knickerbocker
had small, cramped rooms and a badly run-down operating plant,
including an unstable water supply. The lobby bar had an unsavory
reputation as a singles hangout, and the clientele was heavily black.

Clearly in trouble, the owners approached Playboy in 1970 with
a proposition for a takeover. "We came up with a counterproposi-
tion," Lownes said savagely six years later, biting at one of his
inevitable and elegant cigars. "It was so good they couldn't believe
their ears. Among other things, we suggested they get a quarter out
of every dollar we raised room rates. They staggered out of that
meeting in disbelief that anything so good had come their way. You
know that every time you up prices a buck, you do it because your
costs have gone up 90 cents. That's a net loss of 15 cents for us on
every dollar increase. It's just a lousy deal."

One has to have stayed at the Playboy Towers to savor just how
lousy. Renovations totaled $1.75 million but somebody got gypped
—if no one else, the unfortunate guest. Not only are the rooms small,
the windows facing street or courtyard (with the exception of the
"16" line of rooms which offer a view of the lake—through an alley
between the Drake Hotel and an adjoining building), but they were
redecorated to fit an adolescent's tawdry image of a cheap brothel—
presumably one even he could afford.

Enter this piece of surrealism gone amok and you are greeted by
a shaggy yellow rug running up one wall from the floor. Halfway to
the ceiling, the creeper is interrupted by a wall-length mirror. A
brown imitation-leather or vinyl bedspread covers the double bed.
Two uncomfortable orange vinyl club chairs, balanced precariously
on a reedlike center pole, stand at a small, round table with a white
top. Windows are framed by plastic-looking curtains striped red-
brown-orange-yellow-white. There is wood paneling, too oily to look
real or comfortable, two dressers of the same dark hue, three lamps,
a big color TV that rarely works well. Leroy Neiman, a Hefner crony
who grew rich from the pictures he sold the magazines and the art
that hangs in clubs and hotels (and has since gone on to fame and
fortune on TV and elsewhere) contributed two prints per room,
usually a hunt or drinking scene. At its best, Neiman's work is
mediocre. Overexposure to his mass-production output in the Chicago hotel is deadly. Bathrooms feature ceilings lacquered red and
walls striped red and gold. The washbowl is a startling black, tiles
and shower curtains a dead white.

The final chords of this bizarre orchestration are added by the
Gideon Bible, carefully tucked into the top drawers of the night
table. Equally strange is the hotel's stubborn refusal to supply guests

with a Chicago telephone directory. They are supposed to make do with the yellow pages.

Great Gorge was worse, much worse. True, the setting is lovely, and only fifty miles from New York, the largest metropolitan market in the nation. But loveliness and proximity do not make the resort accessible. There is no train or bus service, no major highways, only rambling country roads. Moreover, the huge facility with its two wings, 700 rooms, indoor and outdoor pools, tennis and golf, restaurants and Playboy Club, was completed at a time when more established and accessible resorts were having a hard go. The affluent young, the magazine demographers' darlings, fled to the Hamptons and Fire Island, where they rented summer houses in groups. Those who came to Sussex County for vacations or weekends tended to the lower end of the economic scale. And for years Playboy managers failed to crank up the convention business. With construction costs already ballooned from an initial—dreamy—$15 million to $33.5 million upon completion, the addition of burgeoning operating losses had to bleed the company badly, and they did.

The impending fiasco and its ominous implications for corporate survival were a major reason for Hefner's asking Lownes to come home, at least part-time. Morton had been bumped in 1973 "because he was out of his element," Hefner said. Those who followed him did not improve the situation.

"With Morton gone, the clubs turned into hamburger joints," Lownes said bitterly. "And I am not exaggerating. A couple of idiots ran the division. It was a real mess. I tried every idea in the book to find a formula that would make the clubs more contemporary and exciting. But you couldn't do that overnight, either."

For the first year, in fact, Lownes could do little but try to dam the financial drain. He cut losses in the U.S. club operations as hard as he could and boosted earnings of his chain of British gambling casinos—two in London, one each in Portsmouth and Manchester.

But plugging hotel leaks proved harder. Nothing seemed to work. Lownes tried taking the Playboy name off the hotels, hoping to attract more family and convention business, but found only that it kept away the few customers who had come because of the Playboy label. By the time he put the name back on, the switch had added $1.5 million to hotel losses. By the spring of 1976, Lownes was seriously exploring sale of at least Great Gorge despite the heavy losses the company would have to swallow. Then an old colleague put him onto the time-sharing concept—selling hotel units for fixed periods each year to different customers. If time-sharing didn't save the hotels, it bought Playboy enough time to see if gambling were not, after all, made legal in all New Jersey—in which case Great

Gorge would be a bonanza—and time to attract the kind of topflight management that might make a difference.

The clubs, too, became a holding operation. Lownes knew he had to get "equity sweat" in them to turn a profit, and that he couldn't do that from Chicago. What he needed was more franchising operations, investment of additional funds to move clubs to new locations only where profits looked solid—meaning prosperous suburbs with enough local night-owls to support clubs—and the hard heart to close clubs that could not be turned around.

Again, that took time. While he waited, Lownes was left to his own promotional devices, and occasionally there would be a zinger in his quiver.

The fall 1975 issue of *VIP*, the Playboy Club magazine, features a bevy of bunnies on the cover marching down the stairs of the Chicago Club hoisting aloft a forest of signs. "Wake up Hef, it's 75," one proclaims. "Bunny Lib," says another. "We Want to be Key-holders too," a third. The caption reads: "Bunny Lib Wins in a Walk." Inside, the feature story is headlined "The World's Most Beautiful Walkout." Bunnies, it seemed, were unhappy with the restrictions Hefner had put on their behavior. They wanted to be keyholders too, to be free to date customers and to use their real names if they wished while working. And out they trooped onto East Walton Street to shake their tails and wave their signs to give added emphasis to the protest letter they had sent Hefner.

> . . . there are times when we think you a Male Chauvinist Rabbit. . . . Because of the archaic rules you have decreed for Bunny behavior we are made to feel like strange objects out of step with our times. . . . Our private lives should be our own. . . . You have created a caste system through which we bunnies have become America's "Untouchables." . . . We expect to hear from you in a positive way. . . . We have nothing to lose but our tails and ears.

Coincidentally, TV crews had built up camera stations across the street at the Drake waiting for West German President Walter Scheel to arrive. A dull story. No wonder the reporters and cameras hustled to the Playboy side for action shots and big-grin interviews with the lovely strikers. Bunny Lib made it coast-to-coast on the tube and in print. Hefner sent an obliging letter acceding to all the bunny demands, with one disclaimer: "Some of these rules came about because of specific legal restrictions in certain areas, and these, of course, we must still impose." Afterwards bunnies held a victory celebration in the club and toasted Hefner's favorite still, showing him in a print shirt open past his chest outside his L.A. mansion, with a Bunny Lib button attached.

After Bunny Lib's victory, club business picked up dramatically for a while as men stormed inside hoping to "score" with the newly available bunnies. And it is not a put on, either. Occasionally key-holders do manage to snag dates.

"And who do you think thought that one up?" Lownes grins about his successful hustle.

But hustles were not the answer, and Lownes knew it. "The future of the clubs depends on a mix of services and facilities able to appeal to a regular neighborhood element. The St. Louis Club is a franchise operation, and they closed their central city club and reopened it in the suburbs, and that's doing extremely well. I'm looking to open clubs around Chicago and perhaps maintain one facility downtown for conventions and visitors, but not nearly as big as this monster I have downstairs here." (The Chicago Club in the Playboy Towers building is a rambling two-story affair with showcase theater, two dining rooms, and a capacious Playmate bar.)

"Miami has always made money. It never had a losing year, and the profits have been just in operations—forget the key fees. And that's funny because it's a club many people would say is badly located, off the beaten path for tourists. But what it has is a built-in neighborhood-area clientele who consider it their club. They don't see a lot of tourists and are delighted."

Won't change of format and location demand a changed image, an admission that Playboy has become middle-aged and middle-class?

"That's our customer—that's always been our customer. I can't help it if that's not in our image. We don't get the 'in' crowd at Playboy—we never have. I consider myself part of the quote in crowd unquote and I wouldn't spend a lot of time hanging around Playboy Clubs. But nobody makes a living off the 'in' clubs, except maybe Régine, and she did well in Paris because she knows a lot of people. I don't even know if there are enough 'in' people to support such a club indefinitely. That kind of operation appeals to amateurs. They don't make any money. I spent a summer once at this absolutely gorgeous resort on Fire Island called Talisman. The guy who ran it bought his ashtrays at Hermès, for God's sake.

"There must be other ways for us. I'm bringing in young kids. I listen to almost everything they suggest. Young guys who want to put in a wild discotheque in, say, Cincinnati, I tell them to give it a try. In France, I saw jump suits with Amoco written on them sell for three hundred and fifty bucks. Dressing up as a garage mechanic isn't very prestigious, and yet it is. Antistyle is very chic today. We have to pick up on that wavelength. It comes down to listening to people who can identify with the market and come up with ideas that work. I'm not so much creative as I am willing to be experimental. You have to take chances. Look, change or die, whether you understand it or not."

Can the club concept survive such changes and still make it? Lownes isn't sure, and no one else at Playboy is, either. Clearly, all the answers aren't in yet. Equally clearly, there is hope at Playboy headquarters that someday in the not too distant future, gambling will become legal in all these United States. The clubs could convert into casinos overnight, and gold would rain forever into Playboy's pot. Meanwhile, Lownes has closed several clubs—Baltimore, San Francisco, Detroit—and opened new franchise operations in Tokyo and Dallas, and a new casino in the Bahamas. Playboy is also involved in building a hotel-casino in Atlantic City.

Nor is Lownes the only one in the company pondering a changed and changing club concept. "I think there has to be more thought given to what a contemporary club is in the late seventies," Hefner's daughter, Christie, believes, "because night life in America is changing so quickly. The whole notion of the bunny and what the bunny represents and whether that notion is timeless or a matter of changing costume or appearance are all questions that need to be looked at."

Whatever the outcome, whether the clubs survive, change, or go under, the three dimensions Hefner gave his adolescent fantasies have already entered American folklore. However much a part of the present the clubs may still be, they are already a part of the past. Hefner imbued them with the magic of growing up rich in a newly wealthy America. And the magic, when all is said and done, transcends the tawdry gimmickry that went into them, their plasticity and uniformity.

Those who frequented the clubs in their heyday learned from them a better vision of self. The illusions of style and elegance Babbitt's grandsons bought there surely improved the quality of life in the Gopher Prairie that lingers in so many hearts and memories. Pretending to something finer, like stale sauce béarnaise and chewy cracked crab, was better than eating the juiciest steak in yet another bland steakhouse.

At least the VIP rooms make light sparkle off glass and crystal and create a mood of mystery and festivity even the hardest-charging bunny need not destroy. The clubs did serve the newly and uncertainly affluent, whose education and upbringing had not equipped them for spending money with style and panache. If these men lusted after bunnies, most of them were more relieved than frustrated that they could not satisfy that lust. Clubs were feasts of the imagination and the stimulus of dreams that could not be measured by standards of those who aspire to lunch at Lutèce. The clubs are middle-class and share its posturing.

As such they are easy targets for sarcasm and ridicule, scapegoats for a civilization of freeways and Holiday Inns, McDonalds and psychedelic vans. And though Playboy is inextricably a part of late-twentieth-century plasticity, it has always aspired to be more than that—to make good plastics, achievable dreams. Ridicule is too easy. For every brass-hearted bunny who unfeelingly hustles a drunk, there are kids who have stars in their eyes when ordering beer and steak.

Sure, the food at Great Gorge is barely edible: Hamburgers are dry, roast beef soggy and stringy with blobs of fat on it, spareribs more bone than meat, fried potatoes plastic, saffron rice a mound of glue. Food is served cold. Bunnies are surly. Service is slow. Soup is slopped on tables and the overflow not mopped. But families who come here for Saturday-night dinner and a show don't seem to mind. They wander out through the lobbies and admire the incredible kitsch in the shops with unabashed wonder. They dance in the night-clubs and play with the electronic toys in the game room.

"Isn't this the most marvelous place," one woman said to another. "I'm having such a good time." And out she sashayed from the ladies (Playmates) room in a rainbow pants suit and a cleavage as big as a bunny's, her black face shining with joy.

There is something endearing about bunnies and their robot-who-hasn't-quite-mastered-the-tricks manner. The way most of them shake their ass is a laugh, and anything that adds humor to the dark and desperately serious business that coupling has become is great. Perhaps the bunny is wending her sensuous way into the history of American trivia to take her place alongside the Gibson and Ziegfeld girls. If so, the heartland will miss her, and so will the guardians of culture. Why, in 1984, the Metropolitan Museum may even build a retrospective fashion show around the bunny costume. There may even be a few live bunnies left to serve roast beef to the thousand guests in the museum's great hall set between the artifacts of a Pompeiian village and an Egyptian tomb.

5

Critics and Preachers

In the year the Chicago Club opened, Playboy began, slowly, to be a different magazine—more sober, probing, intellectually curious, striving for excellence. It had begun to change in the late fifties, of course, as Spectorsky made his taste and interests felt. But real quality only seeped gradually into the magazine, largely because serious nonfiction was treated for so long as a stepchild.

Spectorsky had made that point in a memo he wrote to Hefner, Russell, and Kessie in September 1958. Nonfiction, he argued, was not given the same freedom in the magazine that fiction was. Much of it was formula writing, and if *Playboy* turned down a piece, the author could not sell it elsewhere. Editors sat on queries and suggestions too long and demanded too much from their contributors in the way of rewriting and fixing up. To alleviate the situation, Spectorsky suggested a policy of answering all queries within seven days, paying higher rates, creating a $1,000 nonfiction award, and firming *Playboy* ties to New York literary agents and publishers. He also urged recruiting more staff.

By 1960, some of these things were being done. *Playboy* paid higher rates. A nonfiction prize had won the magazine prestige and publicity. Don Gold had added some panache to the up-front sections. But it remained a lean magazine, something Spectorsky realized when Ray Russell quit that spring after six years with *Playboy*. Russell says he had enough and wanted to do something else. Others say he worried that *Playboy* had peaked and would not grow beyond the million copies a month it was then selling.

Since Russell, the executive editor, had doubled as a part-time articles editor, Spectorsky decided he needed a full-time man for the slot, and that while he was at it, he had better expand the overall staff. He found Walter Goodman through an ad in *The New York Times.* Goodman was then a restless editor at *Redbook,* where he handled serious articles. In turn, he brought in Murray Fisher, a writer in NBC's P.R. department. Sheldon Wax heard from a friend that *Playboy* was hiring and applied for a job. All three men would play major roles in the magazine's growth and development. But as articles editor, Goodman would have the greatest immediate impact on a changing content.

His Manhattan connections were similar to Spectorsky's, but they seem to have been somewhat more highbrow. Goodman knew the critics and the politico-literary establishment, and where and how their work could be bought. He was just what Hefner and Spectorsky needed and wanted that year; someone to help them make *Playboy* a "magazine of ideas" as well as "entertainment for men." The focus was clear in Spectorsky's mind and still vague in Hefner's, but the publisher had always nurtured intellectual ambition, no matter how ill-expressed or fuzzy, and it went beyond merely dressing up pretty girls with good prose to make the package more respectable for advertisers.

Hefner admired fine minds. He was never immodest about his own. He thought ideas worth pondering and said as much in the preamble to the first issue. Sex in the raw offended his sensibilities. He required the proper accouterments, the garnish of good conversation—say about Nietzsche, Picasso, and jazz—and tinkling cocktail glasses and hors d'oeuvre trays. In the early sixties, *Playboy*'s content began to reflect that desire. True, sex was the fixed point on *Playboy*'s intellectual compass, but from it ideas could and did start moving in all directions—eventually toward regions that had nothing to do with sex. In fact, by the mid-seventies, there was little *Playboy* had not plumbed, with depth and shallowness, so that Hefner could argue with only a little hyperbole, that for a man from Mars, *Playboy* might be a primer to understanding America's passing parade: literary, social, political, military, moral, religious, even economic; everything from consumerism, ecology, and science to Vietnam and civil rights.

Results of the newly elevated *Playboy* brow began to show up quickly. Some of the pieces were pretentious, others way over the audience's head. But the higher tone was unmistakable. What Goodman had done was to bring in the critics, the names that mean something in New York's cultural establishment so long under Lionel Trilling's sway: Leslie Fiedler, Eric Bentley, Murray Kempton, Alfred Kazin.

In January 1961, *Playboy* published the scrapings from a search of Ernest Hemingway's collected works and came up with a series of quotations the editors titled "Hemingway Speaks His Mind." A subhead staked out the claim made and the reason for making it: "a philosophy of life as trenchant as his prose emerges from the statements and writings of america's foremost literary figure, in a compilation by the editors of playboy." (Art Paul liked to play around with typography, and doing away with capital letters was one of his favorite ways.)

Some fifteen years after the fact, the piece seems a little silly and obvious. But that misses the point. Hemingway and Fitzgerald were *Playboy*'s godfathers. Hefner had not been able to afford a Hemingway story for his first issue. This compilation was better, for the quotes backed *Playboy*'s claim to a slice of Hemingway's life-style:

"The country a novelist knows is the country of his heart."

On Some of the Good Things in Life: "Wine, bread, oil, salt, bed, early morning, nights . . . women, love, honor . . ."

Wasn't *Playboy* all about that? Maybe an extra dash of comfort, but the essential Playboy, surely that was he.

On Love: "It is an old word, and each man takes it new and wears it out himself."

Exactly what *Playboy* had been advising.

On New York: "It's a phony town you come to for a short time. You stay too long and it's murder."

One Midwesterner's confirmation of the prejudices of another.

Six months later, Leslie Fiedler, in "The Literati of the Four-Letter Word," analyzed the erotic styles of major twentieth-century writers from D. H. Lawrence, T. S. Eliot, Joyce, Faulkner, Hemingway and Edmund Wilson to Mailer, Donleavy, and John Barth. All of them, Fiedler argues, fail to come to grips with male sexuality. Literary metaphors for coitus, the physical act of sex, are "hackneyed and absurd." Lawrence's flowery descriptions of intercourse are "the last stand of bad Nineteenth-Century Romantic poetry." Hemingway's portrayals of physical love are downright awful. Norman Mailer writes "tendentious sexual fiction" that turns "good orgasm" into sexual propaganda. Joyce comes off best, but in that context what can a critic really say against Molly Bloom's final monologue?

The piece radiates erudition—and an erudite titillation that showed sex could be written about in that way, too. It was *Partisan Review* material. The prose is dense, the style complex, the points subtle, the conclusions hard to grasp. The most an average *Playboy* reader was likely to have learned is that good fiction had come to terms neither with the act nor its emotional implication. But dismissing Mailer as a writer of "tendentious sexual fiction" made for a good one-liner at a cocktail party or out impressing a date.

The next issue, July 1961, saw publication of the third and so far most serious *Playboy* panel discussion that brought together half a dozen experts or celebrities for a round-table style "conversation" on a particular subject. The first of these panels dealt with "Narcotics and the Jazz Musicians" and plumbed the views of Stan Kenton, Duke Ellington and Dizzy Gillespie. In the second, Mort Sahl, Lenny Bruce, Steve Allen, Mike Nichols and Jonathan Winters traded views and quips on "Hip Comics and the New Humor." That July "the thorny subject of Sex and Censorship in Literature and the Arts" was on the plate.

"Last month . . . Leslie Fiedler discussed the problems of the writer dealing with sex, vis a vis his craft. . . . Our discussion now is far less intramural: to shed some light on the writer . . . confronted with the conflict between his work, as it relates to sex, and the forces of censorship," *Playboy* wrote in opening the "discussion" to which it had invited movie director Otto Preminger, Norman Mailer, Barney Rosset of Grove Press, Maurice Girodias of Olympia Press (both publishing houses with, for that day, heavily "licentious" lists), Ralph Ginzburg (the future publisher of *Eros* and *Moneysworth* and a previous *Playboy* contributor), Thurman Arnold, head of the Washington law firm of Arnold, Fortas and Porter, and Albert Ellis, a clinical psychologist.

Playboy editors had worked out a cumbersome, time-consuming, and often irritating method for putting the panels together. They seemed to be face-to-face, round-table discussions, but in fact were not.

"I started out trying to get them all together," Murray Fisher, who helped originate the concept, says, "but it was just madness. They'd either lapse into shop talk or backbiting or both, and about ninety percent of the tape would have to be chucked. The only way to control it was to ask all the people the same question separately and then edit their answers into a versimilitude of spontaneous conversation, giving them all a chance to see the manuscript and what the others had said, and then let them get their shots in. The manuscripts were sent around two or three times till they sort of ran down. They must have taken two or three months at least to do. The technique is still cumbersome, and the panels were never well read."

Perhaps not. But they did afford *Playboy* an opportunity to explore at unusual length and detail, for a magazine anyway, topics of general and arcane interest, and to make *Playboy* genuine source material for future social historians. Not that this particular panel broke much new ground. But it did highlight then-current definitions of censorship, the burdens censorship loaded on those who practiced professions vulnerable to it, and the problems it posed to artist and society. Extracting a theme from the predictable mishmash is not easy. Obviously, panelists opposed all forms of censorship, but conceded that the tender minds of children should be protected. They deplored the antisexual puritanism of American society. Pornography, they agreed, could not be suppressed, and efforts to do so would only lead to higher prices, as Prohibition had done to the cost of alcohol. Obscenity, they said, lay in the eye of the beholder. Arnold cited the prurience of an asterisk in a 1911 novel. Preminger found virtue in sex without love. Mailer polemicized against masturbation and argued that open labeling of pornographic literature as such was vital for "the health and life of the republic," but that pleading its socially redeeming values was not. D. H. Lawrence and Henry Miller were run down the dog track to see who was the truer depicter of human sexuality. Ellis called Miller's writings after the *Tropics* "trash"; Girodias saw them as an effort to "shake up false values."

The jumbled thinking makes for hard reading, yet the text is sprinkled with perceptive insight—mostly Mailer's—who seemingly can't help turning up fresh blossoms on dungheaps. Much of the controversy seems dated today, but much of it was dated at the time as well. After all, Judge Woolsey had lifted the ban on American publication of *Ulysses* on December 6, 1933. Miller's *Tropics* may still have been banned, but had been the common coin of college reading since the late 1940s, when postwar student travel to Europe had resumed.

What the panel demonstrated, then, was the double and triple vision the many manifestations of sex—from prostitution and pornography to art and literature—still aroused in the American conscience. What had long been matter-of-fact in the East, California, and the "enlightened" enclaves in between, remained anathema for much of the country. And however vague any definition of Middle America might be, Hugh Hefner was emerging as a radical force within it, and one, moreover, out to change the system of values under which that slice of America lived.

In September 1961, Murray Kempton blasted the new sociologists and their sociometric approach. *Playboy* said the piece "diagnoses the condition of modern sociology as an acute case of bombast [and] lances its practitioners . . . with the precision of a surgeon." The editorial note represents a significant trait of *Playboy*'s dealing with ideas: You, the reader, and I, the *Playboy* editor, the subliminal message says, we really know what jerks "they" are, and here is the proof so you, too, can feel, if not superior to, than at least equal to "them." *Playboy* the teacher, protector, friend.

Two months later, in November, *Playboy* tackled "TV's Problems and Prospects" in yet another panel. The medium had always fascinated Hefner, and he had gone into TV analysis earlier than most. For *Playboy* it was a double rival: for time spent reading and for time having sex. Besides, serious treatment of TV added to the magazine's intellectual cachet.

In January 1962 editors proudly announced they had unearthed a batch of previously unpublished letters by D. H. Lawrence: "From his personal correspondence over the 25 years of his writing life there emerges a self-portrait of his evolution from ardent humanist to bitter pessimist." And the same issue featured a "manifesto" from Henry Miller against Massachusetts censors then battling Grove Press' efforts to sell the *Tropics* in that state. An editorial note explaining Miller's role in American literature and his past and current legal difficulties preceded the polemic.

Miller slammed into Massachusetts for murdering Sacco and Vanzetti "in the name of justice" and railed against "dealing with archaic laws. Stone Age mentalities, sadists disguised as benefactors, impotents invested with authority, killjoys, hypocrites, perverts. I am not defending myself—I accuse. . . . Show me your clean hands, your clean hearts, your clean conscience, I defy you."

But it was Alfred Kazin who put the real feather in *Playboy*'s critical cap. His piece, "The Love Cult," was published in March 1962. Spectorsky would claim in print later that he had to "work incredibly hard" to get it, a claim Kazin dismisses as "a lot of bullshit. It was done through an agent. I never met Spectorsky. I've written for a lot of strange magazines since 1935."

Goodman, who actually got the article for *Playboy,* said, "I called Kazin and didn't have a tough time persuading him to write for us. We were paying very good rates. He could use the money. He liked the subject. There was no trouble—oh, maybe about the editing; there always is with Kazin. He was fussy, as he should be, but sometimes he requires editing. As far as getting him, though, there was no trouble."

Kazin's feelings about the magazine, however, have turned bitter. "I have nothing but contempt for *Playboy,* " he says now, his hostility perhaps sparked by the cavalier treatment accorded him by younger editors in the 1970s, after Spectorsky had died and few remembered how grateful *Playboy* had once been for the privilege of printing Kazin's by-line.

And there was nothing "bottom-drawer" about the article below the by-line, either. This was first-rate criticism: erudite, intelligent, clear in its point of view. Kazin was out to scrape the barnacles of sentimentality from the semantic use of "love" in America—and in so doing, he intellectualized the concept well beyond the average college education. He moved from Plato and St. Augustine to Stendhal, Céline, Freud, and Proust (and manages the obligatory faint titillation by pointing out that Swann's great amour, Odette, is little better than a prostitute). Love, as Americans understand it, Kazin argues, is not the ultimate good, but camouflage:

"Love is what we most admire when everything else has failed our admiration. . . . [it] soothes . . . beckons . . . replenishes our stale and disillusioned imaginations with the word . . . which is the incarnation of a better opinion of ourselves."

The article, as a Texas cleric, outraged that someone he respected so highly would write for so lowly a publication, told the author, "could have appeared in the *Princeton Theological Magazine.*" Nevertheless, it was the perfect fit for *Playboy* at the time. It built a bridge from the magazine's central concern, the physical relationship between the sexes, to a more cerebral view of that bond and its emotional underpinnings.

That such a view did not hurt *Playboy* with advertisers has to be a given. Part of the editorial decision to upgrade content and respectability was dictated by such commercial considerations. But they were only a part of the process and did not by themselves define it.

Playboy varied the theme of love in the next two issues with serialization of Françoise Sagan's novel *The Wonderful Clouds.* On one level, Sagan is *Playboy*'s kind of woman. She and her heroines make their own rules, live their own lives with gusto (and sadness), are open about needing men and sex, are tough and vulnerable, smoke, drink, swear, drive high-powered sports cars, and live in reasonable versions of Playboy pads. They can be seen as Hemingway women, though they are not; and they tend to be French, which makes their aggressive side less threatening. *Playboy* was always careful about removing the female fangs then.

They were something to worry about, too, as July's panel on the "Womanization of America" tried to document, albeit inconclusively, as was the nature of *Playboy* panels. Again the names were distinguished: Dr. Ernst Dichter, Theodore Reik, Mort Sahl, Alexander King, Norman Mailer (well on his way to becoming a *Playboy* regular), and Ashley Montagu. There was, as usual, little consensus, few lasting conclusions, and many varied opinions. Montagu contributed clever praise of the "second sex," Mailer dour diatribes against distaff-dominated male weaklings, to wit: "I think the womanization of America comes not only because women are becoming more selfish, more greedy, less romantic, less warm, more lusty, and also more filled with hate, but because men have collaborated with them."

Playboy summed up with an early helping of Hefner's philosophy, which by mid-1962 the editor-publisher was already pondering, and with a sentence of Faulknerian length (a weakness of Hefner's own prose):

> As our nation becomes emancipated from the notion of associating sex with sin, rather than with romance, and as young people are increasingly freed of feeling guilty about a play period in their lives before settling down to marital maturity, so the attitudes of the sexes may well become more healthy toward each other, may acquire a mutuality and mutual appreciativeness which does not entail the obliteration of differences, but rather heightens their pleasures and allows individuals of each of the sexes a fuller and more natural development of psyche and spirit, mind and body.

The design was unmistakable. This was no *Reader's Digest* approach to ideas and thought. Class was in session, Professors Hefner and Spectorsky rapping the gavels. And the fee was more than the 50 cent cover price. *Playboy* required readers' time, attention, and concentration. They could always recover laughing at jokes and cartoons, ogling Playmates and tying the ascot they surely ran out and bought in the wake of *Playboy*'s picture spread on "The Return of the Ascot."

But as Hefner and Spectorsky marched *Playboy* up the mountain of literary and intellectual respectability, there were rumblings in the world outside. The first to spot the emergence of something new and important on the cultural landscape was organized religion—specifically the Protestant churches—and they did it early, back in the fall of 1960. The first ecclesiastical "spotter" was the Reverend Michael Bloy, Episcopal chaplain of the Massachusetts Institute of Technology.

Bloy found the magazine everywhere he went on campus: in dormitories and common rooms and classes. Students stuffed copies in raincoat pockets and packed them into their book bags. They actually read the damn thing, he discovered; read it with greater attention than they did their books. And not just for the pictures of nude girls, either. Intrigued, he began to look at the magazine more closely. What he found was both disturbing and interesting. This wasn't just a girlie magazine or another entertainment book. It was preachy, didactic, combative, eager to foster controversy. It had a point of view. Religion, he thought, might have a stake in taking the publication seriously and in understanding what it was about. If nothing else, the church stood to gain wider student interest.

Bloy called a friend who taught at the Andover-Newton Theological School in nearby Newton Center to discuss the matter. The
Reverend Harvey Cox had already carved a reputation as one of the
hip "new" theologians anxious to make religion more relevant to the
new decade and to reflect the forces of change boiling within the
clergy. Perhaps, Bloy wondered, Cox might be interested in lecturing
about *Playboy* before MIT students. Cox, something of a showman,
jumped at the chance and dug into the magazine to prepare his
remarks.

"I looked for the image of man implicit in the Playboy model and
especially at the correlation between the ads and the cartoons, the
Playboy Advisor and the stories," Cox remembers.

The lecture proved a stormy success. Cox spoke before a packed
auditorium. This magazine had pulling power! The young were interested. They wanted to know more. As Cox pondered that reaction,
he decided that the social and ethical problems *Playboy* raised were
serious enough to merit scholarly attention and serious thought. The
result of his musings was *"Playboy*'s Doctrine of the Male," an
article Cox published in the May 1961 issue of *Christianity and
Crisis: A Christian Journal of Opinion.* With Reinhold Niebuhr as
chairman of the editorial board, no more solid bastion of the Protestant establishment could be found. The cachet attached to a discussion of *Playboy* in so august a publication, no matter how negative
the tone, had to be enormous. It meant that *Playboy* was getting
serious attention as a major cultural force.

Cox called *Playboy* "one of the most spectacular successes in the
history of American journalism" and wondered "what factors in
American life have combined to allow . . . (Hefner) to pyramid his
jackpot into a chain of nightclubs, TV spectaculars, bachelor tours
of Europe. . . . what impact does *Playboy* really have? Clearly,
Playboy's astonishing popularity is not attributable solely to pin-up
girls . . ." Sex, Cox decided, had little to do with *Playboy*'s success.
"Rather *Playboy* appeals to a highly mobile, increasingly affluent
group of young readers . . . who want much more . . . than bosoms
and thighs. They need a real image of what it means to be a man.
And Mr. Hefner's *Playboy* has no hesitancy about telling them."

It is a "Guidebook to Identity" that "fills a special need for the
insecure young man with newly acquired time and money on his
hands who still feels uncertain about his consumer skills. . . . It tells
him not only who to be; it tells him how to be it, and even provides
consolation outlets for those who secretly feel that they have not
quite made it. . . . *Playboy* speaks to those who desperately want to
know what it means to be a man, and more specifically a male, in
today's world."

The ads tell readers what to buy, the editorial copy how and when to use the products, and both do so with an "authoritative tone . . . beside which papal encyclicals sound irresolute." Weskits are assertive, cigars a ruggedly masculine smoke, a fur-lined jacket "the most masculine thing since the cave man." Sex is an "item of leisure activity" to be handled with "characteristic skill and detachment." Girls are a "desirable . . . 'Playboy accessory.' " In short stories "the happy issue is always a casual . . . sexual experience with no entangling alliances." Women "know their place and ask for nothing more . . . present no danger of permanent involvement . . . are detachable and disposable."

Having set up the *Playboy* bull—as so many intellectuals would after him—Cox moves in for the kill of "A Futile Doctrine":
Playboy addresses a

> male identity crisis . . . which . . . has at its roots a deep-set fear of sex . . . that is uncomfortably combined with fascination. *Playboy* strives to resolve this antinomy by reducing the terrible proportions of sexuality, its power and its passion, to a packageable consumption item. Thus in *Playboy*'s iconography, the nude woman symbolizes total sexual accessibility, but demands nothing from the observer. The terror of sex, which cannot be separated from its ecstasy is dissolved. But this futile attempt to reduce the *mysterium tremendum* of the sexual fails to solve the problem of being a man. For sexuality is the basic form of all human relationships and therein lies its terror and its power.
>
> Karl Barth has called this basic relational form of man's life *Mitmensch,* co-humanity. This means that becoming fully human, in this case a human male, necessitates . . . exposing myself to the risk of encounter with the other by reciprocal self-exposure. . . .
>
> Thus any theological critique of *Playboy* that focuses on its "lewdness" will misfire completely. *Playboy* and its less successful imitators are not "sex magazines" at all. They are basically anti-sexual. . . . It is precisely because [they] are not sexual that they deserve the most searching kind of theological criticism. They foster a heretical doctrine of man, one at radical variance with the biblical view. For *Playboy*'s man, others—especially women—are for him. They are his . . . playthings. For the Bible, man only becomes fully human by being for the other.
>
> . . . if Christians bear the name of One who was truly man because He was totally for the other, and if it is in Him that we know who God is and what human life is for, then we must see in *Playboy* the latest and slickest episode in man's continuing refusal to be human.

In 1961 this was heady stuff for someone forced to earn his agnosticism through theological debate, first at home, where example prevailed over dogma, and later at Sunday school, where the young Hefner began to doubt teachers "who laid the Bible on you as if it were historically accurate and I couldn't accept that from an early age." Still later, in high school, one of Hefner's closest friends was a devout Catholic "and we used to go back and forth a lot on organized religion." And if he has ever freed himself from his religious heritage, that freedom came only after writing the heavily religious "philosophy," at the time still a year-and-a-half off.

How had he reacted to the Cox piece back then? "I certainly wasn't angry," Hefner mused. "He was right on certain things, and I disagreed with him on others." Was he pleased about the juxtaposition of his name and product with a theological "heavyweight" like Karl Barth? "Of course, of course." He is, of course, much too smart not to have been. The Cox article created a stir and gave *Playboy* enormous publicity.

"My piece was immediately noted and quoted," Cox says modestly. "For years it was the most widely requested reprint the magazine ever ran."

He had indeed touched a responsive nerve among the Protestant clergy which had begun to feel that *Playboy* should be taken seriously because it was both challenge and opportunity. By 1961 it was clear even to the most hidebound that the Christian churches in America were in trouble, as indeed they were around the world, a fact to which Pope John's proposed Vatican Council attested. American Protestants, especially, were fractured, uncertain, sectarian, feuding, stratified, and class-conscious. The sects were institutions in rapid decline, the churches losing their hold on the young, especially the young who made up *Playboy*'s audience. Yet *Playboy* was laced with religious motives and addicted to religious techniques in making converts.

That fact was noted by the Reverend Roy Larson, the religion editor for the *Chicago Sun-Times*, who wrote in *Motive—the Magazine of the Methodist Student Movement*, that *Playboy* is more than just a handbook for the young man-about-town; it's a sort of Bible which defines his values, shapes his personality, sets his goals. . . . The *Playboy* philosophy has become . . . a sort of substitute religion."

A Unitarian minister in Santa Barbara, the Reverend John A. Crane, echoed that thought in a sermon: "It strikes me that *Playboy* is a religious magazine . . . that tells its readers how to get into heaven . . . delineates an ethic for them, . . . expresses a consistent world view, a system of values, a philosophical outlook."

But this was still isolated jousting between *Playboy* and organized religion, one of the many signs that the sixties would indeed be a special decade. The curtain on the drama "Rake and Preacher" would not go up until after Hefner began publishing the philosophy, and articles on religion became a staple of the editorial diet.

Meanwhile, the guns boomed from another front—the halls of academe. In the August 1962 issue of *Commentary,* Professor Benjamin De Mott of Amherst unloaded a classical education on the *Playboy* phenomenon. The results were awesome. De Mott demolished *Playboy*'s claim to excellence in anything, portraying Hefner and his minions as rodents gnawing at the structure and foundation of Western civilization. He pronounced the magazine morally reprehensible, intellectually barren, devious, and dishonest, raked it with fierce scorn, and dumped what was left into the trash barrel of pop vulgarity. It remains the most savage and merciless annihilation of *Playboy* ever committed to print. After reading the article, it is hard to believe that the magazine is anything but diseased, destructive of social values, disruptive of the social order, and a cancer on the culture. It is difficult to do the professor's rhetoric full justice without copious quotes:

> ... the new girlie books remain hard to write off. They swim, all sleazy bikini voluptuousness, with fewer hake in their wake, to be sure, than most of the great whales of mass entertainment now wallowing in commentators' kens. But when placed in the context of recent publishing history, their emergence ranks as a major popcultural event.
>
> ... The girlie books, severe masters, yield to nobody. "Our philosophy," says the publisher of *Playboy* in his penthouse, "is that you (not we ourselves: we have arrived) should strive to get into the sophisticated upper crust ..." Moreover, his letter columns ... are filled with remarks in which the *Playboy* audience defines itself as doltish.
>
> ... the key to the puzzle lies in the nature of the magazine's simplification of experience. The *Playboy* world is first and last an achievement in abstraction: history, politics, art, ordinary social relations, religion, families, nature, vanity, love, a thousand other items that presumably complicate both the inward and outward lives of human beings—all have been emptied from it. In place of the citizen with a vote to cast or a job to do or a book to study or a god to worship, the editors offer a vision of the whole man reduced to his private parts. Out of the center of this being spring the only substantial realities—sexual need and sexual deprivation.
>
> These magazines are without qualification post-cataclysm, utterly sure that no existing moral language is adequate to modern experience. Their single unironicized clarity (I burn, you burn, she burns, they burn) stands simultaneously as a motto for an emergent masscult school of kitsch existentialism, and

as the ground theme for a whole new age—an age of Multiple Inexpressibles, a time in which *épater les bourgeois* will have become the standard folk gesture.

. . . finesse, taste, adoration of tales instead of truthtellers, cannot possibly place the depravity of the stuff in hand: only the vocabulary of flat moral counters, which finesse scorns, can do that. The paradox implicit here may or may not serve as a fair, if indirect, measure of the vulnerabilities of an age of intense linguistic inhibition (about all plain terms save obscenities). But the chance is strong that hidden in its intricacies lies at least one of the stinking seeds that brought girlie books to birth.

Clearly, De Mott was guilty of overkill. *Playboy* was not up to the role he had written for it, nor could the magazine exercise the power he imputed to it. By denigrating *Playboy* so harshly, he enhanced it. "I would say Mr. De Mott makes unnecessarily heavy weather of *Playboy*," Eric Bentley wrote in *Commentary*. "One would almost think from his account that its readers read nothing else."

For *Playboy* editors, it was a matter of laughing and crying. They were in turn furious, irritated, unimpressed, and delighted.

"We were outraged," Jack Kessie, then the managing editor, recalled, "and we thought De Mott had been completely unfair. There were misquotations, wrong statistics. The overall reaction was far from favorable." Kessie grinned, brushed one finger along his moustache, and admitted that yes, they had basked in the high-domed attention, for good or ill. "We'd been recognized in *Commentary*. We were livid, but we were pleased that the criticism had appeared in so lofty a magazine."

Sheldon Wax, who succeeded Kessie as managing editor in 1972, is more cautious by nature. He is not sure of the impact the episode had. Asked about it in the mid-seventies, he varied Stalin's question about the number of divisions the pope had to the small size of *Commentary*'s circulation. Reminded that circulation and influence were not necessarily synonymous, he conceded the point, though grudgingly. But he remembers no heated meetings or discussions about how to counter the blast. He thinks Spectorsky retreated into his office to craft a reply.

Hefner's memory is even vaguer. He remembers that De Mott had given a set of *Playboy* pictures an "S-M implication" that wasn't there and that he hadn't been very impressed with the article—"not the way I was with Cox." He feels that De Mott failed to give "any great insights" and that the article was "more a matter of style than substance." Recapitulate the content for him, though, and there is a touch of anger. "That is so superficial. Not only doesn't it get to the center of the target, but it is shooting in the other direction. Are

you going to condemn *Playboy* for its low editorial quality? I think
it's a joke. Was he suggesting that our editorial quality was lower
than the *Reader's Digest*, the *Saturday Evening Post, Colliers'* or
even *Look* and *Life*—[De Mott was, of course]. I can't take that
seriously."

Spectorsky did, though. Judged from his barbed reply, he had to
be euphoric at the opportunity De Mott offered him to push *Playboy*
as a sober magazine worth the intellectual community's attention,
and to show that he could be every bit as erudite, sarcastic and
pungent as De Mott, and that he knew as many two-dollar words.
He wrote to *Commentary:*

> It would be a pleasurable challenge to answer . . . De Mott's criticism of
> *Playboy* . . . were it not for two rather confounding difficulties. The first is that,
> from his description of his target, we can only recognize ourselves because he
> gives it our name; in his syllogistic sleight of hand, Popculture is bad (who'll
> arise to deny it?), *Playboy* is the apotheosis of Popculture (a proposition he
> fails to prove), and therefore *Playboy* is bad. The second is that hacking a path
> through the densely prolix jungle of his prose left us not quite certain just what
> the hell he was driving at.

De Mott, he argued, "suffers from plerophoric autism," a phrase
Spectorsky is quick to define as the conviction that fantasies are real
(*Playboy* has an obsession about defining everything). The idea of
women enjoying sex, Spectorsky continued, sends De Mott into a
"logorrheaic snit" and he suffers from a "pathetically revealing
phantasy" in his "rather original notion of what constitutes erotic
pleasure for a female. . . . De Mott's psyche can't tolerate the thought
women enjoy sex and may even, on occasion, seek it." He is given
to "fevered distortions" when he argues that *Playboy* offers "a vision
of the whole man reduced to his private parts" and "is guilty of
exactly that of which he accuses us: preoccupation with sex, oversim-
plification and distortion of reality."

Playboy's reality was different, Spectorsky maintained, and proceeded to lay it out in graceful and eloquent prose:

> We feature girls because they're attractive, stories because they are entertain-
> ing, jokes because they are funny. Our vision is not that of a man reduced to
> his private parts, but of man enlarged through his capacity to interpret and
> enjoy life, one aspect of which—but by no means the only one—is the healthy
> enjoyment of sex. We don't really see Evil as a woman's disinclination to sex
> . . . any more than we interpret Good as non-stop copulation for all. To
> derogate *Playboy* with a discussion limited to sex is to ignore much of the
> substance of the magazine: articles and fiction of high merit. . . .

For all of Spectorsky's verbal pyrotechnics and determined high-mindedness, however, there is in his letter to *Commentary* a sustained implication that De Mott's sexuality is somehow warped and the root cause of his *Playboy* critique. In replying, the professor, not unreasonably, demurred at the inference that anyone who "criticizes my magazine must be some kind of pervert," and took issue with "the bouquet of Mr. Spectorsky's innuendo." And he thanked another correspondent—the piece drew a lot of mail—for "responding with an argument rather than a diagnosis." That, too, is fair enough. To this day *Playboy* editors will, at times, adopt a "what is wrong with you?" stance to critics of their sexual attitudes.

By the time this little tempest bubbled in the intellectual teapot, Hefner had all but decided to launch the exploration of *Playboy*'s— and his own—identity. He had no clear plan in mind, no organized structure for what he wanted to say, or any particular style for how to do it. But he sensed that *Playboy* was on a sharply ascending curve, not only financially, but socially. *Time* and *Newsweek* wrote up "Hefner's Way" regularly. The floundering *Saturday Evening Post* spent lavishly to publicize a feature on him. Church and academy were taking note. Promotion—especially self-promotion—had always been one of Hefner's fortes. If others wrote so much about *Playboy* to appreciative audiences, why shouldn't *Playboy* write about itself? Or, as he described his motives in the philosophy's first installment in December 1962:

> *Playboy*'s aims and outlook have been given considerable comment in the press, particularly in the journals of social, philosophical and religious opinion, and have become a popular topic of conversation at cocktail parties. . . . While we've been conscious of the virtues of seeing ourselves as others see us, we've also felt the image is occasionally distorted: having listened patiently for so long . . . to what others have decided *Playboy* represents . . . we've decided . . . to state our own editorial credo here, and offer a few personal observations on our present-day society and *Playboy*'s role in it. . . .

Trying to summarize what the next twenty-five installments were all about is next to impossible. They were, in fact, about everything. Hefner had Aristotelean pretensions—and a mad devotion to self-imposed deadlines—which helped neither clarity nor flow.

"One of the big mistakes I made in the damn thing, which made it so very repetitious and filled with excessive verbiage, is that I felt it ought to appear in every issue. What I should have done was structure it much more and establish an outline as to where I was going to go and complete certain portions of it before deadlines were set. But I didn't do that."

Over the years, a number of writers and magazines have attempted to put the gist in more readable and clearer form. *Time,* in a 1967 cover story on Hefner said:

> Hefner's thesis was that U.S. society had too long and too rigorously suppressed good, healthy heterosexuality. Since its growth had been stunted . . . all sorts of perversions flourished in its place. . . . And the villain at the bottom of all this? Organized religion, announced Hefner with an unabashed air of discovery. Hefner revived puritanism long enough to condemn it. . . . As it poured through the magazine's columns, the *Playboy* philosophy was often pretentious and relatively conventional. Hefner is a kind of oversimplified Enlightenment thinker with what comes out as an almost touching faith in the individual's capacity for goodness. . . . Hefner also exhibits a tendency to "situation ethics," which calls for judging acts within their special context rather than by a more fixed morality . . .

Theodore Peterson, dean of the University of Illinois Journalism School, has probably done the best summary, (as part of an article entitled *"Playboy* and the Preachers," which the *Columbia Journalism Review* published in 1966):

> As a philosopher, Hefner is not a particularly original thinker. Much of what he says is a twentieth-century version of John Stuart Mill's essay "On Liberty," including a utilitarian basis for freedom. Underlying Hefner's beliefs is a profound concern for the rights of the individual in a free society. . . . Hefner is not concerned exclusively with sexual freedom. . . . His first seven installments concentrated on matters other than sex.
>
> Hefner is for free enterprise. . . . The magazine motivates men by portraying the good life that is the prize for honest endeavor and hard work. He is for a wide arena of free expression. . . . He is for separation of church and state . . . [and] believes that an individual has a . . . right to be free from religion and its influence. And the influence of religion, as he sees it, has been pervasive and noxious. . . . By influencing the state to enact legislation that people do not believe in and will not obey, it has contributed to a breakdown in law and order. By encouraging censorship, it has curbed free expression. By equating sin with sex, it has inspired harmful sexual expression. . . .

That organized religion was a major focus of Hefner's philosophy is hardly surprising. He admits that at least in part the editorial statement was a response to critics like Cox and other clerics who first took *Playboy* seriously. For a romantic pragmatist like Hefner, the mystical and the unknowable held little fascination. Organized religion was clearly one of the better dragons he found to battle. He jousted with history, psychology, sociology, economics, media, poli-

tics, and the humanities, relating most of them back to sex, his
original focus. He approached them all with zest, relish, good humor,
and that touch of Candide that is so much a mark of his personality.
Mr. Smith and Mr. Deeds and John Doe had it, too. There is something giddy about his ingenuousness. Rattling his typewriter as a
singing sword, he sallies forth to battle evil as if no one had ever
dared to do so before him. The glee shines through the pages even
a decade and a half after the fact.

He flayed at organized religion as if he were Martin Luther smiting
the pope. "Please do not consider us impious," he wrote, "if we
suggest that it is American religion that is largely to blame" for the
way the puritan tradition had emasculated the Bill of Rights and
played havoc with individual rights. And Hefner was off to the races.
In the months that followed the philosophy was peppered with asser-
tions and arguments such as these:—

"Presumably, a man's religion should make him a better person
—more tolerant, sympathetic, and understanding toward his fellows.
Too often organized religion has the opposite effect. . . . And make
no mistake—the tyranny of man over his fellow is just as great an
evil when it is wielded in the name of God as in the name of the
State."

—"Constitution and Bill of Rights guarantee freedom from religion as well as of religion but the former has not been enforced as
strictly; the things that are Caesar's and the things that are God's not
clearly separated."

—" . . . we oppose . . . any man's attempt to force his faith upon
others. Religion should be a personal matter between man and God;
it has nothing to do with man's relationship with government."

—"If a man has a right to find God in his own way, he has a right
to go to the Devil in his own way, also."

—"In much of what we have written . . . it may have seemed that
we have little regard for the religious side of life. Nothing could be
further from the truth. Life could be a very bleak and empty experience without faith and hope to fill the black void of the unknown."

—"Religious puritanism pervades every aspect of our sexual lives.
We use it as a justification for suppressing freedom of thought,
expression, and, of course, personal behavior."

The response to the series was overwhelming, but, according to
Anson Mount, then *Playboy*'s promotion manager and football expert (and future religion editor), it wasn't fast enough for Hefner,
who, Mount contends, had hoped for "an outpouring from theologians" by the time the second installment was published in January
1963.

"I was assigned to get letters from clergymen, and good ones. So I sent my secretary over to the library of the University of Chicago's Divinity School. She spent two weeks there going through the catalog of every divinity and theology school in the country and got names of clergymen who taught there, every faculty member and officer. That made for a huge mailing list. I made up reprints of the next installment and sent out batches of them, together with a form letter that had only the name typed in. The text went something like this: 'Dear Dr. X, A friend has asked that I send to you a copy of the current installment of the *Playboy* philosophy. We'd appreciate your comment. Please tell us what you think.' And I signed the letters A. C. Spectorsky.

"Those people had no idea we were fishing for letters. We got hundreds that damned us and said we were leading the young generation straight to hell. But occasionally we got a thoughtful letter. We'd cut the part that took issue with the philosophy and leave in 'you're saying important things.' You know, a lot of professors got their ass in the wringer because they didn't know what was happening to them."

Hefner thinks his ebullient, Southern ex-employee (he was fired in the first of many great shakeouts in 1974 by P.R. V.P. Lee Gottlieb, who got his three years later) may have exaggerated the facts a bit. "I wasn't personally interested in getting fan mail from the clergy," he says, "but we did attempt to promote a dialogue with the magazine. When I began dealing with social-sexual questions, I found there was the same debate going on among liberals and traditionalists within organized religion. We started getting some surprisingly positive and sympathetic letters from the clergy."

And some, as Mount noted, that were not so positive. But still it was a flood of attention; in letters, from the pulpits, and in the Christian journals of opinion. However much the clergy might have been outraged, at least at first, it was also delighted. Hefner had succeeded in making religion exciting again, in having it talked and argued about. He had interested the young in their discarded roots. And was he ever vulnerable to counterattack! The *Christian Century* launched one of the elegant ones in its August 28, 1963, issue.

"An Infinite Number of Monkeys" recalled the mathematical contention that a monkey, equipped with an infinite amount of paper and time, and an ability to type, would sooner or later accidentally type in the correct order all the plays of Shakespeare. It continued:

A comic we know has a time-saving suggestion: get an infinite number of monkeys. . . . Now we find that an infinite number of monkeys do exist, and that they are employed as researchers by Hugh M. Hefner. . . . They pirate hundreds of erudite quotations to be used out-of-context fashion in the apparently interminable . . . series called "The Playboy Philosophy."

We are glad to know that the Midwest's tradition of amateur philosophizing has not gone out of style. In the 19th century the fad was Platonism; now it is Epicureanism—of a sort. . . . Editor Hefner in this installment [the September 1963 issue] discusses "the Sexual Revolution currently taking place in society" and proposes to develop a "new morality." Last month he gave a "brief history of sexual suppression since early Christendom through the Middle Ages"; in the current issue he considers the Renaissance, the Reformation and—of course—Puritanism and Victorianism.

What other popular magazine offers sober discussions of imminent cataclysm, eschatology, sacerdotal celibacy, the Malleus Malleficarum, incubus and succubus, total depravity, authoritarian dogma, theocratic society, predestination? Where else can you in a few pages find strung together Augustine, Origen, Chrysostom, St. Paul, Tertullian, Gregory the Great, Innocent VIII, Martin Luther, John Calvin, John Wesley, John Knox, Aquinas, Oliver Cromwell, Paul IV, Jeremy Collins and John Styles—all of whom, says Hefner, were antisexual?

We must admit that we are rather impressed by Hefner's "Look Ma! No hands!" approach to church history; he can string together more references in an article than Toynbee can in a volume. . . . Sad to say, Christians have often given reason for critics such as Hefner to find fault. But are they to be blamed for as much as he blames them for? . . . We hope the monkeys soon tire and that Hefner, a man of not inconsiderable talents, will think of better ways to employ those talents."

Not everyone had so light a touch. J. Claude Evans' "The *Playboy* Philosophy," published in the October 1964 issue of *Catholic World,* for example, did not:

. . . we can compare the philosophy of *Playboy* with the thought of the First Epistle of John. It may surprise the reader to know that John was wrestling with many of the same problems which *Playboy* confronts in the contemporary world . . . [namely gnosticism, a philosophy that affirmed Christ's divinity over his humanity].

. . . 1 John is a polemic against all forms of Puritanism whether ancient gnosticism or 16th-century legalism or 20th-century prudery. One of the central themes of the whole book is that life in the flesh, life as physical, is good, so good in fact that it became the bearer of God's self-disclosure of Himself in the life and death and resurrection of Jesus Christ . . .

. . . Hefner is simply blind to the facts of life in the contemporary Church if he does not recognize that the Church itself is at war with the superficial and legalistic aspects of Puritanism in our culture, and has been at its battle stations on this subject for at least two generations before *Playboy* was founded. . . .

Dr. William Hamilton, a future *Playboy* contributor, returned to Cox's theme of *Playboy*'s basic antisexuality in a piece he wrote for *Motive* in 1963:

Hefner . . . gives the impression of not really caring much for it. He is both loud and sound when he attacks puritanism. Not that he seems to know much about puritanism. . . . He is really busily engaged in defending the sexual rebellion of the 1920s. . . . He rightly affirms the goodness of the body (this is very biblical of him, even though he doesn't know it), but misses something in sex . . . the power and mystery of sexuality. . . .

As the sixties moved toward mid-decade, the clergy's interest in the *Playboy*-religion debate increased. Articles on the subject appeared in *Christian Advocate,* a biweekly for Methodist pastors, *Arena,* a monthly for young Lutheran adults, *Dialog,* a quarterly published by the Lutheran Theological Seminary in St. Louis, *The Register Leader,* a Unitarian publication, *Eternity,* an evangelical magazine, *Listening,* a Dominican one, to cite a few.

Soon after Mount began to solicit comment from clergymen, the Playboy Forum, a new department Hefner started in the magazine in mid-1963 became a letterbox for clerics. Small wonder!

"We were saying wild things in the Forum," Mount recalls, "like that it was not true that premarital sex will destroy your marriage, that sexual relations can be good, warm and helpful outside of marriage, which in those days was still wildly iconoclastic."

But Mount felt that many of the letters "were long and boring" and came "from readers deadly serious about sex. So I invented letters—outrageous letters from priests, southern sheriffs, and eighteen-year-old girls who said they enjoyed group fucks. Hef loved it."

After a while, though, Mount's swashbuckling approach became a bit too much for Nat Lehrman, the future *Playboy* publisher, who had been hired in 1963 to ride herd on the philosophy. He warned Mount that if he picked real names from real towns for his fake letters, the company risked libel action. "After a while," Mount says regretfully, "they put me back in promotion and gave Forum to Lehrman."

That's where Mount was needed most, too. Religion was getting out of hand. Hefner was inundated with invitations to speak at college campuses, and Mount filled in for most of them. Clergymen literally stormed *Playboy* offices in their eagerness to engage in dialogues. A special clergy subscription rate of $2 was introduced.

Playboy began to look around for articles on religious subjects. On speaking engagements, Mount was put in the debating ring with heavyweights like Notre Dame President Father Hesburgh and McGeorge Bundy. "And I used to get the greatest ovation from students," he says modestly.

Mount is a hulking man with some of the charm of a dancing bear and a gift of southern gab totally out of character for the still-uptight world of Playboy. Words flow from his mouth in an easy, bubbling stream and he has the promotion man's practiced ease with strangers. He is also a quick study. But as the eager churches smothered *Playboy* to their ample bosoms, even Mount began to run out of breath. He simply didn't know enough about religion. So he suggested to Hefner that he spend a summer at the Episcopal Theological Seminary in Sewanee, Tennessee, to study moral and contemporary theology and church history. He rented a large house, set up a well-stocked bar, and had the ministers in for late-afternoon cocktails and after-dinner drinks.

The study shored up Mount's theological credentials; the open bar cemented his ties to the clergy. At one point, he was writing and phoning two thousand clergymen of every rank, denomination, and color—from "celebrity" ministers like Martin Luther King, Bishop John A. T. *(Honest to God)* Robinson, the Reverend Malcolm *(Are You Running With Me, Jesus)* Boyd, Bishop James Pike, the Chicago Divinity School's Martin Marty, and Yale Chaplain William Sloane Coffin, to neighborhood pastors in Chicago and Denver slums. Mount trooped them all to the mansion—once even Martin Luther King came and stayed till four A.M.—where the men of the cloth sat dutifully in the baronial living room, sipped scotch and coffee, watched Hefner chugalug his Pepsi quota, and discussed sex, morality, and the new social roles of religion.

Hefner himself hit the campus trail four times in the mid-sixties, speaking and debating at Northwestern, Johns Hopkins, the University of North Carolina, and Cornell. At Ithaca he first met in person the man who had launched him on the religious circuit, the Reverend Harvey Cox, whose stature had grown considerably since that 1961 article. He now taught at the Harvard Divinity School, and his book, *The Secular City,* had sold 900,000 copies and had become a campus classic.

"We had an enormous audience at Cornell," Cox recalls. "The students shouted and whistled. I thought I'd be the lamb led to slaughter. Here I was on fraternity row as the church spokesman against the new morality. But it went well, perhaps because we agreed on censorship and Victorian sexual mores. Some of the kids must have been grateful we didn't just fulminate. And we hit it off better than I thought. He's not dumb."

The "philosophy" went on radio in 1964 when Murray Burnett, moderator of a weekly Sunday-night interfaith religious program called "Trialogue," broadcast over New York's WINS, asked Hefner to discuss the sexual revolution with the regular panelists: a Catholic priest, a Jewish rabbi, and an Episcopal minister. They were more liberal church establishment than celebrity clergy, and served as "designated hitters" for their faiths on public forums. Father Norman O'Connor was then radio-TV director for the Paulist Fathers, the Reverend Richard Gary was pastor of an Episcopal church in a West Harlem slum, and Rabbi Marc Tannenbaum was spokesman for the American Jewish Committee.

The four one-hour programs were an immediate hit. WINS rebroadcast them in the fall. Dozens of stations across the country asked for tapes. Hefner devoted three installments of the philosophy to edited transcripts. Mount sent copies to thousands of clerics asking for comment. Hundreds wrote in, and *Playboy* printed dozens of letters, approving and disapproving.

Most of the appeal lay in the novelty of the idea. This was real-life soap opera from the halcyon days of radio: God, sex, and the devil. And, as usual, at least from Milton to Goethe and Shaw, the devil was winning. Certainly he won in the heavily edited text *Playboy* printed. For Rabbi Tannenbaum and the others, the editing was too heavy. "We looked like fall guys when we weren't."

Indirectly, however, the three clergymen asked for the putdown. They went easy on their guest, pulled their punches, and they are all heavy verbal hitters; treated him, in short, with the puzzled curiosity some grown-ups reserve for smart children who unfathomably act naughty by talking dirty. Father O'Connor's was the tartest tongue, even in the edited transcripts, but for all that, the discussions were tame and polite.

Gary and Tannenbaum agreed that the puritan Protestant ethic was faulty. Jews, Tannenbaum stressed, did not often suffer from Protestant-style hangups. O'Connor denied that a sexual revolution had taken place, conceding only a reexamination. And he ridiculed the Kinsey Report's statistics on American mating habits. Hefner waxed indignant that anyone dare doubt the findings of *his* bible.

Like most four-hour discussions, this one rambled, was at once funny, dull, witty, boring, stentorian, sarcastic, and at times slightly ridiculous. To wit:

Hefner: The traditional Judeo-Christian concept of sexual morality is not working, gentlemen. People are not living by it in our society today.

O'Connor: Mr. Hefner, do you have a statistical analysis that indicates this?

Or this example of Hefner at his oratorical best:

"Gentlemen, unless you are willing, as the religious leaders of our land, to begin relating to this problem realistically and making suggestions for the establishment of a new, enlightened contemporary morality that works, people will look elsewhere for their answers . . .

As Hefner's theological fame spread to the point where Mount could proclaim him the hottest thing since Martin Luther in the nation's seminaries, and do it without too much demurral, religion began to occupy more and more space in *Playboy*'s nonfiction. The magazine's interviewers listened sympathetically to atheist Madalyn Murray, who had brought suit against Bible reading and prayer in public schools and won. The headline called the interview a conversation with "the most hated woman in America." The Reverend William Hamilton, Rabbi Richard Rubinstein, and Harvey Cox (that meeting at Cornell had for a time made Hefner and Cox friends and Cox a *Playboy* regular) contributed articles on the "Death of God" controversy that was a chic intellectual rage around 1966. Asked whether that was not far-out subject matter even for *Playboy,* Hefner replied laconically that it was a *"Time* cover story." Besides, "the death of God was only a popular packaging of much of the kind of thing related to the reevaluation of religion, its place in society and the erosion of public interest in organized religion. It was one offshoot of that, and a short-lived one. And he bounced back quickly."

To a surprised question of who, Hefner grinned, "God, of course."

While God lay adying, however, He got some lively coverage in *Playboy.* Those were "heavy" articles and clearly mindful of *Playboy*'s circulation among the clergy. Auschwitz and the German death camps loom large to buttress arguments both Hamilton and Rubinstein make about the impossibility of believing in a God who allowed them. Cox sees the dispute in the much tamer terms of church-state relations. But then he has always been careful to expand the the edges of the mainstream, not to explore rivers far from it.

More than any other cleric who wrote for *Playboy,* Cox understood the medium he was using and the audiences he could reach with it. *Playboy*'s reach, of course, attracted all the churchmen, but few wrote as smoothly as he did or tailored their product as neatly. Whether Cox described the revolt shaking the churches in the midsixties, chronicled the religious implications of the hippie movement, took part in learned panels on sex and the new morality, wrote about religion, or pleaded for a more joyful portrait of Jesus, his pieces had the right tone and pacing for *Playboy*—and a sharp sense of what appealed to this audience the most about the religious upheavals of the 1960s.

James Pike, the Episcopal bishop of California who later died mysteriously in the Sinai desert, contributed an article in 1967 proposing that churches in America lose their tax-exempt status. "Worldy power has seduced the church from its spiritual concerns," he wrote, and favored tax treatment was "a hindrance to the fulfillment of the church's mission." Church wealth, Pike figured, amounted to almost $80 billion in real estate holdings alone, and if properly taxed could raise $4 billion a year in revenues. It was a bit more ponderous, but certainly unorthodox.

So was the Reverend Malcolm Boyd, introduced in an "On the Scene" feature as a performer more than a preacher who salted sermons and prayers with obscenities, appeared in nightclubs, wrote best-selling books, and cut records. His message? "The church should get off its ass."

The apotheosis of *Playboy*'s involvement with God, however, came in a panel on religion and the new morality in which "leading liberals of the clergy debate the church's role in today's sexual revolution." It took Mount more than a year to put together and required several rewrites, including a complete reworking of the questions. Nine clergymen representing seven denominations took part. The printed text of the panel ran more than twenty-five of *Playboy*'s large pages and covered the ground with typical thoroughness: premarital sex, adultery, abortion, sex without love, noncoital sex, contraception, obscenity, homosexuality, censorship.

By and large, conventional liberal attitudes predominated, though the clerics put restrictions on most of them, and the lone Catholic, a Fordham Jesuit named Herbert Rogers, stuck down the line with Rome's teachings—with one exception; he expected quick papal approval of the pill. Curiously, perhaps, panel members were quick to spot the reverse puritanism that so often emerges from Hefner's thinking. They worried that pressure on young people to perform sexually could turn into a new kind of slavery able to produce a load of guilt as heavy as puritanism's.

Reaction to the panel was all Mount could have hoped for. The clergy showered *Playboy* with letters asking for reprints. Ministers wrote that they would use it in their sermons. "Simply superb"; "one of the finest statements I have ever seen"; "the best serious feature that has ever appeared in *Playboy*"; "never have I been so enthusiastic"; were typical reactions. The Reverend Milton C. Gardner's (of the first Baptist Church in Vidalia, Georgia) was not: "I found your panel disgusting and repulsive. . . . May God have mercy on your soul."

Paradoxically, by the time the panel appeared, Hefner's interest in religion had waned. The last installment of the philosophy was published in 1966, and it dealt with prostitution. Hefner had made his point—made it already, perhaps, as he surmises, by the audaciousness of calling his series "The *Playboy* Philosophy"—an audaciousness that demanded response. "I suspect," he says, "that if I had run exactly the same series and listed it as an editorial page, it would have caused only a fraction of the interest it did."

Religion continued as an editorial staple through the sixties, and sporadically into the early seventies (with an early version of Garry Wills' "Bare Ruined Choirs" one of the last to be published, and at that as a substitute for an interview with the imprisoned Berrigans that *Playboy* had failed to obtain). But Hefner insists he had nothing to do with that. "I can tell you that my involvement in it ended way before 1970 and decisions to run religion pieces didn't come from me." The unspoken implication: Editors continued to run religious pieces because they thought Hefner wanted them, and he did nothing to stop their publication.

By 1972 Mount had stopped making speeches on religion. Clerics no longer were invited to the mansion, except for old friends like Cox. Religious journals lost interest. And when in 1972 Father Joseph Lupo of the Trinitarians secretly placed a $10,000 ad in *Playboy* seeking candidates for his order, the roof caved in on him. Even the Vatican was angered, and his superiors told Father Lupo, who thought *Playboy* a good medium for reaching "the young men we want," never to do it again.

Three years later, there was an epilogue. With *Playboy* hurting financially and trying to shore up advertising, it used Lupo's appeal in its own promotion. "I read *Playboy* and Found God" the text said above the picture of a devout cleric holding *Playboy*. "When the Order of the Most Holy Trinity needed new recruits, they relied on *Playboy* to do God's work," the ad continued, tongue in pious cheek. The Trinitarians were not amused. They called the ad "irreverent" and said the order does not "believe in the philosophy of *Playboy*." *Playboy* got a lot of needed free publicity.

By then the whole religious experience had faded into limbo. *Playboy* editors who had lived through it barely remembered details and profess to have been bored by the whole thing. "Hefner rammed religion down our throats," Jack Kessie says.

At best, most of the clergymen involved in *Playboy*'s religious decade were ambivalent about their experiences. Some felt embarrassed by it all; others, on balance, that it had done more harm than good. William Sloane Coffin, who as Yale's vocally anti-Vietnam chaplain had been more concerned in *Playboy* with the war than with religion, was turned off by what he saw as Hefner's failure either to understand or to champion the feminist cause. "I'd never write for them again," Coffin said in 1975, shortly before leaving Yale, "mainly because of women's lib." And Cox admits that he "started becoming much more sensitive to the sexist side of things."

Talking to both men in the neo-Gothic offices they had at Yale and Harvard—Coffin's a large, ground-floor study with huge fireplace, Cox's a small one under the eaves of the divinity school—gave the conversations an unreal dimension. Coffin lounged in a chair, dressed in jeans and work shirt; Cox wore a more clerical habit. Both were visible proof that Hefner had penetrated the East to a much larger measure than he had ever hoped.

"I was an early prophet of the women's movement," Cox says, "and in *Playboy* women are still accessories, not for equality and sharing. There was something bizarre about my continuing to write for *Playboy*—except for the payment. They did pay very well. But the consumerism and the sexism, the pushing of products and the raising of sexual fears and anxieties just became too contradictory."

Finally, Cox became bored with the magazine and a little bit with Hefner himself. He found him less relevant to the seventies than he had been in the sixties. During a 1974 visit to the Holmby Hills mansion, he thought the temper of their discussions had become "testier" and that he had "less patience for Hefner's self-promotion."

Cox is more candid than most in explaining why he wrote for the magazine: money and reach. "One article got to seven million people. My religious views couldn't have been disseminated as widely in any other way. Hefner had the vehicle. And it was fair. He profited from clerical support. We used each other."

Dr. Martin Marty, dean of the University of Chicago's Divinity School, sees religion's involvement with *Playboy* as an outgrowth of mid-sixties turbulence and ferment. It was a time, he argued, when the mood took hold that "a utopian world may not be so bad" and that anything was possible. Like Rabbi Tannenbaum, one of the radio panelists, he sees civil rights at the fulcrum of an atmosphere made up of New Frontier, Great Society, Vatican II, and the Beatles, of Watts, Newark, and Vietnam. It was a time when the liberal clergy moved into the "Secular City" and settled there in an effort to become relevant to its own era.

Playboy was part of a brief flowering of "celebrity" theology, or what Marty likes to call the "theology of play" or "mod theology." What they shared was the fight against an already groggy puritanism in American society, a fight, Marty says, in which the churches, not Hefner's "philosophy," delivered the knockout punch. The community of interest did not last long. As the sixties moved to dramatic high points, like the March on the Pentagon, the Chicago convention, and Woodstock, many clerics began to see *Playboy* as part of the problem and not of the solution. "Each side had fulfilled its purpose and moved on," Marty says.

For Marty, the break was dramatized by the 1967 panel discussions. He considers them "a heroic effort" that failed. "I don't think it said a thing. It was repetitive and banal. We thought it would provide a context for us to set forth our ethical positions. But that didn't happen. The questions just piled up without any constructive answers." Besides, Marty feels that the philosophy itself is "a funny kind of contradiction. Hedonism is a philosophy that doesn't need a defense. Hefner was just working his way out of his Methodist past like any American kid. And you can get Hefner out of Methodism, but not the Methodist out of Hefner."

Equally destructive to the relationship was a new asceticism creeping into clerical thinking. The consumer society itself became a new target, and *Playboy* was the most blatant example and prophet of that society. In that context, "the philosophy began to look silly as our attention shifted. We in the Protestant churches took a militant stand against the war in Vietnam, and there was less interest in what *Playboy* represented. We should have seen more clearly what was happening in society. *Playboy* distracted us into thinking that this was the real world, and it took us a while to get disengaged—maybe three or four years."

Marty is of two minds about the ultimate value of the *Playboy* experiences. He feels that some good came from it, but that on balance, it did more harm. Certainly, it did not endear those who took part in the "mod" theology to the body of the church. "Churches are shaped a lot like Li'l Abner's schmoo. They are roly-poly and heavy. Their head is where the greatest psychic mobility is located, but it does not have any great effect on the rest of it. The liberal clerics who read and dream are the head of the schmoo, but the body is middle America, a heavy ballast and tough to shift." For that body, Marty's participation in the panel proved that he had no values. Indeed, he doubts whether the bulk of the clergy really was as positive about *Playboy* as the letters to the magazine would suggest. "My hunch is that clergymen used the magazine to find out what Hefner's secret is, but I don't think too many actually quoted from the philosophy," he says. "Too many of us were identified with the impulse of being at home in the Secular City, with being swingers. The body of the schmoo can't shift that fast and for those who made up that body, *Playboy* was a symbol of our engagement. If the world of Pope John, Martin Luther King, the Kennedys, the New Frontier, and the Great Society had lived on, then the religious critique would have been more valid. But it didn't, and we should have learned that the church has to remain somewhat more disengaged from society than it was."

What did the decade's dialogue between *Playboy* and the preachers really achieve? Probably nothing of lasting value, but surely a great deal of transitory worth. Actually, the clergy, for all its reservations now, had the better of the deal. After all, *Playboy* made for a comfortable and familiar devil. Hefner, they said, was just another Methodist boy trying to work out his problems, and the clergy was happy to oblige him. They knew his kind. But more importantly for them, Hefner knew the other kind in its whole spectrum—from the conventional American sybarite, enmeshed in the good life the consumer society could provide, to the dropout hippies and the counter-culture that grew up around them. Those were people the clergy did not know and could no longer reach effectively. In *Playboy* they could. In *Playboy* men of God were shown as human, adroit, understanding, sometimes radical in thought and outlook, more tolerant than those "out there" remembered their pastors. Moreover, the portrait of an enlightened cleric in *Playboy* made it easier for the public to accept the Grand Guignol spectacle of a turbulent and radical clergy—the legacy of the Vatican Councils—that followed. In the wake of "mod" theology and its celebration of life and the goodness of the body, it was not, after all, that hard to accept the Berrigans and the marriage of priests and nuns. The celebrity clerics had burned a path through the religious underbrush for them to walk on. And *Playboy* had been one of the torches that did the burning.

The rewards for *Playboy* were both more and less tangible. The clergy lent it yet another cloak of respectability that had to improve the magazine's standing with advertisers still hesitant about using this medium. But the very fact of engaging in religious debate heightened *Playboy*'s own ambiguity and made definition of identity harder. As Marty points out, a "philosophy," articles on foreign policy, feminism, and Watergate, impose their own dilemma. Men's magazines that don't print them, but rely solely on pictures and jokes, are entirely unambiguous. *Playboy* took the risks, knowingly or not, that are involved in grappling with the complexities of a fast-changing society. Challenging organized religion was one of those risks, a new burden to carry. How many other more or less general interest magazines of comparable reach and audience makeup bothered? And however much the weight of his own Methodism may have prompted Hefner to engage in the struggle, the fact that he did is another sign of how desperately he craved the stars in the sky—as well as those on the silver screen.

6

Show Business Illustrated

THE stars of the silver screen had dazzled Hefner from childhood on. Show business was the sparkplug that fired his dreams and ambitions. He was the quintessential fan and stargazer, and much of his drive for fame and money stemmed from a fierce desire to pal around with the luminaries of the entertainment world.

"I have always been in love with show business," he says. "Show biz and the people in it are the closest thing to an aristocracy we have in this country. They are the celebrities people relate to in terms of fad, fashion and personal life."

Certainly Hefner related to them. He quickly turned his Chicago mansion into a celebrity salon, and already, at the turn of the sixties, the roster was impressive. Lenny Bruce was a steady visitor. Tony Curtis was interested in doing Hefner's screen biography. Even Sinatra came, and his appearance had to be the apex of Hefner's social ambition. More importantly, Sinatra may have given him the germ of an idea for a show-business magazine.

"Sinatra tried to interest me in putting out a trade paper in Hollywood in competition with *Variety* and the *Daily Reporter*. I think he had some beef with their editoral stance." But Hefner's ambitions vaulted higher. A trade paper lacked class, and he has been hung up on quality—in production, if nowhere else—all his life. And he wanted a magazine that would cover the whole spectrum of the art, not just individual facets.

Other books on the market then "were either fan magazines of no editorial quality or the small circulation, special-interest reviews related to dance or film criticism. The opportunity to do a good,

116

viable, entertaining magazine struck me as one that ought to have potential both in terms of audience and as an advertising medium."

Hefner was confident it would succeed quickly, as quickly as *Playboy* had. His staff was less certain. Kessie remembers favoring the idea. Spectorsky and business manager Preuss did not. Both feared that the new publication would draw funds from *Playboy.* Preuss worried about corporate ability to pay high start-up costs. Hefner, though, doesn't remember any "significant opposition" and if there was any, the nay sayers weren't "saying nay very loudly." But if Hefner didn't hear Spectorsky, others did. They say Spectorsky hated the magazine from birth and did everything he could to kill it—save vigorously oppose its creation.

The decision to move on the project was made on a wave of optimism, overoptimism as Hefner admitted 15 years later. "We went way overboard. Originally, the plan was to start the thing with a low profile and low overhead. But then we got caught in our own enthusiasm."

Hefner dispatched Spectorsky to Manhattan to look for a staff. He did not want to cannibalize *Playboy,* but build the new magazine from scratch. He moved Don Gold over from *Playboy* because Gold had once worked on *Downbeat* and knew the music business. For the rest, he went out of house.

Spectorsky commuted to suites at the Plaza and St. Regis hotels to fish for writers and editors. There was some talk about doing a *New Yorker* of show business (something Hefner denies today, "I wanted to do a broader-based book than that"), and Spectorsky first cast lines to *New Yorker* writers. Calvin Tompkins wasn't interested, but suggested Sheward Hagerty at *Newsweek.* Someone else pointed to William Ewald, *Newsweek*'s radio-TV editor. Spectorsky called Frank Gibney, a top *Life* editor, and asked him for lunch and advice.

Gibney was delighted to accept. He harbored the warmest feelings for Spectorsky, who had once written a glowing front-page review of a Gibney book for *The New York Times Book Review.* During the meal, Gibney gave his host a list of candidates. Almost as an afterthought, Spectorsky asked if Gibney might be interested.

"I said I might be," Gibney recalls. "I was bored working for *Life* and would have welcomed a job that paid better."

Gibney talked the move over with Marvin Barrett, whom he had hired at *Newsweek* (Gibney had been around) as radio-TV editor and who was tired of free-lancing. "We sort of made the decision to go out together," Barrett recalls. Once Gibney had decided on the move, he began to look for an art director and settled on Len Jossels, a former art director at *Look* and *Collier's* and then employed at Time-Life Books.

"I was in the mood to move," Jossels says. "I liked Frank and the way he talked about magazines. We were going to do the *New Yorker* of show business, and that interested me."

As Spectorsky spread his net, he began to interview prospective candidates, and they felt the first touch of strangeness.

"I went for my interview in January 1961. As I stepped into Spectorsky's suite, a girl snapped my picture," Bill Ewald remembers. (Later he was successively a senior editor of the *Saturday Evening Post,* editor-in-chief of the Literary Guild and Pocket Books, a senior editor of *People,* and assistant managing editor of the *New York Daily News*.) "Spectorsky and I talked for an hour, and then he invited me and my wife for an all-expenses-paid weekend in Chicago to meet Hefner."

"I had never written about show business," Hagerty, a senior editor at *Newsweek* and former assistant managing editor of the *News,* recalls. "I was a swing writer at *Newsweek* and had been in the London bureau. I wasn't a critic. I didn't have any deep understanding of show business. I had never read *Variety.* But they told me not to worry, that I could learn. I guess they were out to buy competent and professional journalists."

Gradually a staff took shape. Myra Appleton and Lee Gottlieb came from *TV Guide,* John Appleton from Harper Bros. where he had edited Gibney's books. Gibney looked for quality and education, and the staff for *Show Business Illustrated* took on an Ivy League cast.

The fact that so many Eastern writers were readying their hegira into the heartland to work for that strange man Hefner did not go unnoticed in New York. A *Life* colleague sent Gibney a note saying that his going to work for Hefner sounded like Hamilton Fish, august editor of *Foreign Affairs,* taking over the *Police Gazette.* (Gibney had made a reputation as a Japanese scholar and in foreign affairs.)

Gibney concedes that his major interests are scholarly, but points to stints as back-of-the-book editor for both *Time* and *Newsweek,* and his "corollary interest in American culture" and the appeal a magazine devoted to it had for him.

"I saw no reason why you couldn't put a broad umbrella over American culture. When Hefner and I talked, his ideas sounded compatible. I had looked at *Playboy* and thought the pictures of babes with those huge bosoms were just funny. I assumed they would not emphasize that in *SBI.* If you have one magazine for bosoms, you don't need two."

Jossels, too, liked what he found—at first. He thought Hefner an agreeable man, "honest in his desire to produce a quality magazine," and willing to give his new hands "a relatively free hand."

With the magazine more or less fully staffed in April 1961, the whole crew was flown out to Chicago for an initiation meeting.

"Hefner sort of told us what kind of magazine he wanted and showed us a dummy of the cover," Jossels says, "some picture spreads and a table of contents. That was our first shock because we thought we were coming out to produce a magazine from scratch."

There would be other shocks; an unending series in fact that lasted throughout the magazine's short life. But, for the moment, the new editors shared Hefner's own hopes.

"It was great," Hagerty remembers. "I had an apartment on Lake Shore Drive. We were working on a new magazine for good money and under the aegis of the sex king of America. The whole thing was terribly unreal, but it sounded like great fun."

"Chicago was a city you could live in," Barrett remembers. "Apartments were pretty cheap. New York had already gotten out of control, and Chicago's cohesiveness was quite seductive."

But differences sprang up quickly. Hefner and Spectorsky had done too much spadework on details and not enough on overall concept—beyond wanting an "overall" cover for show business. Gibney was after "a news and picture magazine with a heavy service element," and he hoped to give *SBI* "the voice of urban culture." That included articles on architecture and urban planning, Kabuki theater and Restoration comedy. For a while—a short while—Gibney was able to get favored projects into print. Then he realized that Hefner had other things in mind. "He wanted a magazine about Frank Sinatra, Vegas, girls, shows, and all the avante-garde movies breaking censorship."

But he also wanted class. And when Gibney brought in Richard Avedon to photograph a layout, Hefner was impressed. Not enough, though, to give Gibney a free hand.

"Hefner was always coming back to *Playboy,* and half-consciously he wanted to do *Playboy* twice. Half of him wanted *Playboy,* and the other half something with class."

The split was bad enough, but Hefner's inability to articulate specifics made things worse. Impatient *SBI* editors, used to clean prose and clear thought, never learned to decipher Hefner's rambling memos, his jerky half-sentences, the exhausting length of his directives.

"He talked in such a way that I frequently thought he was agreeing with me," Gibney says. "It wasn't too hard to get him to understand what I was doing, and not hard to make concessions, either. But after I left the office, he would sit there thinking, playing records, padding around in his pajamas, looking at the typewriters, and then decide there was something he didn't like. So he would write a thirty-page memo denouncing that. Often he discussed something still incomplete or that I didn't like, either. Sometimes he'd work himself into such a state that there was a virtual barbed wire strung down the corridor. At other times, I would get to the office early in the morning, around seven-thirty, read the memos, and talk to him because he was still awake then. But he was so exhausted, he agreed with everything. Around six in the evening, when I was bushed, Hefner would come in bright as a daisy and hit me.

"He was an editor who couldn't do the work himself. He didn't understand the need for consistency or flow in a magazine except through regular features. Every page had to explode with something."

For Hefner, as boss, the problem was simpler. "I mean, the relationship didn't work out, and if we had a different man in that key position, maybe it would have." Perhaps Hefner should have known from their first meeting that it wasn't going to work out:

> We were walking through the Chicago mansion. I went downstairs with him to the underwater bar which has a series of backlit nudes from the past on the wall. Gibney, I learned later, was intimidated by sex in a variety of ways. I could sense even then that while not taken aback, his was a less than positive response to the nude ladies on the wall, so I said—and these are almost my exact words—"You might be surprised to learn that most of them are very nice women," And his response was, "That's sadder, somehow." And I thought, "What a sad attitude on sex."
>
> What developed later was not unrelated to that. We were two very different guys. His interests were over there somewhere else. I think he wanted to be ambassador to Japan. We never found common ground where both could benefit. I got from Gibney what I might have expected but happily didn't get from Spec; which was a certain aloofness and even suspicion of these upstarts in Chicago who had all this success with this curious publication called *Playboy*.

The problems quickly filtered down to the rest of the staff. The endless memos drove everybody crazy. "Hefner took four pages to say what could have been said in four sentences," Ewald recalls with the professional annoyance of one trained to the sparse sentence and pithy phrase.

"He wanted every movie in the country reviewed," Hagerty recalls with wonder. "Hell, people hadn't seen half the movies in the listings."

One night Ewald and Don Gold stayed up till dawn writing and editing more than seventy reviews of records, everything from classics and pop to jazz and talk.

"What! All you have are seventy reviews!" Hefner barked at his exhausted writers the next day. "I want three hundred." So they went back to their desks, got every magazine in the country that published record reviews, and rewrote them.

"I looked at one review of a Kodaly opera," Ewald says, "and it was inconclusive, so I gave it three stars anyway. We had the three hundred reviews the next day, but of course there was room for only thirty or forty. . . .

"He was always so protective of people he thought were his friends," Ewald adds. "Tony Curtis was a sacred cow because he was going to star in that damn movie [about Hefner, which was never made]. He wrote Dorothy Kilgallen a letter of apology after it was too late to stop an unfavorable piece about her."

Sinatra was inviolable. "He would instruct us that reviews of his records and films be favorable," Gold remembers.

"His single-mindedness would drive you nuts," Ewald grouses. "If he disagreed with something you did, he'd bring it up over and over."

Paul Newman's movie, *The Hustler,* was a case in point. Hefner demanded that all films be reviewed prior to their release. But the studio knew this one was hot and wouldn't screen it ahead of time for anyone. Hefner insisted. Hollywood columnist Joe Hyams, hired as *SBI* Los Angeles bureau chief, tried over and over to break the ban but couldn't.

"So Hyams poked around the studio and got an opinion from several people and then told us to give it two and a half stars," Ewald says. "We wrote a mediocre review of a movie we'd never seen. When the picture was released, it won terrific reviews everywhere. We were the only ones who panned it. Down came a memo from Hefner asking what was the meaning of this outrage. And from then on, Gibney and I would get regular memos about our gaffe and how come we'd only given it two and a half stars.

"Near the end of that year, *SBI* decided to pick a best film. We knew it had to be *La Dolce Vita* or *L'Avventura,*" Ewald continued. "Hefner had an emotional stake in the former. *L'Avventura* was anathema for being much too intellectual. We were sitting on a long table with Hefner counting ballots. When the count stood 9 to 2 in favor of *L'Avventura,* Hefner looked around the table and said, 'Men, it's my million dollars we've lost, and I say *La Dolce Vita* is the winner,' crushed the ballots, and that was that."

Appleton was asked to do a piece on belly dancers in which he put down the art form. An incensed Chicago nightclub owner called someone in the company to complain. Spectorsky heard about it and accused Appleton of writing a negative piece because he had tried and failed to bed a belly dancer.

Even before the first issues hit the stands in the fall of 1961, it was clear that *SBI*'s chances for success were a long shot at best. "Hef jammed up the works too often," Ewald comments, "and the staff never jelled enough to turn out a magazine that had a single voice or point of view. The result was a grab bag."

"Frank and Marvin tried to bring significance and class. That's why they ran pieces like Louis Kronenberger on Restoration comedy," Hagerty says. "We even discussed one story—and I don't remember if it ever ran—on the political tapestry of the Vatican as a kind of show business. We used to have those five-hour administrative conferences where Hefner sat in his shirtsleeves drinking Pepsis. Frank's approach and style were low-key. He'd say, 'Now Hef, we're going to come on strong with Pablo Casals.' Hefner probably didn't know who Casals was, and he would look at Spectorsky for approval. All this was not the way to make creative tension into something that worked."

"There was a lot of initial excitement," Gottlieb mused a year before he was sacked (after seventeen years with the company). "Had it worked out, tensions wouldn't have surfaced. We were starting something new and worked very hard, often fourteen hours a day. Unfortunately, the magazine didn't sell. The spirit of people flagged. The guys we had tended to be too cerebral for a show-business magazine. The stuff was dry and dull. It had the diction of *Evergreen Review.*"

For Hefner, too, the magazine never fell into place, and as late as 1977, he still had trouble focusing:

"*Playboy* started from a single germ of an idea, an amoeba that grew as an organism in a natural way over the years. *SBI* was an attempt to put together an animal full grown with pieces and parts drawn from different places. It wound up a gerrymander with five legs and one eye and no tail."

"Personally, I feel he would have been more successful if he had aimed for the *Playboy* of show business, rather than the *New Yorker,*" Jossels says. In the end, after everything was too late, Hefner threw the ballast of quality overboard and tried that midcourse correction, but it didn't work.

In fact, the magazine unraveled quickly. Hefner had put all his chips on instant success. At most, he thought the magazine would need four to five months to turn the profit corner, and he felt the $2 million he had budgeted for losses was more than ample. But the money melted like wax. Only the cash generated by the clubs avoided disaster. Without them, *SBI* would have taken the company under. Hefner lost $3 million on the venture, which, at the time, was the company's book value.

"The first premonitions of doom came pretty early," Hagerty remembers. "By November the handwriting was on the wall."

Jossels was the first to quit. "He resigned because Hefner insisted on nudity," Gottlieb says flatly. "It was all about putting more nudity in the book."

Gibney was fired several weeks later, and, after a brief stint as *SBI*'s New York bureau chief, moved gratefully to the editorship of A&P heir Huntingdon Hartford's rival *Show* magazine.

Hagerty saw the end coming—and so did his friends at *Newsweek*. "Before I left, Oz Elliott [the editor] said, 'If anything happens, you can come back.' At the point where it was clear that things were breaking up, Oz had Bill Brink [*Newsweek*'s Chicago Bureau chief] take me to lunch and tell me it was okay."

Barrett left the magazine at the beginning of January. After a month of P.R. work in New York, he joined Gibney at *Show*.

With four top people gone, Spectorsky moved over to *SBI* full time to see what he could rescue. Lee Gottlieb was promoted to managing editor, with Ewald as his deputy.

"Spec called us in individually and asked us to sit on his couch to talk about *SBI*'s strength and weaknesses. It was more therapeutic than real. We were past the point where *SBI* could make it. Circulation wasn't much and advertising was declining," Ewald says.

Up in the executive suite, Hefner, Lownes, and Preuss worried about what to do. Lownes was blunt: A lot of tits and ass could save the magazine. Hefner agreed. More skin was added to the mix, but it was too sudden, too foreign, too much without focus. The strain showed. Lownes proposed a desperate gamble—make the biweekly a weekly—but conceded, "If we had done it, we would have blown our brains out." Cooler heads prevailed, and *SBI* became a monthly. Economies were instituted, but, like everything else by then, they didn't make much sense.

By February it was pretty much all over. Gottlieb had the painful task of firing fifteen people in one afternoon. Girls came out of his office crying. Most of the writers' contracts were honored, but some had to struggle.

"They paid me off," Ewald says. "But most of us were kind of disgusted with the organization. No one got any money to move back to New York. The company should have done that. Sure, the magazine was lousy, but it was terrible to be brought out to Chicago and then to have a good job pulled out from under you."

Blame for *SBI*'s demise has to be divided equally between Hefner and his crew. The Easterners were not ready for the Chicago square in the publisher, and Hefner didn't know what to do with so many well-educated and contemptuous young men. He didn't like winning points by applying financial muscle, but he wanted to make them through the force of his logic and the strength of his ideas. But those snotty Ivy Leaguers all sneered at him! And lost millions doing it.

Nor had the editors even suggested initiatives to give the magazine a personality of its own, one that was commercially viable. Hefner's efforts to inject more skin were resisted. His suggestions, memos, and promptings were treated with derision, often with open contempt. Mostly they were ignored as editors fought among themselves to push conflicting ideas into print.

"Hefner hired a bunch of East Coast squares because he was bemused by the newsweekly mystique," Hagerty contends. "I guess we were all competent, but whether this was the right amalgam for a good show magazine is something else. We were not a bunch of superpeople failed by Hefner. We failed Hefner, and Hefner failed himself."

Gibney, too, does not emerge unscathed from the debacle, even in the eyes of his writers who surely felt more loyalty to him than to Hefner or Spectorsky. Most staffers were ambivalent. His maneuverings were widely viewed as Byzantine. He was not much interested in show business as Hefner knew it, and took little trouble to learn. "Frank's parting words," says one staffer, "were 'Thank God I'll never have to read *Variety* again.'"

Nor was Gibney the only *SBI* editor to think that way. "Show business is inherently boring," Ewald maintains. "One or two pieces are okay, but a biweekly about people who are essentially bubble-heads is something else."

Few mourned the magazine or the fact that they had not been able to erase its hybrid character. It remained to the end a mixture of *Cue,* the news magazines, a pale *New Yorker* imitation, a skin book, a show-biz trade paper (yes, there were streaks of that, too). Hefner feels that if he had been able to devote full time to the project—and been willing and able to absorb larger start-up costs—it would have succeeded. He would like to try editing such a magazine again, perhaps in the 1980s. The concept remains dear to his heart.

Physically, two bound volumes of the magazine remain in a few specialized libraries (like Lincoln Center's Library of the Performing Arts) and in the homes of former staffers. Hefner sent copies to ex-editors after he had unloaded the shipwrecked magazine—in a stroke of commercial genius more typical of his career than the *SBI* failure—onto A&P heir Hartford, who, in effect, bought the *SBI* subscription list for *Show. The New York Times* put the price at $250,000.

SBI is less interesting for what it was—and it never was much— than for the light it shed on Hefner's mind and ambitions—the magazine's failure spurred his determination to make *Playboy* serious, respectable, and influential—and for the clash of philosophies and social attitudes it invited. Both Hefner and Spectorsky, surely for different reasons, had hired their aspirations rather than their needs. Gibney and his crew were competent, professional, opinionated, educated, trained to do a job and to do it well. They had not lucked into their *Playboy* jobs, as most of Hefner's original *Playboy* staff had, but left successful and promising careers to try for something better. They had natural style and firm identities. They could not easily be molded. Above all, they were media insiders.

Playboy had started as an outsider—the Peck's Bad Boy of the outsiders, in fact; a skin magazine that had shocked its competition and done so in Chicago, the Second City, of all places. Something of a bunker mentality had come in the cradle and had been nurtured by success. The staff was insulated. It saw the *Playboy* mystique as magic. Even Spectorsky basked in that protection. His New York reputation was flawed and tarred with failures. *Playboy* was proving to be his most lasting triumph. The others had known only *Playboy,* and they feared *SBI*'s staff more than Kessie had feared Spectorsky.

Not surprisingly, the floor at 232 East Ohio Street assigned to *SBI* was soon known as "The East Coast." Staffers were regarded with distrust and suspicion, and few friendly ties developed between the two magazines. The social chasm was too wide to bridge; background and class were too different.

Hagerty remembers *Playboy* editors as uptight and buttoned down, worried about correct regimental stripes on their ties and properly cut Ivy League suits, and not bruising their gin. By 1961 those concerns were going out of style in the East.

At lunch, *SBI* staffers would go out to the "Navy Pier" park nearby and play touch football. "*Playboy* people thought that was awful," Hagerty says. "They tended to affect a dilettantist, rather elegant style which I thought was Second City inferiority. It was almost foppish elegance. Spectorsky liked that, and Kessie imitated every one of his affectations. Touch football was just out of place in that atmosphere. We were very disliked."

It was the security of roots and tradition of self and place, pushed against the insecurities Hefner had set out to conquer and to exploit; the insecurities of a newly rootless and upwardly mobile generation stuck with more money than its members, or their parents, ever dreamed of making, and burdened, too, with all the hesitation, cant and uncertainty that has afflicted the newly rich since *Le Bourgeois Gentilhomme.* More bluntly, it was a clash between Eastern values and genteel traditions and the raw edge of the Midwest; of Sinclair Lewis, Sherwood Anderson, Upton Sinclair, and James T. Farrell on the one hand, and John P. Marquand, Louis Auchincloss, and Thornton Wilder on the other; of stockyards and stock exchange; of "Hog Butcher for the World" and the Council on Foreign Relations; finally, and perhaps most pronounced, the University of Illinois and Northwestern against Harvard, Yale, and Princeton—and even Oxbridge.

Gibney was a Yale graduate. One of his assistants, Margarete Sutton, was out of Cambridge University. Staffer Dick Atcheson was a Princeton man. Barrett, though Des Moines born, had gone to Harvard on a scholarship and served as an officer in the U.S. Navy. Hagerty was out of Yale, King's College, Cambridge, and the U.S. Marine Corps. Hugh Hefner had been a clerk in the U.S. Army and held a B.A. from Illinois.

Rail at the contrast, attack its unfairness and irrelevance in the modern world, deplore the snobbery of the distinction, the sheer unfairness of the difference—but it did exist, and it did fester. Nor was it only the geographic entity of Manhattan that stuck in Hefner's craw—the street wisdom it teaches, the global culture it has absorbed as its own, the ethnic and intellectual diversity that mark its stones —but the East as myth beyond geography, as center of the American meritocracy whose spirit can flourish in Iowa City but was never really comfortable on East Ohio Street. Somehow, the *Playboy* mystique never meshed with that culture and could not free itself from it. For all the Eastern domination of the magazine that was to follow, the tension and the suspicion remained. Hefner could and did buy Eastern talent, but he never owned it in quite the same way he would own Spectorsky, a special case, and the early members of his staff who gave—and received—quite a different loyalty.

For Hefner, *SBI* was a culture shock he has never forgotten. Of course he won the showdowns, but only because he had the power of money. And that was unsettling. So were the opinions of those who had served him. It was the first cold, inside look anyone had taken at Hefner the publisher, the editor, and the man, the first confrontation of values on the subtle turf of intellectual excellence rather than the rough-and-tumble playing field of social disapproval as embodied by church and Post Office. In some ways, the *SBI* experience foreshadowed the bitterness of cultural differences that surfaced decades later when Chicago and New York became symbols of struggle: the city that works versus the city that doesn't; the real versus the sham; the American versus the foreign. Certainly, some of Hefner's attitude is embodied in Barry Goldwater's 1964 remark about cutting off the East Coast and letting it float out to sea. In the January 1975 layout on the Playboy Mansion West, a *Playboy* executive sums up the underlying outrage by saying, ". . . I'm afraid that some of the New York media have an anti-*Playboy* bias. I guess they just don't dig the fact that the most successful publishing venture of the past twenty years was created by a kid from Chicago."

How much is really bias? Some, of course. But the memories of ex-*SBI* staffers are more than that—a hard-eyed look at one American dream.

Take Bill Ewald's view of the trappings of life at *Playboy:* "They gave us the impression that we would get our work done inside an endless fun party. But actually it was kind of grubby. There would be those office parties on Friday night at Hefner's mansion with a cast of thousands who didn't know each other. The celebrities were slightly seedy, too—Bill Bendix and his daughter. After a while, *SBI* editors didn't go anymore, and were told they had to. Hefner insisted we all have plants in our office, plastic plants. And the bigger the plant, the more important the job. The women in the office were all buxom and wore bouffant hairdos. They were all comely in a Miss Ohio kind of way; too overripe, like the fantasies of a fourteen-year-old boy. Gibney began hiring girls who were not so *zaftig* but could type. Hefner didn't like that. . . ."

As for substance, Ewald felt that "Hefner wanted a magazine better than a gossip sheet, but he didn't get it. Maybe he can only turn out *Playboy.* He did hit with an idea that was right. Yet his magazine appeals to the guy he detests, the Kiwanis or Rotarian in a middle-sized town. You have to remember that he is a Middle Western land-grant college product, with a middle-church Protestant background, that is very much like the Kiwanis. And essentially he still has Rotarian tastes. Johnnie Ray was Hefner's personal favorite, despite all his love of jazz. He remains a Rotarian with money who made it in Chicago with a style of life that is essentially empty and has all the class of Kansas State.

"I am still bothered by his 'centrality.' He had one of everything that was typical; one de Kooning, one Kline. He knew just enough right names. It was a learned response to art. Hefner floats with his time. He has no core. Harold Robbins is a lot like Hefner, with his wild world of fantasies. But Hefner has no more fantasies left. By the late sixties, his had become mechanical, and people no longer wanted them. Now Guccione manufactures the new fantasies."

"Hefner is really not a very complicated man," Don Gold believes. "He thinks Poe is the best writer in the world. When he buys a pipe, he buys two dozen—the same pipe. He likes his mashed potatoes with a dimple of gravy on them. He is Mid-America personified. The Marquis de Sade would have told him to wait in a corner, though he is, in a healthy way, by sex possessed. He is not an intellectual but aspires to be one. Perhaps that was why alliteration was so highly prized, though the way it was used at *Playboy* was almost a parody. One editor kept a card file of attractive or acceptable words. He would flip them for words Hefner might like. That becomes absurd. . . .

"I think Hefner set the style for his empire, recognized his limits, then assigned the carrying-out of style to Spectorsky, whose own was elegant. After all, Spec could go into a French restaurant and not need anything explained to him. Hef thought Spectorsky was sophisticated in that enviable Eastern way. And he had agreed to work for an intellectual inferior. For Hefner, that was one way of manipulating the East. Spectorsky was simply one of the highest-paid slaves around.

"The work atmosphere at *Playboy* and at *SBI* was more relaxed, and there was less pressure than on Eastern magazines (since leaving *SBI,* Gold has been a top editor at *Holiday,* head of the William Morris Agency literary department, and managing editor of *Travel & Leisure*). But in some ways things were more rigid. We had to watch the clock. If someone took too much time for lunch, it was mentioned. We were not supposed to read the papers in the office. You were expected to do an honest day's work for an honest day's pay. There was a puritan streak. Hefner wanted people to work hard. He really believed in the traditional values. The hierarchy had to be recognized, the rules observed.

"But interpersonal relationships were relaxed. It was a friendly place to work. Sex had a place in the office. We saw women walk into Hefner's office and the door close behind them. There was the undercurrent that sex is beautiful. I was separated from my wife, and when I told people at the office about it, I was congratulated on being free and able to swing, free to enjoy the *Playboy* philosophy. . . .

"Those plastic parties at that plastic mansion! The whole thing was a parody of hedonism. He used a Jackson Pollock as a room divider! But his sense of style was his way of being accepted. Like Gatsby, he was on the outside trying to get in. He'd like to be honored by the intellectual and the rich and the famous, many of whom must find him plebeian. He is the personification of the nouveau riche.

"Hefner has spent his life growing up—and at a slower pace than other people. His is still a Christmas-morning view of life. It is as naïve as his sense of hedonism. He peaked early—a case of arrested development, if you will. But you know, basically, in retrospect, I like him."

That, too, is a common Hefner paradox. People do like him. He gets worked over like Joe Louis' "bum of the month" and then is told he is really a great fighter.

"I thought Hefner was a bastard, but a fairly straightforward bastard," Hagerty says. "Spectorsky was devious. But I never felt that Hefner would stab you in the back. He'd blast your head off looking at you. Spectorsky was a kind of Iago figure. I thought he was a snake."

"I don't think Hefner had a brow—low, high or in between," Barrett, later a novelist and teacher at the Columbia School of Journalism, says. "In terms of success, his was a fluke. I don't think he was an editorial genius. My relationship with him was uneasy. I don't think there was any basic trust. He would appear at story conferences or at parties, but there was never a sense of matinees or congeniality. We didn't seem to have a common cause. He had a show-me attitude, a sense of self-consciousness, an anti-Eastern bias, an inferiority complex that made him dismiss people as elitist."

For Gibney, Hefner had at first come on as someone like Henry Luce. "He had the same single-minded devotion to his magazine. Like Luce, he was humorless and very curious. But I didn't realize that he lacked Luce's breadth of interests. It is still hard for me to realize how narrow the man was. He produced a national magazine that mirrored himself. Luce mirrored his own curiosity. I never knew what Hefner stood for. He didn't seem to have anything positive, only a negative antiauthority posture. I think *Playboy* helped propagate a kind of rootless irreverence. Hughie had no values of his own. He was very conscious of being in the Midwest and of not breaking out of his environment. He had a legitimate feeling for the heartland, and yet at the same time Hughie had a real thing about Easterners."

Hefner is never called "Hugh," except by people who dislike him, mostly clerics. But even men of the cloth do not stoop to "Hughie." Over the years, the edge of Gibney's dislike for his onetime employer has remained razor-sharp. Hefner's feelings are lazier. Things didn't work out between them, and that was that. As for the culture shock and the clash of Eastern and Midwestern values, he concedes that, too, and adds the difference between American and foreign ideas to the mix of conflict.

"It's a curious phenomenon that the media of our country are primarily in New York and Los Angeles, and those two cities are not particularly typical of America. New York is more European, and Los Angeles is something else altogether. There were great advantages of starting the magazine in Chicago. We felt it gave us a much clearer finger on the pulse of what was really going on in the country. It made it easier to look at New York than it would be from inside New York. I do think there was a cultural thing—and the snobbish thing that goes with it. It is two-sided. The New York mystique is permeated with a certain amount of 'the world begins and ends here.'

And there is suspicion of the New York attitude elsewhere in the country."

Had the *SBI* experience reinforced his anti-Eastern establishment biases, made him more suspicious of New York than he was already?

"I don't know. To be perfectly frank, I find that none of these generalities really work. They don't have much to do with individuals. Spec was as much of New York as any of those guys. . . ."

Over the years Hefner continued to go to New York to buy talent. But he never bought en masse anymore, and, for a while, he was leery of the Ivy League. In 1978 *Playboy*'s publisher, editor, and managing editor were New York–born and –raised, respectively, out of Brooklyn College, City College, and Syracuse University. One senior editor was a Dartmouth man, the executive editor, a Yalie. And, for a time, a fugitive from fair Harvard—God help them in Cambridge—was the publisher of *Oui*.

7

From Civil Rights to Vietnam

AFTER *Show Business Illustrated* folded in early 1962, Spectorsky sent Murray Fisher into the failed magazine's offices to see if there was anything in the editorial inventory worth salvaging for *Playboy*. Fisher didn't find much he thought suitable, except for a half-finished "candid conversation" feature with black jazz trumpeter Miles Davis. The writer was a newcomer named Alex Haley, a middle-aged man just discharged from twenty years' service with the U.S. Coast Guard. Don Gold, *SBI*'s music editor, had made the assignment a couple of months before the magazine folded. He had long been interested in Davis's music and in his prickly character. As one of the producers of Hefner's 1959 jazz concert, Gold had had two run-ins with Davis; one backstage at the concert, and "a screaming match" on the telephone.

Fisher thought the unfinished piece had potential and got on the phone to Haley, thus starting a lifelong friendship and literary collaboration. (Fisher helped Haley with both *The Autobiography of Malcolm X* and *Roots*.) Fisher realized Davis had a lot more on his mind than merely music, and in 1962 it was high time for *Playboy* to venture on the slippery parquet of civil rights. The magazine had stayed away from most political controversy in the past, but it was becoming too topical to maintain that posture much longer. And music seemed the perfect entry. Even before Haley was finished with Davis, Fisher had discussed an article on race with Nat Hentoff, the protean New York intellectual who had served as *Playboy*'s jazz critic for the past several years.

The result of that discussion was Hentoff's "Through the Racial

Looking Glass," one of the most prescient, incisive, and brilliantly
analytic articles published that year on race anywhere in America.
Risky praise, given its appearance four months before James Baldwin
published "The Fire Next Time" in the *New Yorker* and with it
created a literary and political landmark, which Hentoff's piece was
not. But at the time Hentoff reached a larger and different audience
than Baldwin's—less affluent, less certifiably liberal, and surely less
educated.

What made Hentoff's writing special was his inside view of black
anger and his distance as a white reporter. It was a distance Baldwin
did not have. Hentoff predicted the rapid advent of black power as
the inevitable result of the raw edge of Negro fury. He had seen it
as few whites had. A close friend of leading black jazz musicians, he
talked to them with their "for whitey only" masks off, and cataloged
the evidence of coming black violence with more chilling conviction
than anyone else had that summer.

Hentoff quoted Dizzy Gillespie on the reality of black power,
chronicled the development of "black is beautiful" within the Negro
community and described how pervasive black racism had become.
He cited examples of black musicians who refused to hire white
players, the sudden problems black leaders with white wives encountered in the high councils of the civil-rights movement; told of smold-
ering rebellion against Martin Luther King's leadership at a time
when the Kennedy administration still considered him a dangerous
radical.

In fact, Hentoff previews most of the attitudes, issues, and rhetoric
that would terrorize white and black bourgeois after Watts and the
rise of Stokely Carmichael: freedom now, Afro hairdos, the appalling
teen-age jobless rate in black ghettos, the hate for white liberals and
black Uncle Toms. Negro leaders "agree that this is going to be a
decade of unremitting, organized pressure for basic change," Hentoff
wrote, pressure far beyond white perceptions. Southern blacks talked
political and economic power while ardent white liberals thought
voter registration and passage of a civil-rights law beyond reach.

"The day of accommodating Negro leaders, men willing to accept
partial gains now for promise of more to come is nearly over,"
Hentoff warned. He wrote of stiffening racial pride, the freedom
riders' shattering impact on Southern social structure, the effectiveness of economic boycott, the ferment among intellectual American
blacks watching the rise of black nations in Africa. He predicted new
pressure for open-housing laws, the victory of school integration
based on the "busing" concept (though he did not call it that) rather
than on any upgrading of slum schools, and the inclusion of "black
studies" in textbooks and curricula. Finally, in 1962, he singled out

the Student Non-Violent Coordinating Committee as the most influential new black organization, and one most likely to take the struggle beyond Dr. King's nonviolence. He even warned that the new Negro would soon storm out of the South and invade a complacent North.

Though Hefner personally had always been blind to color bars, had featured blacks on his first TV show and in his jazz concert and had given opening-night proceeds of the concert to the Urban League, editorially the magazine had come late to civil rights. By 1962 the promise of integration was bright, the Negro struggle becoming the major domestic American news story. Violence flared all summer. King had holed up in the red-brick Shiloh Baptist Church in Albany, Georgia, in a dramatic and eventually successful drive to desegregate the city. Negro churches were bombed. The Klan rallied in Georgia. Burning crosses flared. Northern ministers, in the South to push desegregation, were arrested. But despite mounting terrorism, New Orleans lunch counters were integrated; discrimination was banned in El Paso; schools in Virginia's Prince Edward County were reopened.

In September a major state-federal battle brewed over the admission of James Meredith to the University of Mississippi. In early October the campus exploded, and the state of Mississippi stood in open defiance of federal power. The Kennedy brothers first negotiated, then crushed the insurrection. Meredith enrolled behind the bayonets of 3,000 soldiers.

All these stories made nationwide headlines, as did the rise of the Black Muslim movement and its sinister leader, Malcolm X. But civil rights still got skimpy coverage in many national publications. Surprisingly, *Life* was among the laggards, and comparing its treatment of civil rights with *Playboy*'s is instructive. The two magazines had more in common than it seemed; certainly as much as *Playboy* and *Esquire*. Like *Playboy*, *Life* was a packager of life-styles, and for a while it was as sexually explicit as then current mores permitted.

In 1962 *Life* covered only one civil-rights story in any depth—the battle at the University of Mississippi—and the pictures it published were stark and brilliant and much more pentrating than anything on TV. A January editorial protested conditions in ghetto schools, but urged blacks to help themselves rather than appealing to the federal government. A photo essay on two black children in ghetto schools gave the editorial visual shape.

For the rest, *Life* covered the exclusive Cosmos Club in Washington snubbing black New Frontiersman Carl Rowan; published a picture of a New Orleans segregationist pleading with that city's Roman Catholic archbishop not to desegregate Catholic schools; ran

a Gordon Parks fashion spread featuring stunning model Liz Camp-
bell, a classic "high yellow" beauty with molded Caucasian cheek-
bones who could easily have passed; and did a prison story that
featured black inmates but focused on broader issues of prison reform.

In 1962 *Life* still looked at black demands through white glasses.
Hentoff—and *Playboy*—never did. He was clear and sharp about the
obstacles facing civil rights. His hopes for integration were guarded
—so guarded that he had hopes only because in 1962 it was still
unthinkable heresy that it might already be too late.

When Haley got through with Miles Davis, however, that heresy
emerged more clearly, even though Davis, in the end, still believed
in integration. The Davis interview would prove a *Playboy* bench-
mark, and not only because of the searing discussion of race it
presented. It marked the beginning of the *Playboy* interview, which,
in the last sixteen years, has become one of the most vibrant and
important public-opinion forums in the United States.

"Miles is not fond of writers," Haley remembers of his first *Playboy* assignment. "He was difficult to get to. I talked to his press
agent, his wife, and his recording people, but he wouldn't consent to
be interviewed."

Haley was forced into more indirect tactics—like spending many
evenings waiting outside the Village Vanguard, where Davis was
performing. Without success. Next, Haley discovered that Davis
boxed regularly in a gym on 135th Street. When Davis saw Haley
at the gym—and recognized the "stagedoor Johnny" from the Vanguard—"he cocked his head and told me to get into the ring. He
didn't really hurt me, just peppered me a bit and we talked in the
clinches." Afterwards, they talked some more in adjoining shower
stalls. A black man writing for a mass magazine pricked Davis's
curiosity. Outside, Haley bought two magazines with his articles in
them. One was the *Reader's Digest,* the other a men's book. That iced
it. Davis asked Haley to his house on West 77th Street and agreed
to talk.

"Miles was tough to interview. If you got ten words out of him
in answer to one question, it was a lot. Sure, I steered him toward
race. Miles and his music were very much involved in black matters.
He was very intense, very pro-black. He belonged to that era of
musicians who knew what it was like to play on Fifty-second Street
—and then sit outside in his car between gigs."

What remains most striking about the two civil-rights pieces *Playboy* ran in 1962 is the seamless joints between them. The rage Hentoff
analyzed explodes across the entire Davis interview. True, Davis's
temper was not an unknown quantity. He sported a querulous repu-

tation and demanded acceptance on the merits of his artistry. The Uncle Tom shuffle many whites still expected from black entertainers was not for him. Jim Crow had dogged his life, and he called the specter by his rightful name whenever and wherever he met him.

Much of what infuriated Davis in 1962 has since been corrected or at least eased, but then it had bite, and in the pages of *Playboy* a pungent novelty: Negroes are not lazy and shiftless, and he was one living proof. White sexual fears of black men were unfounded. "A Negro just might not want to sleep with your sister." Whites pretend to an expertise on the black condition they do not possess.

"I don't know how many times different whites have started talking, telling me they was raised up with a Negro boy. But I ain't found one yet that knows whatever happened to that boy after they grew up."

Television and movies do not reflect black reality. "I mean, in life they are part of the scene. But in the films supposed to represent this country, they ain't there. You won't hardly even see any in the street crowd scenes because the studios didn't bother to hire any as extras." He refused an offered TV network special for that reason, and was shown one with "a big-name Negro singer" as star to make him change his mind. "Well, just like I knew they had eighteen girls dancing for the background—and everyone of them was white. Later on, when I pointed this out to the TV people, they were shocked. They said they just hadn't thought about that. . . . All . . . races want to see some of their own people represented in the shows—I mean besides the big stars."

The signal was clear. Blacks were about to push themselves into the white heart and mind at every social level, and do it both directly and subliminally. Davis did not alter white perceptions—networks and advertising agencies would, under court and government pressure—but he articulated the demand in a magazine that was being read by a generation of collegians who would execute the changes. They listened because Davis was a star whose music spoke the hidden language of their dreams. But for blacks with less talent, not enough for stardom but enough for lesser jobs in arts and communications, the door remained closed.

"It's a lot of intended discrimination, right in music. You got plenty of places that either won't hire Negroes, or they hire just one that they point out. The network studios, the Broadway pit, the classical orchestra, the film studios—they all have color discrimination in hiring."

They did, and the Civil Rights Act was still two years away from congressional passage.

But for all of Miles Davis's outspokenness and deep sense of "race pride," he remained within the system, eager to change it, but not to break and replace it with another. Sure, he griped and ached, and anger burned deeply inside him. But he had made it and he knew it. Integration *was* the answer:

> I got my music. I got Frances [his wife] and my Ferrari [successful and race-conscious blacks no longer drove Cadillacs, because, like watermelons, they had become symbols of black inferiority]—and our friends. I got every-thing a man could want—if it wasn't for this prejudice crap. It ain't that I'm mad at white people. I just see what I see and I know what's happening. I am going to speak my mind about anything that drags me about this Jim Crow scene. This whole prejudice mess is something you would feel so good if it could just be got rid of, like a big sore eating inside of your belly.

The next man to talk race with *Playboy* would not be satisfied so easily. Nothing cut out of Malcolm X's gut could heal his wounds. He was already a menacing figure by 1962, and the media began to talk about him as the man to take Elijah Muhammad's parochial vision national.

"He was just what *Playboy* wanted then," Haley remembers. "Someone very controversial whom many viewed with alarm."

Malcolm was less sure that *Playboy* wanted him and told Haley he doubted *Playboy* would ever print what he had to say. *Playboy* did, but not without qualms. Fisher was for the idea, Hefner ambivalent, Spectorsky dubious. The editorial director did not want politics in the magazine, and his dislike of the subject was the focus of a battle he waged with his editors to the day he died. But he ran the Malcolm X interview, though richly garlanded with disclaimers and profes-sions of how much *Playboy* despised everything the Black Muslim leader stood for. The kind of man he was, the Playbill said, was illustrated by "a postcard he sent us shortly after we conducted the interview. . . . The message on the card, sent from . . . Arizona, read simply, 'Greetings from the middle of the Desert. X.' On the other side was a color photo of a coiled rattlesnake ready to strike."

The introduction to the interview gave a quick sketch of the Mus-lim movement ("amalgamating elements of Christianity and Mo-hammedanism . . . and spiked with a black supremacy version of Hitler's Aryan racial theories . . .") and of Malcolm himself ("a lanky onetime dining-car steward, bootlegger, pimp and dope pusher who left prison in 1952"). Publication of his views, *Playboy* said, was an "antitoxin against the venom of hate." And it warned that "many will be shocked by what he has to say; others will be outraged. Our own view is that this interview is both an eloquent statement and damning self-indictment of one noxious facet of rampant racism."

The facts Haley brought out in the interview were familiar enough to readers of the press and the news magazines. But never before had they been explored in such depth and at such length in a national publication. Some of what Malcolm told Haley seems quaint, as does so much unachieved 1960s rhetoric. But Malcolm's arguments for black separatism retain their fierce logic. His insights into the Negro role as whitey's entertainer, though commonplace today, had a fresh sting in 1963. His language explains the tonic the Third World's burgeoning strength was for American blacks. "Ten years ago," he says, "you couldn't have paid a Southern Negro to defy local customs." But with the colonial era virtually over, "standing in fear and trembling before the almighty white man is gone." And there is something chilling in Malcolm's prediction that "I know the time is near when the white man will be finished. The signs are all around us." Whites who "reveled as the rope snapped black men's necks . . . will be the victims of God's divine wrath."

Malcolm's crude anti-Semitism was born of Jewish ownership of services like stores and banks in black communities, and it flames from the page. Blacks must emulate Jews and obtain economic and media power to survive a hostile world. "The Jew never went sitting-in and crawling-in and sliding-in and freedom-riding, like he teaches and helps Negroes to do." Only the economic weapon holds ultimate power and the Jews had never taught Negroes to use it. "When there's something worth owning, the Jew's got it."

Malcolm had catholic tastes in prejudice. He hated just about everybody, he told Haley, and usually for different reasons. White people are born devils. The Negro bourgeoisie backs integration because it hopes to ape white comfort. *Playboy* wanted the interview to sell more copies. Jesus was black; so was Hannibal. He preferred racists like South Africa's Vorster, Arkansas Governor Faubus and Mississippi Senator Eastland to integrationists because they were honest men. The $3 million spent to enroll James Meredith should have gone into raising black living standards in Mississippi. Lincoln cared for the Union and not for blacks, and no other American president had ever felt any differently. Whites would have to atone for their fathers' sins by handing over the territory of several states in which blacks could build a civilization and government. The ice in Malcolm's thought and vision seemed unmeltable.

Malcolm told Haley he was pleased with the interview, but that until it appeared he had not believed the white devils would print it. Reaction was phenomenal—an outpouring from across the political spectrum. Haley says, "There were letters that argued the magazine should be shut down for printing such stuff." Not all readers, however, left the interview with negative feelings—certainly not Kenneth

McCormick, Doubleday's editor-in-chief. He contacted Haley and wondered if the interview did not contain the seeds of a book. "It was contracted and written for Doubleday," Haley says of his now-classic *The Autobiography of Malcolm X,* "and when it was delivered, a decision was made over Ken's head not to print it." Grove Press snapped it up quickly.

Playboy stayed with civil rights through the sixties, providing both forum for diverse opinions and probing analysis of events. No firebrands followed Malcolm X. Fisher asked them all—from Roy Innes of CORE to Stokely Carmichael and Rap Brown of SNCC—but was turned down. However, in 1964 he did feature conversations with Dick Gregory (just before the Democratic national convention in Atlantic City where Gregory protested exclusion of Mississippi's Freedom Democratic party), Cassius Clay (after he won the title and came out of his Muslim closet), and George Wallace (just before his first tentative run for the presidency.)

In January 1965, *Playboy* landed Martin Luther King, clearly a coup since the interview was published only months after Dr. King won the Nobel Peace prize. Given the load he was carrying and the demands on his time, even trying was a long shot.

"I was the obvious choice to do it," Haley says. "I would have better entrée, and I was known quantity as a black writer. I contacted his people, but he had a cruel, cruel schedule and I had to pursue him for a long time."

Appointments were made and not kept. Haley became a New York–Atlanta commuter. Finally, King's secretary took pity and told Haley to go to a church barbecue King was attending. "Let him see you there and don't press," she advised. Haley did, sitting with a paper plate of barbecued chicken on his lap and waiting to be noticed. King came over and told Haley they might talk for a few minutes in his office. Taping stretched over several weeks, a period that made Haley an intermediary between King and Malcolm, bitter public enemies but privately interested in one another.

"King was curious about Malcolm. We'd do an interview, and then he would casually ask what Brother Malcolm was saying about him."

Malcolm was less circumspect. Whenever Haley returned from Atlanta, he jumped up to ask, "What did he say about me?"

King was pleased with the interview and told Haley "it was the best he ever had." Certainly the ring of his eloquence was there, and the bite of his thought:

> The projection of a social gospel . . . is the true witness of a Christian life. . . . The church once changed society. It was then a thermostat of society. But

today I feel that too much of the church is merely a thermometer, which measures rather than molds popular opinion. . . . As the Negro struggles against grave injustice, most white churchmen offer pious irrelevancies and sanctimonious trivialities . . . they claim that the gospel of Christ should have no concern with social issues. Yet white church goers, who insist that they are Christians, practice segregation as rigidly in the house of God as they do in movie houses.

Yet before he agreed to the interview, King worried about *Playboy* as a proper forum. "I got to somebody close to him," Haley says, "and gave him a breakdown of the audience. I told him these people were vital to King's interests, for anyone with a cause. Think what you will about the girls, but you can't ignore this audience. That's what I told Malcolm, too."

But the most bizarre exploration of civil rights in *Playboy* had to be Haley's interview with American Nazi leader George Lincoln Rockwell published in April 1966. Playboy was interested in talking to people on the political lunatic fringe then, someone like Rockwell or the Grand Dragon of the KKK. Haley pondered both, but Fisher steered him gently away from the KKK and toward Rockwell. He was not going to chance Haley on the Klan. (Fisher got someone else to interview Dragon Robert Shelton.)

"I got Rockwell's telephone number and called him. He went on about how he couldn't trust the magazines and that he would have to think about it. Then he said he'd take the chance." Almost as an afterthought, Rockwell asked Haley if he was Jewish. "I said no."

A group of Nazis met Haley in Alexandria to escort him to party headquarters deeper in Virginia. "They met me in formal rank—and with considerable consternation," Haley remembers. A hurried phone call to the commander, and he was bundled into a car. "I was in the middle seat with one of them on each side of me and two up front. We drove up to a white house in a clearing in the woods. When I got out, they patted me down to see if I had a gun. Then they took me upstairs. I knocked. Rockwell opened the door. He was livid and shook a finger in my face and told me how much he disliked niggers."

Inside Rockwell's office, an armed guard stood between the two men. Rockwell put a pearl-handled revolver on the arm of his chair. He sat underneath a portrait of Adolf Hitler. It was nothing personal, Rockwell explained as they began talking, he just hated niggers. Haley smiled that he was used to being called a nigger, but this was the first time he was being paid for it, so to go right ahead.

Rockwell did. His racism had the virtue of directness, and the handicap of a grab bag of anthropological clichés on which he drew to prove white mental and physical superiority over "purple" black niggers. Whenever Haley, who had done his homework, raised an objection, Rockwell dismissed it by saying that exceptions prove the rule. His litany was familiar, but no one in the mid-sixties had an opportunity to recite it at such length to so many readers:

Niggers were animals. Some black bucks were in better physical shape than degenerate white intellectuals, mostly Jews. Once he became president—Rockwell expected to win the 1972 elections and correctly predicted in 1965 that a Republican would take the 1968 race—he would ship blacks to Africa, quarantine "queers" on some island—Rockwell seemed to hate homosexuals the most—and exterminate Jews. Yet he denied that Hitler had gassed 6 million Jews and said concentration-camp pictures were actually photographs taken during the Dresden firestorm. Jews were behind the Watts and Harlem race riots, part of a plot to communize America. Communist Jewish traitors should be "fried" like the Rosenbergs had been, but since there were so many of them he feared that he might have to gas them after all. Haley listened, unflapped.

The interview lacked the clarity, drive, and passion of Malcolm X. But Rockwell was saying out loud what many in a growingly uncomfortable lower- and middle-middle-class felt and thought—and what 14 million voted for by backing George Wallace in 1968. Rockwell, incidentally, picked Wallace as Secretary of Interior in his cabinet, with the job upgraded to a European-style Interior Ministry with police powers.

But the strangest and in some ways most touching aspect of the interview never saw print—the near friendship that developed between the two men. Rockwell had never known an educated Negro before, and the experience stirred him more than he knew. Rockwell would come alone to the airport to pick up Haley and drive "quite a way, just him and me, and talk to me about writing. He wanted to write, and I was doing what he wanted to do. He'd ask me about what magazines paid and how much rewriting was involved. In his own way, he was not being hostile, but enjoying our talks."

Back at headquarters the armed guards—and some tension—returned. "But I felt detached and a little surreal. There was so much of the child and baby in that man."

Civil rights continued as a regular *Playboy* feature into the seventies. The magazine excerpted two chapters of CORE director James Farmer's book, *Freedom When?* A tedious and legalistic panel on "Crisis in Law Enforcement" (Hefner enjoys arcane points of legal dispute) focused on harsher police treatment of blacks than whites, a point panelist Bayard Rustin made neatly when he said that "no police are going to stop and frisk well-dressed bankers on Wall

Street, but they don't hesitate to stop well-dressed Negro business-men in Harlem."

The *Playboy* Forum provided space for a broad spectrum of civil-rights opinion and became something of a community bulletin board. One example: a group trucking food, medicine, and books to black strikers in the South asked for financial help to keep their trucks moving. Their seven-vehicle fleet had been vandalized, drivers beaten, and one almost lynched.

Black power was seen in Forum as a kind of "operation bootstrap" that had Vice-President Humphrey's support—and as a call to vio-lence, because only "the worst kind of all out rioting will have any effect on this fascist democracy we call the Great Society." One account in "Forum Newsfront" described black fears that Job Corps camps were being readied as Negro concentration camps.

Playboy deliberately sought out big names to discuss race. Budd Schulberg wrote of his experiences in trying to set up a writers' workshop in the embers of Watts. Later he engaged in a provocative but essentially fruitless dialogue with James Baldwin on the relation-ship between black and white, Negro and Jew. Baldwin refused to concede that blacks had any need of white liberal support. The discussion documented the split in the black-white liberal alliance that had marked the halcyon days of the civil-rights movement and foreshadowed the triumph of reaction under Nixon and the "benign neglect" of black demands that followed. Like so many of *Playboy*'s rambles through the intellectual thicket of the day, the piece is valuable source material for social historians interested in study of the sixties' zanier antics.

New York Mayor John Lindsay talked earnestly and sincerely about race as an urban problem in his 1967 interview. Read ten years later, he sounds like a horse's ass, a judgment as unfair as life itself. But Lindsay did have a gift for turning a pompous and obvious phrase. An article he wrote as part of *Playboy*'s 1969 "symposium" on "The Decent Society" began like this: "Race is the great issue of our time." Football great and Hollywood hopeful Jim Brown laced his discussion of sport and acting with comments on race. Senator Charles Percy (Hefner has made sizable financial contributions to his campaigns) warned that Molotov cocktails would not win black freedom, and nonviolence was the only way to obtain needed white support.

The roster of those who spoke out on black problems in the 1960s reads like a celebrity register: Norman Thomas, William Sloane Coffin, Marshall McLuhan, Bill Cosby, Jesse Jackson (whose opera-tion PUSH received *Playboy* funds almost from the beginning), El-dridge Cleaver, Julian Bond, Joe Frazier, Muhammad Ali (one of the few "repeaters" on *Playboy*'s interview couch), Ray Charles, Hank Aaron, O. J. Simpson, Sammy Davis, Jr. They talked about politics, media, humor, housing, music, baseball, football, boxing, the agonizing superstar problems of being a one-eyed Jewish nigger—Kretchmer, for one, feels the Davis interview is close to a classic—and always about race.

When Charles Evers and Huey Newton sat for their portraits in 1971 and 1973, the "second reconstruction" was over and, more than any fire of future hope, an air of nostalgia for the might have been hangs over their remarks. Both interviews were reflective in tone, plowed over past ground, wondered what they had done wrong, what they felt, thought, suffered—as human beings and as black men. There were few threats and fewer calls for action.

By then, too, blacks had been melded into the *Playboy* package. Fashion layouts featured black models and spreads on the clubs' black bunnies. Eventually, without much seeming fuss, black women were shown nude as Playmates, Afros and all. But it was not an easy decision. Hefner did agonize over black sex. He understood the ambivalence in black communities about depicting their women for white delectation.

"I don't remember it as a conscious decision," he says, "but I suppose it must have been. Black nudes did not appear until after the civil rights and racial pieces. Black women were always viewed as sex objects and made welcome in the white man's bedroom, and not much good would be done for civil rights with that."

In fact, when *Playboy* did publish a frontal nude shot of a black woman, Hefner drew flak from some Negro publications who charged that he had used a black to introduce pubic hair to his magazine and wouldn't use a white woman to do it.

"That was sad and obviously untrue because we had run several white nudes with pubic hairs showing by then. The editors just hadn't seen them."

Did *Playboy* matter? Did it change white attitudes? There are no firm answers, and even polls wouldn't give one. But those who spoke out in *Playboy* about civil rights thought it worth sprinkling their words on pink nipples to get the message across. And if Hefner caught a ride on the black freedom train into greater social respectability, which he did as surely as dance on clerical coattails, blacks, in turn, had a seat in Hefner's caravan into an upwardly mobile society.

Even today, *Playboy*'s life-style appeals to blacks. They throng the clubs and have started some of their own patterned on them. Washington's Foxtrappe club is one. It has 4,500 members who pay $50 a year to frequent a renovated town house at 16th and R, drink in several bars, patronize a disco and use other facilities. "Foxtrappe members admit that the prototype is the Playboy Club," the *Washington Post* wrote in a feature article. It "purports to represent a lifestyle, with an attitude, educational and professional requirements and lots of beautiful people."

But most importantly, perhaps, *Playboy* helped blacks seep into the American mainstream—at least to the extent they have—by depicting them as normal people, or even better as normal celebrities.

"*Playboy* changed a lot of people's minds, especially on the college campuses," Haley feels. "I lecture a lot there and am always asked about *Playboy*. Professors wish students paid as much attention to their textbooks as they do to the magazine. It played as big a role as any other periodical in changing campus attitudes on race. The articles were more open and candid and reaching out, not at all hidebound, kind of daring, really, and the kids identified with that. Their thing was to dare, to be different. *Playboy* symbolized that attitude, and most especially on matters of race."

Championing the drug culture and defending the rights of drug users must have come more naturally to *Playboy* than its involvement with religion and civil rights. Drugs were linked closely to sex and jazz, central concerns both, and they were a cause with which the magazine's young readership could easily identify. A 1960 panel had dealt with jazz and drugs. Two years later, Hefner tackled the history and spread of marijuana in Dan Wakefield's "The Prodigal Powers of Pot." Its publishing history taught *Playboy* something new about its audience interest and concern. The article was to run in March 1962 but was delayed until August. The delay caused reader consternation. The Playbill noted just how much:

"When this article failed to appear . . . as originally announced, an alert colony of columnists and a vexed generation of vipers (as users call themselves) quickly decided that 'pressure' had forced us to put the lid on Pot. As much as we'd enjoy being embroiled in such a dramatic situation, we must admit that the delay was caused merely by a mechanical conflict in scheduling."

Clearly, pot was a popular issue and one *Playboy* picked on quickly. Over the years, freedom to puff a joint ranked second on the magazine's scale of values only to the freedom to fuck. The Playboy Forum quickly become a national pot lobby that urged softening existing laws and easing penalties. The Playboy Foundation gave convicted users legal and financial help and Hefner used its funds in the early 1970s to set up the National Organization for the Reform of Marijuana Laws. Since then, NORML has become as potent a Washington lobby as *Playboy* has a media one.

Wakefield's article is first-rate magazine journalism and an excellent introduction to marijuana. He gives the etymological derivation, describes the botanic origins and the forms in which it can be used, cites actual and alleged powers, and traces its historical and geographic spread. Napoleon's soldiers brought it to Europe from Egypt, foreign seamen introduced it to New Orleans, and Mexican laborers to the Southwest. There is an account of early medical experiments, and of the use of the drug found among artists and intellectuals in expanding mind and spirit. He notes passage of the Marijuana Tax Act in 1937, and the disregard of the La Guardia report in 1944 that found the drug's dangers vastly exaggerated. Penalties for users continued heavy. But—and this, too, is a hallmark of a basic fairness—Wakefield lists pot's then-known negative effects, including time distortion and anxiety. And he ends with this warning from jazz musician Mezz Mezzrow: ". . . I know of one very bad thing the tea can do to you—it can put you in jail."

In November 1963, *Playboy* published a package of three articles on hallucinogens written by Wakefield ("A Reporter's Objective View"), Allan Harrington ("A Novelist's Personal Experience") and Aldous Huxley ("A Philosopher's Visionary Prediction"). In general, they extolled the drugs' virtues, but also warned of their risks. The Playbill's assessment is fair: "This month, in a definitive three-man report on Hallucinogens, we present a full spectrum of views on that controversial group of vision-inducing drugs which has suddenly and dramatically highlighted man's ageless and ambivalent attempt to find—or escape from—himself. . . . Together, we believe, these three pieces form the most comprehensive study of hallucinogens to appear to date."

The package also introduced Timothy Leary to *Playboy* readers and began nearly a decade's uneasy relationship between magazine and drug guru. *Playboy* often championed Leary and his causes, but in the end became disenchanted and discarded him. Nevertheless, the Leary connection was important for *Playboy* because more than anyone else who handled the subject in the magazine, he articulated the link between drugs and sex. At the same time, society's "persecution" of Leary and his various communards made his cause somehow part of the civil-rights revolution. In a way, therefore, Hefner looked upon Leary much the same way the clergy had looked on *Playboy.* The sixties had a habit of suspending belief in contradictions.

In all fairness, however, publication of Leary's 1966 *Playboy* interview was a newsworthy event. Leary had become everybody's devil. He had been chased from Harvard, cited during congressional hearings on LSD, arrested and convicted for marijuana possession and transportation. That spring, G. Gordon Liddy had led a force of

Dutchess County sheriff's deputies in a postmidnight raid on Leary's borrowed estate in Millbrook, New York, and arrested the guru and three of his followers. The threat of a second conviction and yet longer jail term made him an even more romantic figure.

What Leary said about LSD and sex enhanced the image. LSD releases enormous amounts of sexual energy and "increases your sensitivity a thousand percent." Comparing conventional sex with LSD sex is like making love to a department-store dummy. He made love every time he used LSD. That's "what the LSD experience is all about . . . it's all love-making . . . the sexual impact is . . . the open but private secret about LSD . . . the psychedelic experience is basically a sexual experience . . ." Curiously, Leary warned that LSD wasn't much help in casual making-out. The relationship had to be lasting; otherwise the aphrodisiac powers of the drug would be dissipated or turn ugly.

The interview drew a huge response, most of it laudatory, and *Playboy* printed a wide cross-section of short letters praising the piece. But almost a page was given to a thoughtful and critical appraisal by two young UCLA research psychiatrists. Drs. Ungerleider and Fisher had amassed a large dossier of bad LSD trips, and it did not make for pleasant reading. Another correspondent, Charles L. Tart of the University of California, charged Leary had left "the overall impression . . . that psychedelics are primarily aphrodisiacs," and that "emphasizing the sexual area is very misleading especially in a publication whose readers are primarily interested in sex."

The controversy over Leary's interview worried *Playboy* editors enough to commission a piece on sex and LSD. The intention was surely laudatory; the result was not. Dr. R. E. L. Masters's "Sex, Ecstasy and the Psychedelic Drugs," published in November 1967, is one of the greatest "yes but" jobs in magazine history, and as ambivalent a piece as *Playboy* ever published.

Masters's data is clearly fragmentary. It is based on 300 drug-related sexual experiences had by 94 persons, "two-thirds of them male" with 19 homosexual experiences included. "The interview subjects were almost all college graduates from middle-class white Protestant backgrounds. Most of them took the psychedelic drugs outside any formal research or therapeutic context and reported their experiences to me." As a scientist, he worried about milking more from his numbers than reliable statistics allow, but blamed laws restricting psychedelic drug research for his inability to base conclusions on laboratory verification. Small wonder that Masters's findings read like an ad for any patent medicine. Qualifications accompany nearly every statement he makes, and they are not much more enlightening than the relief Preparation H promises "in many cases."

Trouble is, the author's heart yearns for the goodness in drugs: the vision of Faust without Mephistopheles holding out his hand for the purse of the soul. So he trots the devil out first, as a kind of apology. If only Leary had never made the nexus between sex and drugs, the problems they posed might have remained manageable instead of raising so many irreconcilables. But since he did, it is true that the psychedelic drug family, from pot to mescaline, does affect sexual functions. They can give some men better erections, prevent ejaculation, anesthetize parts of the genitals. Much of their impact depends on individual psychology and personality structure. The young and ill-educated do not experience their effects as intensely as older and better-educated people. LSD does little to reverse homosexual tendencies.

There is conventional copper-plating throughout, specifically warnings against bad trips, how to recognize them, what to do, what to avoid. But the subliminal message, to those who want to interpret it that way, seems clear— ". . . and yes I said yes I will Yes."

Hefner himself wasn't even that sure. "I don't remember our ever having taken a pro-LSD position," he says, and contends that his relationship with Leary never progressed beyond a casual friendship. "We met on a number of occasions when he was in town, and he stayed at the house on more than one occasion, but that's pretty much it." For the rest, "I think you see most of it in the magazine. He was obviously a pop-culture figure." Hefner remembers *Esquire* once doing a piece on the subject that had illustrations of "Leary, myself, and Billy Graham. Fascinating trio. Patti, Laverne, and Maxine." As a vision of a latter-day Andrews Sisters, the idea is far out.

But Leary was instrumental in anchoring *Playboy* into the counterculture, while Hefner made sure it did not slip the establishment moorings. It was one of the neater tricks that decade and perhaps possible only in the sixties when both sides were so desperate for bridges. *Playboy* championed drugs and sex and the link between them, and gloried in flaunting the consumer society. The counterculture bought the former at the price of the latter because *Playboy* did more than offer drug apostles a forum for their views. It cared— sometimes passionately so—and the care showed. Listen to Hefner on drugs, and the tone is all there:

"My concern about the drug culture was its Prohibition-like aspect, the prosecution of relatively innocent people, the treating of a very legitimate social and medical problem as if it could be solved simply by putting people in prison. That made it a major target area for us. Along with the war, attitudes toward drugs have really torn our society apart in terms of the low opinion young people have of law enforcement. When you make a major part of the population outlaws or criminals by definition, you hurt society in a very real and deep way. I think that's what our attitude toward drugs has done. We're beginning to come out of that now."

If society really is, *Playboy* made a major contribution to the change. Indeed, many people who are opposed to decriminalization of marijuana have singled out NORML and its *Playboy* support as major villains. Over the years, *Playboy* has given some of the best sustained news coverage in the country to the social and legal aspects of the drug controversy. And it has taken an unequivocal advocacy position. Month after month it ground out horror stories, large and small, of harsh sentences for possession of marijuana, inconsistent legislation, willful interpretation of the law, and has, moreover, provided legal and financial aid to imprisoned offenders.

By 1962, then, *Playboy* had expanded rapidly into a host of new areas: literary criticism, religion, civil rights, drugs. That November, Spectorsky fitted in another of the missing pieces: public affairs. The vehicle was a panel discussion on business ethics, one of the hotter and more controversial subjects of the period. Though Spectorsky disliked partisan politics and fought his editors for years about putting it in the magazine, he enjoyed controversy and was very much a public man; bright, aware, knowledgable about the world. In 1962 his problem was not content, but finding the right kind of contributor.

In the wake of *SBI*'s folding, it was not a good year for that. Most ex-staffers drifted back to New York and told horror stories about life on East Ohio Street. But money and good assignments can trump most things. The solution to Spectorsky's public affairs problem was Alvin Toffler, a young editor just off *Fortune* and testing his freelance legs. Paul Krassner, publisher-editor of *The Realist* and a *Playboy* contributor who often found new writers and editors for the magazine, introduced Toffler to Spectorsky. Polished professionals both, they got on well together, and the business ethics panel grew out of their first discussions. Not only was the topic newsy, but Kennedy had added a touch of high drama that spring when he forced the steel barons to roll back prices. Expense-account living and high-cost dealmaking had the meat of scandal in them, but few of those involved wanted to talk. The American Management Association had tried to organize a conference on business ethics the year before, but had been forced to cancel it for lack of participants.

Toffler was a resourceful reporter with good contacts both in the business community and in Washington. It took time and a tough hide, but he lined up two senators—Michigan Democrat Philip Hart and New York Republican Jacob Javits—columnist Marquis Childs, author Vance Packard *(The Hidden Persuaders),* James Carey of the electrical workers, William Benton of the Encyclopedia Britannica and Robert Barnet of Pepsico. Toffler conducted the panel with a no-nonsense professionalism that must have gladdened Spectorsky's sometimes-worn heart. Like most magazine editors, he often had to settle for less.

What Toffler got out of his panelists was a huge amount of information, judgment, and analysis. When a reader finished it, he had covered the subject, and learned something of the subtle nature of shifting power and its uses in America. He had some background on the history of ethics and corruption, had been briefed on the background that led to price-fixing scandals involving General Electric and others in the late 1950s, knew about conflict-of-interest charges against the heads of Chrysler and Prudential Insurance, about the Billie Sol Estes case, and the DeAngelis salad-oil scandal in New York. Moreover, the information had been synthesized for him into a recognizable pattern, and yet not predigested into newsmagazine format. Carey expounded organized labor's views with some eloquence, and in so doing demonstrated the growing role unions played in shaping the nation's economy. In fact, Carey was flexing the AFL-CIO's new corporate muscle. For all his scathing criticism of business and union corruption, his was no longer firebrand rhetoric, but the language of secure power.

For the rest, the panel touched on these issues: the dangers of deceptive advertising; expense-account padding; definition of "acceptable" gifts in ethical terms; tax laws as an invitation to cheating; opportunities and pitfalls of stock options; impact of conglomerate growth on price fixing (still a nascent thought in 1962); adequacy and degree of antitrust law enforcement; top management responsibility for corrupt practices; stockholder rights; insider dealings on Wall Street; proper functioning of the Securities and Exchange Commission.

Like exploration of civil rights, this panel moved *Playboy* into a new arena which sex touched only at the edges—a brief reference to use of call girls as business perks. Like Hentoff in July, Toffler helped *Playboy* stake out radical new turf in November. In so doing, he also witnessed an example of Hefner's editorial courage, which firmed his ties to the magazine and kept him working for it.

Before publication of the panel, Toffler was in St. Louis on assignment for another magazine. *Playboy* called and asked him to stop in Chicago to see Hefner on his way to New York. When he arrived at the mansion, he found Hefner slumped in a chair, dressed in a bathrobe, the panel galleys on his lap. They were awash in thin red lines which Toffler recognized as lawyers' objections; standard procedure given the tender subject matter and its libelous implications.

"We went through the objections line by line," Toffler recalls. "Hefner would ask me where I had gotten such and such a fact or statement, I would tell him, and he'd say, 'That stays.' In the end, everything stayed, and I thought to myself, 'Well, three cheers'."

If the foundations for intellectual excellence had been laid by 1962, the walls went up rapidly in 1963 and 1964. Murray Fisher moved forcefully to shape the *Playboy* interview into a new literary form, a vehicle large and sturdy enough to carry sharply differing loads of freight, both intellectual and trivial. Thus Peter Sellers and Jackie Gleason followed Miles Davis.

Then, in February 1963, *Playboy* published a coup—an interview with "The King" himself, Frank Sinatra. It had taken Hollywood columnist Joe Hyams and photojournalist William Woodfield, a Sinatra friend, months to collect bits and pieces of conversation and put them into shape.

The Sinatra who emerges from these pages is not the conventional "King," the bully, slugger, womanizer and friend of underworld bigshots. Rather, he comes across as a thoughtful man, concerned about the society in which he lives, and for the liberties and rights that are its heritage. That he is a totally unbelievable Sinatra can only have heightened reader interest. Show business is dismissed in one question, which Sinatra answers with one word: honest. That quality transcends all others in his performances.

Then he buckles down to discuss religion, civil rights, politics, and foreign affairs, exhibiting strong interest in all of them. Despite a Catholic upbringing, his religious views are surprisingly protestant: Man should be allowed to come to terms with his personal God and to read the Bible. Clerics, Sinatra says, destroyed the library in Alexandria, began the Spanish Inquisition, burned witches in Salem. Too many in the public eye talk up religion because they are afraid to talk it down. In doing so, he, Sinatra, is risking boycotts of his records and films, "maybe a picket line at my opening at the Sands. Why? Because I've dared to say that love and decency are not necessarily concomitants of religious fervor."

He opposes bigotry and would have broken his daughter's back had she married a bigot. What about disarmament? He is for it, within limits set by national security, but thinks these limits allow conclusion of a nuclear test ban treaty and the admission of Red China to the UN. Poverty is the breeding ground of communism, but as long as American workers can climb into their " '63 Chevy" and drive "to a steak barbecue behind a $25,000 home in a tree-lined subdivision" they aren't going to trade what they have for a Communist party card. And Sinatra is a one-worlder: "We're all neighbors. But didn't somebody once go up on a mountain long ago and say the same thing to the world?"

Much of this was radical rhetoric for the time, and showed a side of Sinatra rarely if ever in the public eye. Sure, he palled around with the Kennedys and was presumed a liberal. Despite John Wayne, Ronald Reagan, and George Murphy—whose political persuasion had not penetrated deeply into the public consciousness in the early sixties—most Hollywood creative types were perceived as pinkos anyway. But that Sinatra could be so articulate on major issues had to come as a surprise, and to wield great influence. He was still a heroic figure then, a man who had taken on the establishment "to do it my way," the leader of the rat pack, heir to Humphrey Bogart's legend of cool courage.

But there were much bolder things to come. In late 1962, Fisher received a letter from British journalist Norman MacKenzie. Would *Playboy* like an interview with Bertrand Russell? *Playboy* would. The Nobel Prize winner's remarks were published in March, six months before Kennedy concluded a test-ban treaty, and ban-the-bomb agitation was peaking.

For *Playboy*, Lord Russell laid on the agitation with a trowel. It was better to be red than dead. "The essential thing to understand is that no conceivable solution to any problem is worse than a nuclear war. It is necessary to realize before it is too late that any act— whatever its motive or rationale—is to be considered wicked if the consequence is an atomic holocaust." Such a holocaust would wipe out Britain and Western Europe, kill half the population of both Russia and the United States.

But that wasn't all. Nuclear bases should be dismantled. The UN cannot be effective without Red China as a member (twice in two months—what other mass magazine dared advocate it so often in 1963?). Civil disobedience is effective propaganda, no more. Russia and America "both have abominable systems" of government with neither "wickeder than the other. They are both wicked." Nationalism is abhorrent and should not be taught in schools. ". . . the flag is a murder symbol, and the state is a pirate ship, a gang of murderers come together." Salute the flag and you salute "the symbol of bloody murder."

To *Playboy*'s obvious delight, Russell also championed his lifelong unorthodox sexual views—and did so unasked. Personal causes that had mattered the most to him, he said, were international peace, mathematical logic—"perhaps the source of my deepest intellectual gratification"—and his efforts to change "sexual morality and behavior." Most of the "cultivated unreality" in relations between the sexes had disappeared, but the battle was far from won. "We still need much more freedom and frankness in sexual instruction."

Much of what Lord Russell advocated in this interview would become standard New Left rhetoric; yet when *Playboy* published his remarks, the Students for a Democratic Society had only just signed the Lake Huron Manifesto. Mario Savio's "free speech" movement would not hit Berkeley until more than a year later. Herbert Marcuse, not Russell, became the New Left's guru. Still, those who read the interview, no matter what their politics, must have better understood—and perhaps helped frame—the student rhetoric when it came.

That Helen Gurley Brown should next recline on *Playboy*'s analytical couch was part of Fisher's careful pacing. He felt that the serious interview could prosper only inside a frothier mix. Therefore, Brown was followed by Malcolm X, and he, in turn, by film director Billy Wilder. July and August were given over to a tedious panel on 1984 and beyond. It was mostly science fiction stuff: computerized population control, space travel beyond the moon on which the Russians would land first (hindsight can be so embarrassing), sex in the future.

Richard Burton sat for his portrait in September, and Indian Prime Minister Jawaharlal Nehru for his in October. Or did he? Well, no, he didn't. Not really. After a year of doing the interviews, Fisher had stumbled. Earlier in the year, he had met the editors of *Wisdom,* a hardcover magazine devoted to what Fisher calls "heads of state and other great minds thinking great thoughts." It seemed a perfect interview source. One of the editors was willing to sell a few. He had one lined up with Nehru.

"We understood that it was original material and that he had Nehru's permission to do with it as he wished—which was less than candid," Fisher says. "He never did have an interview with Nehru. He had taken the stuff from printed material and woven it into a fabric—a fabric of lies, as it turned out. We published the 'interview' in good faith and discovered too late that it was a fake and couldn't pull it."

The Indian embassy in Washington got wind of the planned interview, checked with Delhi, found it was a fraud, and zinged *Playboy* with a denial. Fisher squeezed a graceless and grudging retraction into the October Playbill, stressing that there had been "no reason to doubt its validity." And in one sense it had been valid. *Playboy* readers were given a careful synthesis of Nehru's stand on major world issues: the bomb, Gandhi, pacifism, China's 1962 attack on India, the dispute with Pakistan, India as peacemaker and as armed power, the UN. A tightly written introduction on Nehru and his career preceeded the "interview." Moreover, there was as much, if not more, information packed into the piece than the average reader of *Time* or *Newsweek* got about Nehru that year. And for the uninitiated it was a rounded introduction to one of the giants of the age —with warts, such as Nehru's invasion of Goa, showing.

Nevertheless, the episode did little to enhance *Playboy*'s quest for seriousness. The magazine had been taken—painfully so. But Fisher learned his lesson. "I never again bought anything by someone else. I worked out questions with the interviewer and insisted on getting the tape to check on the answers."

In November 1963, *Playboy* printed a long-delayed interview with the Teamsters' Jimmy Hoffa. Mike Wallace, an early Hefner friend, had begun it, but tired of Hoffa's stalling, so that Toffler finished it. Six years had passed then since *Life* labeled Hoffa public enemy number one, and the Teamster boss had lost none of his pugnacity. In *Playboy* he also displayed great mental agility, and a crooked kind of charm. Toffler threw enough darts, but the portrait he drew is one of an American original: quick, shifty, down to earth, almost endearing, like a stubborn working-class Pooh Bear. Here was a whole man in the pressure cooker of his career, not a bunch of truncated newspaper clippings.

(A dozen years later *Playboy* scored a Hoffa exclusive: the last interview he gave before his presumably fatal disappearance. By then, both *Playboy* and Hoffa had forgotten each other. Hoffa told his interviewer that he didn't want to be in a "magazine with tits on the back of my shoulder," but then relented. *Playboy,* in turn, did not mention the first interview in the introduction to the second.)

Albert Schweitzer showed up in December, victim of another casual letter that had landed on Fisher's desk. An American newsman in Africa wrote to say he was sure he could get one with Schweitzer if *Playboy* wanted it. Fisher said okay. The reporter showed up unannounced at Schweitzer's hospital in Gabon and spent several days there as his guest. The interview was short, and except for the incongruous combination of interviewer and interviewee, contained little of note—perhaps because of the transcription method. Schweitzer permitted neither tape recorder nor notepad, so the reporter had to develop a fast case of the trots—he rushed out every twenty minutes to jot down what had been said.

Toffler had spent the summer of 1963 teaching at the Salzburg Seminar of American Studies and looking for suitable interview subjects. He tried both Orson Welles and Vladimir Nabokov. Welles said no, only relenting three years later to discuss film-making, censorship and pornography in the March 1967 issue. Nabokov was agreeable, but set peculiar ground rules: no tape recorder, no face-to-face question and answer sessions. Toffler submitted written questions, waited in his Montreux hotel room for the written answers, then submitted more questions. The interview stretched over ten days and although Toffler and Nabokov chatted socially, they never talked substance. "It was the only nonverbal interview *Playboy* ever ran," Toffler says. But Nabokov must have been pleased with the results because soon after it appeared in January 1964 he began to publish his fiction regularly in *Playboy* and the magazine excerpted *Ada* before publication.

The Nabokov experience confirmed Fisher's theory that the interview could be used as a lasso to snare authors unwilling to write directly for the magazine. Moreover, once they had done an interview, many were willing to write for it. Lord Russell, for example, followed up his interview with an article deriding "The Conflicting Ideologies of East and West" as "merely an elegant decoration." Love of power, he argued, was the real source of Soviet-U.S. tension.

But in the early years it was not easy to persuade the prominent to do *Playboy* interviews. And even those who agreed had scruples. "Public figures were the toughest to get," Fisher says, "because they had the most to lose (as Jimmy Carter found out as late as 1976). So we tried the buckshot approach, and the further we moved away from this country, the easier it became."

Experience bears Fisher out. Harvard economist John Kenneth Galbraith turned down a Toffler request in the mid-sixties because his friends thought it risqué that he wrote for *Esquire*. (For Galbraith, the risk diminished quickly, and by the late sixties he had become a regular contributor and polemicist against the Vietnam War.) But Jean Genet, Salvador Dali, Ingmar Bergman, Ian Fleming and Jean-Paul Sartre (*Playboy* got to him through Simone de Beauvoir) all agreed to interviews in 1964–65.

But the real bird of paradise Toffler captured for *Playboy* in 1964 was Ayn Rand, the first female intellect given voice in the magazine. Miss Rand did not disappoint. She dominated the interview with sharply phrased opinions that rode over Toffler's questions like the charge of Czarist cavalry. And nowhere did the firmness of her views emerge more rigidly than on sex. It was, she said, an expression "of a man's self-esteem, of his own self-value," and "must not be anything other than response to values." She judged promiscuity immoral, opposed hedonism because it was irrational, dismissed the Don Juan type as a man who despised himself, denied existence of biological instincts or nonrational biological urges, extolled love as "the most profound assertion of your own needs and values."

But most startling was Miss Rand's crisp espousal of feminism some years before it became a popular cause. "I believe women are human beings," she replied to a question about women working, and "what is proper for a man is proper for a woman. The principles are the same. I would not attempt to prescribe what kind of work a man should do and I would not attempt it in regard to women. There is no particular work which is specifically feminine. Women can chose their work according to their own purpose and premise in the same manner as men do."

For a magazine that spent years struggling with its own ambivalence about the role of women in society, this was a radical opinion, and yet another illustration of a willingness to stick its neck out—and into controversy, even if it ran counter to what editors perceived as the magazine's own interests.

But Fisher could afford the risks because he edited the interviews with such meticulous care that craftsmanship alone could balance off negative impact. He has a sense of "architecture" that appealed to all the writers who worked with him and made the *Playboy* interview a form of literary expression that neither the looser models—from *The Paris Review* to *Redbook*—nor the televised version ever matched.

"They are a literary form, not a spoken form," Fisher insists. "They have the versimilitude of conversation, but nobody talks like that except William Buckley." (And Fisher even had the gall to press Buckley's *Playboy* interview into that mold.) "The technique is to tape and then to transcribe the tape. Take the transcript and break it into subject categories so that everything that fits one subject is put in one pile. There are constant echoes and digressions in the course of an interview that belong somewhere else than where they occur.

"You [the person being interviewed] come back to a subject and reflect on it further. In most cases the reflection and the original subject belong together. I'm very Germanic in my linearity, and it seems to me that there should be a natural progression to invite accessibility to the eye which is much more critical than the ear. You wouldn't have to do that kind of editing if it were a spoken interview because your ear doesn't listen as hard and is less critical.

"Next, I would label the subject categories by topic and order them into a sequence, guided by whatever form the interview ought to have in terms of logic. I wrote a kind of scenario for the interview. It had to have flow. I have a pathological aversion to abrupt changes of subject and to things out of context. Once subject categories were arranged according to sequence, with logical and very tight hooks between one and the next, I would sit down with subject A, part one, distilling, condensing, reflecting, in some cases adding a line or two myself, sometimes more than that if the subject was unavailable and something had to be filled in. I knew how they felt by then. In a way I had become that person. I could give an interview for them. Everything had become internalized in the editing process. We took no egregious liberties. Interviews were always sent back to the subject —and they always changed what they had said, never what I added."

As the sixties marched on, the mix broadened, partly because the magazine became a better product and partly because Hefner himself had blossomed into full-fledged celebrity status. He attracted prominent people to the mansion. His intellectual late-night sessions became as well known as his ritualized—and much-satirized—buffet-cocktails. Gradually, some of the best minds in the country were drawn into *Playboy*'s orbit.

Columnist and historian Max Lerner met Hefner on a TV show, and despite disparity in age, social, and educational background, they became friends. Lerner enjoyed debating Hefner and found him open to argument and new ideas. Hefner persuaded Lerner to write for *Playboy*—on political violence and, again, on admission of Red China to the UN. Lerner and Hefner both favored Peking membership. But for Lerner, such advocacy was a truism of East Coast liberalism—a given—for *Playboy,* it was not. Lerner's piece appeared in 1966 with the United States already deep in the Vietnam quagmire and the threat of Chinese intervention a constant fear. It could antagonize readers and advertisers. But on that one the idealist in Hefner had no trouble prevailing over the huckster. A fuzzy and often naïve internationalist, he has always been fiercely critical of postwar American foreign policy. And China still stirs his juices.

"About that there is no legitimate debate," he said in January 1977, sitting cross-legged on the couch of his Los Angeles library under a bust of Barbi Benton, framed by a lead-embossed window. The view behind him dropped across a splendid valley, lush green in winter, to blue hills melding into the horizon. "Accepting Red China into the UN was part of something that for me is so fundamental in terms of saving the planet. I mean, you don't have the first vague trappings of a world government and leave out as some kind of outlaw group so large a people. Our attitude toward China . . ."

He stopped for a moment, struck a match from the big box on the coffee table, puffed, and said, "Luce can have all the credit for Chiang Kai-shek. The case for keeping Red China out was not a case. But an awful lot of what passed for political insight since the Second World War is predicated on the same bullshit. The real motivations don't surface. They're economic, and people would be embarrassed to lay them on the table. The notion that after a major country in the world had clearly changed its government to suggest that the little dictator living down there on an island was the real head of government is just madness if one wants to save the planet. All the beginnings of a world government are for is to get communications going so that the planet's problems can be solved with something else than war and annihilation. How do you do that by keeping out a major part of the world's population? We could live with Russia but not with China? It's crazy, just crazy."

That was Lerner's view, too, although he said it a bit more elegantly, more to the point, and with few digressions about saving the planet.

During 1966 Hefner also wound up the philosophy with a critique of the "patently antifemale" character of U.S. laws against prostitution, printed a strongly worded plea against capital punishment by former Ohio Governor Michael di Salle—and plunged a Playmate's dainty foot—and with it, *Playboy*'s own—into the Vietnam War.

It started with a letter Second Lieutenant John Price wrote to Playboy in November 1965 from Bien Hoa enclosing a money order for a lifetime subscription to the magazine. It was his understanding that the first issue of such a subscription is delivered in the United States by a Playmate in person. "The loneliness here is a terrible thing—and we long to see a real living, breathing American girl," he wrote and hoped the delivery policy could be stretched to "include us." Any Playmate would do, Price wrote, but Playmate of the Year Jo Collins, if possible.

It was a promoter's dream. Magnanimously, Hefner overlooked the fact that his subscription offer was limited to cities with Playboy Clubs in them, and at once "began drawing up plans for the successful completion of Project Playmate." After cutting through wads of Pentagon red tape, "Playmate First Class Collins and her party" were on a Pan Am jetliner bound for Saigon on January 9, 1966. The picture spread and text *Playboy* ran on the voyage was embarassingly rah-rah—self-conscious, badly written, inept. A Bob Hope–style tour without Bob Hope. Imitative, unfeeling, conventional. The justness of our cause. The battle to stop godless communism. The danger of VC ambushes. The "hi, gorgeous" from a badly wounded GI. The flow of tears from beauteous eyes. The dabs of lipstick on soldier cheeks. A World War II morale builder with the Playmate taking the place of Betty Grable and Rita Hayworth pinups—something Hefner was careful to note.

Back in Chicago, some of the newer editors, already dove converts, had stomach cramps. Others rationalized the trip as a morale builder for men doing the dirty work of fighting. Few realized that the innocent pictorial and its cloying text would prove to be *Playboy*'s ideological bar mitzvah, and crossing that border into manhood would be much tougher than tackling drugs, sex, literature, religion, or civil rights.

A decade later, Hefner would call Vietnam "one of the sadder chapters in American history," but *Playboy* edged into the sadness more than meeting it head-on. First there were scattered letters about soldiers busted for pot smoking in the field or from officers who found penalties out of whack for an offense that gave the jungle fighters a little "harmless" relaxation. Then, in the summer of 1966, *Playboy* interviewed Norman Thomas, the six-time Socialist presidential candidate, and first came to grips with the war and what it was doing to the country. The interview was published in November, presumably because Leary and drugs still took precedence.

Nevertheless, the war's impact was becoming hard to overlook. Vietnam had already begun to tear the nation's social fabric. There was a nascent peace movement. Lyndon Johnson attacked "nervous Nellies." Campuses were shaken by antiwar "teach-ins," and the U.S. buildup in Vietnam reached 300,000 by the year-end. Uncomfortable liberals sought for ways out with honor.

Playboy asked Thomas if he favored unilateral U.S. withdrawal from Vietnam. For all his criticism of U.S. involvement, he did not: those who fought the Vietcong would be massacred once the Americans left. He urged that negotiations replace military action and suggested reconvening the 1954 Geneva conference on Indochina with both Vietcong and Peking at the table. Free elections under UN auspices would follow the talks. The United States would withdraw after formation of a new government, hopefully a coalition. At home, antiwar demonstrations should be augmented by political action, specifically targeted support of antiwar candidates in the 1966 election. (The magazine with the interview in it was on newsstands in October, before the voting.) Proven political clout would make the peace movement a much more potent political force. And Thomas dismissed LBJ's famous polls showing popular support for the war as demonstrating that "the majority . . . is . . . in a very confused state of mind."

(Thomas did not limit the interview to Vietnam. He had not had so large an audience for a long time, and he made the most of it, ranging broadly, and with badly needed historical perspective, over such issues as the New Left, the Great Society, changes shaking Russian communism, developments in China, and prospects for his own democratic socialism. It was another of *Playboy*'s crash courses in history and current events, and, judging from the large volume of mail the interview drew, *Playboy* had used Thomas to build a bridge across the gap of cultures.)

In April 1967, historian Arnold Toynbee took up the cudgel

against U.S. Vietnam policies. (With Lord Russell to his credit, Norman MacKenzie had little trouble persuading Toynbee to do the *Playboy* interview.) Toynbee's approach was more leisurely, but no less stinging. The United States had become another Rome, he charged, and always supported the rich against the poor. By fighting the Vietcong, the United States was "making herself the heir of European colonialism in Asia." Washington saw itself as St. George and international communism as the dragon. "I happen to think it is an imaginary dragon . . . that the U.S. will not look at the realities."

Reality in Vietnam, Toynbee argued, meant an independent and united Vietnam under Ho Chi Minh that would act as a buffer against communist expansion in Asia much as Tito had done in Europe. Ho was a nationalist first, a communist by unhappy necessity—and the best solution to the mess in Southeast Asia. Once the United States left the area—with apologies—Vietnam would again oppose Chinese expansion as it had done for two thousand years. Moreover, with the war settled and the United States gone, Russia would seek insurance from Washington against Peking, and that could result in a new global stability, one in which the United States might even reach an understanding with China. Peking did not have global ambitions, and wanted only return of its traditional hegemony in East Asia and the lands lost to Russia in the nineteenth and early twentieth century. The latter aim, Toynbee predicted, would lead to armed skirmishes along the Ussuri river.

For the rest, the interview was another tour of past and present: Toynbee worried about a growing North-South confrontation, thought racial integration in the United States inevitable, saw nuclear proliferation as "one of the greatest menaces in the world," downgraded the space race, and thought LBJ would build the Great Society in the United States if he could get out of Vietnam. He saw the U.S. student revolt against the war as a "coming generational revolt" against the American way of life as exemplified and sold by Madison Avenue. He cited Thucydides, Buddha, Jung, and Freud, touched on his own theory about the influence of personality on history, and expounded at some length on his opposition to Zionism and the state of Israel.

In August 1967, *Playboy* ran an eyewitness account of the Vietnam fighting by Tom Mayer, a twenty-four-year-old Harvard graduate. "The war is very complicated and I knew nothing about war or the Orient. So I went out on a few missions and talked to people and tried to learn."

John Kenneth Galbraith got in his licks in December. Whatever tentativeness might have marked war critics in mid- and late 1966 was gone now. The march on the Pentagon was history. Norman

Mailer was writing his seminal *Armies of the Night.* Gene McCarthy had issued his incredible challenge to a sitting president. Johnson himself was becoming a prisoner of his war policy, afraid to move freely among his own people.

In "Resolving Our Vietnam Predicament," Galbraith hacked away the roots of U.S. involvement. ". . . the American people have watched the collapse of the assumptions on which the Vietnam war was launched. In vindication of an intelligence none should mistrust, a very large number have reached the inevitable conclusion: The assumptions that took us into Vietnam have been shown by history to be false. Therefore, we should not be there."

The year that passed between publication of the Thomas interview and the Galbraith article (adapted from a speech Galbraith had given in Washington) saw the gradual emergence of *Playboy* as one forum for liberal establishment dissent from the war, and almost by definition one of the most unusual. But tits and ass take on a special quality in war, and Vietnam was no exception. Soldiers read it, and those who wrote for *Playboy* knew that. Opinions on the war became firm, analyses acute, suggestions for policy changes concrete. Still, solutions were more cautious than those propounded by the New Left. This was the responsible opposition, anxious to channel dissent into the political process, out to guide and instruct readers in the arts of constructive change. The tone was Olympian, the credentials of those who spoke out on the war impeccable, the suggested solutions still clearly within the parameters of the American mainstream.

Response is hard to measure, and the best available yardsticks— letters and readership surveys—inconclusive. But *Playboy* no longer needed them to confirm its reach. Those who used the magazine as an anti-Vietnam forum over the next five years knew that *Playboy* mattered, that it influenced the campus and the battlefront. That a radical like Robert Scheer would ever write for *Playboy* was inconceivable in 1967. But in the years that followed, those who did prepared Scheer's way. Consider this cross-section:

——In February 1968, British critic and longtime *Playboy* contributor Kenneth Tynan wrote an "Open Letter to an American Liberal" in which he condemned, as *Playboy* put it, "U.S. involvement in Vietnam and castigates those passive dissenters among us who have learned to live with horror."

——In April 1968, Senator Charles Percy said that "bombing . . . population centers in North Vietnam will not disunite that country . . . [but] . . . give them visible evidence . . . that we want to overthrow their government."

——In June, Galbraith, having succumbed to *Playboy*'s blandishments for an interview, enlarged on his earlier Vietnam criticism. He

praised Coffin and Dr. Spock for opposing the war, condemned
Johnson for embracing Dean Rusk's "obsolete" foreign policy, insisted on U.S. responsibility for "our" Vietnamese, and chastised his
"liberal colleagues" for ignoring their plight.

——In July, Senator William Fulbright pleaded "For a New
Order of Priorities at Home and Abroad" in which he criticized the
negative impact U.S. Vietnam policy had abroad, and pointed to U.S.
inability to supress the "war of national liberation" in South Vietnam, "even with an army of more than half a million men, and
expenditures of $30 billion a year."

——In August, William Sloane Coffin laid out his opposition to
the war—having agreed to the interview because he wanted to meet
interviewer Nat Hentoff and because he was dazzled by *Playboy*'s
reach. Government efforts to crush the peace movement had failed,
he said, because they gave "dissent a kind of respectability it didn't
have before." The interview was published just after Coffin, Dr.
Spock, Marcus Raskin, and several others were put on trial (and duly
convicted) for conspiring to counsel young men to violate draft laws.

——In September, Hentoff explored further government efforts to
stop dissent. The FBI had snooped into his life because of his antiwar
stand. Hentoff warned of a McCarthy era "rerun," cited a legislative
proposal backed by nineteen senators to make peacetime treason a
federal crime, and told of draft boards canceling deferments of antiwar activists.

——In November, *Playboy* printed an astonishing cross-section of
comment on the Coffin interview that had clearly struck hard at
exposed nerve-endings:

"Once again you have met the challenge of a disturbed nation with
journalism of import and urgency."

"That was an awesome and inspirational interview . . ."

"It is a long time since I have been as deeply moved."

"How ironic that the best interview ever to appear in *Playboy*
should be with a chaplain. But what a chaplain."

"I hope your interview with Coffin will be as widely read as its
relevance demands."

"Those of us who have been exposed first hand here in Vietnam
will understand the terrible truth of Coffin's words . . ." (and that
signed by a marine, no less).

And on the other side were comments such as these:

". . . under the guise of 'constitutional freedom' Coffin and his
followers can advocate acts of treason." "The bromidic formulas
suggested by Coffin are the same blindly indignant . . . solutions
advocated by most of the unreasoning antiwar saints." "Coffin's logic
is like an old pair of blue serge trousers: shiny but full of holes."

This outburst of reader feeling sealed in brass what had been clear for some time: The war moved this audience as much as sex and drugs.

But it took Hefner's "brief encounter" with Chicago police during the 1968 Democratic Convention for the "political rabbit" in *Playboy* to penetrate the popular mind. Media accounts made it seem like the conversion of St. Paul. The wrath of God, in the form of Dick Daley's cops, dumped Hefner on his rump. A chastised lecher arose an enlightened crusader.

The facts of the oft-told tale: During the convention week, Hefner had turned his mansion into a USO stand for his celebrity friends. On the night of the "police riots," Hefner, Max Lerner, and Jules Feiffer went out to see what was going on. Enraged cops told Hefner and his friends to get off the street. When Hefner protested, one of the officers whacked him. The story made for nationwide headlines —and quick *Playboy* exploitation.

For once Hefner moved too instinctively and too fast. Those who now began to look at *Playboy* more seriously—after all that furor, it must exercise some social and political influence—found more social and political articles than they had expected. The conclusion of such instant analysis: exposure to the real world at the convention had shattered the fake work of Hefner's dreams. Though a bum rap, Hefner has never been able to shake it. Repeated pleas to interviewers to look at what *Playboy* printed before 1968 fell on deaf ears.

But the incident did shore up *Playboy*'s interest in politics—and weakened Spectorsky's hand in opposing it. Hefner had begun to move out of his hermit life-style anyway. Now he took a more active role in partisan politics, something he had not done before. The Playboy Foundation stepped up support of candidates and political issues. Hefner was active in the McGovern campaign. His mansions —both in Chicago and Los Angeles—were thrown open for political fund-raising parties. More quietly, when David Halberstam still struggling with *The Best and the Brightest* needed money to pay legal fees arising from his connection with Daniel Ellsberg and the Pentagon papers, Hefner contributed $1,000.

With Nixon in the White House, *Playboy* grew increasingly political, radical, and antiwar. Hefner still had reservations about involving *Playboy* in political partisanship, but his heart was not in them. Besides, the war was touching every particle of American life, and however splintered, it was reflected in *Playboy*'s nonfiction:

Marshall McLuhan discussed the impact of televised war. Allen Ginsberg talked about the Chicago convention as street theater, calling it "an exercise in black magic and mass hallucination—just as the Vietnam war has been." Ramsey Clark defended his handling, as attorney general, of the march on the Pentagon. Senator Frank Church of Idaho saw Vietnam as part of a "global crunch" that would make the United States stop interfering in the affairs of smaller states. A September 1969 panel on the student revolt focused on the impact the war had on campus and found it all-pervasive. An article published in early 1970 centered on the war's cost and the disappearing "peace dividend" for social programs that Nixon had promised.

David Halberstam wrote a searing piece on the Americanization of Vietnam that crackled with anger and venom and a verbal passion that does not often clatter off his cool typewriter. William F. Buckley, Jr., riposted in a *Playboy* interview that the American position in Vietnam was the best of all possible positions. He was as optimistic about Vietnam as Halberstam was pessimistic. In October 1970, Tom Wicker took apart Nixon the president and the personality in a long, rambling article whose most trenchant point was the missed opportunity of ending the war quickly—something, Wicker argued, a conservative Republican could have done more easily than a liberal Democrat. A *Playboy* poll of 7,300 college students found disenchantment with the war high on campus. Jesse Frank Frosch summed up the My Lai massacre in another massive and exhaustive account. The piece was a final wrapup, the last word rather than the first, and it drew approving comment from senators and soldiers. Joan Baez told her *Playboy* interviewer that organized nonviolent resistance could "end police terror" in the United States. Such nonviolence, she suggested, might have saved Jews from Hitler's gas chambers. An Auschwitz survivor picked apart that piece of political stupidity in a barbed reply which *Playboy* printed without comment.

Halberstam was back with a second, even angrier article in January 1971. "The Vietnamization of America" burned with pain, anguish, despair, a special hate. Halberstam described the failure of American values in Vietnam and the damage that failure did to "belief in our democracy." As the liberal U.S. center came apart, he wrote, it spawned an angry left, which, in turn, sparked "a new menacing nationalism" and the splitting process bedeviling American society.

He recalled a 1970 New York dinner with Nelson Rockefeller —all black tie and glittering women and Cuban cigars—that left him choking with rage at the governor's "Rotary Club speeches" and bland assumptions that talking about the war still mattered or could heal its wounds. Divisions ran so deep that a girl in his party at a Yankee Stadium ball game refused to rise for the national anthem. And he cited Polish writer Jerzy Kosinski's pessimistic appraisal of America as less centrist and more European at the end of the sixties than it had been when he first arrived here in the fifties.

No summary can do justice to so impassioned a piece of writing. The searing polemic had a point of view most *Playboy* readers simply could not find anywhere else. It had shock value. Read it and dare believe the nation does not shudder with trauma!

In August 1971, *Playboy* published Washington columnist Milton Viorst's interview with Senator George McGovern and gave the South Dakota Democrat's views the in-depth mass-media exposure they had not had before. The interview made the man believable, compassionate, wise, humane, a viable candidate for the fragmented liberal center. *Playboy* alone did not "make" McGovern presidential, but it could not help but give his candidacy a vital push.

The introduction showed him touring the Bronx and talking to municipal workers. "McGovern made no speeches. Instead he sipped coffee from a paper cup and listened—which is unusual for a political candidate." In fact, the glimpse of the Bronx gave McGovern, the farm boy, a crash course in urban affairs that he could weave into a presidential campaign for social regeneration. "When the tour was over, he collapsed into the air shuttle back to Washington, his body exhausted and his head swimming, but with the feeling that this had been an indispensable experience."

In the interview, McGovern said all the conventionally liberal things about Vietnam that marked his campaign, and, perhaps thanks to Fisher's skillful editing, said them particularly well. Whether you ended up liking McGovern or not, *Playboy* provided succinct information about where he stood on issues to base an intelligent decision upon.

The same issue featured John Kerry's antiwar testimony before the Senate Foreign Relations Committee—a document of veteran disenchantment with Vietnam—and an article about the demoralized American soldier slogging through the last year of the war. Arthur Hadley's piece could have used defter editing—a lot of *Playboy* think pieces could have—but the writer had captured the sights, sounds, smells, and feel of a decaying war.

As the war wound down, *Playboy*'s coverage slackened. The polemics gave way to soberer articles so that Joe McGinnis's raking over the Ellsberg coals in October 1972 seemed already overdone. In fact, it was written more in terror of "four more years" of Nixon, inevitable after McGovern's nomination, than in opposition to the war. In mid-1973 Gloria Emerson rounded out *Playboy*'s Vietnam coverage with a series of vignettes on people she had known in the 'Nam—almost a foretaste of her 1977 book about the legacy of the war and which won a National Book Award in 1978. It was already reflective and about the bitterness of pain past.

How much *Playboy* mattered on the war is as difficult to measure as its impact on civil rights. It had impact on the campuses and on the soldiers in the field. There were enough letters and enough personal comment from those who were there to attest to that. Of course, Playmate pictorials were the opening wedge. Lieutenant Price's 1965 letter made that abundantly clear. Everything critics at home put down about the pictures—the milk and honey, the rosy glow, the absence of warts and blemishes, the glossy perfection, the bursting health of all those corn-fed blondes, their undemanding prettiness and those sweet, safe, innocent, and empty smiles, the gouda cheese of vaulting breasts, the dazzling whiteness of their skins —was magic to the soldiers. Fighting a war without conviction, they turned Playmates into talismans, symbols of hope. Every bivouac, every encampment, every army post or helicopter pad was plastered with Playmates.

"I've been told," Hefner says, "that you could walk into any army base rec room in the 'Nam and know how long the men had been there by the month in which the Playmates on the wall began. A writer for the *Washington Post* once said that if *Stars and Stripes* had been the publication of World War II, then *Playboy* without doubt was the publication of the Vietnam war."

"I always felt there was something reassuring about that publication," says Frances Fitzgerald, who won a National Book Award for her Vietnam book, *Fire in the Lake.* "All those healthy American girls. But there was nothing specifically sexy about them, I don't think. They were like a set of icons, a desire that could not be satisfied. The magazine was in all the barracks and compounds and in many ways it was like the home fires. There would be references to that in the way people talked about *Playboy.* It is perfect for a place where there are no women. Because of the framework of the clubs and because of the magazine itself, the women seem to be there. Yet they are not. There was something abstract about *Playboy*'s pictures. They could have been taken from baroque paintings with their notion of the beauty of the human body."

"*Playboy* was desperately widely read. If the soldiers read anything, they read *Playboy,* " Gloria Emerson says. "The pictures were more important to them, of course, but *Playboy* did make a difference in Vietnam. Whenever I went up into the lines with the soldiers, I'd find Miss March or Miss January all over."

She remembers coming back from the war and attending a Harvard seminar where feminists became enraged when she argued that *Playboy* was not all bad. As a feminist, her position was curious: "I felt that these women simply didn't understand the problems of an

army. Those nineteen-year-old boys with cowlicks in their hair, they
needed to see a fat, pink Miss January."

Did the polemics matter? Both women are less sure. Fitzgerald
believes average soldiers were too ill-educated to follow a Galbraith
or a Fulbright. Emerson thinks *Playboy* exercised more influence
through the ambience the magazine presented. David Halberstam,
however, feels that more than any other magazine *Playboy* was read
—as well as looked at—by "the kids who did the fighting. It was
influential."

Playboy's editors don't pretend to any great editorial impact.
They know the magazine sold thousands of copies, that soldiers
bought lavishly at Vietnam PXs products advertised in the magazine—hi-fi equipment, shoes, photographic gear, toiletries, and
had them shipped home, perhaps as down payment on staying
alive—that pilots plastered decals of Little Annie Fanny, *Playboy*'s
dumb blonde with big tits cartoon feature, and of Granny, the sex-
starved old hag with touchingly sagging breasts, onto planes and
helicopters, and that thousands of soldiers wrote letters detailing
their feelings about the war, drugs, sex, the military, the agony of
combat, the pain of groping for meaning. But beyond that even
Hefner is stumped.

"There is just no real way for me to know what kind of influence
Playboy had there. I'm just not certain about our changing any
attitudes. For the guy in Vietnam, *Playboy* was the magazine. It
represented home and what the guys out there were fighting for. We
felt the cause was wrong but were supportive of the guys. So we'd
run a Galbraith piece and sent over a Playmate of the Year. That's
not contradictory, simply part of the ambiguity out there."

Add up a dozen years of Playboy quality in nonfiction, efforts,
succesful or not, to reflect the major issues and concerns of the day
and what have you got? For critics, a lot of window-dressing to make
girls respectable. Ideas, they say, merely served as an adjunct to lust,
something to occupy the time between contemplating tits and ass or
masturbating over them. Worse, unlike the fiction, whose level is
generally conceded as high, especially from the mid-sixties on when
Robie Macauley signed on for a decade's stint as fiction editor, the
nonfiction was often uneven. Sometimes it was downright asinine,
frequently pretentious, rambling, badly or carelessly edited. Every so
often, *Playboy* went off on a "respectability strut," especially in the
late sixties and early seventies, that made even the most ardent
Playboy fan—let alone some of the magazine's sharper editors—
wince. Year-end packages on such topics as "a new set of national
priorities" or symposia on the "decent society" exhibited noble intentions, noble names, and a fairly acute ear for what's on TV news.

They are intended to impress the reader, and their obviousness embarrasses.

Yet long before the economic storms of the mid-seventies forced *Playboy* to reassess its identity and purpose, there was no need for the self-conscious hawking of the magazine's intellectual wares, the implied "look at me, how bright and smart and advanced I am, and you too, with me. So stay with me." Readers did. And intellectual critics notwithstanding, *Playboy* was rousing people to think serious thoughts who had never done so in quite that way before. On balance, it mattered.

8

The Editors

"A conscious decision was made in the late fifties and early sixties that if the magazine were to grow, not change, but grow in a natural way from what it already was, then we should be paying attention to major social issues that were keeping a good number of people from enjoying the Playboy life we were espousing in the rest of the magazine."

Hefner sat on the library couch dressed in brilliant white pajamas under a rainbow-colored kimono. He had invited me to lunch that day—the last of our interviews—in the mansion's "Mediterranean room." Indian and Chinese sculpture. A glass and wrought-iron table. Carefully manicured grounds through french windows. Hefner is fond of eclectic things. Would I like a drink, the polite young waiter asked. A gin gibson? Of course. It was properly dry and made with good English gin, a radical departure from the "wet" and metallic martinis served in the Playboy Clubs.

I lunched in solitary splendor on a delicate cheese omelet, a crisp salad, and firmly textured fruit. After lunch Hefner appeared for a guided tour of the estate that included a view of his exotic fish in the pond, the birds and plants in the greenhouse, the early American furniture of the guest house (done over by Barbi Benton) and the game stable with all the pinball machines of Hefner's—and my—youth. Hefner wore slippers and chatted amiably about how he had found the place and how he had done it over. The landscaping had been extensive and costly. The result had a Shangri-la quality, especially for a visitor from the freezing East to that balmy California January. Small wonder Hefner left the place so rarely and so unwill-

ingly. Unlike the Chicago mansion, this was the total environment
—the Enlightenment's cultivated garden.

"I was very much involved in that evolution," he continued back
in the library, where coffee had been poured, ashtrays emptied, and
the first Pepsi uncapped. "It was a conscious decision," he repeated,
almost as if trying to convince himself. "You don't think, incidentally," he said somewhat belligerently, "that it happened from bringing in a bunch of people who then pushed Spec or myself in that
direction, do you? That direction came from myself and Spec, etc.
That's why you can look at the *Playboy* philosophy as the beginning
of that . . ."

Well, you can't, really, and really Hefner doesn't. The philosophy
was a creative response to the quality already in the magazine and
an attempt to enlarge it. And "bringing in a bunch of people" had
not only made the initial quality possible, but was responsible for the
expansion that followed. New blood had to make a difference. There
was so little editorial blood to begin with. As late as 1959, the
editorial staff consisted of Hefner, Spectorsky, Russell, Kessie, copy
chief Arlene Bouras, and four contributors from the East: food and
drink editor Thomas Mario, fashion director Robert Green, travel
editor Patrick Chase, and car buff Ken Purdy.

Eugene Troobnik, a displaced New York actor, came aboard in
1959, and, after finishing up with the jazz concert, so did Don Gold.
Both men still fitted the accidental-hiring pattern of the fifties, but
Gold, at least, already had solid editorial credentials. A year later,
Spectorsky found Walter Goodman.

"I had a good job with quick advancement and handled all the
social issues. But women's magazines didn't really get into the kinds
of things I was interested in. *Redbook* had good intentions, but I felt
limited. When I saw the ad in the *Times,* I sent off a short letter and
a copy of a book of mine that had just been published, a collection
of articles on advertising and public relations. I got a quick reply
from A. C. Spectorsky who knew the book and had seen my stuff
elsewhere and was quite interested. He came to New York. We had
a talk—I guess he must have interviewed several other people then
—and he asked me to come to Chicago for a tryout. I did and finally
got the job. They wanted to get classier writing on what was for them
more serious subjects."

Like everyone else lured out to Chicago, Goodman first tried the
New York ploy, but again Spectorsky wouldn't buy it. They agreed
on a year "and if we were happy with each other, I would go to New
York and be their New York editor." Goodman was to be the first
articles editor, though he never got the title. But the staff was still
small, so Goodman, the quintessential New York intellectual high-

brow, was asked to write copy for the Playmate of the Month. Confident that he could write anything, Goodman plunged in. "I thought it was all right, but it was a disaster. I didn't know what I was doing. I was a dead loss at stuff like how to fix up your office, so they never asked me to do any of that again."

Luckily, Sheldon Wax was hired a few months after Goodman, and Wax brought the skills needed for that side of the magazine. In New York he had worked for auto, movie, and fan magazines. He had heard that *Playboy* was hiring from his old boss at Popular Library, applied, and was taken on. Over the years of his long tenure, he became an anchor of stability and common sense for an often volatile magazine.

Goodman, freed from the mysteries of the flesh, settled down to handle the more serious side of the magazine.

"I enjoyed the stuff I was doing, and they wanted it. I even wrote a short story. But my relationship with Spectorsky was edgy," largely, Goodman suspects, for the reasons he had been hired in the first place—his New York connections which seem to have rivaled Spectorsky's own.

"He was conscious of his position in Chicago. He often talked of the creature comforts he had gained. It was on his mind and because of that, our relationship was always a little peculiar. We had run-ins on articles. I'd say, 'Let's not run this, it's crap,' and he would explain to me the nature of the *Playboy* audience. I guess he was right. He was more attuned to the audience, and he was an excellent editor for that magazine. He wanted to open it up and make it more serious. His values weren't mine, and we had different interests, but professionally he was very good."

Spectorsky was still looking for more "up-front" staff strength though: someone, Goodman remembers, "in his twenties, who had been around a bit, knew something about show biz, and could write." Before leaving New York he had talked to a man who seemed to fit that bill, and once ensconced in Chicago, he wrote to Murray Fisher. "I asked him to send me some of his stuff, and it was bright, and you got the sense that he could do some rewriting and handle captions, so I went to New York and brought him back. Murray worked out very well."

In 1960 Fisher had been in the NBC P.R. department for five years, handling magazine relations. He had approached Goodman in 1959 with an idea about publishing a "conversation" between Huntley and Brinkley. On TV they never talked to each other, except to say goodnight. Goodman liked the idea and *Redbook* bought it.

Fisher's initial reaction to the *Playboy* offer was bewildered and negative. Leave New York and live in Chicago? Work for some

magazine no one took seriously? But then the idea began to intrigue
him. "I'd been at NBC for five years; it was beginning to pale." He
talked to his boss, won a half-promise of being able to come back
(also standard for early prospective *Playboy* employees) and went to
Chicago for a three-week tryout.

Initial signals were not encouraging. Fisher remembers Jack Kessie's acting the tough city editor, satisfied with little the new writer
submitted. "I'm not running a journalism class," he snapped when
Fisher asked why a piece had been rewritten. Fisher lived in a cheap
hotel near the office and ate hamburgers. As the three weeks neared
to a close, Fisher told Kessie that he guessed he'd be leaving on
Friday. Kessie growled for him to see Spectorsky—who asked how
Fisher liked the French restaurants in Chicago and whether he had
found an apartment yet. Months later, Fisher was feeding Spectorsky
names of possible *SBI* staffers.

Goodman enjoyed his year in Chicago, but never felt that *Playboy*
could become a serious magazine. "It could be a magazine that dealt
in a more stylish way with important issues, but I don't know if that
makes for seriousness. It had serious components, but the whole tone
was fun and games. Though I enjoyed it more than *Redbook,* it was
the same thing. You had a large audience and were doing a kind of
social welfare by putting in virtuous articles. At *Playboy* it could be
done with more style and pizzazz. That was more fun, and you could
get better writers."

When the year was over, Goodman wanted out of the Windy City.
He went to Spectorsky and said his time was up, he was ready to open
Playboy's New York office. Spectorsky wasn't interested. He wanted
Goodman in Chicago. They finally agreed on a deal where *Playboy*
paid Goodman $10,000 a year to keep his eyes and ears open for
material in New York. The arrangement didn't work out—"they
were right; to do it well, you had to be in Chicago"—but it lasted
for several years, and gave Goodman a more detached perspective
of both Hefner and Spectorsky than the *SBI* staff had. His judg-
ments, however, are similar:

"I don't know what Spectorsky would have done if he hadn't
gotten the *Playboy* job. *The Exurbanites* was an interesting book. I
understand he didn't write it—everyone knows that. So I don't know
what terrific talent he had beyond that. Whenever I went back to
Chicago after leaving *Playboy,* he would take me into his office and
show me his latest gadget. This terrific TV set or unusual tape
recorder cum clock. But he knew what he was showing off. He was
earning a lot of money, and in a sense, he had sold out. He felt I was
disdainful of his life-style, which was not totally true. But he identified me with that New York crowd that he felt looked down on him

for associating with *Playboy*. He must have thought they'd all say, 'Oh, Spectorsky has gone to make a million dollars and given up whatever serious pretensions he had,' and of course they'd say that. Spectorsky talked a lot about this terrific book he was going to write to follow up *The Exurbanites,* and he was looking for a million-dollar advance. But he never wrote the book. He wasn't committed to writing or committed to any cause—certainly not to politics. You had to have some passion for the subject to keep up with what was happening in the sixties. That was not for him. His passions lay in having a good life—sailing in the Virgin Islands, taking his boat out, entertaining in Chicago. He never had Hefner's attachment to the magazine. It was a vehicle that allowed him to live a very, very pleasant life."

Goodman seems to have liked Hefner rather better, though the gap between them was infinitely wider. They must have looked upon each other as strange animals in a zoo. "Hefner was not a reader. He was interested in cartoons and selecting girls. He picked them single-handedly. You were asked to make your comment when the photographer sent in the pictures, and I never guessed right. Hefner knew what he wanted there. But he was very ignorant, and his comments on larger subjects were absurd. He wasn't doing much of that when I knew him. He hadn't become a public figure and was quite diffident, sucking his pipe and drinking his Pepsi. He was comfortable with things he knew—good-looking girls, a good spread on design of an apartment. He was a natural editor for that. But have a serious discussion with him? No, I wouldn't walk in for that. He didn't really have street smarts. He didn't know enough about the world. He knew about his audience.

"Political savvy? Not in my experience. He doesn't know anything about anything. But he was always a very decent guy as far as I was concerned. He wasn't out to hurt anybody. There was nothing nasty about his character. I think he hardly looked at anybody on the staff, though he was kind of interested in me. He worked these strange hours. When I came to work, he'd prowl around in his pajamas and say, 'What, are you still here?' "

With Goodman gone, Fisher began to throw his considerable weight around with greater authority—and probably with more authority than he possessed. A mercurial man, he blew hot in *Playboy*'s cool. Speech poured from him in effortless torrents. His sheer physical size must have overwhelmed even Kessie, a husky man. Fisher towers close to six and a half feet, with the shoulders of a plunging fullback hulking over a wasp waist, and a face of worn granite. He could model the "sexy" American man—the effortless Playboy who need not claim to have laid all the bunnies, drunk all the wine, known what to eat and wear and drive, even to have read all the books. Those who met him knew he had. Not surprisingly, he was abrasive, combative, something of a bully—Kretchmer says he used to write "yuch" and "blech" on copy, both on in-house and on outsiders— hard to fit into a corporate mold. Fisher says he both attracted and repelled Hefner, got along with him and didn't. The swashbuckler in his editor must have charmed the slight and at times frail-looking Hefner. And he probably enjoyed Fisher's readiness to fight the boss —and anyone else who crossed him. That included Spectorsky and business manager Preuss. Fisher seems to have been the first hell- raiser on the staff—both intellectually and physically. He worked hard and could handle both the sybaritic and intellectual ends of the magazine. Writing up-front sections on restaurants, books, and nightclubs, rewriting food and fashion, or editing Mario's cook- books, came as easily to him as fighting Spectorsky's caution on running interviews with Ralph Nader, Malcolm X, and Fidel Castro. Fisher claims to have won most of the fights on interviews, save on Castro, where Spectorsky insisted on putting some ideological dis- tance between the Cuban premier and *Playboy* magazine.

Moreover, for all their personal disagreements and abrasions, Spectorsky approved the direction Fisher was taking. He liked hav- ing Lord Russell, Dali, Genet, and Sartre in his magazine. They reflected the search for quality and added to Spectorsky's editorial reputation. The infighting with Fisher and other editors was part of the price he had to pay for that quality. (What Spectorsky clearly had not counted on, however, was the battle the young Turks would force him to fight in the late sixties when they pushed *Playboy* to the fringe of the radical left, and into bitter opposition to the Vietnam War.)

Fisher calls the move to quality "an impulse to go after the best we could get, not just the names but the best writing," and thinks it was part of Spectorsky's "own longings to be the editor of *Harper's* or the *Atlantic Monthly*. He went after their authors and subjects, went into competition with them, and he paid better prices." But Fisher insists it was not something Spectorsky or Hefner had done alone. "What we did reflected individual and collective concerns. It was the imaginative exploration of all staff members in a position to decide what to look for."

Fisher sprawled on a king-size couch—an endless expanse of chocolate-colored pillows—that filled one corner of his living room on Mulholland Drive outside Los Angeles. A sheet of glass made home and the blue valley below it one canvas. He had quit the Playboy wars in 1974 to try his writing luck in California where he helped Alex Haley with "the architecture" of *Roots* and contributed interviews and panels to *Playboy* (including one with Haley).

"We didn't think about audience. Basic to *Playboy*'s success is that Hefner never edited for the readership but for himself. And so did Spectorsky, for himself, not for Hefner. There was a receptive readership because we did not pander to the demographics but simply edited the kind of magazine we'd like to read if we weren't the editors. I think that's why it worked. When you start playing around, second-guessing, and tailoring content to a mythical or actual readership, you either become arbitrary or you limit it to the readership you have. It doesn't ever grow. We didn't, and I think that's why it began to grow so geometrically."

Girls, he concedes, were the magazine's foundation, but patterns of expansion were dictated by a more sophisticated editorial package. Yet he argues that any split existed "only in the minds of our critics. You couldn't pull the pieces apart." And in 1977 he was as critical about the "double-dome" charge *Newsweek* had leveled in 1960 as Hefner was when writing the philosophy. Interests in girls and matters of the mind, he says, go together. You can talk existentialism and look up when a pretty girl walks by.

"It's the whole spirit-and-flesh dichotomy. The magazine catered to the widest possible spectrum of what most intelligent men were interested in. It is an intelligent magazine. It is also interested in tits and ass. So are men. So are women, for that matter. *Playboy* didn't think one more important than the other, nor see any contradiction between them.

"Millions enjoyed the merchandising features who without them would not have had access to articles about social conscience. They'd be reading the *Reader's Digest* and *Popular Mechanics* and not given a shit about their fellow man. Preaching to the converted is jacking off, in my opinion. *Playboy* was the most radical mass-circulation magazine in history at the time it started doing all this. It served a positive and profound social purpose in arbiting between social classes, between rich and poor, young and old, in building bridges of understanding.

"That sounds very cloying, but I think it really did to the extent that any magazine can perform that function. There were twenty-five million readers. Some of them must have read it. If you were getting it as a jack-off magazine, there were better masturbatory outlets. We weren't getting the good stuff as window dressing. It cost too much for that. The magazine started to leap upward in circulation as the good stuff started being published. Any other conclusion is irrational."

The staff that found "the good stuff" shaped slowly in the early sixties. Spectorsky didn't pick up any real talent from *SBI*. Lee Gottlieb vaulted into a P.R. job, and Victor Lownes's brother Tom, an *SBI* editor, moved over to *Playboy*. Some think that Tom Lownes was the first in a long line of editors groomed as Spectorsky's successor. But he died in 1963, at the age of twenty-nine, when the car his girlfriend—Hefner's secretary Bobbie Arnstein—was driving crashed into a tree.

Jeremy Dole, now a senior editor at *Reader's Digest,* stayed for a while in 1962–63, and was followed by Peter Andrews, who also moved on to the *Digest.* Both added some professional sheen. In 1963 Spectorsky went east again to hire two key editors. Michael Laurence came to *Playboy* just out of Harvard and quickly teamed with Fisher as another hellraiser. He rose through the hierarchy—with time out for writing sabbaticals—to become a senior editor, publisher of *Oui,* and *Playboy*'s business manager. He added financial and business know-how, and when the war became an issue, lined up quickly on the anti-Vietnam side. So did Nat Lehrman, brought in from editing *Dude* and *Gent* in New York to ride herd on the philosophy. He ran Advisor and Forum and soon took over the "human behavior" articles and interviews; i.e., he became the resident expert on the study of sexuality.

Each new man added to the growing *Playboy* mix. None seems to have been Spectorsky's ideal. Perhaps *SBI* had frightened him from hiring those cut too close to his own jib. Perhaps he feared Hefner would not approve. He may have worried about a rival, someone with the stature to eclipse his own. At the same time, he had a knack for spotting moldable talent, for finding men who would move the magazine along his own lines, while providing it with things he could not give, even things he opposed—like politics.

Hiring could not have been easy after the *SBI* debacle. Editors talk, and most of the *SBI* hands drifted quickly back to New York with stories of Spectorsky's prickly nature and Hefner's eccentricities, stories soon picked up by other media as Hefner's reputation as the mansion hermit grew. Besides, Spectorsky did not believe in editorial fat—not even in the mid-sixties, when *Playboy* was awash in money. Gradually, however, he admitted to himself that growth mandated more help, and once again he turned to Gotham.

In 1966 he landed two fat fish—though both were as tall and lean as picket fences—named James Goode and Arthur Kretchmer. Goode saw an ad in the *New York Review of Books* and answered it. He was fed up with Time, Inc. Spectorsky had heard of Kretchmer, then managing editor of *Cavalier,* a men's book, and asked Paul Krassner to see why "the only good editor on *Cavalier*" had not applied for a job at *Playboy.* Krassner did. Kretchmer called Spectorsky and was hired. For the next four years, Goode and Kretchmer played Blanchard and Davis, the Mr. Outside and Mr. Inside of West

Point's wartime football powerhouses, in *Playboy*'s shocked offices.

They could not have been more different. Goode is a Wasp Hoosier out of Wabash College in Indiana; Kretchmer the grandson of White Russian Jewish Mensheviks. He scraped out of New York's City College just before the sixties ruined that potent cannon of Jewish upward mobility by stuffing open enrollment down its barrel. Kretchmer was twenty-six when he hustled onto the *Playboy* scene, the kid brother of a rising New York City politician named Jerry Kretchmer whose career reached a temporary apex as John Lindsay's sanitation commissioner. Goode was ten years older. He learned his trade first as a researcher for *Life* in New York and then as a reporter in *Life*'s Los Angeles bureau. When Hefner started *SBI,* Goode had just completed a book on the making of Clark Gable's last movie, *The Misfits* (with Marilyn Monroe) and was looking for new worlds to injure. Gibney hired him as a writer in the *SBI* Los Angeles office. After *SBI* folded, Goode drifted back to New York and a job with Time-Life Books. He was editing a cookbook when he stumbled on Spectorsky's ad, and, incredibly, was hired.

Kretchmer must have seemed much more moldable editorial material. Physically the classic schizoid of his German namesake's typology, his spirit burns with a lean blue flame. Arthur Kretchmer cares. "You're going to the hottest book in the country," someone told him after he had accepted *Playboy*'s offer (at a salary nearly twice of what *Cavalier* was paying him), and Kretchmer believed it. *Playboy* had just published Max Lerner's piece on recognizing Red China.

The dynamic duo hit Chicago the summer Stokely Carmichael climbed on a flatbed truck in Grenada, Mississippi, and asked hundreds of blacks what they wanted—and taunted millions of whites with the answer the next morning: black power. Vietnam had begun to claw at the great society. The sixties were preparing to burst into full bloom. Spectorsky seems to have empathized with his Menshevik offspring and to have hated the Wasp anarchist who had slipped out of Henry Luce's loins. No matter. They raised hell.

The atmosphere was ripe for it. Kessie, the managing editor, acted as a lightning rod for editorial discontent. Much of the wrath that by rights should have been unloaded on Spectorsky descended on Kessie instead, much of it invited. Or so the younger editors claim. There was a good deal of chaos. Goode fought Spectorsky virtually all the time. Fisher says Goode used to get on top of a desk and harangue the editorial director or march into his office and bend his elongated form—Goode, too, towers close to six and a half feet; at six-two, Kretchmer is a veritable shrimp in that company—over Spectorsky's desk and wag a finger in his face. Not so, says Kretchmer. That's not how it was. But he cannot make the case for *Playboy* as an orderly Time, Inc., with clearly defined roles and disputes carried on in whispers. *Playboy* was a loud place to work, and underneath the noise, Spectorsky practiced the wiles of Byzantine politics; not always with good effect. He had an open side that prevented imposing the kind of corporate discipline *Playboy* pretended to have, but in its bowels didn't. Didn't because Hefner did not. For Hefner, "corporation" was something he had read about or seen in the movies, something he didn't and couldn't quite believe in. And his lack of faith seeped down through what seemed rigidly hierarchical structures but weren't. How else to explain the Goode-Kretchmer approach:

"I think Jim is a brilliant editor," Kretchmer remembers. "Not a trendy editor in the sense that Clay Felker or Harold Hayes or those guys are trendy editors, but an editor of tremendous substance. He spotted stories long before they came due. He was radical and aggressive. He hates hustlers and criminals in a social sense. The world is full of them, and *Playboy* represented that hatred for a while. He is against all ripoff artists, so the magazine got to be about ripoff artists. He was the blunt edge that shook up or at least traumatized the magazine's basic approach to its nonfiction, and I was the scalpel that got some of it done, that cut through the body and did some of the transplants. Jim doesn't know what the word 'indirection' means, and I do. That's one of the things that made us a great working team."

That Goode had no use for indirection is as sure as that he and Spectorsky hated each other on sight. Goode is an angry moralist who smells corruption and conspiracy at every level of American society and sees their uprooting as his personal mission in life. He is an anarchist through and through. And when he came to *Playboy* in 1966 he saw a God-given opportunity to smite the Philistines.

"When I arrived, there were no articles, no inventory, not even of those articles on the joys of absinthe that Spectorsky assigned to his old friends in the East and then rejected because the authors had let him down. Spec loved playing games like that. I immediately stitched together some articles the week I arrived."

All those who have worked with Goode agree that he is an intellectual catalyst, that he has a special gift for spotting the essence of things. It is something he proved not only at *Playboy*. In the early seventies, he took over *Penthouse* and gave Guccione an editorial content and bite—from articles denouncing the CIA to a series on the problems of Vietnam veterans—the *Playboy* imitator would never have dreamed of reaching for without him.

"Spectorsky used to say that we were bleeding hearts, that we were too political. He didn't care what the politics were, really, in the way a political person would care. I mean if John Gardner (Goode, of course, despises Common Cause as merely another establishment plot) had had A. C. Spectorsky's job, we would have been told exactly what to print. Spectorsky thought we were erring on the side of humanity, on the side of causes, that we were cause-oriented. He didn't like that at all. He didn't understand that a social revolution had begun the year before he hired Arthur and myself. The international social revolution began in 1965, the first social revolution in the history of mankind. Everyone alive knew it. The record dealers did. But Spectorsky didn't know about it. He just wanted articles in the magazine. And we said, 'Let's do this or that,' and he would agree, however reluctantly. You had to have five or six articles a month. That's a lot of articles."

But why had Spectorsky allowed the new strain of radicalism to seep into his magazine? Why had he given Goode so relatively free a hand? Part of it was surely due to Kretchmer's indirection—Goode was articles editor and Kretchmer his associate—and because, as Goode put it somewhat bitterly, "Spectorsky looked upon Arthur with friendliness, and I don't remember that he looked upon me with too much friendliness." Partly it was because of the reasons for Spectorsky's dislike of Goode, reasons Goode explains this way:

"I became known as intransigent, cantankerous, and hard to deal with, so no one would come up and talk to me. Once I had a conversation with Spectorsky in his office about money, and he asked Kessie to come in and be a witness. I was so obnoxious that he wanted a witness. Now, if you are that obnoxious, nobody is going to come up to you and start a gratuitous conversation about the nature of an article. You have to project a kind of compliance before people come up to you to talk. I didn't. Sure, we would clear all titles in monthly meetings, and if Spec had hated something sufficiently, he could have killed it after it came in. But that would have been damaging to his own image—especially after other people had read the same article and said, 'Wow, that's really nice.'"

What would have made it more damaging was the response some of the articles Goode assigned drew. "The most significant article we did was called 'The Death of Politics' by Karl Hess. (Hess started out as a political operative for Barry Goldwater in 1964 and then flipped onto the anarchist-libertarian side of the political coin.) It drew more mail than the Playmate in that issue, the first time an article had done that."

Nor could Spectorsky have faulted Goode's analysis of the response: "It told me that if you speak with candor about anything of importance without censorship, without processing the material, without interposing the magazine between author and audience, you will get a strong audience response." Moreover, such response added to Goode and Kretchmer's editorial power, and to their ability to make *Playboy* reflect social change.

In fairness to Spectorsky, who seems overly maligned by those who worked for him, maligned, incidentally, even in their praise of him, he was at least of two minds about the new subject matter. It had quality. It drew attention. It made *Playboy* significant. These were all goals he espoused. What he worried about most was pushing the magazine over any radical brink that would make it lose the hold on the vital center.

Nor was Hefner hostile to such innovation, and his claim to have created the environment in which it could take place is surely valid. Thus Goode could, within certain limits, follow "my interest as an anarchist in disturbing myths. I don't care whose myths, as long as they are widely held. I get off on myth busting. *Playboy* as a religious and political forum disturbs a myth. You had to have been around the pieties of *Time* and *Life* for fifteen years to see how disturbed they were by the rise of *Playboy* and *Penthouse* as legitimate opinion forums."

But Goode wanted *Playboy* to reflect social change not only in the articles, but in the whole look and approach it took. He wanted "a larger use of photography for subjects other than women," to change the "morbid graphic look" of the magazine into something lighter. "It looked like a Bavarian wood carving, and a lot of it was. They hired people to carve illustrations in wood. It's dark, man, the magazine is dark. It's heavy."

That, of course, ran counter to art director Art Paul's expressionist biases. Besides, those areas of the magazine stayed out of editorial's control. Hefner remained too fascinated—and still is—to ever let them go. Goode became increasingly despondent and restless. So he set out to raise money to start a magazine of his own. Possessed by the growing threat to the environment—his and Kretchmer's interest had triggered *Playboy*'s, and they had made ecology a fashionable *Playboy* subject long before Earth Day in 1970—he started *Earth* in San Francisco in 1970 and in it dealt chiefly with ecological issues.

Spectorsky heaved a sigh of relief when Goode left, delighted that he would not, after all, have to psych himself up to the point of firing him, or have Kessie fire him.

Goode's departure did not relieve everyone. Kretchmer was glad for him because he was a friend, because he felt that Goode had been only half an editor while scrounging for start-up money, and, because the open slot meant his own promotion. But he and Fisher, at least, knew the magazine had lost a personality of power and conviction, and that Goode's voice would be missed. Creative cantankerousness causes problems, to be sure, but smooth pap does not make up the loss.

More importantly, Goode's departure made the question of finding a successor for the already ailing Spectorsky—he was past sixty, then, and had been with the magazine for fourteen years— much more urgent. Goode had the editorial vision and the required skills for the job, as everybody involved attested, but neither Spectorsky nor Hefner had ever considered him for the top job. Neither could handle Goode's obstinacy.

So if not Goode, who? There were no logical successors on the staff. Spectorsky had complicated the situation by promising a string of editors (including Bruce Jay Friedman, in the early sixties, who did not accept the job offer) the succession if they came to work for him—and then quickly disabusing the "groomed" editor of his hopes. And he had had a falling out with Kretchmer who had for a while seemed a viable prospect.

"The man men call Kretchmer," as novelist Herbert Gold once sardonically called him, was singled out early for Spectorsky's attention, and a special, intimate relationship developed between the two men, nurtured perhaps by their common White Russian and Jewish heritage.

"The Spec whom I knew was very different from the Spec everybody else knew because he and I had a very complicated and very varied relationship. He showed me a side he didn't show others, and he rarely showed me certain other sides of him. Spec thought I was special, and he wanted to be special with me. He gave me a chance to grow tremendously, to become much better at what I did. He was a seducer, a consummate seducer. One of my favorite lines was that before I went into his office, I used to open my belt so that he wouldn't have to take so much time to seduce me."

Paradoxically, perhaps, in what clearly seems to have been a father-son relationship, Kretchmer's attraction for Spectorsky lay as much in his maturity as in his youth. "Arthur was born forty years old," Fisher says unkindly, and Lownes displayed shocked surprise in 1976 when told that Kretchmer was only thirty-five.

"I thought he was my age," he growled disbelievingly.

The incident that clarified Kretchmer's special status in Spectorsky's mind occurred a couple of years after Kretchmer arrived in Chicago. Eric Norden had been assigned a piece on the paramilitary far right. More than a year in the researching and writing it consumed 38 of Playboy's outsized pages when it was finally published in mid–1969. At approximately 20,000 words, it is overlong even by

Playboy's generous standards. The beginning, especially, drags with its endless compilation of right-wing organizations and what they have done when and where. But Norden can be a crisp and swift writer, and once he has gotten the preliminaries out of the way, his narrative has pace and bite. The description of a trip he took to a right-wing hideout in Pennsylvania is a cunning mix of Eric Ambler and a Tony Lewis column in *The New York Times*—of adventure and polemic. A companion interview with Minuteman leader De Pugh, conducted in Kansas City in 1968 and clearly destined at one point for an interview slot, is folded neatly into the body of the piece. The end of the article though, is disappointing. It lapses into the heavy rhetoric of the late sixties, replete with the threat of race war and a mournful dirge for the dead in the rice paddies of Vietnam.

Needless to say, Spectorsky hated the whole idea, the writing, the execution. It was anathema—another issue to fight with his staff about—and in the late sixties he fought with his editors a great deal. "It was one of my great moments in my early life here," Kretchmer remembers. "Norden hung out with guys who were going to shoot leftists. It was a great piece for us at the time. Yet, when we gave it to Spectorsky, he was very upset. He didn't want to run it."

That was all Fisher and Goode needed. Fisher wrote a memo that attacked Spectorsky personally, his long and fiercely held disdain flaming off his typewriter. "Murray and Jim both wrote memos praising the piece, and they attacked Spec for being gutless, for not seeing a good story, for fifty other things."

Knowingly or not, Kretchmer saw the need for a different approach. If banging the line head-on didn't work, maybe a sneak around end would. "I wrote a note saying that this was the most responsible kind of reporting, that it wasn't a leftist piece, that it was simply journalistically pure, that it was not a leftist position to be against the extreme right wing. Spec read my note and said, 'Okay, we can publish this thing. The only one with any sense about it is Kretchmer.' So I became the judicious editor on the staff. Jim and I used to manipulate Spectorsky that way."

It is hard, really, not to feel sympathy for Spectorsky's near-desperate position. He had come to Chicago to edit a magazine he hoped would be called *Smart Set*. He liked P. G. Wodehouse and Oscar Wilde and English country-house parties. What was he doing out here with these barbarians and chained to young Massa Hefner's whims? And whatever he had experienced in New York of the McCarthy hysteria must have festered at such moments. He never articulated that pain, just let enough show for someone like Kretchmer to sense the hurt and stomp it, because "the times they were changing."

But because Kretchmer, more than the others, showed that he sensed his mentor's pain, he was anointed. With Goode gone or going, Spectorsky pondered about moving his young protégé up the hierarchical ladder. He went so far as to discuss it with Hefner, who says he had no objections, but did not exhibit any great enthusiasm either. For a while, Spectorsky opposed making Kretchmer the articles editor—the logical next step—because he feared it would limit him too much and not allow his growth into magazinewide responsibility. Kretchmer was briefly listed on the masthead as a senior editor; then he was given the articles editor's job, anyway. But without Goode's battering ram to run interference, Kretchmer slid into trouble. He is, today, still full of praise for Spectorsky's flow of seminal ideas in the nonfiction area, his interest in behavior and psychology, and the tests and quizzes he devised. But Kretchmer concedes that in the months before Spectorsky's death, "My relationship with him was terrible because I wouldn't assign his lousy ideas."

The issue was politics and *Playboy*'s identification with the left, at times the radical left. And however hard Spectorsky fought against the identifying labels, he kept losing. Thus, before the 1970 congressional elections, Kretchmer ran a sarcastic piece in which he baited most of the establishment candidates, Republicans and Democrats, writing, for example, that there was less to big Ed Muskie than meets the eye, a tipoff (however unconscious, as Kretchmer claims it was) that the left was out to tomahawk the Maine senator and willy-nilly throw the 1972 election to Richard Nixon. The piece incensed Spectorsky, but he could not stop it. It angered Hefner, too, who remembers it as having run in 1968 or 1972 and as having endorsed the Democratic presidential candidate, and who vows that Playboy would never endorse candidates again, that it would not—repeat not —become a Democratic sheet. Talk about the impotence of power! Neither Hefner nor Spectorsky could stop the leftward drift of the magazine, largely, one suspects, because their hearts were not in it, and their heads lacked the necessary passion.

"Arthur and I were burrs under Spectorsky's saddle," Fisher says. "We were disputatious, and that exasperated Spec." He cites the fight over running the interview with Ralph Nader as an example. Spectorsky didn't want to touch the consumer crusader, whom he regarded as a "vindictive Savonarola." Fisher's open contempt didn't help; neither did his "clenched typewriter teeth" that showed on his memos to the boss. But the Nader interview ran, with Kretchmer lining up behind Fisher in support.

A certain amount of disillusionment was inevitable, and by 1970, Spectorsky shelved the idea of grooming Kretchmer for the editorship just yet. But he needed someone. He was ill and growing worse.

Hefner had hired a brash young New York publisher, Robert Gutwillig, to run the newly created book division, and Gutwillig was displaying real panache. There was room within the corporate hierarchy for someone savvy to move up, and to move fast. Spectorsky had neglected corporate business for years, preferring to stick to his editorial duties, and he knew that his lack of business acumen annoyed Hefner. The corporate fences needed mending, but Spectorsky could not attend to that task unless he had covered his editorial rear.

So he turned east toward home, to the towers of Rockefeller Center that harbored the Luce empire. He found Michael Demarest, then *Time*'s national affairs editor, and a veteran foreign correspondent. Kretchmer contends that Demarest was ripe for making the move because he had lost the sweepstakes for the managing editor's job, that *Time*'s politics being what they are, he had no choice but to leave.

Demarest's explanation is more prosaic: "I was offered a lot of money at *Playboy,* and I was hired as Spectorsky's successor."

But Demarest was not prepared for the hothouse *Playboy* atmosphere, for the ideological battlefield, for the scrambled chain of command, the feudal editorial setup with its independent fiefdoms and baronies, the incestuous clawing for power and influence. Spectorsky had talked rationally to him in New York, with charm and wit, explaining that he needed someone who could infuse his editorial staff with news-magazine savvy, a professional editor able to overcome the magazine's inertia. Then Spectorsky abruptly suffered his first heart attack. Demarest concluded negotiations with business manager Bob Preuss and moved to Chicago to take over.

"The editors were all graduates of *Dude* and *Stud,*" Demarest said with some distaste over a mid-seventies lunch at the King Cole Bar of the St. Regis in New York after he had returned to *Time* as senior writer. "Their knowledge was abysmal. I don't think they read the *Times* or the *Wall Street Journal* or the *Washington Post* or *Harper's.* They were just not reading people." ("I've never read *Time,*" Goode said munching a hamburger at the Hyatt Hotel near the Los Angeles airport in 1977. "I know how it is produced, that the final story is always 180 degrees from whatever the writer sent in.")

Perhaps Demarest should have known better from the beginning. "It was a vague lunch over which he hired me. Spectorsky never sat down to discuss my duties beyond my running the magazine when he wasn't there. But he was a good salesman. He represented himself as an Easterner filled with an intellectual mystique. And I got greedy."

So one day in mid-1970 Demarest arrived on the tenth floor of 919

North Michigan ready to go to work. Spectorsky was still in the hospital. The staff glowered. He was eaten alive, Fisher says matter-of-factly. Certainly, Demarest was bewildered by what he found. He came on with an urbane civility, was, according to Fisher, "affable, breezy, egalitarian, and talked and looked the part of an executive editor." But he clung to the illusions of *Time*-style rationality, that there was such a thing as an orderly editorial process. Instead, *Playboy* was a battlefield of personality and ideology wrapped in the cotton candy of too much money and too much success. It did not have to be rational to work; it could afford an insular eccentricity, the endless debates on purpose and identity that marked the dispute between Spectorsky and his editors in the mid and late sixties. The rest of the publishing world may have felt the cold sting of the first Nixon recession in 1970, but *Playboy* did not. It was still all lobster and cream sauce.

"There was no chain of command," Demarest said, years later, still amazed by the chaos of it all. "Things were put to a vote. When I wrote a piece, the others would comment on whether to publish it or not. Anarchy, ineptitude, inertia, and sloth are the only ways to describe it. If *Pravda* were edited by a collective, that would be it. It was a group grope, a disjointed cottage industry. People would go and do their own bit. Pieces of the book were going to press practically every day, and no editor was keeping an eagle eye on what happened. There were no logical, simple rules you could describe. There was no normal procedure. At *Time,* we would have a cover conference, but *Playboy* didn't—not even about the lines of type on the cover. Hefner decided all that. No one had the reins in hand for the whole magazine. The research system was chaotic. I tried to bring in a *Fortune* researcher, but someone screwed it up with Hefner. I tell you, I was someone from another planet."

Coming from the East, Demarest was bewildered by the ideological infighting. He felt *Playboy* had come rather late to liberal causes such as the Vietnam War and could not understand the opposition he encountered to writing an article against the CIA and ended up writing a spoof. (Yet *Playboy* had published an anti-CIA piece as early as 1967.) But he liked the people he worked with. He thought Fisher extremely intelligent and his one ally on the staff, at least as far as quality went. He thought Shel Wax intelligent if innocent, and Kretchmer very bright but journalistically naïve.

New York Times columnist Tom Wicker had been assigned a piece on the Nixon administration. "I got a note from Kretchmer. We must have an emergency meeting on the Wicker piece. (It needed one —even the printed version rambled on at near-uncontrolled length.) We're running a cover line on it. Kretchmer was almost hysterical and kept saying, 'We have to stop the cover run—the piece is unsolvable.' I looked at it and thought it was mostly a matter of reorganization. I did it in one evening in my hotel room."

Kretchmer and Fisher contend that Demarest simply didn't understand how *Playboy* worked and didn't learn fast enough.

"He was busy trying to placate everyone," Fisher says. "He didn't have any power, and Arthur had buying power as articles editor. Where did that leave Demarest? And he had no feeling for the sybaritic side of the magazine, any more than Luce ever did. He was out of his pond, and the pond he found was too shallow for him. He was a good writer—and he ended up as clean-up articles assistant. Only someone who had worked there could run it. You had to understand the structure, the infrastructure, the psyche, the labyrinthine office politics, the exceedingly strange types that had to be managed, all the interests that had to be served. You needed years of experience and sophistication, and the cost of acquiring it might have meant Demarest's life. Everyone was aggressive and proprietary of their bailiwicks—including me. I didn't let anyone meddle with the interviews, even Hefner (something of a hyperbole, for Hefner did meddle on occasion, especially with the Jim Garrison interview, feeling—correctly, it turned out—that the New Orleans district attorney was using *Playboy,* and that the questions asked of him were not tough enough). Arthur felt the same way."

Still, Demarest might have survived had Spectorsky not returned from that first heart attack, convinced he had made a mistake even before he saw Demarest in action. Certainly, he told all his staffers that if he had not taken ill, the *Time* editor would not have been hired, that the final details had all been Preuss's doing. It was becoming fashionable at *Playboy,* even then, to make the business manager responsible for all the mistakes—his own and those of others—a penchant that would ultimately lead to Preuss's downfall.

Spectorsky was disturbed by many things about Demarest, both large and small. For instance, when he had hired him, Demarest wore a beard; in the Chicago office, he had shaved it off. Was this still the same man? And all that energy. Demarest was a workhorse, Kretchmer says. "Demarest did more work than anyone else. He was a very qualified man who did his job well. But he wanted to rewrite everything and to run everything. He was an information animal, a political guy, but not a *Playboy* guy. None of his skills applied to *Playboy.* He liked everything and he wanted everything to work. We were slow and fussy. It was all much too refined for him. People say that Kretchmer got Demarest. That's not true. Spec got Demarest. I went out of my way to make the transition possible for Demarest, and then I guess because it was me, we became enemies. Demarest wanted to usurp my role because he needed a base from which to project his skills. Where else does a *Nation* editor of *Time* who had written some forty-odd cover stories go but to the articles job? It was logical, rational on his part. I felt enormous pressure from him. Demarest found it easier to ingratiate himself with the younger editors than with the more senior staff. So each of those gunslingers took his place and fired. Demarest couldn't figure out who kept the lock on the arsenal."

Toward the end, Spectorsky had Demarest writing service features with Kessie. And Spec treated Demarest with the same mixture of contempt and seductiveness he did everyone else. "He treated his executive editor like a copy boy," Demarest complained mildly. "I would get notes saying 'Please don't talk so much' or 'Get Kretchmer in here.' "

"When he left," Kretchmer said, folding his hands under his chin, watching a late-afternoon sun streak into his office window across the roof of the Maryland hotel where Hefner's secretary, Bobbie Arnstein, killed herself, pouring apple juice into one glass (his) and Fleischmann's gin into another (his visitor's), "I told him, 'You have skills and instincts this magazine could use, but because you came in here as the heir apparent, as the successor, there was no chance to work those things out. No chance for you to adapt to us and for us to adapt to you. You came in here with clout and rank, so from the very beginning'—this was literally my closing speech to Demarest, and I told him that with great affection—'there was something wrong. We were looking to you for leadership, and you needed some time to get used to it.' " Kretchmer paused to swig some apple juice. "Today a Demarest can come to work here. Today it is a different magazine—less patient, more topical . . ."

But not in 1971, so Demarest drifted from Chicago to help Gutwillig organize the international editions—after all, he was one *Playboy* editor who knew a language besides English and who had been abroad—and eventually leave the company for Ralph Ginzburg's *Moneysworth* and after that to return to *Time*. The question of the succession remained unresolved.

Were the reasons buried in Spectorsky's psyche? In the festering contradictions that ravaged his mind? His fierce joy and pride in what he had made of *Playboy*, and the despair he felt over being only at *Playboy?* Every foray he had made in the East to hire seasoned talent had been a failure, largely because he had willed it to be a failure. It was bad enough with the kids, and he even had to go east for them! Brooklyn, City, Syracuse. Demarest had been educated in England. One kid out of fair Harvard, another out of Dartmouth. But kids!

"Spec was always ambivalent about *Playboy,*" Fisher says, articulating what everyone who ever worked at *Playboy* knew and said. "He felt he was destined for something better. The editorship of *Harper's,* but at $150,000 a year. He needed a sailboat and an apartment with a thirty-foot living room, a Mercedes, fine wines. Because of these necessities, he did not feel free to leave, and he was ashamed about what he was doing. And he played on our sympathies because of it. He was contemptuous of Hefner and always badmouthed him. He used to call him 'Godzilla.' There was a serpentine, manipulative, subterranean quality to the man. If Spec nursed you too close to his heart, it was time to start worrying. He was always trying to neutralize people, to stop them from embarrassing him in front of Hefner."

And Kretchmer must have done that most often. Yet he was the one Spectorsky relied upon in those traumatic editorial meetings with Hefner at the mansion, meetings he dreaded. Kretchmer went and served as Spectorsky's crutch and tranquilizer. With Kretchmer in the room, Spectorsky felt he could function. Without him, things became, well, difficult. But Kretchmer was one of those who kept shoving politics down his unwilling throat. And was he properly grateful for the favors Spectorsky had shown? The editorial director began to think not. "Spectorsky became disenchanted with Arthur because Arthur didn't kiss his ass enough," Fisher says pungently. "Politics was the issue of dispute. Arthur stuck to his guns. He's responsible and enlightened. Spectorsky was more concerned with image and advertisers. Being antipollution was too liberal. Some of our biggest advertisers were polluters. And they wouldn't like our stand on the war or on Ralph Nader."

"Spectorsky was a complicated man, a corrupt man, a devilish man," Kretchmer mused about his predecessor, "and not a very gutsy man, but he was also a very talented man. A beautiful man, small, small-boned, well-tailored, stylish, totally hip, totally aware of current fads. Hef used to say about him that he was too sophisticated to commit adultery or take drugs. He liked dirty stories. He had a streak in him that was ribald, scatological. He had an old man's humor. He was a con man, but he was very committed to this magazine. Yet, there were many times in his life when he was disturbed about his relationship to Hefner and about being here in Chicago at *Playboy.* He had misgivings about all these things."

And misgivings about his staff. He downgraded their abilities, never talked seriously about any of them taking over his job, not after the initial pitch had been made and discarded. "Until I surfaced, he thought nobody was strong enough to succeed him," Kretchmer says. He is quietly self-confident now with little braggadocio about him, even when his surface calm is cut by flashes of dark temper.

"And there are some very talented people here. Wax and Lehrman are both talented; so is Fisher. But Spectorsky had them all slotted and didn't believe they had the dimensions to take over the magazine."

Demarest departed in mid-1971. Spectorsky's health worsened. Talk about the succession grew more common. It was clear to everyone that managing editor Kessie was out of the running. According to a rare consensus, Spectorsky had told him that years earlier, and Kessie had dutifully replied that he didn't want the top job anyway. He probably did. Most men who wait for seventeen years do, whether they admit it or not. But Hefner had crossed him off the list years earlier, also, and Kessie knew that, too. Fisher, who is not the most unbiased observer of the *Playboy* scene—but then none of the principal actors are, and who disliked Kessie even more than he did Spectorsky—says Kessie stopped being a bastard when he realized how the wind was blowing, and that his efforts to become a nice guy were worse. "He became a kind of ghost," Fisher says. "People went through him like an open door."

As Spectorsky's hold on the magazine weakened, he kept trying to rebuild the fraying ties to his onetime protégé. Even today, Kretchmer remains torn. "It was a bipolar relationship," he mused, "good filial and bad filial." Still, Spectorsky seems to have done more of the courting, right down to the end, and if not in person, then by memo, of which the following were not untypical:

When I threatened to work directly with you, I don't think you had any idea of how much I would continue to bug you. What I'm bugging you about right now is the belief that nobody appreciates my political precognition as much as I do. I remember being dismissed when I said I thought that John W. Gardner and Common Cause were worthy of being solicited for a piece . . . I know that scene doesn't warm your personal political heart, but I think of it as valuable. . . .

And again:

Here is the memo you gave me on ideas for Kenneth Tynan . . . The suggestions you got from Butler, Demarest, Standish et al . . . I would have been . . . embarrassed to suggest to Tynan. . . . Alternatively, your suggestion . . . makes a lot of sense. I think you might try him on that in a letter, unless you are planning to go to England, in which case you might discuss it with him. . . .

Kretchmer had suggested that Tynan write about the brutalization of American society by the Vietnam War at the same time as an "anything goes" liberalization in sexual-cultural matters was sweeping the country. The offer of a trip to England, a fairly subtle piece of bait, was not accepted—nor was Kretchmer's ambivalence resolved.

In October, Spectorsky, growing sicker all the time, built himself one last monument—the Playboy Writer's Convocation held in Chicago and at the Lake Geneva resort. It would be the last and greatest test of the literary pulling power he had worked so hard to develop all his life. Though Fisher organized the fiesta and pulled together all the big names, it was Spectorsky's show—fifty-five *Playboy* contributors in all, including John Cheever, John Kenneth Galbraith, Arthur Schlesinger, Jr., Ken Tynan, Studs Terkel, Dalton Trumbo, Alex Haley, Evan Hunter, David Halberstam, Art Buchwald, Murray Kempton, Gay Talese, Nicholas von Hoffman, and Tom Wicker.

It seems to have been rather a self-conscious affair with an expensively printed program and panel discussions on everything from "The Future of Sex" to "The New Urban Life-Style." Many of those who attended made fun of it afterward, but most said they had a good time. "It was a little stiff," Halberstam admits. "I thought Spectorsky was embarrassed by his role, and Hefner is a stiff, not a graceful host. The whole thing had some of the flavor of a twenty-fifth college class reunion where nobody knew anybody."

Calvin Trillin of *The New Yorker* noted, "I had a bit of a feeling that people who attended were ripping Hefner off. They'd order the most expensive wine because it was Hefner and these people were giving a bash, and that's how they lure writers. I got an invitation from *Esquire* to their Christmas party, and it was a Xerox of a drawing. It looked like an invitation to a block party. Of course, *The New Yorker* doesn't give parties."

Trillin remembers Hefner's throwing the floor open to questions one evening and Gay Talese's asking, "Why did you start showing pubic hairs?"

Hefner replied that he got tired of airbrush jokes and of being made to feel like a prig.

Several months later, the *Atlantic Monthly* poked more fun at the conclave in a piece entitled "Gathering at Bunnymede" by Richard Todd. Most of the writers, Todd reported, did enjoy the caviar-stuffed crepes and Beefeater gin (the only kind served) and rack of lamb, but there seems to have been general grousing about the lack of sexual opportunity, a grousing aptly summed up by Wicker, who is quoted as saying, "You know, Ah really did think there'd be some tushy-pinching."

And Michael Arlen voiced the general expectations when he said, to no one in particular, in the writers lounge before the first evening's parties got under way: "Proust is coming, but he won't be here until later. We'll be whipped at Spec's house. Oriental ladies will walk on our spines."

Nicholas von Hoffman complained that no one read the magazine, that he hadn't even gotten beyond the first page of his own piece "and then—boob alley!—I was lost in the boobs." *Newsweek* called the panel discussions "a Nembutal factory."

But they had all come, and in coming, proved Kretchmer's remark, which he would attribute to "the late A. C. Spectorsky," that "we are here to deal with writers in the way they understand best —with praise, money, and alcohol."

In December, Spectorsky prepared to clean up his affairs in Chicago before going to St. Croix for two months of rest and rehabilitation. Kretchmer was still one of the most pressing. Three days before leaving, he wrote his articles editor a memo. Dated December 13, 1971, it is titled "Spectorsky's Unfairness":

I think it is very unfair of me to be bugging you about having pieces about whole subjects, as opposed to pieces about individuals who typify whole subjects, because it wasn't so long ago that I was bugging you to have more pieces about people.

However, I think the pendulum has swung too far in the people direction, and in ways that worry me. It also worries me that you feel so deeply and so passionately about things that it is very hard to get you to be as expressive about them in face-to-face meetings as we would both like you to be. I think you sort of choke up—which is why I am putting this in memo form. Let me give you a couple of specifics . . .

Instead of a personality piece on a Mafioso, Spectorsky wanted an article on the Mafia "as a subculture, rather than purely as a criminal organization;" and, second, he wanted to explore the "new breed of freewheeling, entrepreneurial international businessmen" as a phenomenon, and not a story on one man who typified them all.

I certainly don't want to stop having pieces about people. They are essential. But I also don't want to stop having pieces on what I guess we can call phenomena, or trends, or new movements, or whatever you want to call it. I'm sure you know. And I also don't want to stop having pieces on issues, which we seem to be slighting. . . .

Please talk to me about these things, Arthur, if they gall you or if you feel I have been even more unjust than I admitted to being at the very beginning of this memo. Or, if it makes you more comfortable, answer me in writing.

You are far too important to this magazine for problems to exist between you and me. You are also—if I may raise another sore point at the very end of a memo—far too important to this magazine to be so insufficiently backed up by strong professionals. . . .

I'm available at any time to talk about this until the 16th, when I will be gone for two months. It's up to you to decide whether or not you want the meeting, and my professional feelings about your professionalism and the job you are doing will not be influenced (to my knowledge, if I can prevent it) by whether or not you want a meeting. In fact, I honestly don't know which way I would predict my own reaction, so I am trying to enforce upon myself no reaction whatever.

Except that I hope you pay attention to this memo and don't feel offended by it.

Kretchmer accepted the olive branch. A couple of days later, he went to lunch with Spectorsky at the Pasta Vino, a mediocre Italian restaurant in the Playboy Towers the editorial director loved because they always gave him a special booth and "he didn't eat much anyway."

"The memo overwhelmed me," Kretchmer remembers. "Sure, it was manipulative, too. Spec always knew the effect he was going to have. He could be sincere and manipulative. But during the meal, I sensed that he was trying very hard to keep us together and I responded to that, to his efforts to end our estrangement. We parted as friends."

It was the last time they saw each other. Five weeks later, Spectorsky was dead, succumbing to a stroke on January 17, 1972, at his vacation home on St. Croix.

"He was a great literary act," Kretchmer reminisced years later. "He gave Kurt Vonnegut the idea for the short story, 'Welcome to the Monkey House.' He dealt with Ken Purdy and Arthur Clarke and Ray Bradbury—and he got their love and devotion. He came from a time when stories were stories and not 'properties.' He worked on a personal level. The first time Scott Meredith (a New York literary agent) held an auction on a manuscript, Spec was incensed. Because he'd have to pay more, sure. But also because his world was on its way to becoming a marketplace rather than a drawing room. Spec ran one of the great drawing rooms. His ideas were those of the salon—chatty, convoluted, witty, expansive, delightful, irreverent. He was a true gentleman editor who could be tough, curt, miserly when it was necessary. But he was an awful lot of grace and style as well."

Locked into its three-month lead time, *Playboy* did not get around to publishing Spec's obituary until the May 1972 issue. It was a graceful page, bordered in black, that eschewed *Playboy*'s verbal mannerisms in writing a touching tribute. When the obituary appeared the matter of the succession had been resolved.

It took Hefner several weeks to make his decision—weeks marked by long conversations among the contenders, a little politicking, and a lot of waiting. Kretchmer and Lehrman told each other with that deep, deep sincerity contenders must display that the other had the better chance—and agreed that the most likely solution was for Hefner to go outside his staff for a new editor. Wax says now that he never expected to get it and just did his job. But Kretchmer remembers Wax coming "into my little office in back where I used to sit drinking wine all day, to talk to me about what was going to happen. He didn't go to Nat, who was his good friend, or to Murray, because Shel figured I wasn't going to get it. Therefore, maybe I would share some information with him. He said, 'Of course they should give it to me,' and I said, 'Shel I don't think they will.' He said, 'Why not?' He was taken aback and we were never friendly.

"I said, 'Because you don't assume power that hasn't been given to you. You don't make decisions and walk away from them, you don't do that.'

"He said, 'Give me the power and I'll make the decisions,' and I said, 'You haven't learned the key thing around here, which is that you have to take the power before they give it to you. You have to assume it; then you can have it. They don't ever bestow it on you.' (A neat summation, incidentally, of why the hierarchically oriented Demarest didn't make it.)

"Shel said 'That's just bullshit. I can run this magazine.'

"And I said, 'I don't disagree. You can probably run this magazine better than anyone they may be considering,' I said, in my fucking duplicity. 'But I don't think you are going to get it.' "

"When Spec hired me," Lehrman remembers, "he told me that he wouldn't be around forever and that Kessie didn't want the job. He had an idea for breaking up his job into three parts and that I would get one of them. It was all part of Spec's seductiveness. The assumption about Demarest was that he'd been brought in to avoid making a decision in the office. When he left, I thought I had a shot, but there was no evidence to support that. I didn't do any politicking. I wasn't hooked."

Fisher figured that he, Wax, and Lehrman were the finalists, and, he says now, he knew that none of them would get the nod. "Shel wasn't going to make it because he was too narrow, too low-energy, not receptive enough to innovation. He is a superbly competent managing editor, and he performed that function for several years even while Kessie kept the title, but he just lacked the qualities for the top. Nat, who at the time was wrongly regarded as too much of a lightweight by Hef and Spec, had too little contact with the rest of the magazine. I was immediately eliminated because of my abrasiveness. If I had gotten it, I probably would have done a good job and not been abrasive."

Fighting for the top is more of a Rashomon experience than most other events in life, so it is not surprising that Kretchmer has a more activist version of Fisher's candidacy. "Hefner's line on Murray," Kretchmer says, "was that Fisher proposed a triumvirate to run the magazine—Fisher, Wax, and Lehrman. And at a lunch with Doug Bauer and Laura Babb (two junior staffers), Murray said, 'I can handle it if Lehrman or Wax get it, or the three of us, or any two of us. The only thing I can't possibly handle is if he gives it to Kretchmer, and he won't do that.'

"The day I got it, Murray was on vacation and called me and said, 'Of course you know you have my complete support.'

"I loved Murray for that. I thought, 'Oh, that fucking Murray, he's the only one—at least he went to the movies and saw *Executive Suite* twice and he was the only one who had the sense to know how one is supposed to react in that situation.' "

And what about Hefner? He smiles a Buddha smile about all the commotion at the lower levels, a smile to wipe away the struggle, the frustrated hopes, the searing expectations, the suppressed emotions that the old Playboy image—the fifties image—did not allow showing. He is still in pajamas as he talks about it, the sun bursting through the leaded windows of his Los Angeles library and hugging his shaggy head like a golden halo. There are already three empty Pepsi bottles on the coffee table.

Though Spec had been ill, the timing of his death had come unexpectedly, Hefner says. "There had been plans in terms of a transition, and he had been doing that. I can't remember the chronology very well at all, but it was Spec who reached down for Kretchmer and planned to bring him up as executive editor. Both Spec and I had the notion that the job would be split when necessary (Spectorsky had been both editorial director and associate publisher). And then, somewhere along the way, something occurred to change Spec's mind about that—and I don't know the details at all—so that no real plan was being implemented. There was a period of looking inside first and then also outside because there wasn't a logical strong person."

Hefner and Spectorsky agreed that Kessie was not qualified for the job, though he was next in line. "Spec and I agreed that we needed someone stronger brought up underneath." But when Spectorsky died, nothing had been decided, and Hefner had to make the choice alone. On what basis had he made it?

"On the input from all of the guys. I sat down with the individual guys and got their evaluation of their coworkers. Very democratic. Didn't actually hold a vote, but that's how it was done."

And the vote had gone to Kretchmer?

"The majority. There was no strong second choice." Hefner hesitated a moment, and then said quietly, "I'm sure there was a little political maneuvering going on, etc."

But no matter how democratic these proceedings may have been, Kretchmer held the high card: Spectorsky may not have cast his dying voice for him (though that last memo comes close), but Hefner remembered the earlier enthusiasm for Kretchmer and chose to ignore the doubts Spectorsky expressed about his sometime protégé.

"Spec used to tell Hefner that I had the most depth and the most resiliency and the most integrity, though God knows what Spec meant by the word 'integrity,' that I was the brightest, that I would be the most responsive to the entire magazine, and I'd be the most sensitive to the staff," Kretchmer says of Hefner's decision. "And then Spec and I did have this famous falling-out. What Hefner did was make a conscious decision that Spec was being vindictive about me and that he had to discount the last reports because he felt that towards the end Spectorsky had suffered a diminution of his judgment and had become too vindictive and too personal. Something had begun to go wrong with Hefner's relationship to Spec as well, and he assumed that would also affect Spec's relationship with me."

Just before announcing Kretchmer's promotion, Hefner sent executive assistant Dick Rosenzweig to break the news to Lehrman and Wax in person, to phone Murray Fisher, and to tell fiction editor Robie Macauley (though not a contender, he was considered too senior to ignore). All their disappointments were sweetened with raises.

"Arthur was grumpy and cranky as articles editor," Fisher remarks, "but as editor he became Gandhi: kind, intelligent, compassionate, a superb executive . . ."

Anyway, an executive who had also seen *Executive Suite*. On April 27, 1972, Kretchmer announced Shel Wax's promotion to managing editor, an announcement coupled with that of Kessie's resignation. The skids had been greased for that move a long time, but Hefner agonized over the decision—or so he says—and Kessie left, if not wealthy, then pretty well off.

Kretchmer was thirty-one years old and had been with the magazine for five years. His initial yearning for New York—strong enough at one point in the late sixties to dicker for a job on *The New York*

Times Book Review—had ebbed. He took over a surging magazine whose circulation topped 7 million in September, the first issue that bore Kretchmer's exclusive editorial imprint.

"Spectorsky was aloof and distant from us," Lehrman remembers. "Things had begun to stagnate towards the end. Kretchmer brought youth and energy—but no conscious change."

That wasn't needed then. Still, Kretchmer wanted youth and energy other than his own, eventually a younger, looser staff than the one he had inherited. Within a week of taking over, he took a first, unconscious step in that direction. He flew out to Chicago a young writer named G. Barry Golson to show his appreciation for a Golson piece he had liked and bought some months earlier, and to look over the "new young man." Golson turned out to be more than just one more new young man. He was a breed not seen often at *Playboy* since the demise of *SBI:* the compleat Ivy Leaguer, late-sixties model, and he had that touch of class Kretchmer found appealing.

Born in Massachusetts, Golson had been raised abroad by parents in international business. He came home at sixteen to attend first Exeter, then Yale and Stanford. Fluent in French and Spanish, he was, at a precocious twenty-four, managing editor of *Atlas,* the world press review. Tiring of preaching to the converted after a while, he decided "to peel off and try some free-lancing and cooling-out on a farm in Connecticut." Some months later, "when I was running out of money as a writer" and Kretchmer was recruiting staff, "the original contact was remembered. I was called, came out, and was hired as assistant articles editor."

It would prove an important acquisition. Golson was the next generation. And in the time of trouble that lay only a year away from that 7 million issue, Kretchmer needed all the help he could get.

9

The Sexual Revolution and Beyond

IF the beginning of social upheavals can be pinpointed in time—the way Lenin's arrival at the Finland Station signaled the Bolshevik uprising—then the publication in 1948 of Alfred Kinsey's report on male sexual behavior marked the official start of the second American sexual revolution. For Hugh Hefner, as for most American collegians, the appearance of Kinsey's book was like switching on an electric light bulb in a dark room. Moreover, the light went on at a time when the age of the first revolution, the 1920s, was again becoming the vogue of young men in school. Fitzgerald and Hemingway novels were assigned reading. Jazz, which had begun as whorehouse music, and, together with Prohibition and the 1920s stock boom, had first made sex acceptable to a large segment of the middle class, enjoyed a new creative surge. The war had loosened some of the sexual strictures the depression and the 1930s had reimposed on American life. Returning GIs crowded the campuses and told tall stories of their sexual exploits in Europe, Asia, and at home, where the renewed influx of women into the labor force, especially into factory jobs previously reserved for men, had made sex more open and frank.

Yet conventional morality showed little sign of loosening its grip on public attitudes toward sex. If anything, the coming cold war tended to associate loose living with the communist conspiracy, an association reinforced by the excesses of the McCarthy period. By and large, sex was still frowned upon, a subject of furtive discussions and sly winks, the purview of "that notorious Viennese quack" as smart young men called Sigmund Freud.

The issue Kinsey's findings posed so dramatically, therefore, was the continuing discrepancy between private behavior and public attitudes, and in articulating that gap, Kinsey helped narrow it. By treating sex as a subject of scientific study to which he applied rigorous statistical analysis, he helped move discussions of sex out of the locker room and into the drawing room. It became respectable to discuss Kinsey in mixed company. Sexual behavior was no longer naughty. Science had stripped away its frivolity. Nor could it remain totally evil in a society newly burning with the scientific spirit. It was, after all, the Year Three of the atomic age.

For Hefner, Kinsey was the confirmation of his own vague feelings, first discovered in the two years he spent in the army, that something was rotten with the state of American sex. "I'm not sure why sex became a cause célèbre for me at an early age but it did become a social issue for me at a time in my life when I was still very tradition-bound about my own sexual habits," he says now. "My folks had very traditional puritan values in terms of sex. In high school I really thought I would not have intercourse until I got married. Oh, I went steady a couple of times and engaged in some petting sessions, but I didn't change my views until I got out of high school."

Today Hefner views the postwar years—the late forties and early fifties—as a mixed bag in terms of sexual permissiveness. Introduction of Christian Dior's New Look in fashions in 1947, Hefner believes, was a definite step backward. Hemlines plunged. Bell-shaped skirts and loose blouses replaced tight-fitting dresses. The leggy and bosomy look of the war years faded. Girls told boys they'd have to use their imagination, and there was quiet cursing among the jock-strap set. Hefner hated the Dior creations. One of his earlier cartoon efforts for a college magazine showed a "smiling co-ed with short skirts" in the opening panel. The next three or four drawings saw the skirts grow longer and longer while the smile faded from the girl's face. The caption said, "This is progress?" For college boys, Hefner maintains, "those were important social issues," akin to the fact that the bikini "couldn't establish itself"—something Hefner would help along later by championing "more natural" fashions in *Playboy*.

On the other hand, *Esquire* had won a landmark decision against Post Office efforts to suppress the magazine for its sexual content. And after the war, "We all got cars again and had the drive-in movie, and a lot of other things were going on that made it more permissive. I'm very aware of that because I was in high school during the war and couldn't get a car. Also there were no drive-in movies. Drive-in movies had big impact on adolescents after the war. And mobility is what changed our whole social-sexual strictures."

The first Kinsey book, Hefner feels, "produced a tremendous sexual awakening," largely because of media attention. Even women's magazines commented. "Not too many people were damning it. The general thrust was: 'Here are the realities. We've been keeping our head under a stone.' I really view Kinsey as the beginning. Certainly the book was very important to me." Important enough, at any rate, to prompt Hefner to write a rave review for the University of Illinois humor magazine, *Shaft*. He stressed the importance of the book and deplored, as he remembers it now, "our society's very hurtful hypocrisy related to sex, and the gap that exists between our behavior and our supposed beliefs."

A couple of years later, while pursuing graduate work in sociology at Northwestern, Hefner expanded on the theme. He wrote a term paper for a criminology course on Kinsey and U.S. sex laws. "If successfully executed, they [the laws] would have virtually everybody in prison," he wrote and suggested major revisions in the penal code similar to those incorporated several years later in the American Bar Association's Model Penal Code. "A very interesting thing happened on that," Hefner says. "I got an A on the research, marked down to a B+. I got two grades from the professor because he didn't approve of my conclusions. Yet they were essentially what almost any right-thinking guy would agree to today on the whole matter of victimless crime."

In a way, that term paper was a first draft for the philosophy, something Hefner realized only when he began research on his "editorial statement" and discovered that he had carried the germ of the idea since college days. The paper did something else, too. It confirmed Hefner's abiding interest in sex as a subject of study and concern separated from any prior sexual activity. Sexual freedom for everybody became social cause long before Hefner turned into a freewheeling man about town "making out" with the girls. In other words, sex for everybody came first; sex for Hefner second. The crusader was born before the libertine, and the teacher before the cause.

Hefner is a didactic man whose relationships from childhood on were instructional—teacher-pupil, father-son. "I was the neighborhood guru," Hefner says about his childhood. "All the kids used to come to me to discuss their problems. And that has remained true for most of my life." He is not certain how conscious any of that has been. "I am a teacher, yes. That I set out to be a teacher, I'm not so sure. It has been suggested that there was an evangelical fervor, a teacher plus in a lot of Hefner and *Playboy*, but not too much of that was a conscious driving force when I started."

Conscious or not, Hefner approached *Playboy* with a prophet's fervor. Sex was good, abstention almost a moral wrong. Moreover, lust was not exclusively a male passion, as generations of Victorian guilt had led American men to believe. Women did not, after all, invariably follow mother's advice "to close your eyes and think of England" while the beast in their husbands unloaded his bestiality inside them.

Kinsey had once again demonstrated the fallacy of that canard. His probe of female sexual behavior had been published only months before Hefner put the first issue of *Playboy* together, and could be read as evidence that women really want it, want it worse than men do. Not only did they want it, but Kinsey had shown that in substantial numbers they went out and got it, bouffant hairdos, bee-stung lips, corsets, merry widows, petticoats, long skirts, fussy blouses, and all.

Nor was age a barrier to indulgence or to dreams about it. Kinsey straight-facedly records the response of a ninety-year-old woman who said that yes, she had sexual intercourse regularly. The point is less the reality than the yearning, the pervasive nature of the urge across time.

Thus, from the beginning, *Playboy* huckstered the goodness of sex as much as it did the naked female form upon which it could be practiced. Hefner made nudity a celebration and sex a vaulting joy. "You, too, can have a good sex life," he preached. "Enjoyment is as much right as privilege." And, in a sense, as author Gay Talese puts it, Hefner's nudes replaced the girl who wasn't there in the dream life of thousands of young Americans who still had never seen a woman naked any closer than on a burlesque-house stage where their vision was marred by pasties and stars in all the wrong places.

Better than anyone else in the communications business, Talese says, Hefner understood the nature of male frustrations in the early 1950s. Having experienced them himself, he was able to externalize that experience so that it applied to thousands and then millions of others. Hefner himself likes to use the word "decontaminate" and believes that *Playboy*'s single greatest contribution to the common weal is the sexual decontamination process the magazine helped start. And the beginning of that process was the conviction, the absolute, certain and unshakable conviction that nude was clean, not dirty. In *Playboy,* that first year, the conviction was demonstrated with a solid twelve months of calendar art. For Hefner had not only bought the Marilyn Monroe transparencies, but other calendar pictures thrown into the original $500 pot. Marilyn Monroes they were not, but pink-nippled and warm-fleshed, good enough to deliver a warm promise of fulfillment. The nudes were in color. The flesh tones shone. You could forgive the goopy mascara and purple lipstick and the come-hither looks. And once Hefner and Art Paul discovered the girl-next-door concept, readers could fantasize in absolute safety. No one threatened or demanded in that stillness of placid flesh.

Critics argue that Playboy's antisexuality fomented male fears of women and prevented men from finding fulfilling relationships by building a protective wall against the dangers and terrors of sex. Perhaps so. But millions of men bought *Playboy*'s message that sex was safe and fun anyway. And even those who didn't, who feared sex or commitment, must have found much of the *Playboy* message soothing—maybe even soothing enough not to pass their insecurities on to their children.

Much of *Playboy*'s sexual tone was subliminal. It emerged from the total package more than from any individual piece. And the underlying motif was approval. "Enjoy yourself," a tired Lee Gottlieb told the author after ten uncomfortable minutes negotiating his entry into a *Playboy* party at the Rainbow Grill. The phrase can serve as a *Playboy* slogan. Certainly it is the way most early readers responded. They drooled over the girls with innocent pleasure. The leer is notably absent. One reader in the mid-fifties was happy in his Miami "paradise," but for Playmate Dawn Richard he was ready to trade his Jaguar for a pup tent and spend time with her in the northern woods. "I'm getting married next month," wrote one reader in 1957, "because I thought I'd been around and seen them all, but your buxom Betty Blue really does . . . I mean she's . . . ah, you know what I mean."

Sophomoric? Of course. But *Playboy* began life with the irreverent and experimental look which Art Paul himself described as still part college-humor magazine. And it did not fully lose the collegiate flavor until the mid-sixties. *Playboy*'s Sin City features, for example, were not that different from those in the Magazine Management books—certainly not in layout and subject matter. But their attitude was something else. Like the magazine, the features were a little wide-eyed, curious, inquisitive, slow to damn, eager to praise. Take Sam Boal's January 1957 story on "The Girls of Shepherd Market," a look at some of London's well-mannered prostitutes who patrol Shepherd Market in trench coats and sleep with men in return for "presents" rather than cold cash (well, presents can be money). The piece, illustrated with black-and-white photographs of pretty, trench-coated English girls, does lard the "whore with a heart of gold" theme with a trowel, but the underlying message is clear: it is all right to pay for sex, and there are parts of the world where you need not be afraid of those who submit for pay—i.e., any kind of sex is better than no sex.

Indeed, the availability of women was a constant theme. "Jayne

Mansfield appears in these pages for the third February in a row,"
a 1950s Playbill said, "but this time it's a Mansfield with a difference;
she was never a plain-Jayne, but wait until you get a load of the new
improved version! Sally Todd is another young lady who will pique
your interest, we feel—you may remember her as the girl who took
the Champagne Flight to Las Vegas last June. This time she's our
Playmate and you have a date with her." If not in real life, you can
at least indulge your dating fantasies in these pages. Permission has
been granted. Believe us. It is okay.

But perhaps the most provocative of the sex-is-all-right articles
written for *Playboy* in the mid-fifties was by an eighteen-year-old girl
—Pamela Moore—whose novel, *Chocolates for Breakfast,* had a
naughty vogue in 1956. "Late last year," the February 1957 Playbill
told readers, "Pamela Moore brought out a tart novel about sex-wise
teenagers . . . one of those her-body-was-suddenly-alive-with-an-
awareness-she-had-not-known-it-was-capable-of sort of things—and
thereby shocked a lot of people who thought young ladies' bodies
should not come suddenly alive until voting age, if ever. For *Playboy,*
Pam has written a controversial indictment of the American male,
called *Love in the Dark.* "

Miss Moore's savaging of the American male is conventional. But
Playboy worried enough to write an introduction absolving readers
in advance from the author's indictment. "Some of us will forgive her
blanket denunciation . . . others will find their hackles rising. And
there will be those (we suspect a good many *Playboy* readers among
them) who will suspect her of having what must be a limited acquaintance with Homo Americanus in his more relaxed and carefree
manifestations."

"Are American men ashamed of sex?" the subhead asked. Yes,
answered Miss Moore with the absolute self-assurance of one just
back from exposure to "relaxed" European sexual attitudes. The
trouble is, she wrote, that Americans make love in the dark and close
their eyes while kissing. Moreover, such attitudes are bred into people from childhood on. Authority in America conspires to make men
and women ashamed of their bodies, and that shame stunts a child's
emotional development, thus assuring crowded psychiatrists'
couches later on. Fathers reject their childrens' physical tenderness
as somehow perverted. Parents guiltily excuse themselves on Sunday
afternoons to make love upstairs. Men are afraid of being found
sexually wanting, and flee to the bottle to avoid testing their manhood. Morality, she argues, stems not from conviction but from
repression. How Hefner must have loved that! And thoughts such as
these: "Years and years of repression, of being taught that sex is evil,
that it is something carried on in the dark, can, and often does, lead

to impotence." Her conclusion was equally scathing: "The guilt-ridden, convention-ridden American male will be a better father when he's no longer ashamed to be his wife's lover."

Reader reaction was all the editors could hope. Playboys howled. They accused Miss Moore of gathering experience for her piece as a prostitute in Shepherd's Market, said she should see a psychiatrist, suggested—what else—that she needed a good fuck, accused her of suffering from a father complex, contended it wasn't the male's fault, women liked to make love in the dark, charged her with engaging in voyeurism, told *Playboy* the piece belonged in the Party Jokes section, and urged that Miss Moore be kicked hard "on that part of the anatomy usually reserved for the purpose of kicking, at least once a week."

On the other hand, there were a surprisingly large number of readers—many of them women, thus confirming the early interest of the distaff side in the magazine—who agreed with Miss Moore's indictment. One reader called her a sexual Paul Revere, bringing light to the unenlightened, another agreed with her complaint and said that "American men rarely live up to their advance billing." "The sooner the American male wakes up to the fact that he is a sexual failure, the better off everyone will be," wrote a third.

But this was almost too serious a probe into sexual dysfunction, and it was not something *Playboy* pursued often in the 1950s, being content with the Miss of the month, jokes, cartoons, and the steady parade of airbrushed girls next door, showing more or less nipple, depending on the moods and mores of the moment.

For even nudes are subject to the whims of fashion. Hairdo, makeup of lips and eyes, the way the female figure is presented, the nature of provocation, change with the years. An upswept hairdo, mouths penciled onto faces with bright and caky lipstick, eyebrows plucked into filigreed arches, a Varga girl pout, the swirl of fabric draped to expose flesh with discretion—they all can be used by clever art directors and photographers to achieve a portrait far different from nature or another combination of these same elements. Hefner's nudes reflected their times. They were much more artificial in the fifties—even after the calendar art had run out and *Playboy* was finding its own models and using staff photographers—than they would be in the sixties; while the girls of the sixties, in turn, had a different look than those featured in the seventies.

The "girl next door" was personified by Charlaine Karalus, who worked in *Playboy*'s subscription fulfillment department. In fact, she *was* the subscription fulfillment department. The story of her rise to fame is something of a Playboy classic. She needed a new Addressograph machine. Would Hefner buy her one? The publisher hedged.

Then inspiration struck. He would if she agreed to pose in the buff. After some coaxing, she said yes, and Hefner ordered the office equipment. He also changed her name to Janet Pilgrim. "I invented the name," he says, "and picked Pilgrim for all its puritan implications."

Twenty years old and blessed with an hourglass figure (36 up and down), she does not, in retrospect, have the "natural" look *Playboy* would favor later on. There is white fur and lace in the picture. Her hair is swept up, her mouth thick with lipstick, her smile almost a smirk. But she had the requisite big breasts and pink nipples and her face seemed friendly—for those who bothered to look at her face. Her impact on college campuses was kinetic. Students loved her. Dartmouth had her visit one winter, and she broadcast over the college station to the oohing delight of undergraduates.

But since Hefner did not like fussy fashions, he moved relatively quickly to a different look: looser, nuder, more windblown, more active, limbs swinging, breasts bouncing—and not always gouda-heavy. In fact, one ex-editor claims that *Playboy* published more pictures of girls with normal breasts than with the watermelon kind, Hefner's taste in that direction notwithstanding. Maybe so. But to this untrained eye, Playmate breasts shrank only after lensmen aimed at the lower extremities and *Playboy* published pubic hair. Certainly breasts dominated the early pictorials, while the erotic possibilities of the female face were explored only after Playboy went pubic, and only fully after nudes were banned from the cover—a 1976 marketing decision to push checkout-counter sales. In the fifties breast were it, and their exposure fulsome.

A new decade dawned in 1960, and it brought a vigorous and handsome new president. Change was in the air. Perhaps, Spectorsky mused, more sexual content could be added to the nipple shots. What else did readers want? He thought of a joke, a spoof of Dear Abby, a takeoff on the lovelorn column, done with *Playboy* style, spice, and wit. He suggested the idea to Hefner. Hefner loved it. He had thought about something like it himself. Only not a spoof. Ann Landers wasn't comic. People who wrote to her had serious thoughts and serious problems. So did people who wrote to *Playboy*. Years of letters to the editor documented that. Why not separate out those asking for advice and treat them with dignity in a column of their own? Readers deserved that much care. And so the Playboy Advisor was born—a joke made legit. Still, the humorous cast Spectorsky had wanted to give the feature has remained. Answers are often frivolous, sometimes sarcastic, sometimes funny.

Nor was sex a major focus. Readers were more interested in other things. What is correct dating behavior, for example, and is it proper to kiss the girl after the first date? Were they really in love, those seeking counsel wanted to know. How did they feel about themselves and their girls, why their ambivalence about virginity?

One letter expressed that particular ambivalence with dramatic effect. The young man wrote that he had spent months trying to make his virgin girlfriend without success. Then he left town for a while. When he returned, she told him that his arguments had been so persuasive, she had popped her hymen for another—and was gratefully ready to resume their relationship. The reader was uncertain he wanted to, now that he had lost her maidenhead to someone else. What should he do? Grin and bear it, *Playboy* advised, and while you're at it, look at your own feelings about virginity.

Sum up the quality of *Playboy*'s advice in one word, and that word has to be "sensible." Readers were counseled not to marry in haste lest they repent at leisure, but one was told that unwanted pregnancy by itself was no barrier to matrimony. The Advisor did not urge defiance of convention for defiance's sake, but only for pragmatic advantage. There is no playing fast and loose with reader emotions, no advice to take risks where risks seem foolhardy.

In fact, the early Advisor was not that far removed from Dear Abby or Ann Landers, and the difference was expressed more in attitude than in content. *Playboy* displayed greater tolerance and seemed less wedded to the rigidities of the Protestant ethic. It applauded premarital sex and condemned sexual guilt. The sisters took a more astringent position on both. But through the mid-sixties, at least, there was little in the Advisor's counseling they could find objectionable.

Much of *Playboy*'s advice, however, focused on areas outside sex or personal relationships. Questions about sports cars, hi-fi equipment, clothes, shoes, and wines occupied as much space as sex (and were a major reason why critics like Cox called *Playboy* antisexual —in that context, sex was a consumption item). In commenting on them, *Playboy* remained cool and pragmatic. Advice was packed with useful information and seldom marred by factual error, whether the subject was vaginal sprays (they don't do anything soap and water doesn't) or the meaning of tinfoil wrapping on German wines (some are *Trockenbeerenauslese,* some are not, and the German is spelled correctly).

Into the early seventies, the tone of the column did not change much. But when the raunch wave hit around 1973, the Advisor became much more explicit and sexually oriented. More letters inquired about oral sex and its techniques, and generally about improved sexual proficiency. Readers looked to *Playboy* for approval for things they had not thought about doing five or ten years earlier.

And by the mid-seventies letters asking about fist-fucking—what is it and how do you do it?—had become routine.

But the Advisor marked only the beginning of *Playboy*'s expanded sex coverage. The real breakthrough came with publication of Hefner's "philosophy" and its focus on sex and society. Hefner devoted much of his 250,000-word ramble through the condition of man to the curbs law and convention placed on free sexual expression. He worried at length and with passion about definitions of obscenity, the dangerous spread of censorship, the cruelty, injustice, and illogic of "archaic" laws governing sexual conduct, and about the role of such social institutions as church and state in enforcing restraints.

Hefner was smart about exploiting controversy and turning it into copy. He attacked the media early as "outriders" for the establishment—and for having criticized *Playboy*. *Newsweek* was a target because in 1960 it had called *Playboy* "double-domed" for putting nudes on top of good prose. The charge stuck, and the magazine has never been able to shake it. It is a measure of Hefner's media savvy that he tried to put that one away quickly; that he failed was documented as late as 1976 when candidate Carter's *Playboy* interview became an election issue. The double-dome image had lingered in the public mind. Still, in 1962, Hefner gave it a good whack.

The trouble with the *Newsweek* writer (unidentified but personalized, thus doubly villainous), and the generation he represents, is their schizophrenic attitude toward sex (I'm not double-domed, you're schizophrenic). *Newsweek* likes the good prose but not the nudes. Yet normal men look for both in a men's magazine. Ergo, "*Newsweek*'s editor is projecting the uneasy and quite hypocritical and unhealthy attitude . . . that sex is best hidden away somewhere, and the less said about it the better." Everybody enjoys sex, Hefner continues, "but it's rather distasteful business at best" because it pits the animal in man against intellect and spirit.

> This nonsense about the body of man being evil while the mind and spirit are good, seems quite preposterous to most of us today. . . . Body, mind and spirit all have a unique way of complementing one another, if we let them, and if excesses of the body are negative it is the excesses that are improper rather than the body, as excesses of the mind and spirit would be also.

But the media only reflected a broader sickness about sex in the society as a whole, Hefner said. "The erotic and sexually attractive have got to be sinful and objectionable." The inner self insists on it and rejects "the very idea that the sensually pleasing may be clean and pure." The older generations, he charged, were hung up on sex.

Playboy was not. It believed that sex was to be enjoyed and savored, not put down and restricted by law. Moreover, those who formulated the laws feared to define what they were banning. Most statutes refer to "vile and contemptible crimes against nature" and leave more specific definitions to the courts. Presumably, a judge could rule that holding hands was illegal. Even worse, Hefner contends that only a short and logical step leads from laws governing sexual behavior to those restricting public communications about sex: e.g., censorship of allegedly obscene material.

The evidence he marshals to support these conclusions is, as usual, vast and badly organized. It is not clearly targeted, seems collected at random, and is thrown at the reader in a slapdash fashion. If there is a pattern, the reader must put it together himself, and at that he is likely to be left with a simplistic one: censorship is bad; sex laws should be relaxed.

The fate of two men seems to have struck Hefner particularly hard. One was a relatively obscure University of Illinois biology professor named Leo Koch; the other, comedian Lenny Bruce. Koch was dismissed from his university post in the wake of a letter he wrote to the student newspaper arguing that wide availability of contraceptives had removed barriers to sex among mature adults. Predictably, Chicago's Catholic establishment rose in wrath, talked darkly of moral decay, cultural collapse, and of free love as part of the Red Menace. Hefner commented that "it may not be too far-fetched to suspect that sexual intercourse outside marriage will soon be attacked as a Commie invention." It was a safe comment. In the McCarthy years, it already had been.

Bruce was something else. He haunts the *Playboy* philosophy as half-saint, half-ghost. Hefner must have seen the comedian as the point man of the sexual revolution; someone who put his body and his life on the barricades of struggle and took risks Hefner applauded and supported, but did not take himself. *Playboy*'s admiration for Bruce has lingered long beyond his death.

For the rest, Hefner deplored censorship with a litany of examples: An Atlanta housewife who doubles as film censor wants the word "whore" excised from *Never on Sunday* and replaced by "tramp" in the English dubbing. A Kansas film board objects to "slut" and "bitch" and "pelvic motions," to cite two. Hefner built a First Amendment defense of obscenity and drafted everyone from Thomas Jefferson to Justice Hugo Black to man the barricades. But he is careful to include a censorial enclave for children. Minors should be protected from smut. One way, he suggested in 1963, might be a kind of "family hour" on TV.

Why did Hefner care so passionately about censorship? It was not, he argues cogently and prophetically, for "any commercial self-interest." Indeed:

> a freer, less taboo-ridden, less hypocritical society would probably have less interest in the rebel part of *Playboy*'s personality. . . . An easing of the censor's tight control would only bring to wider distribution and sale a host of bolder imitators . . . that have long been a bane to our existence and a source of not a little embarrassment. Nor would *Playboy* change very much in such a censor-free society. The magazine has never attempted to push to the outer boundaries of what was censorable or what could be considered objectionable by the more sophisticated part of our society.
>
> Our interest in a society free of the shackles of censorship is as a citizen who believes he will be happier living in an America in which all men are allowed to exercise full freedom of speech, of press, of religion, and of association. It is the kind of America we believe in. It is the America our founding fathers meant us to have. We believe we should have it.

"Touching" may seem a curious word to describe Hefner and his writing, yet it fits. There is a stubborn willingness to risk becoming a figure of fun, to be ridiculed and reviled, especially by the intelligentsia. He has something of a Don Quixote about him, as well as of a Candide, and both qualities help account for the enormous response the philosophy elicited. In a painful and clumsy way, Hefner was talking about things his audience had only begun to feel, and to feel just as painfully and clumsily.

For the *Playboy* millions, freedom to enjoy pleasure needed defending. Puritanism remained the reality of life for many, and in a growingly libertarian atmosphere it was becoming a heavier burden. Hefner commanded the authority to lift that burden, or at least to lighten the load. There is the ring of absolute conviction in his voice, and he has an uncanny ability to make even the banal and the trivial glisten with fresh sparkle. However naïve he may appear in the philosophy (and in personal interviews), he burns with righteous fire. He smites the Philistines with the torch of truth. When he is finished, he drops the torch and hucksters the images made from the scene. It is a unique gift, and in the sixties it made him all but invulnerable to attack. Hefner the sexual thinker had impact. Students penciled "how true!" in the margins. Against so much faith, the laughter in academe rang hollow.

Even the turgidity of his prose and thought helped. The sixties were not noted for lucidity and clarity. Revolutionary periods seldom are; they tend to the pompous and self-important. In the sixties, a "happening" had weight. Satire did not float like a feather but raged like a jet engine. And Hefner brought that force and drive to his battle against puritanism. It had a Calvinist strain, and one, moreover, that gave his comments on sex and morality so much weight. *Playboy* preached hard work and the virtue of accumulating material possessions. The notion that the more you have, the more you can enjoy is almost an updated version of the Calvinist thought that wealth was one expression of the inner certainty of salvation.

Taken whole and judged more on social impact than literary merit, Hefner's philosophy emerges as a major manifesto of the sexual revolution as millions of Americans first perceived it. It was not the only one, of course. Others wrote voluminously about sex in the 1960s. But few had Hefner's reach or influence. For many readers, the thoughts expressed were true revelations. More than Kinsey, more than Masters and Johnson, more than the sex manuals of the day, the philosophy made a mass audience aware of sex as a social issue, something that had a life apart from the act: an attitude, a life-style, a right, a joy, a matter of both individual and collective concern.

As for *Playboy,* the series not only added excitement and controversy, but in the process opened the most vibrant channel of communication between editor and reader—The Playboy Forum. The feature was launched in July 1963 with a descriptive subhead, "an interchange of ideas between reader and editor on subjects raised by 'the *Playboy* philosophy,'" and an invitation to readers to "write and express yourselves" on issues "facing our free society today." It triggered a huge response, so diverse in content and opinion as to make the Forum the most uninhibited "town meeting" in the nation.

Over the years, no subject has been taboo: Vietnam, drugs, world federalism, religion, nationalism, law, government, politics, the CIA, civil rights, sexual practices of every kind, censorship, obscenity, abortion, imprisonment of sexual offenders, marriage, divorce, population, big breasts and small breasts, penis size, impotence, surgery to correct it, breast feeding, feminism, the mating habits of whales, sexual and social roles for men and women.

The basic focus, however, has been sex and society, and it is an area where the wild things dwell, as a sampler of comment will testify:

What this country needs, one reader wrote in 1963, was not a philosophy but a good 5¢ contraceptive. "Small breasts are beautiful," said another and opposed surgery to enlarge them. "Promiscuity would crack the foundation of our society," someone warns. Large penises are terrific, the "big cock society" claims, a claim *Playboy* denounces as without scientific basis. The trouble with puritanism, a Californian wrote, was that it bred Prohibition and bad food. "Is there some significance in the fact that Hitler loathed good food and drink?"

A professor in Buffalo promised to use the philosophy in class "as a means of critically analyzing the basic assumptions" underlying censorship. "If the sex drive in man is evil," a doctor wrote, "then so is the hunger drive and all other components of his instinctually endowed nature; and if this is so, then it must follow that God, if he be, is also evil." Five graduate students forced the Stanford library to put *Playboy* next to *Daedalus* and *Ethos* so that *Playboy*'s "sprightly covers" would enliven the "fusty" atmosphere of the place.

A girl from Boulder, Colorado, resolved a searing conflict between sex and Catholicism by ramming a crucifix up her vagina, achieving orgasm with Christ, and then joyfully fucking her brains out with the suitor who had besieged her virtue. One youngster complained about his inability to escape from Onan, which trapped him in "this cheerless chasm of corruption from whose semen-stained wall I cannot escape." A young couple planned to marry and sleep with other partners to break laws against adultery, just as they had laws against fornication.

Playboy editors argued in Forum that exposing children to nudity did not foster penis envy and cited an impressive array of evidence, from *The Encyclopedia of Sex* to Dr. Spock and Margaret Mead, to buttress their position. Forum gave down-the-line support to sex education—from underground comics like "Facts O Life Funnies" to Mary Calderone's Sex Information and Education Council of the United States (SIECUS). But it also printed a broad range of comment, both pro and con. One of the most touching chronicled the consequences of no sex education. The girl first had intercourse at fifteen, became pregnant, married, dropped out of school, and at age eighteen was saving money to leave her nineteen-year-old husband. Knowledge of contraceptives, she wrote, "has come too late."

But this little soap opera of a tragedy in a small Connecticut town did not soften those who saw a Communist plot in sex education. *Playboy* reported the remarks of a GOP congressman who believed that sex education and rock and roll "are part of a Communist conspiracy to destroy America." Another crusader, *Playboy* noted, told an audience in St. Paul that the UN and "some of the largest U.S. corporations" were involved in "the communist sex-education plot." America, he warned, is "heading for Sodom and Gomorrah on a greased slide."

Homosexuals were given sympathetic treatment despite *Playboy*'s aggressive heterosexuality. Freedom of sexual choice was too basic a commitment for Hefner to abandon. And some of the letters he printed in the sixties, before the dawn of the gay rights movement, were wrenched from bleeding pain. Men told of being busted in toilets, of having their homes rifled, their mail stolen, of losing their jobs.

"I remember last New Year's Eve," a Los Angeles reader wrote. "The police raided a small, friendly 'gay' bar and beat and kicked some of the customers into submission. One cop kept yelling, 'Save a queer for me.' Why should innocent people enjoying the company of their own kind be subject to such brutality?" Another man chronicled twenty years of his double-life, his stay in mental institutions, his breaking marriage, his fears for the effect his homosexuality might have on his sons. "Describing homosexuality as the gay life is one of the sickest jokes around," he wrote.

But for all its tolerance and defense of gay rights—advanced for the sixties—*Playboy* could not bring itself to regard homosexuality as anything but a phobia and a compulsion. A 1971 panel on homosexuality went further in expressions of tolerance—and in predicting a coalescence of the gay movement along the lines laid down by blacks, women, and the antiwar protest. But *Playboy* continued to define homosexuality as an aberration, not a variant on normal behavior, as the American Psychiatric Association has done.

Extramarital sex is given evenhanded treatment. Forum does not proselytize for it, but rather served in the sixties as mirror for the conflicts that resulted from a growing ambivalence about such activity. Some women wrote that extramarital relationships had awakened their sexuality, made them more human and tolerant, even improved their marriage. Others said that while they approved of premarital sex, they could not condone adultery.

"Love and fidelity go together, they give sex a pleasure that the sense alone cannot impart," one women wrote.

Another recounted the bliss of a ménage à trois in which a famous artist lived joyously with wife and mistress and fathered a child with each.

"I found adultery to be a bad habit that ate at me like a chronic disease destroying my morals, my ideals and my pride," wrote a third sadly in 1968. "I no longer felt I was a clean, decent person." It had taught her one thing, she added—greater respect for her deceived husband.

Yet another woman's tale was all the more pitiful for its lack of resolution. She had married young and inexperienced, then met a man who woke her sexual passion. He kept her in a state of suspended ecstasy, unwilling to risk his marriage. Professions of love were taboo, he decreed, yet she could not give him up. So she tried suicide, survived, and watch John's "rational, antiseptic, plastic universe" crash down together with her own life and marriage.

"I don't know whether to try suicide again," she concluded, "enter a convent, join women's liberation or go into psychoanalysis. But this much I do know: There is something dangerously wrong in the belief that sex and love can be put in hermetically sealed compartments with an iron wall between them. The only really cool people are in the icebox at the morgue."

But the subject most discussed in the Forum was the importance of penis size and penis performance. Thousands of letters asked the same basic question over and over: Is mine long enough? Why isn't it longer? *Playboy* was big on reassurance. One reader summed up the essence of *Playboy*'s counsel with a variation on a cigarette commercial: It's not how long you make it, it's how you make it long. Women wrote soothing letters—most of the time—and *Playboy* printed them, varying the diet occasionally with anxiety-provoking ones.

One correspondent wrote from twenty years' experience in the sex business (so she said) that included stints as prostitute, call girl and nude entertainer:

"I am familiar with penises of all types and sizes. In my experience the size of the penis has no bearing whatsoever on the ultimate pleasure."

"I prefer men with talent and a willingness to explore to a well-hung dummy or an athletic stud," wrote another woman.

Playboy editors quoted Masters and Johnson over and over that vaginas adjust to penis size. But it didn't help much. "It's still a role we fill," sighed thirty-three-year-old executive editor G. Barry Golson in the spring of 1978. "We get an awful lot of letters on that one."

One of the more perceptive, again from a woman, was published in 1973—even though it took a resigned crack at *Playboy* itself:

I've learned men are worried about the size of their penises—another body-fear neurosis this society mass-produces . . . I gather [men] spend a lot of time wondering if their organs measure up; but most women are not really very penis oriented. Women spend their time worrying about their tits. . . . They scarcely ever notice a penis until it's in action, when you almost can't see it at all . . . I went to bed with seven men over a period of two years before I finally had an orgasm with one. He happened to be the one with the smallest penis. . . . To the average woman, the most important thing is still what the man does with what he's got. . . . I don't discount the possibility that women with large or slack vaginas get more physical satisfaction from someone who can fill 'er up. But I doubt that most of them think of this in terms of the man's adequacy. They probably just feel inadequate themselves for not having the prescribed tight vagina. . . . The point is, we are all so intimidated by the impossible and irrelevant standards set by society and the media (and I'm afraid *Playboy* isn't exactly innocent in perpetuating women's fears) that we hardly ever function at our optimum level sexually and emotionally. This nonsense about big breasts and big penises is just part of the great American bigness fixation. The function of these organs is not enhanced by gross size.

Still, myths die hard. One woman wrote that if *Playboy* took a poll of experienced women, "I'm sure you would learn that we derive more pleasure from a penis that fills us adequately than from one . . . 'groping in darkness in search of something to lean against.' All I can say is: before I'll play, show me."

Forum also provided continuous coverage and editorial comment on the issues Hefner had raised in the philosophy: censorship, sex laws, suppression of obscenity, and pornography. No injustice is too small, no incident too trivial, to find space in Forum, or its newsier offspring, "Forum Newsfront." Post Office snooping or attempts at censorship are faithfully chronicled. Judges are reviled, blue noses rubbed raw, lack of confidentiality in VD clinics relentlessly exposed. Let a city pass an ordinance forbidding nude bathing at the beach where there had been no restrictions before, and *Playboy* will report on it. Do institutions, from business and the law to the military, object to the hirsute look? *Playboy* will puff with indignation.

But *Playboy*'s real fire and brimstone is reserved for the defense of imprisoned sex offenders. Their letters are printed regularly, their punishment is deplored, their cases often adopted by the Playboy Foundation and given legal and financial support. Of all his varied political activities, Hefner takes the greatest pride in the number of convicted sex offenders he has helped to free.

Over the years, this personal interest has infused *Playboy* with something close to a passion for law and led to arcane discussions of legal points in obscenity cases—and to blanket, in-depth coverage of obscenity trials. *Screw* publisher Al Goldstein and actor Harry Reems, for example, both had their cases aired at indignant length in *Playboy*.

Outside the Advisor, Philosophy and Forum, *Playboy* has published a steady stream of sexually oriented fiction and nonfiction, picture layouts, jokes, cartoons, and the ribald classics that have been a feature from the earliest issues. (In March 1978 Count Cagliostro concocted potions magic and not so magic to trap a philandering wife.) The "light" pieces are sometimes funny, sometimes vulgar, occasionally boring. The serious articles have become lighter and defter. For all of Hefner's insistence that the sexual revolution is far from over, his editors treat sex with ease and familiarity. If Hefner has not fully "decontaminated" the subject, he has gone a long way.

Certainly the culture is more comfortable with it than it was ten or fifteen years ago.

In 1965 Ernest Haveman contributed a thoughtful *Playboy* article on Kinsey, the man and his work. In 1978 Keith Mano took a sober, though sometimes wry, look at the dildo industry and found it booming. Subject matter aside, the great difference the thirteen years have made is in tone. Haveman is still describing an ideological battlefield; his is a story of struggle. Mano writes about a business; just another way to grow and make money.

In 1965 there were people who still tittered nervously when Kinsey's name was mentioned, despite his two monumental studies on American sexuality, and the global reputation of the institute he had built in Indiana. In 1978 one dildo manufacturer is embarrassed enough about his line of work to say that he is in plastics, but his unease does not go much further than cocktail party conversation. Yet when Haveman published his article, American society had, in a large part thanks to Kinsey, already traveled a long road toward making sex a bearable condition. And without Kinsey, without Masters and Johnson, the dildo manufacturer would never have been in business.

Haveman swiftly sketches the nightmarish quality of growing up in the Midwest before Kinsey, the dozen little tragedies he had witnessed as a youngster that permanently scarred lives. The portrait he draws of Kinsey blends perfectly into that background. He was strict, puritanical, uptight, with little charm or wit, dedicated only to his work. He abhorred prurience, disdained critics of his statistical method, was never tempted to turn his findings into a preachment or into the kind of "gospel" Freud and Jung had made of their teaching. In America, Haveman argues convincingly, only a man of such harsh moral fiber was free to probe an area of such public sensitivity. And even in the mid-sixties, his memory needed crusading defenders like *Playboy.* By the late seventies, sex merchants were just that. They didn't peddle flesh or smut, but hardware.

Wardell Pomeroy, for twenty years a Kinsey associate, provided intellectual services similar to Haveman—for example, a learned discussion on the problems of defining sexual normalcy. Pomeroy concluded the term defied simple semantic resolution because too many cultural, legal, moral, historical, social, and statistical factors had to be considered. "Am I normal?" he wrote. "It would be better to banish 'normal' from our vocabulary than to answer that question." And in the seventies, few bothered to try.

Sex as science received another important boost in *Playboy* in 1968 when Nat Lehrman interviewed Masters and Johnson, just two years after publication of their first book on the physiology of sexual processes. It was one of the first times—if not the first—that the famous couple spelled out their findings in nontechnical language to a mass audience. Lehrman first led them through a simple description of their research, explored some social and sexual implications of their work, then probed his subjects' views on issues more central to *Playboy*'s concerns—censorship, sexual dysfunction, pornography. Those views included Mrs. Johnson's harsh criticism of *Playboy* and Madison Avenue for fostering America's breast fetishism. Overall, however, Masters and Johnson approved of the magazine. Masters told Lehrman he thought *Playboy* "the best available medium for sex education in America today." *Playboy* returned the compliment with long-term financial commitments to the couple's research.

In 1970 Lehrman sat down with Dr. Mary Calderone, long the focus of right-wing attack for championing broader sex education. The John Birch Society had taken after her Sex Information and Education Council of the United States, which Birch founder Robert Welch called "a subversive monstrosity" linked to the all-pervasive communist conspiracy. But fire from the right was more admission of defeat than signal of new repressive dangers to come, as *Playboy* suggested in the introduction to the interview. In 1970 the country stood on the threshold of an unparalleled period of sexual openness and frankness that began to ebb only in the second half of the decade.

Nothing could document changes to come more dramatically than a sixty-five-year-old grandmother's advocating in the pages of *Playboy* discussion of oral-genital contact in sex-education classes and dismissing sex manuals as unnecessary. What counted, she said, was to make children look on intercourse as something joyful, "an exalted, wonderful, exciting gift from God." She could not approve of casual sex because "my puritan conscience" wouldn't let her, but conceded it was finding "widespread acceptance." *Playboy* and Dr. Calderone made for curious allies, but most revolutions do, and, again, the sexual revolution was no exception.

By 1973 the "new sexual life-styles" had taken hold and transformed the way large chunks of the American people behaved. *Playboy* wrapped it up in a panel discussion that covered all the current fads from open marriage to group sex. It encompassed *Screw* publisher Al Goldstein's aggressive male chauvinism and sedate opinions about what had really happened to sex in America. Was it a revolution accomplished or only more talk? Is living together better than marriage? Is there too much sexual freedom, or not enough? The panel went on and on. Richard Warren Lewis, who put the panel together, spent a week watching Disney movies after he finished to recuperate from the bewildering variety.

Meanwhile, the *New York Daily News* ran a series on teen-age sex in a Newton, New Jersey high school. Newton is a gentle town, the seat of Sussex County, where Playboy owns the Great Gorge resort complex. The reporter had graduated from the school a decade earlier and found things hadn't changed that much—except that sex was the common coin of social relationships the way dating had been in her day. And she was talking about fourteen- and fifteen-year-olds, not high school seniors.

Study after study bore out her findings, beginning with the Sorensen report in 1970 which pointed out that virginity had become a "minority position" among teen-agers. Starting age levels for sexual activity have been dropping all through the decade. Derek Calderwood of NYU's Health Education Department, where he conducts a human sexuality curriculum, believes intercourse among sixthgraders in some urban areas is now as common as it used to be among twelfth-graders—with accompanying behavioral problems and communications difficulties; e.g., children of that age are neither emotionally nor intellectually ready for the relationship.

Dr. Michael Correra, a vice-president of SIECUS and professor at New York's Hunter College's School of Health Sciences, says that "we now have enough evidence to show that more people are involved in normal sexual relationships at earlier ages than at any other time—and far beyond population changes." Most of Dr. Correra's numbers come from a telephone sex-counseling service he has run in New York City since 1971.

But the most comprehensive new data of the 1970s on changing sex mores across the country came from Hefner himself. The Playboy Foundation put up $125,000 for a national sex poll, conducted by Research Guild Inc., an "independent market survey and behavior research organization." The techniques used were the same as those first honed in the Kinsey Report, though Playboy's sample was much smaller and differed in makeup. Research Guild queried 2,026 persons—982 men and 1,044 women—compared to Kinsey's 12,240 subjects. Kinsey's sample was all white; Playboy included 10 percent blacks, but no one from rural areas or without a high school diploma, then adjusted statistically for the difference.

People were studied in 24 cities closely paralleling "the composition of the adult (over 17) American society." Some 71 percent of the respondents were married, 25 percent had never been married, 4 percent were divorced. The Research Guild developed a 1,000-item questionnaire to probe sexual attitudes, practices, and histories. Morton Hunt, who fashioned the findings into five *Playboy* articles, and subsequently into a book, did follow up taped interviews with 100 men and 100 woman.

"America is in the midst of a sexual liberation movement," Hunt's first article in October 1973 began. "In the quarter century since Dr. Alfred Kinsey made his celebrated census of American sexual behavior, there have been dramatic increases in the frequency with which most Americans engage in various sexual activities and in the number of persons who include formerly rare or forbidden techniques in their sexual repertoires."

The numbers bore him out: three-quarters of under-25 women in Playboy's sample had intercourse, only a third in Kinsey's. Among young marrieds (18 to 24), 80 percent had lost their virginity before marriage. College-bound boys of 17 had twice the rate of intercourse Kinsey's sample had. The female orgasm quotient was way up, but the number of married women who claimed they always had orgasms rose only from 45 to 53 percent. Anal and oral intercourse rose dramatically. Kinsey had no figures for the former; Playboy put it at 25 percent. Oral intercourse, overall, was up 50 percent from Kinsey's sampling. Homosexuality may have become more visible, but the statistics hadn't changed much; both studies showed that about 25 percent of the population had had homosexual contact.

For all its careful statistical work, some scientists criticized the poll because it had not been conducted by trained social scientists, and because sex polls tend to attract people both willing to talk about sex and to lead more active sex lives. But Playboy had not told its subjects in advance that they would be polled, and Kinsey Institute director Paul Gebhard thought the survey looked "pretty good," adding that "the figures they're getting agree with our research, and they're in line with pre-existing trends toward more liberal activity."

Few experts in the field of sexual research and adjoining disciplines, from psychiatry to sociology and history, doubt that *Playboy* had a role in shaping these "pre-existing trends." But like everything else *Playboy* has touched, the question is how much? How great has its influence been? How much for good, how much for ill? Reliable yardsticks are hard to come by, and while opinions are not, most of them are touched by ambivalence. The "yes, but" and "on the one hand, and on the other" are more common reactions than any clear-cut "yes" or "no."

Dr. Calderone retains "a good feeling" about her *Playboy* interview. She is grateful for the help the magazine provided when she was under fire from the right and for the forum it gave her views. "I was flattered that they thought highly enough of my work to interview me," she says. "And I knew that Hefner and the editor (Nat Lehrman) were fond of me." But she is more guarded on *Playboy*'s overall approach to sexuality. "I find some of the material childish, and some in poor taste—and I have nothing against explicit sex. But of course some of the material they publish is very good."

Masters and Johnson make no secret of the financial support they have received from the Playboy Foundation and the importance they attach to it. Asked to comment on *Playboy*'s influence on sexual matters, Masters pondered a reply for some time, then wrote out this answer:

> For almost a quarter of a century, Hugh Hefner has significantly influenced our culture. Starting with the PB philosophy, which, when first printed, had a realistic impact on our traditional, channelized approach to human sexuality, Hefner has sincerely tried to inform while he bent every effort to entertain. The Playboy Advisor and Forum columns have been responsibly based upon available facts, far more so than the imitator magazines or the how-to-do-it books that have multiplied like his talisman bunny since Hefner pioneered the field of media-oriented sex education.
>
> When *Playboy* turned its enormous profit, Hefner chose to distribute some of the gain through the Playboy Foundation to encourage legitimate research in human sexuality and to attempt reversal of wrong occasioned by indiscriminate, biased application of our archaic body of sex laws. In short, he sought the truth in this controversial field and marketed the information in a most readable package, a parlay hard to beat.
>
> In recent years *Playboy* has displaced much of this creative energy looking over its shoulders at the rapidly closing competition. The clarity of its position has been shaded and some of its vitality lost. Neither of these diversions from original direction need continue indefinitely.
>
> Any adequate definition of the depth of the *Playboy* influence upon our culture will remain for sociological research to establish. But that Hefner has created a prominent place for himself in the history of this vital field of human sexual interaction there can be no doubt.

That view is not universally shared. The head of a New York sex clinic, for example, feels "there has been a verbal revolution about sex, more sex is out in the open," but he is frankly contemptuous of *Playboy*'s role. He dismisses as "bull" the idea that it was in the vanguard of sexual change. At best, *Playboy* caught a ride in the caboose of that train, and he isn't even sure of that. "I don't think *Playboy* has anything to do with sex. There was more sex around in World War II than when *Playboy* started. Sexuality was rampant then, especially in the European theater." Whatever changes in behavior have taken place, he feels, are at best "a rerun" and adds that "we've had those for thousands of years. We're like puritans compared to some periods of history."

Paul Gebhard agrees with the idea of a verbal revolution "in terms of change in mass media. . . . In roughly one decade sexual censorship has essentially collapsed in all media save TV." While considerable, change in sexual behavior has not been sweeping enough, he believes, to qualify as a "revolution." Instead, he expects behavioral changes to "continue at a moderate and inexorable pace as we evolve toward what one might call a Scandinavian model."

Playboy, he feels, should get high marks as a vehicle for sex education because it reaches so large an audience with "generally sound" advice. But he does not think that many people ever got "initial basic information" from it. That's probably true about the facts but not about the illustrations; e.g., initial exposure to nudity. Gay Talese's observation that early Playmates were the first nudes many young men had ever seen is born out by a workshop survey Derek Calderwood conducted at NYU. He found that 90 percent of the participants had seen their first nudes in *Playboy.*

Calderwood believes that public acceptance of nudity was an important development in sex education because it helped break the prewar "conspiracy of silence" about sex. People no longer lock the bathroom when undressing, and they make love in the nude. The naked human form is seen as decent and clean, where it was perceived as pornographic and dirty only a short time ago.

"I can see *Playboy* having a role in that. It may not have been family to begin with, but it was soon brought into the home, and was big on college campuses. That girl-next-door art was a real innovation. Playmates were not one of 'those' women, but someone with a family and roots in reality—regardless of whether the story was made up or not. *Playboy* made nudity respectable. Even the old dodge about getting the magazine for the articles helped the process of social acceptability."

But for Calderwood, *Playboy* is no longer the sexual avant-garde. He rates the quality of its advice as "conservative and Ann Landers to liberal," largely because of *Playboy*'s "guarded" endorsement of nonintercourse sex. "The fastest change in sexual attitudes has been in the acceptance of mouth-genital contact," he says. "Ten years ago, the average person didn't know what cunnilingus and fellatio meant (and couldn't find out in most dictionaries). Among wide strata of the middle class it was considered abnormal. Today the vast majority see that as very normal behavior." Calderwood concedes that *Playboy* "had some part" in that because it discussed the subject in print. On the other hand, it shied away from explicit visual presentation of oral sex.

Dr. Correra of SIECUS and Hunter College agrees with nudity's cleansing function, but worries about the visual message getting into the way of the verbal one. Lumping *Playboy* and its raunchier competitors into one bin, he says that much of the guidance in them tends to be "synthetic" because of a visually related focus on the genitals.

"It is always penis and vagina, penis and penis, vagina and vagina. I think that does violence to the study of sex. If it is to become a real discipline, it must go beyond the genitals. Penis and vagina don't love each other; only people do. I'm for free portrayal of sex. But it should be a manifestation of our totality. Sex is essential to being human. Genital manifestation is only one aspect."

But it is the one that threatens to overwhelm all others, Correra thinks. For all the glut of available sex information, ignorance of basics remains rampant. "Until you concentrate on the facts about our bodies, the focus will continue to be genital. Skin magazines titillate and turn you on, but don't go into fundamentals: How does it smell? Am I going to get sick? How does it taste? Is it okay to do it? What about my own reservations and fears?"

Fear of sex underlies much of its fascination and here, some sex therapists believe, *Playboy* sends out conflicting signals that both soothe and agitate the uncertain.

"I don't think *Playboy* adequately responds to male fears," Dr. Correra says. "The solid and substantial information in the response to a letter is not left to stand. Jokes and cartoons confuse the issue, and often they are not supportive. The pull of the glossy things in the magazine tends to overwhelm everything else."

"Humor is the basic source of education," Dr. Bernie Zilbergeld, author of *Male Sexuality* and a California sex therapist, says. "And sexual humor bolsters all the old crap and all the old fears. It counts. Sex is loaded with anxiety, even for ten-year-olds. There are too many double messages in the media and in society." Cartoons that poke fun at impotence or other male inadequacies "would outweigh any supportive things said in the advice column. Cartoons are simply more compelling. Some things are." And *Playboy,* Zilbergeld says, constantly whipsaws readers between reassurance and new anxieties.

"And my cake didn't rise either," a disappointed miss says to her bedmate in one *Playboy* cartoon. "Think metrically, Mr. Lester," a buxom nude in a 1976 John Dempsey cartoon advises a droopy-moustached and middle-aged denizen of a nudist colony. "Then it would be at least 100 millimeters long." (Readers who whipped out their slide rule quickly found it was less than four inches.) "It's a poor workman who blames his tool," a suntanned blonde tells her flabby bedmate, while in another drawing a clearly miffed lady says to her lover, "Don't give me that premature ejaculation bunk—you just come too fast."

"I have no idea how much *Playboy* may engender fear and concerns," Paul Gebhard says. "Any cartoon with an impotence theme would distress an impotent male to some extent and perhaps plant the seed of worry in another male's mind, but such inadvertence cannot be avoided nor its effect measured. On the other hand one could equally well argue that making sexual dysfunctions the topic of cartoons and jokes suggests that they are commonplace, and hence a sufferer might feel relieved."

Playboy editors believe that jokes about sexual problems are part of decontamination. They relieve anxiety by sharing it.

"Jokes are supportive," Hefner himself says flatly. You decontaminate stupidity and fears by the right kind of humor, as long as it isn't hostile. If these things can be talked and joked about, then you feel less alone. A lot of problems about sex are related to people feeling what is the matter with me, I must be a pervert, or what's wrong that I can't get it up. Being open in a humorous way is helpful."

Much harsher criticism of *Playboy*'s influence on sexual mores and practices has come from the ranks of psychoanalysis, and no one has been harsher than Dr. Rollo May. In his book *Love and Will* (published in 1969), Dr. May lumps *Playboy* among "the new puritans," who converted the Victorian "thou shalt not" into the present's "thou shalt." In that transformation, sex dehumanizes love by putting technical proficiency ahead of emotion:

> The old Puritans repressed sex and were passionate; our new puritan (purposely spelled with a small p to dramatize the distinction) represses passion and is sexual. . . . I define this puritanism as consisting of three elements. First, a state of alienation from the body. Second, the separation of emotion from reason. And third, the use of the body as a machine. . . . Making oneself feel less in order to perform better! This is a symbol, as macabre as it is vivid, of the vicious circle in which so much of our culture is caught.

Such demands on performance, May argues, breed insecurities greater than those that spouted out from under Victorian sexual repression. And *Playboy* has been part of that scene, which May, quoting the "poet-sociologist Calvin Herton," says is an expression of "the new sexual fascism." Open an issue of *Playboy* and you "see the curious ways the new puritanism shows itself," Dr. May wrote.

> You discover the naked girls with the silicated breasts side by side with the articles by reputable authors, and you conclude . . . that the magazine is certainly on the side of the new enlightenment. But as you look more closely you see a strange expression in these photographed girls; detached, mechanical, uninviting, vacuous—the typical schizoid personality in the negative sense of that term. You discover that they are not "sexy" at all but that *Playboy* has shifted the figleaf from the genitals to the face. . . .

Playboy gets its "dynamic," May continues, "from a repressed anxiety in American men that underlies fear of involvement. This is the repressed anxiety about impotence. Everything in the magazine is beautifully concocted to bolster the illusion of potency without ever putting it to the test or challenge at all."

Asked to respond almost a decade later, Nat Lehrman, the resident sex expert turned *Playboy* publisher, pondered the issues raised, then tapped out this counterattack:

> May not only misunderstands the concept of new puritanism, but confused it with sexual fascism. Sexual fascists do indeed adopt a "thou shalt" attitude. They reject the repressive attitude of the traditionalists, and insist that to be "modern," the individual must screw with the same mindlessness that his predecessors avoided screwing. This is not at all true of *Playboy*'s stated and implicit philosophy.
>
> *Playboy* advocates freedom of sexual choice. The sexual attitudes of society should be open enough so that the individual can refrain from sex, or can choose to indulge in it, under conditions of his own making.

May's assault on *Playboy* in *Love and Will* was an early blast at unbridled, anything-goes sexuality. Since *Playboy*, sexual barriers have tumbled like ninepins, and triggered their own reaction. The Burger Supreme Court has refused to enlarge the area of privacy. It is less a matter of reversal than holding the line at the status quo— with that definition dependent on local option as laid out in the 1973 Supreme Court decision. The growing number of obscenity cases in such tradition-bound states as Tennessee, Kansas, Ohio, and Georgia supports that interpretation; so does the conviction of actor Harry Reems, *Screw* publisher Al Goldstein, and Larry Flynt.

However these are finally resolved, and whatever the lasting impact of the Flynt shooting may be, Hefner and *Playboy* now have fresh ammunition in their war on bluenoses. Certainly Hefner revels in the new challenge. Just how much became clear in our interview in early 1977. Trying to sum up the discussion of sex, I said, "So we agree that by and large the sexual revolution has been won in this country."

Hefner would have none of it. "I don't agree with that at all."

"Where has it not been won?"

"It certainly hasn't been won in the courts yet. People are serving time in prison for publishing salacious material and are going to serve time in the future." As evidence, he cited a high court decision to let stand a West Virginia ruling that allows states to keep sodomy laws on the books. Sodomy statutes, Hefner says, cover every sexual activity "other than coitus." In Wyoming and Indiana, even mutual masturbation falls under them.

"The sodomy statutes tell husband and wife what they can do in their bedroom. They make it a felony for a husband and wife to have oral sex. No, I don't think the sexual revolution is over."

He admits that "we were getting so close" to Scandinavia "in terms of communicating ideas and images related to sex," but have drifted far from that ideal model. "The Supreme Court as now constituted is moving in the other direction. That does influence a lot of things. There would be major motion picture companies making hard-core films today were it not for that shift. Social attitudes are being affected. I think you are going to see censorship boards in some cities. The very ambiguity of this community standards concept throws a lot of questions up in the air. Most forms of mass communications—films, books, magazines, etc.—are directed at a national audience. When the Court says that each community—however that is defined—has the right to set its own moral values on sex, the First Amendment protects citizens only up to a point. We face an uncertain transitory period.

"I do agree, though, that the general thrust of our society is toward a more humanistic, permissive, open attitude toward sex, and I have no doubt that eventually this will prevail—hopefully within our lifetime. I do think we're going to win. I just don't think it's time for a victory celebration yet. There are still a lot of people being killed out there. You can't say the war is over when they're still bringing in the bodies. I hope it is a cleaning-up operation, and it would be except for the Supreme Court. It's not that the general thrust of the Burger Court is so much antisex or antiobscenity as it is 'We don't want to bother with it anymore, so let's turn it back to the local courts.' And that is the most dangerous game of all. That, and the fact that the Court is going to be there a long time."

Hefner does believe, however, that there are social forces working against the Court. Popular attitudes toward sex are changing. TV has helped homogenize public opinion and wipe out class differences about sex. And TV, Hefner believes, is the great barometer of public feeling:

"Johnny Carson has tremendous impact on our sexual attitudes by the kind of jokes he tells and the conversation he allows on his show. I mean, Jack Paar walked off 'The Tonight Show' after a big hoopla about a joke using the word 'water closet.' You have to keep reminding yourself—because everything fights it—where we were as a society in terms of values and attitudes only a very short time ago."

Even more than television, *Playboy* has made the transition possible, as Hefner states with force and conviction:

"I think it can be said with reasonable certainty that no other single thing in popular communications has had more influence on the changing social-sexual values in the last twenty-odd years than *Playboy*. Without question. And its influence is far more dramatic than most people realize, especially on young people growing up, both male and female. Outside of one-to-one relationships, I think it would be difficult to find anything on a general, universal level that had more impact in establishing a whole set of values and attitudes about social-sexual problems. *Playboy* is almost twenty-five years old. The generation now running society is the first *Playboy* generation—the first to grow up with this significant influence on their lives —and their influence has been felt across society."

But doesn't that generation have a totalitarian strain running through it? Has it not made the idea of chastity obsolete and its practice difficult? Hefner does not allow the question to be completed.

"But that's not true. You have more choices than you did twenty years ago. You can be chaste today."

"You'll get laughed out of your society."

"I don't think so. I'm not disagreeing that such an implication isn't in the shift that has taken place. But it certainly isn't true that there aren't a great many people who are still virgins when they get married. That's probably not the best way to get married, in my view. But those people have that choice. And I don't think they have been laughed out of society. The truth is that while there are strong pressures now to have sex, they are not nearly so strong as the pressures not to have sex that existed while we were growing up. And we are sexual beings. I'm not suggesting that someone who decides never to have sex"—Hefner interrupts himself "—though, of course that's impossible. You have to have some sexual response. I'm not saying that such a person is forever crippled, but he is only living a part of his potential. He has lived a little less. And furthermore sex is more than simply a good and positive part of life. It is a key and touchstone of life. Sex, not religion, is the major civilizing force on this planet. Clearly and obviously it is the best part of us. It is the part that brings us together, the beginning of the family, the tribe, of cities, of civilization. If we lived on this same planet but reproduced in some other way that did not involve sex and there were only one sex on this planet, it would be a very, very different world. And if we think the world is rather bleak and cold and hostile now, I would suggest that without sex it would be much, much more so. Much of the hurt related to sex on this planet is what we have done with it, the way we have twisted and thwarted and disfigured it."

How well informed are Americans generally about the subject of sex, does Hefner think? In New York Dr. Correra's telephone sex-information service seems to suggest a hunger for details. "Where to put it?" Hefner quips, and adds, "I'd like to put a footnote to that. You remember what you said a little while ago that implied the sexual revolution was over? Well . . ."

But without the sexual revolution, without the overexposure to sexual explicitness, without the feverish sexuality in society, such people would never have sought the information in the first place, or thought that much about sex. The question pricks at Hefner's emotions. He is shouting now:

"I would hope they would think about it. For Christ's sake, someplace along the way, one would hope—somewhere in the bed there, as the marriage came apart, they thought about it. Wham bam and unhappy lives. I mean, what about the woman?" The outburst is over. "What about the female role in bed today and what she expects and has a right to expect and the part *Playboy* has played in that? There have been tremendous changes in the whole area of female gratification—and in the recognition on the part of men that women have a right to the pleasures of the bedroom. There is a problem for men in terms of greater expectations on the part of his partner and concern about that on the part of the male. It was a much simpler, but clearly a much less humanistic and less loving kind of society we had in the not-too-distant past where if the man got the job done and had an orgasm, that was successful sex. Today there are other expectations. The man knows going in that he is also expected to perform in such a way that the woman will also have some response and satisfaction. Sex isn't a problem of too much communications, I think. It is just that now we are more sensitive to the implications of our sexuality. There are greater expectations to be fulfilled. Those are intimidating to some people. And that is a problem."

The war continues—the war to establish sex as the great civilizing force on this planet—now that religion has failed us, if indeed religion ever was a civilizing force—at least organized religion. For Hefner "sexual" and "erotic" are interchangeable words whose different meanings he will admit only when pressed to. When he talks lyrically of sex, he means to encompass the universe, to sing with Schiller *"seit umschlungen Millionen, dieses Lied der ganzen Welt"* (after all, he has a house down the block from Schiller Street), while the celestial orchestra plays the choral movement from Beethoven's Ninth. Sex may be the underbelly of love—the dark side of the moon —but Hefner means to expose it to the sun. He may never have heard of agape (I feared to ask after we slipped into the verbal quicksands of sexus and eros), but *Playboy* is about God and love, that dreadful word which threatened to strangle sex for so long.

"The war isn't over," Hefner murmurs. "Honest, the war isn't over."

He has a vested interest in its continuation, of course—ideological, commercial, and personal. The sexual revolution defines his world and his achievements in it. Maybe he is a clown. Perhaps he does see himself as a messiah, as Harvey Cox maintains. Certainly he and his life-style are easy to ridicule. Eccentrics and their eccentricities generally are. Everyone who has met him, however briefly, has his favorite "Hefnerism" to recount. Walter Goodman's probably sums up the naïve essence of *Playboy* and sex the best. He was waiting for the elevator at 232 East Ohio Street one evening when Hefner bent over the desk of a new receptionist—the tragic Bobbie Arnstein—and said to her, as Goodman remembers it, "don't think of me as your boss or the publisher of this magazine, think of me as a guy looking for a date."

Millions of men were in the same quandary when *Playboy* rode high—and alone. Millions still are. The decontamination of sex may well be a continuous process rather than one that can be completed. Fear and loathing, awe and mystery, remain a part of growing up sexually. Men are clumsy, women unsure. Perhaps Freud did not, after all, rob man of his fear of the cloaca. . . .

The pendulum swings back and forth. Hugh Hefner watches it swing. He has told his editors to start a new monthly sex poll "in which our roving pollsters survey changing sexual attitudes and practices." You could read a new conservatism into the numbers. Out of 100 men polled, 68 preferred to reach orgasm through intercourse rather than oral sex. Or does that make Calderwood's point about the sexual conservatism of *Playboy* readers?

"Whatever happened to fucking?" Hefner grinned almost wistfully.

Perhaps, like the counterculture, sex has been coopted by straight society. Cleaned up a little. Made more respectable. Touched by a nostalgia for virginity. After all, even Republicans do it. John Dean's wife "Mo" was an eye-opener. Now, that was a Playmate! People still listen to Wagner's "Liebestod" from *Tristran and Isolde,* the fleshiest music ever written with its cadenza of postcoital blues.

"Howie, there are are other things in life besides Marxism," a young Brooklyn girl said at a Trotskyite meeting on Fourteenth Street in New York in the 1940s. "Dere is lit'rature and music and poeetrye." Howie remained a Marxist, but got the point. His interests broadened beyond revolution. Maybe, in the late seventies, some are saying that there are other things in life besides sex—perhaps, again, even Marxism. Even in *Playboy.* The current editorial director is a socialist and the grandson of socialists. And Hefner says the publisher is a socialist, too, sort of—a utopian socialist. . . .

10

The Target of Outrage

"WE wanted to do a piece on feminism because it was the right time to do it."

For Nat Lehrman, turning forty that year, six years with the magazine, a senior editor now, in charge of all the human behavior sections, the right time was late summer 1969. High time, too, in a year when militant feminism crackled across TV screens and searingly into the public consciousness. And more than any other publication in America, *Playboy* was the target of feminist outrage.

Angry women had tramped down the Atlantic City Boardwalk the previous September, crowned a sheep Miss America, stuffed a trashcan with false eyelashes, boxes of mascara, stenopads, copies of *Cosmopolitan* and *Playboy,* symbols of male oppression all, and lit a bonfire of liberation. Others had stomped past Playboy Clubs, stripped at Grinnell College, Iowa, during a lecture on the Playboy philosophy, and left few opportunities unused to harass, needle, and annoy the magazine.

Lehrman, a liberal intellectual out of Brooklyn College at the bare-ass tail-end of the old left and with an M.A. in English literature from NYU, realized that *Playboy* could not afford silence or an unreasoned counterattack. It had to develop a rational position on the issue, or at least provide readers with a factual account of what the noise was all about. The din had become so deafening that sorting out the pieces was difficult.

In the years that had passed since Betty Friedan's book, *The Feminine Mystique,* women had pushed a ban on sex discrimination into the Civil Rights Act, formed the National Organization of

Women, taken to the streets to protest oppression, bludgeoned the government into enforcing Title VII, and fought for abortion on demand and the addition of an Equal Rights Amendment to the Constitution. Gradually a new strain of militancy entered the movement. Valerie Solanas shot Andy Warhol, and Ti-Grace Atkinson published Solanas's SCUM—Society to Cut Up Men—manifesto. Kate Millet wrote *Sexual Politics.*

Moreover, *Playboy* was already late. Other media were getting the message. Articles on the difficulties women faced in a man's world, from unequal pay for equal work to lack of professional advancement, proliferated. The tone ranged from the stridency of *Ramparts* to the sedateness of *The Saturday Review* and the sober objectivity of *Business Week* and *U.S. News and World Report. Life* and *Look* were preparing major text and picture stories.

Although Lehrman considered (and still considers) militants "the enemy," his initial approach was sober and professional. He knew that male writers were being excluded from feminist meetings and that he would have to hire a woman for any inside reportage on their feel and flavor.

"I called seven women to do that piece," Lehrman recalled while still editor and publisher of *Oui.* A tall, rangy man with silvered sideburns and an owlish face puckered behind rimmed glasses, he sat in a fifteenth-floor office in the Playboy building, fitfully flicking the switch on the hi-fi behind his desk and punctuating the conversation with gushes of rich classical music. An abrupt lakefront vista hung outside his window: proud apartment towers marched up Lake Shore Drive, and, flung into infinity behind them, the deep blue waters of Lake Michigan.

"They all turned me down. I know Nora Ephron. She said no. I wrote to Gloria Steinem. She didn't even answer."

Finally, articles editor Jim Goode put in a call to New York literary agent Lois Wallace, a serenely confident woman liberated at birth, and asked her if she knew someone who could do the piece. Mrs. Wallace did. Her name was Susan Braudy, a graduate-school dropout making a name as a free-lance writer for articles in *New York* and the *New York Times* magazines. In an account for *Glamour* ("that great feminist publication," Lehrman groused) on her *Playboy* experience, Braudy says she was "wary" about accepting the assignment. If she was, neither her agent nor Goode remember the caution.

"Goode called me and asked me to do a fair and objective article, descriptive of the movement, but that I shouldn't draw any conclusions," Braudy said some years later.

Goode followed up two phone conversations with a letter confirming the assignment—a fair, descriptive, nonjudgmental piece—and a phrase that caused Braudy some soul searching. The piece, she quotes Goode as writing, should be "in a tone that is amused, if the author is amused, but never snide."

"This remark puzzled me," Braudy wrote in *Glamour* in 1971. "I reread it anxiously several times with the conviction, I suppose, that if I could understand it, I would know if I could win out—keep my integrity and write an article which would surely help my career."

Thus armed with a proper ethic, Braudy set out to discover the women's movement. She attended consciousness-raising sessions near Columbia, met Roxanne Dunbar and Robin Morgan, listened to Betty Friedan talk about "male lib" in Philadelphia.

"I had a sense that *Playboy* wasn't for me," Braudy says now, "but not that *Playboy* was the enemy. But the more I did the piece, the more uneasy I became. I rationalized that I would reach an audience no one else could. I'd say that to the feminists I talked to."

The argument won her pitying smiles. Movement women were sure that *Playboy* would not give her a fair crack, that her piece would never run—certainly not as she wrote it.

"Gloria (Steinem) said to me you'll never make it. Lindsay Van Gelder (a *New York Post* reporter and early feminist) was angry and wouldn't let me come to feminist meetings. She said I was doing women in. Ti-Grace was furious. She's crazy, though. Robin Morgan wrote me an angry letter saying I was ripping off all women, so I sent her a couple of hundred dollars as a contribution. I seemed to be a target at meetings when women learned that I was writing for *Playboy.*"

When Braudy delivered the finished article in early December, feminism had become an even hotter issue. *Time* had done a major takeout in November. The *Life* and *Look* articles had been published; and the *Look* author was a man, Richard E. Farson, who wrote about the issue with sympathy and perception, detailing not only the prejudice of the present but the slippage from the past. (The number of women receiving graduate degrees was down from the 1930s.)

Braudy's article was more impressionistic than descriptive or analytic. It focused more on Robin Morgan and Roxanne Dunbar than on Betty Friedan—the three pillars on which her article was built—more on the radical groups WITCH and Redstocking than on NOW. Consciousness-raising sessions and the Atlantic City demonstrations were given greater attention than problems of jobs, homes, children.

Playboy's initial reaction seemed favorable, Braudy thought. Goode told her he liked the piece, and that, she believed, was that. (Goode today remembers little about the episode, says he always stuck by his writers and defended them, but that when the hand of censorship appears, he tends to walk away from the situation.) She felt vindicated and a little smug. She was sure she had broken the *Playboy* barrier.

In fact, Braudy had not. If Goode liked it, Lehrman did not. And many other *Playboy* editors didn't, either. The article quickly became a focal point of dispute. Women employees, long resentful of male domination, took strong stands on it—both for and against. A memo blizzard began to inundate the editorial office.

On December 16, 1969, Lehrman sent a memo to managing editor Jack Kessie that summed up the problems as he saw them:

> ... A lot of the resentment this piece appears to be engendering relates to the fact that it seems to lump all people who are concerned about female rights together with the militant feminists. Since this piece is in fact only about the radical fringe, and doesn't touch at all on the really important issues of the movement, I think we should clearly label it—either in the subhead, or early in the piece—as being what it is: reportage on a tiny and noisy segment of women with no following among the great majority of females. To fail to do this would be analogous to identifying all civil rights advocates with the Black Panthers; all conservatives with the Birch Society; all student activists with the Weathermen.

Lehrman attached memos from Henry Fenwick and Toba Cohen, two editors who were "pretty savvy about the subject of women's rights." Fenwick, a young Englishman, wrote:

> A very silly, shallow piece. If we are going to touch this area, our identity as *Playboy* necessitates that we do a very thorough, scrupulous job—not just hack reportage. The scope of this is much too narrow—there is a much wider range of feminism than shown here, and they have much better points than this article ever gets into. Susan Braudy seems very fuzzy-minded, and her descriptions of some of the leaders are stomach-turning starry-eyed. Haven't read anything so bad since The Chalet Girls Go to It.

Toba Cohen, who had only recently moved from researcher to assistant editor on Lehrman's sections, was just as negative, but more cautious and aware of her complex role as a woman editor:

> Nat, I have just read the article by Susan Braudy—thank you for the opportunity to express my views. It makes hard-core feminists sound so utterly unattractive both physically and ideologically that any sympathizers for the basic "cause" would blanch at the thought of identification. To say that all females interested in equal opportunities for women agree with the battle-

ground tactics and combat clothes of the groups depicted here is to say that all people opposed to the war in Vietnam agree with the Weathermen philosophy of destructive action.

Not all feminists use bad grammar to express their views. Neither do they wear outlandish clothes and "walk out" on their families. There must be room in an article on this subject, for the female who believes in working from within —one who does not believe that in order to compete on an equal basis with men one must look like a man. These "feminine feminists" believe they are nearer a compatible victory in their way than are their combat boot "sisters." Let the bra wearers be heard.

Cohen, managing editor of a medical magazine in the mid-seventies, felt strongly about Braudy's piece because "I thought it would be our only shot to say anything. I didn't want to waste it. She did not write a good piece. There were other people more capable of writing a sharper article."

For all the division, however, sentiment on the magazine was for running the piece—after some rewriting and heavy editing. Kretchmer wanted to print the article as written, reasoning that it was the best putdown of militant feminists available, while getting *Playboy* off the hook they could all see forming: *Playboy* had asked a woman to write a piece on feminism—and then had turned her down.

Lehrman held out for reworking the article to give it better structure and smoother flow. Fenwick drafted a sixteen-point outline on how to improve it. Then the Christmas holidays intervened and everybody slowed down. Kessie ran into Hefner at a party and told him about plans to run an objective piece on the women's movement. "Hef, you'll love it," the managing editor said and moved on. It was an offhand remark, but Hefner stewed over it for several days, and his reaction, when it came, was explosive.

Early in January 1970, Susan Braudy arrived in Chicago on assignment for another magazine. She called *Playboy* to say hello, and Goode invited her to lunch. But when she arrived, he turned her over to Julia Trelease (whom Braudy incorrectly identified in *Glamour* as *Playboy*'s lone woman editor). For Braudy the atmosphere was charged. She felt on enemy territory; unsure, uncertain, unsafe. Her memory of what happened focused, naturally enough, on herself. She remembered that several secretaries came along to lunch.

"One secretary mentioned that the joke going around the office before I arrived was that I would be instantly recognizable because I'd be wearing combat boots and battle fatigues. Actually, I had deliberately worn a soft pink short dress and even managed to wash my hair the night before," Braudy wrote.

During lunch other storm clouds formed. "One secretary told me that she didn't think my article would ever see print, a statement that stunned me." The girl's reason? "Oh, I just don't trust people around here when it comes to women." Braudy also discovered that "these *Playboy* women knew much more of women's liberation than I would have expected. A few said they had read my article and liked it. . . ."

At best, memory is a trick mirror of reality. Julia Trelease, reminiscing years after leaving *Playboy,* remembers it differently:

> There were four of us at that lunch; myself, Susan, Jim Goode's secretary Connie Segur, and Sherry Ratliffe, who had just been made a writing editor. What we talked about mostly at lunch was Sherry's promotion and the fact that another woman, Laura Langley, was coming in as an editor in June after finishing school. She had interned at *Playboy* the summer before and done very well. When the Braudy piece appeared in *Glamour,* I drafted an angry letter but never sent it.

Lehrman had spent a hectic and at times frantic morning. As he was sorting out notes for a revision meeting that afternoon with Braudy, a Hefner memo plunked on his desk—the delayed reaction to that chat with Kessie. A note from Spectorsky was attached requesting an urgent meeting with Lehrman and Kretchmer. It was needed. The memo, dated January 6, 1970, was a blockbuster:

> From a brief conversation with Jack Kessie a couple of days ago, it sounds as if we are way off in our upcoming feminism piece. . . . Jack indicates that what we have is a well-balanced "objective" article, but what I want is a devastating piece that takes militants apart.
>
> Jack seems to think that the more moderate members of the feminist movement are currently coming to the fore . . . I couldn't disagree more. . . . What I'm interested in is the highly irrational, emotional, kookie trend that feminism has taken. . . . These chicks are our natural enemy—and there is . . . nothing we can say . . . that will convince them that we are not. It is time to do battle with them and I think we can do it in a devastating way. That's the kind of piece I want. . . .
>
> We start by conceding that women have had traditionally a second-class citizenship throughout the world. . . . This is less true today, than ever before, however . . . and many . . . suggest that women have it at least as good as men today. . . .
>
> What the militant feminists are looking for is something else altogether. They are rejecting the overall roles that men and women play in our society —the notion that there should be any difference in the sexes . . . other than physiological ones. Now this is something . . . to which we are unalterably opposed and I think we should say so in an entertaining, but highly convincing

way. The society they want is an asexual one. We believe women should have truly human roles in society, and that each individual—male and female—should be able to explore the broadest aspects of their nature, but the notion that female emancipation is in any way similar to the racial problem . . . is nonsense.

. . . We certainly agree that a woman's place is not in the home, that a woman should enjoy a career, that she should not be limited to a double standard in sex, etc., etc. But the militant feminist wants much more than this . . . she wants to play a role exactly comparable to the male's. . . . It is an extremely anti-sexual, unnatural thing they are reaching for. . . .

. . . The only subject related to feminism that is worth doing is on this new militant phenomena and the only proper *Playboy* approach to it is one that devastates it . . . if you analyze all of the most basic premises of the extreme form of new feminism, you will find them unalterably opposed to the romantic boy-girl society that *Playboy* promotes. That's the piece I want—and I wanted it several months ago. . . . It is now up to us to do a really expert, personal demolition job on the subject. Let's get to it and let's make it a real winner.

Whatever Lehrman and Fenwick had planned to fix up Braudy's piece would no longer do. A fresh approach was needed. When the women returned from lunch, Lehrman walked out into hall and was introduced. After an exchange of initial pleasantries—"I didn't know feminists wear pink," which made Braudy "grimly pleased about the pink mini-dress"—Lehrman ushered the woman into his office.

"I sat down with Susan," Lehrman remembers, "and explained to her that the basic problem was that she didn't know where she was. She had written a piece with two points of view. The changes we had proposed would make it internally consistent. But of course Hefner's memo had made that whole approach obsolete."

Braudy wrote in *Glamour* that Lehrman had read her article that morning and "written a few suggestions which he said pointed up the differences between the 'radical crazies and the moderates.' . . . Lehrman showed me his early corrections apologetically. 'It might have been so easy,' he said nervously. . . ."

"I said, Susan, here's the memo, and this is what we can do about it," Lehrman continued his story. "You can do what we ask and make the changes to conform, or you can give us the piece for the full price we promised to pay you, and we'll use it as research and give the assignment to someone else."

Braudy's reaction—as Lehrman remembers it—was to say she couldn't make up her mind, that she had to talk to her husband.

Next, he came up with a third alternative: *Playboy* would run her piece alongside another, giving the male side of the feminist controversy. Lehrman says Braudy asked for time to think the whole thing over. She ran into Goode, who was sympathetic but noncommittal. She talked to Fenwick about redoing her article. He, too, was sympathetic (and in her *Glamour* piece she treasured Fenwick's sympathy), but wondered whether she shouldn't go home and not redo it— perhaps as much because he didn't like it to begin with as for the embarrassed pity he felt for the troubled writer.

"Susan felt new and unsure of herself," Toba Cohen says. "She did not know how to deal with men used to having what they say done. She cried and was stubborn. She did all those things that make men say, 'Isn't that typical for a woman!' "

What she did by her own account was let Goode check her into a room at the Knickerbocker Hotel next door (now the Playboy Towers), call her husband, and then "cried out of self-pity, ordered a solitary dinner . . . took two tranquilizers and went to sleep."

The next morning, she and Lehrman again debated making the changes that would fit the piece to Hefner's new guidelines. She saw Fenwick and went over what had to be done, point by point. She took notes. To staffers who passed through the office assigned her, she made no secret of her unhappiness, confusion, despair. Some offered sympathy. She could not remember their names. And she could not decide whether to fish or cut bait.

Lehrman showed her a memo to Hefner proposing to run both her article and a male author's, under one headline. She grew more depressed. At 7:30 that night Fenwick left. She was alone. "Here I am and I am the enemy, I thought. They are so sure of my civilized sense of myself that they have left the enemy alone within the walls of their camp. I sat down at a typewriter and copied the two memos. Then I called the airport and fled," she wrote in *Glamour*.

Back home in Manhattan, Braudy vomited and slept for thirteen hours. The next morning, when Lehrman called, she refused to make the changes. *Playboy* paid her the agreed-upon $2,000.

Faced with a gaping hole in his schedule and mindful of Hefner's instructions, Lehrman got on the phone to *Playboy* regular Morton Hunt (author of *The World of the Formerly Married* and *Woman: Her Infinite Variety*) to discuss his writing a substitute article.

"Lehrman called, explained the Braudy situation, and asked if I could rapidly write a piece on what men and women's roles are in the world today, what is changing about them, and what is not," Hunt remembered some years later.

"Before I accepted the assignment, my agent wrote *Playboy*, saying that the conclusions would be my own. They said that was okay and told me I could use Braudy's material as research. I called her because I knew how badly she must feel. She was cordial and seemed to understand why I had been called in."

Hunt suggested a story line to Lehrman pegged on changing sex roles and a delineation of those differences between the sexes that can't be erased or altered. Lehrman liked it and Hunt set to work. Hunt admits to having seen parts of Hefner's memo and finding it "reasonable and rational. It did say the radical women were the enemy, but I saw nothing wrong in that. As for my piece, I was trying to state what the facts led to."

Both the time bind and Hefner's memo must have compounded Hunt's problem. He had to write fast, and, though he claims that did not influence him, to the specifications laid down in the memo. The result was "Up Against the Wall, Male Chauvinist Pig" (a title Hunt did not pick and says he would not have). It is a sometimes meandering but skillfully written piece—Hunt is no mean stylist—that first made the feminist case for equal pay and equal opportunity, then tried to trim off the radical wing and its excesses. As befits a major *Playboy* article, it was opinionated and packed with facts.

Hunt told readers to pay attention to the serious thrust of women's lib and not to what he felt were kooky demands like ROTC membership and karate classes. He called the movement "a major drive by American women, the Labor Department and the Equal Employment Opportunity Commission to give women an even break in the job market." And that he applauded; doing away with biological differences he did not.

"The fiery evangelists and raging nihilists of neofeminism want to wipe out all role differences—not just the socially prescribed but the psychobiologically determined as well."

And he concluded that such feminist extremists as Roxanne Dunbar and Ti-Grace Atkinson would surely end up "in the discard pile of history."

Predictably, Braudy's misadventures and Hunt's rescue expedition had repercussions within *Playboy* and in the media. A *Playboy* secretary was caught copying Hefner's memo and was fired. But she got it out anyway—to a Chicago paper. *Newsweek* picked up the story, asked Braudy for comment—she refused, she wasn't up to that yet—and dumped on Hunt's piece as being too long and too boring. A New York underground paper charged that Braudy had been pressed into a classic female mold—a researcher whose material men rewrite under their by-line. Gloria Steinem went on TV to protest.

Though friends told Braudy her experience was "pure gold," she let a year pass before putting it down on paper. She admits that the clash with Lehrman and her exposure to Hefner's wrath, however indirect, had traumatized her. But the article she wrote for *Glamour,* she says, was important for her development as a writer:

"In a sense it was the payoff for me. It allowed me to examine my own conflicts and I found I was interested in that kind of journalism. It embodied me as a woman and allowed me to write about myself as one. It gave me my first sense of using my own voice instead of the objective voice I had used in other pieces."

At *Playboy,* the furor produced a gratifying amount of mail, both pro and con, and fueled a debate on various feminist issues that raged into the mid-seventies before abating. Internally, it caused some soul-searching among the more perceptive senior editors and acted as a sparkplug for the growing discontent among women who worked on the magazine.

"I felt the feminist attitudes toward *Playboy* were wrong," Lehrman says, "because I think of ourselves as a humanist outfit and am in favor of ninety percent of the things feminism stands for. Hefner has always said the sexual revolution did more for women than for men. Men can always get laid. But women say we're doing that just to make it easier for ourselves. . . ."

Even Hefner had second thoughts about the Hunt piece. In response to a blistering memo from a female staffer—in-house dissent is always encouraged at *Playboy*—he wrote that "we would never suggest that a man who preferred bachelorhood to marriage was abnormal; why treat a woman any differently in this regard?

"Instead of listing alternative life styles—and attempting to weight the virtues of one over another—I think we should have concluded our article with the recommendation that a more truly free, humanistic, rational, society should offer both sexes a wider range of choices in establishing their identities as individuals. . . ."

As for specific positions *Playboy* should adopt toward the movement, opinions in the wake of the Braudy-Hunt caper were divided. "Some said, 'Let's recognize this as the wave of the future,' " Lehrman recalls, "but others felt that as long as libbers were treating us mindlessly and pushing us against the wall, we should not give in."

The division was reflected in articles and interviews published over the next few years, and endlessly in the letters and comment of Forum and Advisor.

Hefner's memo of January 6 was used as a guideline for developing an initial editorial position. In April 1970 Lehrman wrote a reply to a letter from a female reader who urged *Playboy* editors to "take a good look at what is happening with women and how it will affect national life." In it, he drew heavily on Hefner's thought and approach:

Though we are opposed to the destructive radicalism and the anti-sexuality of the extremist fringe . . . our position on women's rights . . . is as consistently liberal as our position on all human rights. We've been crusading for . . .

universal availability of contraceptives and birth-control information [and] for the repeal of . . . abortion laws; we believe a woman's right to control her own body is an essential step toward greater personal freedom. . . . We reject the Victorian double standard, which applauds sexual experience in men and condemns it in women. . . .

We are opposed to the traditional stereotype that relegates women to domestic drudgery. We believe that any woman who wants to shun the homemaker's role for a career, or who wants to combine both, should have the opportunity to implement that decision—recognizing, without inflexibility, that some occupations are better suited to most members of one sex than the other.

It should be needless to add that we believe women ought to be given equal pay for work of equal value. Although we clearly recognize that there are certain inequities in these areas, which are in obvious need of reform, we feel, nonetheless, that American women have never had more freedom of choice than they have today.

As for the "radical liberationists," no quarter was given:

"In our view, these 'Weatherwomen' are more anti-masculine than genuinely pro-feminine. We believe that many distinctions . . . help form the very basis for heterosexual attraction. This leads us to conclude that there should be distinct social roles for men and women in a society in which they complement one another rather than compete with one another."

It was a neat summation of *Playboy*'s difficulties: how to be for and against women's rights, how to pick those to support and those to oppose without sounding contradictory, how to keep abreast of the women's movement without being pushed into rigidly fixed positions.

Just how keenly editors were aware of the sensibilities involved was demonstrated in a heated debate that flared around the turn of 1971–72 over the March 1972 cover. It depicted a nude inside a wine bottle. Shel Wax and Murray Fisher, both assistant managing editors that year, were outraged. The cover, they argued, was the ultimate in showing women as objects. Both predicted heavy feminist flak if the cover were printed. They lost on both counts.

Wax, cool, consciously unflappable, careful, somewhat uptight, will say only, "There was a discussion, just a staff discussion about whether that particular artistic approach might be interpreted as turning women into objects. My feeling was that if we did something like that, it would be subject to misinterpretation by some feminists. We debated it. Discussions can get lively. We were in the minority and that was that. Anyway, I was wrong. There wasn't any big brouhaha over it." Maybe not. But clearly *Playboy* was growing more sensitive to the heat from "Up Against the Wall, Male Chauvinist Pig."

Gutwillig, who had blossomed into a commanding figure in the company by the early seventies, to the point where he was considered an heir apparent to Hefner, pushed hard for greater *Playboy* involvement in the feminist issue, and for a more positive approach. His reasons were pragmatic. He felt that *Playboy*'s readership was less sophisticated and more blue-collar than market research indicated. It needed guidance for coping with the new feminist phenomenon. *Playboy* should publish "how-to" articles on dealing with the new woman at every level, from the social to the sexual. If *Playboy* continued as the prime chauvinist symbol, the magazine risked loss of touch with the real world and isolation in the ghetto of skin magazines, where inevitably it would lose circulation and influence.

But Hefner and his editors were not willing to go that far. They continued to explore the subject and to write about it, with their ambivalence hanging out like shirttails. They supported abortion, sex education, equal rights, and job opportunities, and polemicized against the "crazies" out to eliminate sexual differences. More women were featured in roles other than that of sex objects. In 1971 alone, Mary McCarthy, Joyce Carol Oates, Janis Joplin, Joan Baez, and Virginia Johnson showed up in *Playboy*'s pages as writers or interview subjects. But as Gutwillig had foreseen, the cloak of male chauvinism remained glued on.

Playboy editors tried to rip it off by discussing the issues with feminists, but it wasn't easy. The women didn't want to play. After Kate Millet's *Sexual Politics* deepened the growing rift in the women's movement, *Playboy* decided to try for a panel discussion among leading feminists. Researcher Barbara Nellis (who has since risen to research supervisor and book editor) was told to moderate the panel and put it together. Excited by both the opportunity and the subject matter, she thought first of having this one be a real panel —e.g., have all the participants sit around a table rather than questioning each one separately and then weaving the answers into a "conversation."

"I went on the road," Nellis remembers, "and had lunch with Betty Friedan at The Ginger Man in New York. But it was no dice. She didn't want to air the movement's dirty linen in public, and not on a panel with other feminists. She wasn't even all that much against *Playboy*. She would have been happy to debate Hefner." (In her book, *It Changed My Life*, Friedan dismissed the overture in two sentences: "*Playboy* had asked me to do an article about the disagreements in ideology within the women's movement, but I refused. I offered instead to do a critique of Hugh Hefner and the Playboy

Bunny as sexual philosophy, but they didn't want that.")

"I went to Washington and tried to contact Ti-Grace Atkinson, but I couldn't get past her bodyguards." A request to Germaine Greer elicited "a semi-snippy post card, saying she didn't appear on panels, and certainly not in *Playboy.*" Efforts to contact spokeswomen from organizations as diverse as Redstocking and the National Organization of Women proved equally fruitless. The project was abandoned.

Three months later, Germaine Greer changed her mind about appearing in *Playboy,* but not about a panel. She agreed to an interview. Bearing the scars of feminist rejection and outrage, Lehrman set off for Tuscany where she had rented a farm. Soon he was tooling north of Rome in a rented Fiat to see what he could pry out of the author of *The Female Eunuch.* He returned, as Hefner would chuckle later, "quite smitten. Nat was really taken with her."

Small wonder. On one evening of their talks, she offered to pose in the buff for "an enormous amount of money . . . enough . . . so she could tell people she ripped off Hugh Hefner," or to pose for pictures of her fucking any one of a hundred men. She promised Lehrman a list but never delivered, perhaps because "we'd had too much to drink." On another night, she gave him dinner at the farm and "made it clear she wouldn't appreciate an offer to help clear the table," a gesture that made Lehrman all but delirious: "I hope my revealing this does not get her into trouble with the movement, which sometimes behaves as if the kitchen were its real battleground." (Which, of course, it was—one of them, anyway.)

In the interview, Greer belted *Playboy* with energetic gusto, pretty much ignoring Lehrman's technique of pointing to contradictions in what she was saying. She had attended a *Playboy* orgy in Amsterdam. Lehrman quickly interrupted that "It must have been some other company's orgy. We don't merchandise them," a remark Greer dismissed with a "says you." The girls at the orgy, Greer continued, "were blonde and long-legged and lovely. They had taken their clothes off . . . and you could see they'd never had any children, which is one of the essential characteristics of your Playmates. No signs of actual use of the body. . . . Your girls are so excessively young."

Then she settled into the specifics of her disapproval:

". . . it's not just the centerfold I disapprove of. It's all the other images of women in *Playboy.* Why, you even ran a shoe advertisement that showed an Indian squaw stroking some dude's damn shoes! And those *Playboy* parties are so awful. All those bleary faces and those haggard men and those pumped-up women in their see-through dresses, with everyone's nipples poking out and those fixed, glittering maniacal smiles. . . . They all give the illusion that fifty-year-old men are entitled to fuck fifteen-year-old girls . . . while fifty-year-old women are too repulsive to be seen with. . . . You display your girls as if they were a commodity. Sex ought not to be that. It ought to be a means of communicating between people."

Lehrman repeatedly tried to get the conversation off *Playboy*, but Greer would not let him:

"But it's important for me to talk about *Playboy* because I'm going to get shit for giving you an interview in the first place. It's got to be very clear with what kind of cynicism I do it."

Lehrman then asked the pivotal questions: "Why did you grant the interview? Other feminists won't come this close even to insult us!"

And Greer gave the answer that once again explains the Tantalus in *Playboy:* its vast and heterogeneous readership, and the chance to persuade and convert it. Like catnip or Chateaubriand and sauce béarnaise, the audience compensates for everything—presumably even the savaging *Playboy* receives at its critics' hands.

"I guess it's because you seem to be trying to go in a decent direction. Although I disapprove of the entire subliminal message in *Playboy*, your editorial matter is more liberal than that of other large-circulation magazines. And I probably feel that some people will read this interview and drop some of their more ridiculous notions about the women's movement."

That may have been an idle hope—though Greer eventually did settle down to a discussion of her brand of sexual politics and was given the space to do it properly—but did *Playboy* readers love her! Love her raunchy vocabulary, sexual liberties—"every man should be fucked up the arse"—even her cannonading of capitalism. A year later, Greer published a blistering attack on tolerance of rape, an article that foreshadowed *Against Our Will*, Susan Brownmiller's definitive 1975 book. Again she drew favorable response, even from Jill Johnston, the *Village Voice* columnist and lesbian proselytizer. Her letter, however, reflected continuing feminist schizophrenia about *Playboy:*

"I don't know why *Playboy* would encourage such an intelligent, enlightened and sophisticated view of rape and seduction in apparent contradiction to its own philosophy. I suppose your more yahoo readers might have gotten off vicarious jollies while perusing Greer's article, but in the process they were treated to a serious indictment of their sex. . . ."

But however split feminists may have been about the content of *Playboy*, their charity did not extend to Hefner himself. He remained the most blatant symbol of male oppression, and his public appearances did little to dispel that feeling. He went twice on the Dick Cavett show in the early seventies to square off against feminist spokeswomen, and gave a wooden and ineffective performance. He could not match the feminist barbs with his own, and he gave ground with obvious reluctance.

On one program, Cavett asked Susan Brownmiller to define sexual equality. "When Hugh Hefner comes out here with a cotton tail attached to his rear end, then we'll have equality." The audience roared. Hefner looked pained. Cavett devoted a subsequent show to the *Playboy*-feminist controversy, and, docilely, the editor-publisher came back to slug it out—courteous, opinionated, unflappably cool, and inexhaustible in his ability to take verbal punishment.

Nothing illustrated that ability as dramatically as a conversation with Gloria Steinem at the Chicago mansion in 1970 which was duly published in *McCall's*. Hefner remembers it as a relaxed and funny occasion, "a rather good-natured back-and-forth with a lot of joking. I didn't expect her to do what she did. I really felt I would get a fair shake because I have a rather high regard for Gloria. And what appeared in the magazine was only a sliver of what that evening was all about and not reflective of our conversation."

But what a sliver—more like a bear trap baited with cavalry lances! "What *Playboy* Doesn't Know About Women Could Fill a Book" the title proclaims in thick black letters, next to a demurely smiling picture of la Steinem ready to close the trapdoor. She began with an anecdote about a playwright mansion guest who is asked whether he wants a girl, and when he says yes, is sent one. He was still making her a drink when the phone rang and an excited *Playboy* executive asked, "How was it? How was it?"

(Originally, Hefner says, that story was told around New York by Gloria, "and I learned later that the playwright was Jules Feiffer and the executive was me—and it is of course complete fantasy. When Jules confronted her with that fact, she changed it to anonymous people. Gloria knew it was untrue and put it in the introduction, anyway.")

". . . the anecdote is a parable of all that is boyish, undeveloped, antisensual, vicarious and sad about the *Playboy* phenomenon," Steinem wrote in her introduction to excerpts from the conversation. For the next thousand or so vitriolic words, Steinem devastated *Playboy*'s commercialism, its buy-for-status philosophy, the attitude that women are "like a prize for collected Green Stamps," the lack of joy in the empire. "Today the young know better. A lot of them reject the idea of middle-class status-buying . . ."

She moved into the mansion next, sniffed the chlorine around the pool, and compared the swimming grotto to the YMCA, knocked

Hefner's casual clothes—when Steinem's around, God help any poor bastard who doesn't wear his jeans and Dunhill pinstripes with the slim-hipped panache of a Michael Korda—his penchant for big words, and his coltish eagerness to write down the names of writers he did not know.

When they sat down to talk, Steinem wanted to discuss politics, social issues, women's rights, *Playboy*'s consumerist philosophy. She chastised Hefner for his lack of social involvement, scolded him for not knowing Saul Alinsky, a Black Panther or Mayor Daley, for not remembering whether he had contributed to the campaigns of Jack and Robert Kennedy. Hefner ambled through his 1968 escapade with Chicago police, said the incident hadn't raised his social consciousness much, and that he still believed in the same basic things.

"People are getting killed in the streets, in Vietnam, and you're fighting the Post Office," Steinem told him, and warned him later that "you may be the first magazine editor to be killed in a socialist revolution."

Nor did things go much better when they talked about feminism. Hefner hadn't changed his mind about the "crazies"—he was still quoting from his memo on the Braudy article. "Women shouldn't be wasting time on this foolishness"; there were other, more important problems around. He had never talked to leaders of the movement, but kicked one out of a mansion party after she stuck anti-*Playboy* stickers on the walls and on "one of my paintings." Women, he argued, "have all the opportunities that are really important to their human potential. . . . I think the militant feminists really want to be men."

Steinem shot back statistics, facts, names, numbers in a point-by-point rebuttal of Hefner's comment. "Now we want to celebrate blackness, womanhood, and make it our own way."

"I still think the militant feminists are pathetic," Hefner replied. "There's no comparison with the racial problem because racial differences don't matter and biological ones do."

"They matter for nine months if one choses to have children. . . . You've made women objects. . . . It's like being on a meat hook. . . . There are times when a woman reading *Playboy* feels a little like a Jew reading a Nazi manual. . . . You sound a little like a good-hearted plantation owner who's deeply hurt when his childlike slaves start rebelling."

Like a wounded bull, Hefner kept coming back for more—and got it. Finally, when Steinem asked him if there was anyone in history he really identified with, Hefner shot back: "Jack the Ripper." But even that didn't flap the unflappable Steinem. She calmly asked why, and Hefner admitted that he wanted to be as outrageous as she had been in accusing him of Nazism. In print, it wasn't even a standoff. Steinem had annihilated him, more savagely, perhaps, than anyone since Benjamin De Mott.

Nor did the feminists ease up. In 1971 the Playboy Foundation, which does not support institutions but causes, wrote to NOW's legal committee asking if it were involved in cases to which *Playboy* could give financial support. The initial response was a letter requesting the profits of one night's operation of all Playboy Clubs before the fifty-first anniversary of women's suffrage.

Playboy charged that this was "crude extortion" but wasn't much happier with a more formal communication stating that no amount of money "would compensate for the low rating of the source. We hold the Playboy Club and all it stands for in such contempt, that to accept money from the foundation bearing the same name would only contaminate us."

Yet the Playboy Foundation would not be deterred. It had contributed funds to the proabortion battle since 1966, and has helped fund an impressive list of causes and organizations since then:

—The Association for the Study of Abortion

—The Illinois Committee for Medical Control of Abortion, a group active in changing antiabortion laws, until the Supreme Court acted

—The Clergy Consultation Service on Problems of Pregnancy, a referral service for women in the Chicago area

—NARAL; the National Association for the Repeal of Abortion Laws

—The Texas Citizens for Abortion Education, which took the case that finally overturned the abortion ban to the High Court. *Playboy* also helped finance the amicus curia brief in the case prepared by Professor Cyril Means

—The League of Women Voters

—Three day-care center projects, two of them national, one in Chicago

—The National Women's Project of the American Civil Liberties Union

—A research project for chemical abortion techniques

—An IUD project

—The Citizens Committee for Victims of Rape, a Chicago group

—The National Conference of Woman and the Law

There are half a dozen others, including down-the-line support for the Equal Rights Amendment, support that over the years blunted some of NOW's hostility. But the *Playboy*-feminist truce is an uneasy one, at best. Some now concede it a good side as well as a bad. Others allow *Playboy* no redeeming social value whatsoever.

Susan Brownmiller, for example, considers *Playboy*'s financial contributions to women's causes as "hush money," and says flatly, "Hugh Hefner is one of our enemies. I believed that when I was on the Cavett show with him, and I believe it now." She argues that Hefner opened the door to hard-core porn. Centerfolds and snuff movies are linked. *Playboy*'s contribution to sex has been "a lot of misery." Liberal men who write for the magazine are contaminated.

"I remember a time when writers were embarrassed to be in *Playboy.* It was just not a place to be published. You have to be particular about whom you sleep with and whom you write for. We are soiled by handling it. You go from stereo to naked women in a straight line. Women are something for men with a couple of bucks to acquire. When I see *Playboy* in the home of a man I know shouldn't have it, I see it as something from a foreign culture, as if I've caught him at something that's not quite on the up-and-up. *Playboy* is a world without women except for twenty-year-olds with big breasts.

"Women have to be perceived as creatures without minds. They never had Frances Fitzgerald or Gloria Emerson writing about Vietnam, now, did they? (Emerson has.) Does Emma Rothchild write for them? Of course not. It would fight their own editorial content. The feminist message in *Playboy* would be distorted. Any woman speaking through the vehicle of *Playboy* is taking her clothes off in a frat house on Saturday night. The confusion of the women's movement with sexual lib was bad enough, and any appearance in *Playboy* enhances that confusion. That audience is just looking for beaver shots. I know they take surveys that content is read, but I don't believe it for a minute."

Betty Friedan has relented to the point of giving the same Barbara Nellis a "mini" interview for the magazine's up-front section to coincide with publication of *It Changed My Life,* but she can still turn her not-inconsiderable polemical talent on *Playboy*'s "distorted" view of sex and society, and singe Hefner's hair doing it.

For all the feminist controversy, however, Hefner has a valid point when he says, "I think that by and large *Playboy* is a good place for women to work." And he is not talking about bunnies. Copy chief Arlene Bouras has been with the magazine for twenty years. Gretchen McNeese is a senior editor (*Newsweek* has only one, too). Mary Ann Stuart heads up the book division. Michelle Urry doubles as cartoon editor for *Playboy* and *Oui* and as head of the product-licensing division. Both women are corporate vice-presidents; so is Marilyn R. Smith, who is in charge of merchandising the clubs. Hefner's daughter Christie is also a vice-president, and while her name helped get the corporate stripes earlier than if it were, say,

Papadopoulos, she would have landed a top job even as Miss Papadopoulos.

This is not to suggest that life for women was easy at *Playboy* or that advancement came automatically. But talk to a few who have made it at PEI, and their story is not very different than those of women on magazines from *Business Week* to *Time*. The transition may have been hardest for Mrs. McNeese. She learned to write on newspapers on the West Coast and in Puerto Rico, and, traditionally, women were treated more as equals in the newspaper business than in other branches of communications—at least once they had become reporters and broken out of the women's-page ghetto.

She had then married a doctor, brought up a couple of kids, was divorced, and returned to work on *VIP*, Hefner's club magazine. Murray Fisher rescued her and put her on *Playboy* because "she was a writing machine" and had a special talent for turning a tart and pithy phrase. She has conducted several major interviews including a tough and incisive one with Erica Jong in September 1975 that did what Gutwillig had advocated three or four years earlier: explain the liberated woman to men fearful of her sex and drive. McNeese had to fight to get and keep the assignment, but she won. And it is perhaps a measure of *Playboy* under Kretchmer that she can hew to her own conventional, home-oriented life-style without too much flak from other staffers. She found the problems of making it at *Playboy* difficult and perhaps compounded by the magazine's attitude toward women. But at least she was never told by a male editor that he felt uncomfortable working with a female writer, something that happened in the late sixties to the then lone woman on a news magazine, who was transferred out of the editor's sections and subsequently left.

Toba Cohen did not have McNeese's professional credentials. She had come to *Playboy* from a proabortion lobbying job in Illinois, where she had first met Lehrman and others at the Playboy Foundation. She started as a researcher, but within a year had worked herself into a writing editor's job (in the late sixties, an all-but-impossible feat at the news magazines).

"I worked in the front of the book, known as Nat's magazine. And Nat played by different rules. He allowed his people more freedom. But for a woman, he was difficult to work with. He claims to have had his consciousness raised, and he doesn't understand why women can't work with him. Many men in their forties find it difficult to make that connection. I still feel cowed by him. Ours was an avuncular relationship. I was new in the business, and you are always treated as the kid you were when you started."

But Forum was into a broad range of issues, from opposition of capital punishment to support of abortion on demand. "That gets into women's rights and then very quickly into equal rights. I became the women's-rights representative, the token everything. And I had a lot of input. We were saying things not said anywhere else. Nat ran the Playboy Foundation, and he was giving money to causes like abortion and day-care centers. A lot of good was coming out of this magazine. And I was being treated very well."

On balance, Cohen felt, the opportunities made up for the disadvantages, the fighting to get her husband's name on mansion party lists (and then not attending), the lack of advancement, the putdowns. "They were letting me play."

In the sixties, few women were allowed to do that much, not at *Playboy* and not at most other mass-circulation magazines. When they were put behind a typewriter, it was more accident than design. Julia Trelease's *Playboy* career was not untypical. She had started out as a secretary with a knack for picking talented bosses—Goode, Lehrman, and Fisher.

"I guess it was around 1968 when I was working for Fisher and going through a divorce. I had been screening the 'After Hours' items and writing some of them, and I also submitted party jokes— we all did—and some of those had been printed. One day Mike Laurence came over and told me, 'I hear you want to be a writer.' "

A memo had come from on high suggesting more in-house promotion rather than outside hiring. Barbara Smith, Spectorsky's then secretary, had gone for drinks with Laurence, and, Trelease remembers, "told him the memo was a crock of shit. There's a lot of talent around here, and if they're serious, they should talk to Julia."

Laurence pulled Trelease into his office, showed her the layout for a Playmate feature, gave her the available information on the girl and her phone number, and told her to see what she could do. "So I took the material home, wrote it up, and brought it back. Mike liked it and took it to Murray and said, 'Guess who wrote this?' " Fisher sighed that it must be Julia, and the two editors cleared her promotion first to editorial assistant and then to assistant editor with an office of her own.

But Kessie stood between her and the masthead. He was nervous about "lady editors." Could she go up as J. Bainbridge (her name then)? When she refused, Fisher and Laurence went over Kessie's head to get approval for the "Julia." In her *Glamour* article, Susan Braudy used the story as an example of male chauvinism in action. "When she insisted that she be on as Julia it was done. But nobody had enough nerve to point it out to 'Hef' and maybe he never noticed." Maybe if he never read the masthead. By 1972 there were four women editors named on it, and half a dozen others in various administrative and editorial positions.

Trelease found her stay at *Playboy* pleasant and uneventful. The pay was good. She was glad for an opportunity she had not sought. Discrimination was slight; nothing that she couldn't handle. "It was tough, but not that tough. Sometimes at meetings I noticed the men wondered about how much rough language I could take, and occasionally someone would say, 'Julia, why don't you take notes?' But I just said, 'Why don't you?' and that was that."

Bobbie Arnstein told her she could not bring dates to mansion parties, as she had told other *Playboy* women, and like the others, Trelease fought and won. "Murray got angry and started shouting at Bobbie and threatening to go to Hefner, so Bobbie said that wouldn't be necessary. 'I will add her husband's name to the list.' "

But the pioneer who carved out the most spectacular female career at *Playboy* was a young Canadian, now named Michelle Urry. She took a design degree at Berkeley and worked for a while in a Los Angeles architect's office. On her way to New York to live, she stopped off in Chicago and fell in with a chic Near North Side crowd that clearly delighted in the dark-haired, sharp-tongued, loose-hipped, good-looking girl. She liked the city, the Mies van der Rohe houses on Lake Short drive, the wide, tree-lined streets. When somebody suggested she try for a job at *Playboy,* she jumped.

But when she applied for an editorial position in 1964, she was told there were none for a man—let alone for a woman. She took the battery of tests the company required, anyway, and was told that "I seemed to be bright and that I made no mistakes in grammar. They even called the architect in L.A. I had given as a reference—and offered me a job as a receptionist." When she refused indignantly, *Playboy* suggested a post in the bunny department to answer letters from would-be cottontails.

"I took that, and for three months I wrote replies to letters from girls who asked what they should do—they had a twenty-nine-inch bust and wanted. . . . I told them to stay put until they had blossomed. Then I started photostating the letters because I wanted to do a book."

Instead, a job opened up at the mansion as a girl Friday; it mainly involved being nice to people. "I was dying to see what the mansion was like. I had access to Hefner's files and began copying them, but needless to say, loyalty overtook me and I stopped. . . . One day Hefner said, 'I need a new assistant. Mine's quit. I'll give it to that girl—I don't remember her name—the one with the good sense of humor.' "

A comic-book fan since childhood, Urry had a good sense of

design, a sharp and bawdy wit to add to Hefner's own—and a shared passion for cartoons. Soon she was helping Hefner pick cartoons for the magazine. He offered her an apartment in the mansion "with no strings attached—you're fun to have around." She accepted. "It was heaven. I had outside friends. Bobbie and I were the only ones allowed to date and bring men into the place (Mansion bunnies were not). I could take a steam bath and had access to the Sunday movies."

Access, however, cut two ways. Hefner kept her up working into the wee hours. The night before she married her first husband, Hefner worked her till dawn so that cartoons would be up-to-date for the six weeks she would be away. Two years into the job, she made the masthead, and, shielded by her ties to Hefner, slugged toe-to-toe with male editors. "People were afraid to tangle with me. Most women at *Playboy* didn't fight back. For those who did, there was room to move up. Intention was three-fourths of it. Women with gumption got ahead."

By the early seventies, Urry felt uneasy with her charmed *Playboy* life and approached a half dozen other women in semimanagerial slots to see if they couldn't figure out new approaches to upgrade women's jobs—a kind of delayed consciousness-raising group. She encountered suspicion and mistrust. "Why would you want to help us?" one woman editor asked. "You have it made." Despite the hostility, the women attended a few meetings and then dropped out —to continue behind Michelle Urry's back. One of those who did, Mary Ann Stuart, rose to head *Playboy*'s book division.

A short time later, Urry left Chicago and settled in New York, flying out to California a couple of times a month to discuss cartoons with Hefner and to show him what she has selected for his approval. "I have total freedom in that I bring him what I like. And occasionally he will buy something for me because I want it."

For all Urry's success, it has not been an easy life. For a woman, the *Playboy* stamp can be a mark of Cain, saddling her with the *Playboy* mystique everywhere. At parties she would be asked what she did and then plied with questions about how she had gotten where she was. Women always asked if she were a bunny, wanted to be one, or how to become one. Few people believed she was an editor. But as feminine militancy mounted, interest and curiosity gave way to hostility and condemnation—especially in L.A., Chicago, and New York. "In New York, I am regarded with suspicion at best. I still get a lot of 'How could you work for that ghastly magazine?' "

But Urry is a vice-president now. Derick Daniels, the PEI president, adores her, admires her taste and style, and pins great hopes on her ability to upgrade the quality of Playboy products. Daniels does not share Hefner's distrust of the "crazies." All revolutions need them. "Revolutions are not led by gentle, pretty, reasonable people. Leaders are tough and sometimes unreasonable. It's too easy for men who chose to write the whole thing off because of their physical appearance or their ravings." Daniels thinks feminism has been good for society and has not hurt *Playboy* any.

For executive editor Barry Golson, feminism is one of the givens of his adult life, not an issue that needs much examination or rumination. In July 1976 he wrote a breezy piece titled "So You Want to Be a Sex Object" that dissected women's sexual oglings with good humor and good nature. Male behinds and craggy features, he found, topped the list of desirable traits.

Hefner isn't really convinced. He is loath to give up the position he enunciated in his 1970 memo. He likes old crusades. Besides, he thinks there are a "couple of other priorities" in society now and sees "no need for major efforts to help downtrodden women." Feminism has faded as an issue for *Playboy* magazine, too, as it has most other places. But bright girls coming out of Smith or Sarah Lawrence hoping for a publishing career could do worse than *Playboy*. They might even stay out of the typing pool that surely awaits them at Doubleday or Harper & Row. Women who have won a niche at PEI tend, by and large, to be nicer, less aggressive, and not as sharp-tongued as their New York–bound sisters. And if men still dominate the top job at the women's magazines, why shouldn't women move into the men's books—even women who aren't linked to the publishers? *Cosmopolitan* reserves the managing editor's slot for a man. Maybe *Playboy* should set aside a similar position for a woman. Maybe when Christie Hefner takes over the company, it will.

11

The Business of Pleasure

ON November 12, 1971, Loeb, Rhoades & Co., one of Wall Street's most prestigious firms, put on sale on the New York Stock Exchange 1,158,812 shares in Playboy Enterprises Inc., and thus opened Hugh Hefner's "very personal type of company" to public scrutiny. The opening price was $23.50 a share and investors snapped up the stock quickly. Loeb, Rhoades had put together a gilt-edged list of underwriters that had on it some of the biggest names on the Street: E. F. Hutton, Paribas Corporation, Lazard Frères, Walston & Co., and L. F. Rothschild & Co., which together bought a million shares for their customers. The rest went to individuals who often bought only a single share. In fact, PEI sold a record number of singles. Clearly, many people were more interested in the piece of paper with a reclining nude on it than in prospects of financial gain.

Hefner, his family, and his friends all profited handsomely, both on paper and in real terms. Hefner owned 80 percent of the stock; the rest was scattered among some fifty shareholders, including a man who had taken stock for a writing fee in 1954. It was his most lucrative sale ever, and it made him rich. Hefner sold 300,000 shares, adding $7 million to his personal wealth while reducing his stockholdings only 8 percent—to 72 percent. His father sold 100,000 shares, banking $2.3 million. Arthur Paul, with 3.2 percent, or 280,-350 shares, the second-largest single stockholder, sold 70,000 shares, realizing better than $1.7 million. Preuss sold 20,000 shares and netted more than $450,000.

"Why did we go public?" Hefner mused in 1977 when he thought it was the "least likely thing" he should have done, "the wrong thing" for *Playboy.* "It was the era of the conglomerate, the era of 'you can't get the kind of executive talent you need unless you can offer them stock options.' The big-is-better syndrome played a role, too. So did the idea that you can't expand properly unless you can make a stock offering, and the only way to do it is to go public. I was sold on it by the business people inside the company who had a very bullish attitude. It was only a matter of how far up the market would go. In no way was it gravity-related. No one thought that what comes up can come down, too."

Business manager Bob Preuss thought growth and diversification would be easier "that way" and allow "us to grow up as a company. And it would help Detroit look on us better. (The Big Three auto makers have always been leery of *Playboy.* Ford and Chrysler advertise sporadically in the magazine, but General Motors never has, despite years of persistent *Playboy* efforts.) The ramifications were all-encompassing. We wanted the image of the New York Stock Exchange. Hell, we only sold 1.2 million shares. Half was Hefner's stock; half went into the company. We didn't need the money at the time, but we might need $25 million someday, and with a small amount of stock in public hands, you get people watching."

Preuss and Hefner's father, Glenn, the company's treasurer, prepared the ground carefully. They wanted a prestigious image much more than a quick buck. Some firms turned them down—Playboy remained too brash for the starchier investment houses—but "others looked on it as a good risk. We picked Loeb-Rhoades because of its stability, name and reputation, which were good. They were, too. They produced a good issue."

The explanations are on the lame side. In truth, Playboy went public in order to keep up with its incredible expansion in the sixties and to find a more orderly way of handling its cash flow. The decision was untouched by the go-go mentality that infected Wall Street during the overheated boom years. Hefner is a fiscally conservative man who distrusts banks and borrowed money. His company would have been the perfect target for any of the Wall Street sharks eager to swallow so cash-rich a corporation. But there was no way anybody could crack a firm that was so closely held, and one, moreover, that owed so little.

It was typical, therefore, that Playboy decided to go public before the full shock of the first Nixon recession in 1969–70 had worn off. Unlike most other publishing enterprises, Playboy was not touched by the recession. Sales and profits surged while other communications businesses cut back and laid off. The insulation may well have clouded in-house judgment. And Wall Street enthusiasm must have removed any lingering doubts. Despite Playboy's salacious image, which would hurt the company later, there were not many privately held companies coming fresh on the market anymore. And many speculators on Wall Street welcomed the arrival of so fat and delectable a fish.

Privately held or not, Playboy's corporate performance in the sixties easily matched—and even surpassed—that of the bounciest go-go stock. And that performance blinded everybody to the basic corporate flaw: Playboy hit the big leagues and grew within reach of the Fortune 500 with what was basically a small company's management team.

In the early fifties, Hefner managed his own business with a little help from his accountant father and, later, from Robert Preuss, his University of Illinois roommate who owned a Certified Public Accountant firm. There wasn't all that much to manage. Hefner ended his first year in business with sales of $268,380 and a net loss of $23,482, largely in unpaid bills. In 1955 sales had climbed to over $1 million and earnings to $65,000. Three years later, sales hit $4.2 million, advertising revenues totaled $730,000, and earnings topped $90,000. Three years after that, in 1961, sales had doubled to $8.6 million, with ad revenues bringing in $3 million with profits of $108,000. Gratifying growth, certainly, and much more spectacular than anything Hefner had hoped for when he began, but still manageable for an accountant of Preuss's shrewdness and ability.

Besides, setbacks were few and easily digested. In 1957 Hefner dropped $95,000 on a short-lived humor magazine named *Trump* and had, as he puts it, "a very rough go" for two or three months because the American News Company went under at the same time and that "caused chaos in all newsstand publications." Hefner stopped paying himself a salary and cut staff, but the crisis passed quickly. What annoyed him most—and influenced his fiscal thinking deeply—was his bank's refusal to grant him a $250,000 tide-over loan.

The same thing happened in the wake of the *SBI* debacle, which cost Playboy $3 million, almost the book value of the company. Again a bank refused to extend a loan. But the clubs were making enough money that year to cushion the blow. Still, the snub reinforced Hefner's careful and cautious approach to handling money.

In the sixties, however, everything turned dizzy. Sales in 1962 totaled $18 million, more than double the previous year, large enough to allow the company to write off the *SBI* losses and end the year with a modest $84,000 in red ink. Four years later, in 1966, gross sales topped $62 million; net earnings were $4.7 million. Advertisers bought 712 pages at an average cost of $20,000 a page and ad revenues totaled $12 million.

By 1969 all that was chicken feed. Sales crossed $100 million, and net earnings amounted to $7.5 million. In seven years sales had risen more than fivefold, and pretax earnings had leaped from $2.5 million to $16.4 million. Advertisers were clamoring to buy space. Hotels and clubs were coining money. Lownes's British gambling operations were becoming a cash gusher. Expansion into book publishing, films, and records beckoned. *Business Week* confirmed the surge in June with a laudatory story of *Playboy*'s growing acceptance on Madison Avenue, and on its editorial formula "that suits the young man of today."

In 1971 the stock-offering prospectus gave the picture of an even sturdier company—healthy, growing, with relatively small debts, large assets, surging earnings, and a hefty cash reserve. It owned seventeen clubs—and Lownes was buying a second casino club in Manchester—one downtown hotel, three resort hotels (and was busily building a fourth, Great Gorge), 275 undeveloped acres on Spain's Costa del Sol, film, book, record and music-publishing divisions, a modeling agency, two movie theaters, a limousine service, a college-marketing firm, and a line of Playboy products—everything from martini pitchers and playing cards to T-shirts and tote bags.

But the prospectus also hoisted a couple of storm signals, warnings that it might not all be smooth sailing. It noted that almost $4 million was tied up in the production of two films, *Macbeth* and *The Naked Ape,* and there was no guarantee of return on investment. Hotel losses were mounting. The Miami Plaza had dropped $1.9 million in the first year PEI owned it; the Playboy Towers in Chicago, $400,000 in seven months. Almost $3 million had gone into renovating the two hotels. Further losses were anticipated, "substantial" ones after Great Gorge opened. Records and books had dropped $750,000.

But optimism predominated and seemed more than justified by the corporate balance sheets for PEI's first year of operations as a public company. Results for the fiscal year that ended June 30, 1972 were nothing short of spectacular. Sales were close to $160 million, with net earnings of $10.6 million. Per-share earnings were up 9¢ to $1.16. Hefner's personal DC-9 was valued at $5.8 million, land at $5.7 million. Cash reserves totaled $4 million.

A new magazine, *Oui,* devoted to a more sophisticated "European" outlook on sexuality and life-style, and aimed at a younger market than *Playboy,* went on sale in September with an unheard-of initial press run of 800,000—and commitments for 185 pages of advertising worth $800,000. A German edition of *Playboy* had been published in August with an initial print run of 350,000. An Italian edition was due to go on sale later in the fall, a French one in the spring of 1973, and exploratory talks were underway in Japan. *Play-*

boy was setting new advertising revenue records month after month. November had racked up $4.5 million, December $5 million, and the year-end issue had topped September's 7 million circulation figures with 7.2 million.

However, there was some red ink. Hotels topped 1971 losses of $1.7 million, dropping $2.1 million. The fledgling film division lost $299,000 (and Preuss knew already that losses would mount higher despite a confident speech he gave to security analysts earlier that year about Playboy's bright future in films). Records dropped $150,000; other businesses nearly a million. The U.S. clubs began to show unmistakable signs of floundering, but British gambling profits more than covered the deficits. Moreover, some clubs were moving out of decaying urban centers, while new management was taking over the club-hotel division.

If there was one really disturbing sign in a basically healthy corporate record, it was the erratic behavior of the stock. Initial investor reaction had been buoyant. In early 1972, the stock hit its all-time high of $25.50 a share. But then it began to stumble and touched as low as 14 and a fraction before recovering, and, for a time in 1973, trading as high as 19. There seemed to be little reason for the stock fluctuations—at least not for the first two years after its listing. In February 1973, *Forbes* ran a puzzled piece about the decline, noting that corporate performance could not be blamed—not with a return on equity of 24 percent and an operating margin of better than 16 percent. But investors were embarrassed about owning Playboy stock, and there was public reluctance to buy it. Reuters ran a story on its financial wire about the same time that talked of psychological barriers. "Institutions with very visible portfolios, such as banks and pension funds, stay away from Playboy stock because of the type of magazines and clubs it has."

But a year earlier, in May 1972, Lawrence Rice, then a security analyst with du Pont, Glore Forgan, Inc., had sent out a purchase recommendation which laid out Playboy's problems and opportunities more neatly than that. Competitors like *Penthouse,* he wrote, were hurting, but Playboy was doing something about it "through greater market penetration and the tapping of new markets." Playboy's second major problem, Rice noted, "is an image problem, which management is resolving through greater corporate exposure and, more importantly, through demonstrated earnings growth." Rice recommended the stock for those willing to take modest risks, and predicted satisfactory future growth.

But Rice had speared the salient points and done so at a time when action could still be taken to correct the problems. Playboy had to meet the competition and offer Wall Street a better corporate image.

In fact, it did neither. *Oui* proved too feeble to stop *Penthouse,* and PEI did little to court the financial community beyond inviting a group of analysts—including Rice—to meet with Hefner in the fall of 1972. The interview was duly published in PEI's 1972 annual report. But little sustained effort was expended on bolstering stockholder relations. Perhaps no one saw the need, though Robert Gutwillig, the marketing vice-president, told Lownes in 1973 to sell his stock when it was trading at 15, and was thought treacherous and demented for doing so.

Certainly corporate performance for fiscal 1973 gave no immediate cause for alarm. Sales surged an incredible $30 million to $190 million; net earnings were up $650,000 to $11.25 million. Per-share earnings were up from $1.16 to $1.20. Net working capital was $18.2 million, and net worth passed $76.9 million.

But through the more narrowly focused lenses of hindsight, trouble—big trouble—is easy to spot: movies lost $2.5 million (*Macbeth* bore out the gloomiest Wall Street forecasts; it was a financial disaster), records and music publishing dropped $2 million, hotels nearly $3.5 million, up substantially from the previous years. *Oui* added nearly a million to profits; so did Lownes's second London casino, the Clermont Club. *Oui*'s profitable year would prove a fluke; Clermont's earning power the corporate lifeline, given, even in 1973, slower growth of sales and profits, the 300,000 circulation loss *Playboy* suffered in the first six months of calendar 1973, and the decline in advertising pages (though not in income, thanks to higher rates). Most important, perhaps, only *Playboy* magazine and the British gambling operations were solidly profitable.

The business press began to look at Playboy's deficiencies in early 1974, a few months after publication of PEI's 1973 annual report. In February the respected *Dun's Review* decided to "take a measure of Playboy's management." The up-front introduction summed up the problem as Dun's saw it: "In its 21st year, Playboy is experiencing some serious growing pains. Its magazines are running into stiff competition from even brasher imitators. Its resort hotels are something less than booked solid. Even its fabled key clubs . . . are being put down . . . as passé." But as the subhead to Lee Smith's article made clear, Playboy's troubles still seemed manageable. "Despite all the bad news emanating from the mansion these days, the bunny at twenty may finally be growing up."

Smith pointed to all the warts: the money-losing film, record, and hotel divisions, the money—much of it borrowed and for the first time—that had gone into building Great Gorge whose occupancy rate was still far from the 60 percent breakeven point, the sliding circulation of the flagship magazine.

"On recent performance, then, the record of Playboy at twenty seems one of careless squandering that promises a dismal future," Smith wrote. "Yet there is evidence that PEI has finally put its adolescent ways behind it and begun to grow up." Smith cited the hiring of "profit-conscious" executives who were trying to straighten operations out and "make some important changes that may well get the company moving again." He was particularly impressed with marketing head Gutwillig's innovative ways that had given PEI a growing book club with 150,000 members, and *Oui* magazine, which showed signs of turning into a solid money-maker. And Smith thought club-hotel chief Paul Kilborn had the needed savvy to turn that losing operation around.

But some barriers threatened to defy executive talent. Though *Playboy* lagged behind some of its lustier competitors, it was still too racy for institutional advertisers. "Most banks, mutual funds and, with one exception, insurance companies balk at advertising in the magazine." Nor did the raunch *Playboy* displayed—and it was growing—ease distribution at a time when the number of big-city newsstands was shrinking. Supermarkets and convenience stores were natural substitutes, but how much sexual explicitness could the checkout counter stand? As evidence for corporate drift, Smith also cited Hefner's refusal to grant an interview (there had been a foul-up, it was a mistake, executives said later) and his failure to show up at the annual stockholders' meeting (Hefner was sick, his minions said).

The criticism stung. Countermeasures were needed. Hefner was pushed front-and-center where the financial community could not miss him—in the business pages of *The New York Times.* On March 11, 1974, the *Times* ran a feature story on Hefner, his mansion, his empire, and his bunny logo. The headline was encouraging: "Hefner Sees Bright Future for Playboy Empire Despite Critics."

But little in the story backed up that claim. It was merely one more Hefner interview in which he described his life-style and how he had achieved fame and success with *Playboy.* He was "the right guy in the right place at the right time" to take advantage of changing attitudes. About the only business news was a list of advertisers that ranged from seventeen for liquor and fourteen for audiovisual equipment to three each for condoms and satin sheets. Nothing there to interest security analysts or bolster institutional confidence. If anything, it reinforced the belief that Hefner was disinterested in business and that his company was badly managed. That view had long been reflected on Wall Street, and long before the facts warranted it. The stock slide showed no signs of ending. When the *Times* story appeared, PEI was selling around $5.

A month later, when *Business Week* picked up the story, it was already bleaker. The first signs of corporate dissensions had begun to surface. Robert Gutwillig's meteoric career—he had zipped from heading up a nonexistent book division to marketing vice-president in less than five years—was derailed, and he was shunted aside, as vice-president for corporate planning. Days later, Paul Kilborn resigned.

"At the heart of PEI's troubles is a basic marketing failure," *Business Week* noted. The company had failed to transfer *Playboy*'s magic from the magazine to its other products. "While parts of the Playboy empire are prospering, most of them are piling up bigger losses each year," *Business Week* said and cited the same problem list *Dun's Review* had: Hotels and clubs were losing money. Movies were a disaster. Records stalled. Magazine circulation was down.

There were grudging admissions from management. One executive said the hotels suffered from "mismanagement and inadequate marketing expertise." Chief operating officer Robert Preuss conceded that "we got caught up in our own growth. Instead of looking for more executives we took on more roles for ourselves." But he bristled at criticism. "We are not being allowed to make the same mistakes that other companies make as they expand."

Yet some of the toughest language came from in-house, from the sliding Gutwillig, and from Robert Adelman, a Chicago real estate tycoon and member of Playboy's board. Adelman blamed Hefner. "He listens to what people tell him and is very polite about it. But he doesn't always follow up. Hefner runs that company on impulse and ego." Gutwillig thought "inconsistent marketing" was at fault. "If we are selling an image, then we should be in projects where we can tie in all aspects of our businesses. The magazine, movies, the clubs should all have something in them that overlaps." Too often, Gutwillig noted, only the Playboy logo did.

Business Week's conclusions were succinct: ". . . whether PEI will be able to solve its problems depends on its ability to recognize that its marketing must be more than a reliance on a rabbit-head symbol and faith in a certain life-style." And it quoted an approving senior vice-president Dick Rosenzweig as saying: "We've started to understand that. Now we are digesting it."

Perhaps. But digestion was slow. Few at Playboy thought the company was in real trouble or that much needed to be done about its current status. Executive turnover had quickened as Preuss and Gutwillig went repeatedly to headhunters for new talent. But more often than not, they turned up bummers. Top flight people did not break down Playboy's doors, and the company found it difficult to attract competent personnel.

Trouble of a different sort surfaced in late March—trouble that had seethed for months, and that would, before it was finally dissipated, end in tragedy, and plunge Playboy into trauma and crisis. Agents of the Federal Drug Enforcement Agency (DEA) had been watching Hefner's executive secretary Bobbie Arnstein for many months. She was under suspicion on a drug rap, specifically transporting and trying to distribute a half pound of cocaine. The narcs had grabbed a Miami dealer from whom she allegedly obtained the drug; he had turned state's evidence and implicated the girl. An indictment with her name on it was handed down on March 21, 1974, and agents arrested her outside the mansion. She was found to have one gram of cocaine in her purse. It was the first solid link the DEA had to Hefner and possible hard-drug use at the mansion. There had been rumors for a long time, of course. After all, the mansion was a home-away-from-home for rock groups and other entertainers in Chicago. If the government could nail Arnstein, a case might be built against Hefner himself.

Bobbie Arnstein had been a Playboy fixture for fourteen years. She was smart, bright, quick, ambitious, pretty enough under most circumstances but not under Playboy's, wisecracking, funny, rudderless, often despondent, sometimes near despair. She had gone to work as a receptionist in 1960, soon after high school, and moved up a complex stepladder of jobs to become one of Hefner's closest personal aides. She managed the mansion, served as his executive secretary, handled a string of other jobs for him, including, it was widely rumored, that of sometime mistress. The relationship, personal and professional, gave her entree to Chicago's jet-set society. It was a world she could not quite handle.

Her looks troubled her. She felt eclipsed by Playboy's beauties and developed a bawdy sense of humor to hide her vulnerability. But the shell was never thick enough, and it seems to have cracked permanently when Tom Lownes was killed in 1963. Bobbie had hoped to marry young Lownes, Victor's brother and a rising *Playboy* editor. Worse, she was driving the car when it crashed into a tree. Loaded with guilt, she landed on an analyst's couch, and bounced through the years on an emotional roller coaster: more analysis, random sex, unmet career demands. As she grew older, she picked up younger men (a habit Hefner applauded as part of the new sexual freedom he espoused) and gradually became dependent on them.

Ron Scharf, aged twenty-five, was one, and together they were involved in the drug traffic. Anxious to hold him, worried about competition from younger women, she carried half a pound of cocaine from a Miami dealer to Chicago. DEA agents had the dealer under surveillance, and when they saw who was swimming into their net, moved quickly to exploit the connection. Phones were tapped legally, other evidence gathered. Then the trap was sprung.

Shortly after her arrest she attempted suicide with an overdose of pills but was rushed to a hospital in time. In April she underwent psychiatric treatment. The months that followed must have been nightmarish. Feelings of guilt and depression mushroomed as she saw fear creep through the corporation. She blamed herself for having brought down the wrath of the law on those she loved. Hefner remained in distant touch from his Los Angeles mansion, promising support and corporate payment of her legal fees. He seems to have been aware of the complex relationship that tied the young woman to him, to have cared and worried about her, but not known quite what he could do to give her emotional succor.

Playboy executives were concerned about the arrest and its corporate implications, but no one seems to have knocked heads or moved with force and direction to clean up the situation. In July, Playboy's security chief, Allan Crawford, quit, charging that hard drugs were used in the mansion, but that no one had listened to his demands that something be done about them. Crawford conceded, though, that he had not talked to Hefner personally about drugs, and it appeared as if no one else in the organization had, either.

As the months passed aimless corporate drift continued. A few Cassandras raised warning voices and were listened to more closely —mostly because they were such a novelty in a firm that had never had any before—but little action was taken on their advice.

The first hard news of serious financial trouble was made public in the annual report for Playboy's fiscal year 1974, which ended June 30. It put the bad news in black and white—despite all the four-color printing used to hide the unpalatable facts. The press was given advance copies of the report on Friday, September 6, and the stories that appeared in the newspapers on subsequent days did not make for pleasant reading.

Joe Cappo wrote a marketing column for the now-defunct *Chicago Daily News,* and on September 10 he crafted a careful analysis of Playboy's problems. It was as fair a deal as PEI would get for a long, long time. Cappo conceded that Playboy suffered from excessive press attention. *Fortune,* he noted, listed Playboy in 1973 as the nation's 590th largest company, "sandwiched between Chelsea Industries and Maryland Cup. There's no doubt about which one got all the ink."

But he also noted that Hefner and the bunny were respectively the nation's best-known chief executive and business logo. "Unfortunately, these factors have contributed to making Playboy the year's best-known and most recognizable bummer in the securities market." Playboy, Cappo wrote, was struggling through "a sour year," and he set down the dreary details that helped explain PEI's closing price of $2.87 a share the day before:

Net earnings were off a whopping 48 percent from $11.2 million in 1973 to $5.9 million, and from $1.20 a share to 64¢, despite a 7.5 percent increase in revenues to a record $204.3 million. *Playboy*'s circulation continued to slide, was down to 6.4 million. Magazine sales were off by $1 million, pretax earnings by more than $7 million. Hotels lost $3.3 million, the entertainment group—film and TV, records, and music publishing—$4.6 million. *Oui* lost $351,000.

Cappo interviewed Preuss and senior vice-president Rosenzweig and dutifully recorded their public optimism about foreign editions, the lucrative marketing prospects for magazine, club, and Playboy products in Japan, condominium sales at the Lake Geneva resort, the outlook for mail-order insurance business, and the expansion of Playboy boutiques in chains like Sears and J. C. Penney. Both executives told Cappo that the company had problems but insisted that new management was being brought in to handle them—pretty much the same thing they had said six months earlier to *Dun's Review* and to *Business Week.*

Cappo, though, had his doubts:

> How extensive can any management changes be when one person remains as chairman, president and chief executive officer of the corporation, as well as editor and publisher of *Playboy* magazine and publisher of *Oui* magazine? His name: Hugh Hefner. Can he handle all these jobs? It seems not. And there's no secret that his interests lie primarily with the magazines. . . . Hefner didn't take time to attend his . . . annual meeting . . . even though confidence is low and he still owns 72 percent of Playboy's stock. . . . Hefner has been available for guest appearances on TV shows but not for security analyst meetings. *Business Week, Dun's Review, Newsweek* and other publications have all run articles on Playboy without getting Hefner to sit still for an interview. He also was not available for an interview in connection with this article.

Preuss told Cappo that Hefner would rather deal with his strengths which are editorial and pictorial. He really didn't know how much to charge for a room at Great Gorge. "That he delegates. To meet with stock analysts is not his strength," Preuss said. To which Cappo commented: "Unfortunately, that often is the kind of strength it takes to be an effective chief executive."

And, Cappo argued privately later, Hefner had not been an effective chief executive. "Any corporation started by an enterpreneur grows within certain limits. When it reaches a second phase of growth, that enterpreneur normally is not the right person to take the company into any spreading-out operation. Airlines are typical examples. Pilots usually start them. Look at Eddie Rickenbacker at Eastern. Suddenly the airline makes millions, and he doesn't know how to handle the money. That's the time to turn the operation over to the professional managers. But Hefner didn't. He made all the important decisions himself. He was the company."

Perhaps he did, at a distance. That summer and fall, however, he did not seem to be making many decisions. Certainly he was far removed from day-to-day operations. "He spent all his waking hours playing backgammon and he watched a movie every night of the week," Gutwillig groused. But as the Arnstein case moved to a head, Hefner's isolation began to end, and the general unease that had gripped the company was given a sharp and painful focus. Bobbie went on trial in October. The first quarter of Playboy's new fiscal year ended on September 30. Results were still solid, and the company pulled out a net profit of $2.5 million.

On October 30, the *Chicago Sun-Times* reported, Bobbie Arnstein and her two codefendants were found guilty "of conspiring to distribute one-half pound of cocaine." Sentencing was set for November 26. Several weeks after the verdict, the psychiatrist who had treated Bobbie in the spring following her first suicide attempt (there was a second later, also with pills, but this one was hushed up) wrote a letter to one of Arnstein's attorneys—at her request—stating that the young woman was likely to commit suicide if she were imprisoned. The letter and results of previous psychiatric tests were in the judge's hands before he pronounced sentence. They seem to have been instrumental in shaping his decision. Miss Arnstein was given a conditional prison term of fifteen years and ordered to undergo ninety days of psychiatric tests, to be followed by resentencing, and, presumably a lighter penalty. Arnstein's lawyers appealed, thus delaying the tests.

Perhaps there was no direct connection. But as the weeks passed, Playboy's losses mounted. Even the London gambling operation looked wobbly. And on Wall Street the stock continued to fall, sometimes as low as $2 a share. Management watched in disbelief as the foundations of an empire began to shake. But the worst was not yet.

On December 8, 1974, the time bomb that had ticked so dangerously for months exploded. The *Chicago Tribune* broke the story that federal narcotics agents hadn't stopped with Arnstein but had been after Hefner and his empire all along.

"Hugh Hefner has emerged as a prime target of a federal narcotics investigation," the *Tribune* story began. "The year-long investigation centers on suspected illicit drug activities inside Hefner's Playboy mansions in Chicago and Beverly Hills."

A key source told the *Tribune:*

> Investigators are shooting at him [Hefner] and he's in a helluva lot of trouble. There's no doubt about it. Word of the extensive probe became known recently when several present and former Playboy employees were subpoenaed to testify later this month before a Chicago grand jury. . . . Findings believed to be in the hands of DEA investigators detail the concealment and use in the two mansions of cocaine, barbiturates and marijuana by some employees.

Arnstein's initial arrest, the *Tribune* account continued, had sent

> shock waves through the Playboy empire and, according to inside sources, prompted what is now regarded by investigators as a coverup attempt by Hefner. Investigators have been told that Hefner, upon hearing of the woman's arrest while in Las Vegas, issued orders the same day for aides to search the mansions in Chicago and Beverly Hills and remove all drugs. The orders were promptly executed. In Chicago, it was learned that drugs, including marijuana, were removed from the mansion and reportedly taken for safekeeping to corporate offices in the Playboy Building."

Once the papers hit the streets, the January issue of *Playboy,* displayed on newsstands next to the bold-type headlines, became a second bomb that exploded with equally devastating effect. On the title page, below a denim-clad rabbit engulfed by bulging bosoms, was a cover line that said: "The Truth About Cocaine."

On page 131 writer Richard Rhodes began "A Very Expensive High" like this: ". . . now at the beginning of 1975, a blizzard of cocaine is blowing over us, little spoons hanging from our necks like crucifixes. . . . In the past two years, cocaine has spilled from the ghetto and the mansion to become the illegal drug of choice, second only to marijuana, of many prosperous middle-class Americans."

The timing of the piece, former articles editor Geoffrey Norman argues, was a total accident. "We knew coke was around. I used Rhodes because he knew nothing about it and I didn't want any heavy-drug-culture terminology. It was locked up three months before the *Trib* story hit the stands. The first thing I knew about Hefner's troubles was when I opened the *Trib* that night."

But that was not how the world saw the "coincidence." The piece had to nail down the popular perception of *Playboy* as a champion of the drug culture, and to strengthen the government's case against Hefner in the public's mind. Certainly Chicago's newspapers had a field day. Scorn and vitriol seared the empire like spray paint. And this time they could not be washed off with money. Attacks like Bob Greene's column in the *Sun-Times* on December 17 had to hurt:

"This current scandal is a fitting reward for General Lee Gottlieb, supreme commander of PEI's Allied Army of flacks . . . now they finally have something they can all sputter and fume and call Kup [columnist and TV host Irving Kupcinet] about. Idle hands are the devil's tools."

It was too much. The corporate gloss was being rubbed off with sandpaper. Sex, drugs, scandal, and a lousy financial performance! Too much even for those in the financial community who had forgiven Playboy everything for that lovely bottom line. Soon after the *Tribune* broke the story, Robert Adelman and Philip Erard resigned as outside directors.

Adelman had long been critical of PEI management, but his withdrawal had more than personal impact. As a substantial Chicago businessman, his resignation signaled the disillusionment of the city's financial community with the Playboy empire. The loss stung. Acceptance was still of too recent vintage.

Erard's resignation was even more devastating. As a partner in the underwriting firm of Loeb, Rhoades, he was PEI's link to Wall Street. His departure meant that those ties, too, had been ruptured. "These guys had to face people every day," Lance Hooper, Playboy's financial vice-president dismissed in the wake of the poor 1974 performance, told Bryce Nelson of the *Los Angeles Times*. "They cannot let it reflect badly on their companies. They were getting snide remarks from acquaintances. They resigned because of the heat."

As the winter wore on, and 1974 turned into 1975, corporate bravado began to wear thin. The company and its executives increasingly felt under attack—from government, the media, the financial community, the city of Chicago. Bewilderment spread. No one knew how to protect the sliding bunny image. The corporate tone grew shrill and whiny. A sense of paranoia, never fully absent from the Playboy Building, haunted the corridors. The "enemy"—whoever he might be—lurked everywhere.

"For a while there," Gutwillig told Nelson later, the drug investigation "had a strong, psychologically depressing, and distracting effect on the employees. It was very hard for the company to explain what was going on. The company didn't know itself what was going on." Advertising continued to drift downward. Any hopes of landing institutional advertisers—let alone General Motors—were fading. "It has not been helpful to us," Rosenzweig deadpanned.

For Bobbie Arnstein, the agony mounted. Free on appeal, she wondered what to do next. Hefner wanted her to work out in California, but she was not sure she wanted to go. The U.S. attorney's office had put more pressure on her to implicate Hefner, or so she felt. There was talk of a contract out on her life. On Saturday, January 11, 1975, Bobbie went to share a pizza dinner with some friends, Richard and Shirley Hillman, in their apartment on West Diversey Street. They talked about how to behave at parties and about California. Bobbie was slated to fly out on Monday to take another look, to make a final decision on moving there. If she went, the Hillmans might follow later. Perhaps they could share a house.

"She wasn't depressed," Shirley Hillman would say later. "She was in a very good mood. She was very upbeat." Maybe. Richard was less certain. He described her spirits as "good or mediocre."

Arnstein left the Hillmans around 11:00 to take in a late movie with a boyfriend. Around 1:00 she returned to the Playboy mansion on North State Parkway, where she had an apartment. "Parkway" does not fit the narrow and elegant street which is more commonly known as North State. Substantial town houses built in the eclectic turn-of-the-century style, and soaring glass-sheathed apartment towers derived from Mies van der Rohe's lakefront architecture, crowd the tree-lined sidewalks.

The "mansion" at 1336–1340 North State is actually a complex of two linked town houses, with the annex smaller and farther back from the curb than the much-photographed facade up front. The block is bordered on the north by Schiller Street and on the south by Goethe Street. The juxtaposition has its irony: two of literature's great playwrights and poets as mute guards to this princeling who gilds his court with the best writers of his day; just as Goethe and Schiller had been ornaments of earlier courts.

Arnstein walked through a wrought-iron gate, past a forlorn evergreen, up a few steps and through the mansion gates.

Inside, she asked the night butler (Hefner had a twenty-four-hour staff on duty then) for a bottle of liquor, stopped to drink a glass of orange juice, and went into her off-white apartment near the street-level entry. It was the last time anyone saw her in the mansion that night. The time was about 1:30 A.M.

In the ensuing hour, she may have drafted a couple of letters, taken a drink, gathered a few things into her vanity case. Around 2:30, she slipped into her coat, picked up her vanity case, and left the mansion. No one saw her leave. She walked or took a cab—no one knows—down North State to the seventeen-story Hotel Maryland at 900 North Rush Street. The area is mottled with change, part Tenderloin, part new elegance, and just a couple of blocks from the Playboy Building on North Michigan Avenue. If she looked up, she could have seen the bunny beacon atop the building sweep the sky.

She pushed through the revolving door of the hotel—nondescript brick, faceless, characterless, save for the Carton coffee shop at one end and the "Alfie" discotheque at the other—and walked across a brown and gold rug to the desk. She signed the register as Roberta Hillman at 2:44 A.M. and then took the small, slow elevator up to room 1716. She hung a "do not disturb" sign on the door and fastened the two security locks.

The next day, when a maid tried to get in to clean the room and couldn't, the hotel manager had the lock broken and called the police. Bobbie Arnstein was sprawled near the edge of the bed. Several loose pills lay on the night table. Authorities found enough drugs in her vanity case to kill five people. The autopsy revealed she had taken three different drugs—Mebral, Placidyl, and Valium—each dose of lethal size.

There were two notes. The first alerted the hotel manager to the second, a letter addressed to R. Keith Stroup, a close friend and one of the defense counsels at her drug trial. According to one account, the envelope bore the legend: "This is another of those boring suicide notes."

The news of Bobbie's suicide shocked Hefner to the core, shocked him more deeply, perhaps, than any other event in his life. The weeks since the drug investigation was made public had seemed like months —and still do. Even two years after the fact, he could not believe that only five weeks had elapsed between the *Tribune* story and Bobbie Arnstein's tragic end.

"That's incredible. So short a time? That's impossible."

The story broke on December 8, 1974, he is told. She killed herself on January 12, 1975.

"I don't think that's possible. I really don't think that's possible."

The dates are recounted again.

"Maybe it is. Maybe it is. It seemed many, many months."

His voice is near a whisper. He looks haunted and suddenly aged. His face is a ravaged battleground. Even in 1977 the pain is still sharp and vivid.

When the news of the suicide came, Hefner's lawyers told him the same thing they had told him all along: Sit tight, don't say anything. He had obeyed for months, though reluctantly. Now he could sit still no longer. He ordered his plane readied for a flight to Chicago the next day and told his public relations people to prepare a press conference at the mansion for Tuesday, January 14.

"I didn't get any sleep the night before," Hefner remembered in his library in 1977. Night had fallen. Lamps glowed softly. "I have a portion of the tape of that press conference if you want to look at it." The videotape machine unspooled the memory.

A bank of seven TV cameras is built up around the fireplace at the far end of the living room in the Chicago mansion. A Picasso floats on the wall above them. Zoom lenses aim at the pretzel of microphones set up on a dais at the top of the steps near the entrance. They pan past the paintings on the wall, the Frank Gallo busts, across the electronic console that acts as a room divider, over the heads of reporters, technicians, soundmen, worried Playboy flacks. Hot lights blaze and lend a new glow to dark oak paneling, parquet floors, and heavy leather furniture—all in the muted, burnished earth tones Hefner loves.

The media like to call Hefner the Prince of Pleasure. He does not look the part today. The fabled cool is gone. His palms sweat. He is drawn, tense, gaunt. Pain has surprised his face. He looks haunted in his patterned silk shirt open at the neck, slacks, and brown corduroy jacket.

It is not a good room for a press conference. The decor takes away from the content. So do memories of other, brighter occasions. The fabled parties with first-run movies and "sumptuous" buffets. The celebrities that attended them. The big-busted bunnies stationed around the room to complement the other decorations.

The reporters who once carried *Playboy* and its life-style to the ends of the earth are less friendly now, geared to falling idols—a president has been dethroned, a power structure collapsed—and eager to see another topple.

Hefner steps to the lectern, takes a crumpled yellow legal pad from a black folder, and smooths the scrubbled pages. His hands shake as he grips the lectern. There is stubble on his chin. His black hair hangs over his ears, stringy, showing occasional streaks of gray. Blue veins lace his pale face. His eyes are red with fatigue, watery.

"Ah, excuse me, if I look a bit harried," he begins. "But I'm very upset." He takes a deep breath as if to pull himself together, says "Okay," and starts to read his prepared statement.

"For the last several weeks, I have been the subject of a series of sensational speculations and allegations regarding supposed illicit drug activities at the Playboy mansions in Chicago and Los Angeles —attempting to associate me with the recent cocaine conspiracy conviction of Playboy secretary Bobbie Arnstein," Hefner began laboriously.

"Although I had no personal connection of any kind, I reluctantly agreed to make no initial public statement on the subject because our legal counsel was convinced that anything I said would only be used to further publicize what—in our view—is not a legitimate narcotics investigation at all, but a politically motivated witch-hunt.

"The suicide of Bobbie Arnstein makes any further silence impossible. Whatever mistakes she may have made in her personal life, she deserved better than this. She deserved—among other things—the same impartial consideration accorded any other citizen similarly accused."

Reporters, sensing the coming break in Hefner's voice, looked up from their notes at Hefner's face, especially his brimming eyes. Would he cry in public?

"But because of her association with Playboy and with me, she became the central focus of a cocaine conspiracy case in which it appears she was only peripherally involved. There is ample reason to believe that if she had provided the prosecutors with evidence to support any serious drug charge against me, she would never have been indicted . . . an already emotionally troubled woman was pushed beyond endurance—and she killed herself.

". . . she was one of the best, brightest, most worthwhile women I have ever known. She will be missed—by me and a great many others as well."

Those looking for that special lead had it now. As the *Daily News* wrote: "*Playboy* publisher Hugh Hefner broke down and cried."

Face muscles alternately taut and twitching, Hefner collected himself enough to continue.

"What the Chicago prosecutors apparently couldn't or wouldn't accept was the lack of any connection whatsoever between their cocaine case against my secretary and my own rather conservative antidrug predilections. For the record, I have never used cocaine, or any other hard drug or narcotics—and I am willing to swear to that fact under oath, and penalty of perjury. . . .

". . . The true motivations for this so-called narcotics investigation are clear enough. As an outspoken critic of all forms of authoritarian repression in our society, and as the major financial backer of the National Organization for the Reform of Marijuana Legislation, I'm an all-too-obvious 'prime target' for such an inquisitional witch-hunt. . . . It appears that the 'enemies list' mentality of Watergate is still with us; and the repressive legacy of puritanism that we challenged in our first year of publication remains as formidable an opponent to a truly free and democratic society as ever."

When he finished his prepared statement, he looked drained. Pearls of sweat beaded his forehead. His throat was dry. He asked for a bottle of Pepsi, took a long pull, and settled down to answering questions.

Now he directly attacked James Thompson, the U.S. attorney who brought the case. Thompson was using the publicity to further his political ambitions for the governorship of Illinois (which Thompson went on to win in November 1976). *Playboy* was vulnerable to political attack from the right because of its "liberal philosophy on drugs and on social, political and racial values."

And Hefner had his flacks distribute copies of Miss Arnstein's suicide note. The operative quote from the rambling, five-page letter: "I don't suppose it matters that I say it, but Hugh M. Hefner is—though few will ever realize it—a staunchly upright, vigorously moral man and I know him well and he has never been involved in the criminal activity which is being attributed to him now."

But in the weeks and months that followed, the heat did not let up. Hefner won some sympathy in the wake of his press conference —especially after he was photographed as one of the pallbearers at Bobbie Arnstein's funeral. There was something humble and tortured about him in those pictures. His face was all lines and hollows with lips penciled in as an afterthought, and the yarmulka—the skullcap devout Jews wear during religious ceremonies—made his grief somehow touching.

Some of his supporters continued to attack Thompson and the DEA. Lawyer Keith Stroup, head of the National Organization for the Reform of Marijuana Legislation, hurled harassment charges against Thompson: "The cheapest and most immoral tactic I've ever seen the U.S. attorney's office use." But Hefner's financing of NORML and Stroup's increasingly intemperate language dimmed his credibility. The ACLU also backed Hefner, even detailing charges of harassment in a letter to Attorney General Edward Levi. But Playboy was a heavy contributor to ACLU too.

Thompson refused to back down. Press attacks on Playboy continued. A *Tribune* writer accused Hefner of trying "to cop a plea through publicity" and put the Justice Department on the defensive. Magazine and newspaper feature writers moved in to do "in-depth" stories about the Playboy phenomenon and its tarnished image. The magazine and life-style it propagated no longer fitted the leaner and sour seventies, nor were Hefner and his editors able to perform the surgery needed to make it relevant again.

On March 8 Thompson stepped up his own attack:

"Not one ounce of the power of the prosecutor's office or the DEA is being used to investigate the conduct of anyone, including Hefner . . . to the point of making a bullshit case. I do not have to pursue bullshit cases. I've got enough of the good kind. . . . No one, including Hugh Hefner, is above the law. . . . We will not abandon our priority to bring a nonsense case."

But his most telling sentence, the one that wrapped up reams of newspaper copy in one neat bundle, was this:

"I'm not sure what Hefner stands for these days is all that relevant, or that any prosecution of him would mean much."

The implications of that statement had to be devastating. At age twenty-one Playboy was through, finished, washed up. Hefner could take his Big Bunny airplane and stuff it up his 007 life-style. What could be sillier, anyway, than his playing Jay Gatsby, as he had in a layout on the Playboy Mansion West that graced the cocaine issue. He had himself photographed in front of Holmby Hills dressed in a white suit and white hat, a 1928 Rolls-Royce in the background, with Barbi Benton on his arm simpering as a Jewish Daisy who passed. For many who watched the antics from the public sidelines, it was all too much.

Playboy's financial performance began to match its bad press, and to confirm corporate disarray. Second-quarter results, made public in February, showed that for the first time in a dozen years, Playboy had chalked up a losing quarter. Sales were down $2.7 million, and the company had lost $356,000. Preuss blamed the recession for hotel and gambling losses; high paper and printing costs for troubles on the magazine end. But in PEI's quarterly report to stockholders, Preuss and Hefner said that entertainment-division losses had been pared, an agreement in principle reached for starting a Japanese edition that would open Japan's lucrative market to Playboy and its products and services.

The two executives also announced an economy drive. They both took 25 percent pay cuts and ordered all other salaries frozen. "Broad-scale cost-cutting programs have been instituted that should aid in offsetting any continued decline in revenue and profits," the report said. Inside the company, living high off the hog would end. No more lobster and cracked crab at editorial meetings. Pampered editors would have to munch sandwiches.

Weeks later, Hefner made his first tentative move toward changes and a reassertion of his own authority. He stripped Preuss of his titles of executive vice-president and chief operating officer, assuming the latter duties himself. Preuss slid down to senior vice-president–group executive. At the same time, Hefner set up a seven man office of the president, which, in the cumbersome language of the P.R. handout, would "be responsible for the establishment and review of the corporation's goals . . . and seek to improve the present organizational structure. . . ." It included Rosenzweig, Hefner's long-time executive assistant and a rising corporate star, Kretchmer, *Playboy* assistant publisher Richard Koff, Preuss, Donald Lewis, the new financial officer brought in to replace Hooper the previous November, and entertainment division chief Harvey Markowitz.

Gutwillig's name was not on the list. He had either resigned or been fired, depending on whose story you believe. Kretchmer says Hefner fired him. Gutwillig contends that "I stayed two years longer than I should have, out of loyalty to Hefner and the others." Officially, the third-quarter report said Gutwillig "has resigned to pursue other interests."

Hefner signed the third-quarter report alone, not, as had been his custom, together with Preuss. But his solo did not improve the numbers. Sales were off almost $6 million from the previous quarter and $3 million below the comparable year-ago period. Net losses totalled $387,000, or 4¢ a share. *Playboy* and *Oui* circulation and advertising were down, with losses only partially cushioned by a hike in cover prices. On the bright side, Hefner could point to renewed strength in the British casinos, reduced entertainment-division losses, publication of a Japanese edition with an initial print run of 430,000, and German and French editions holding up well. He also announced payment of the 6¢ semiannual dividend to all shareholders of record save one. "The Board has accepted my offer to waive receipt of the dividend on my personal holdings," he wrote shareholders. "Your dividend check is enclosed." Hefner was giving up $400,000.

At midyear Hefner moved to strengthen the Chicago operation. He persuaded his old friend Victor Lownes III, the London Playboy king, to divide his time between England and the United States to help shore up the troubled club-hotel division, and see what else he could do to turn the company around. Lownes moved swiftly and savagely to cut fat left untouched by the quasi-hysterical efforts undertaken in late 1974 to reduce costs by chopping blindly with a halberd.

"What Vic was trying to accomplish was very valid," Hefner commented later. "Cut down, cut through the shit to the nitty gritty. One of his early suggestions when there was going to be some cutting was to take away X number of desks and have people run back to Ohio Street. The first guys to find their seats got their old desks. But at the same time he very quickly got the nickname of 'Jaws' in Chicago. That's part of the mixed bag you get with Vic. That was too bad because it was a serious morale problem when we really didn't need that."

There were a lot of other things Playboy didn't really need in the summer of 1975. Like media attention. The brash Lownes had barely settled back into Chicago—where he lived in a twelfth-floor suite in the shabby Playboy Towers, in itself an ostentatious cost-cutting move for the luxury-loving gambling czar—when he breezily told the press that Hefner's customized DC-9 would have to go, and that he planned to put the Chicago mansion up for sale. It was a headline-making story. So was Hefner's denial a few days later. He wasn't going to sell either the plane or the house. The dispute had its comic side, but the publicity was not designed to help Playboy's image.

No publicity that Playboy got that summer helped. Tony Jackson, the company's highest-ranking black, was fired for alleged incompetence and insubordination. Incensed black employees took to the streets to protest. TV cameras recorded the event. For a time, race was added to sex, drugs, poor management, and a red-ink-splattered balance sheet on the roster of Playboy woes.

The uproar bewildered Hefner and his top aides. Their record on hiring blacks was good. Hefner's friendship with black celebrities and their promotion in *Playboy* magazine was well known. Briefly he toyed with the idea of trading on them. Perhaps football great Jim Brown could talk to the disgruntled blacks. It was a poor move, and the idea was quickly abandoned. But when word got back to Playboy, blacks grew even angrier. "What do I have in common with a guy who pushes women off a balcony," one black Playboy staffer said angrily (Brown had once been charged with doing that). "I live in the ghetto. My problems are different."

Things got so bad that Hefner had to fly to Chicago again and hold another press conference. This one was angrier than the Arnstein one had been. Black reporters were furious. Jackson had run Playboy's affirmative-action program, and opposed moving part of the clerical operation to Boulder, Colorado, because he feared that minority jobs in Chicago would be cut. Also, he charged that blacks weren't paid as much as whites at Playboy.

Hefner was patient and courteous. Jackson had been a "nonproductive man" who was "undermining the company's affirmative action program." If he had been white, he would have been fired long ago. But Hefner admitted that Playboy had not done all it should. "As far as numbers are concerned, our record is good. But as far as opportunity within the company, our record is unsatisfactory. We will be doing something about it."

Other reporters peppered him with questions about business—or, more accurately, about his prospects for survival. A *Sun-Times* columnist noted that "the white, middle-class TV reporters—the very 'sort of men who read *Playboy*'—were cranking up their basso profundos to render such incisive queries as: 'Mr. Hefner, we've all seen the rise of *Playboy*. Some people say we're now seeing the fall. (Theatrical pause.) What's your reaction?'" Other questions weren't much better, but they did typify the attitude of a gleeful press eager to see Hefner and his empire come crashing down. That summer, many people felt they would not have long to wait.

Red ink continued to leak over Playboy ledgers—so much red ink, in fact, that Playboy decided to hold up publishing the bad news. In September newspapers began to wonder about the delay and speculated about new disasters yet to come. Lownes's announcement about plane and house fueled the rumors. Weeks turned into months. Nothing happened.

On a bright fall day in New York, Robert Gutwillig munched a croissant and sipped coffee in the dining room of the Park Lane Hotel on Central Park South. He lived in California now and came east only rarely. Six months out of Playboy, he had both distance and intimacy, and his critique was dispassionate and devastating. Small, slender, intense (no one at Playboy is ever fat except for Ray Russell, the first executive editor), Gutwillig had carved out a successful Manhattan literary career (two novels, top editorial jobs at McGraw-Hill, NAL, and World) before deciding he was tired of talking to his own kind and jumped for the mass audience Playboy promised.

What had soured the promise? Mostly, Gutwillig thought, the departure of two men—Hefner and Spectorsky. Spectorsky was dead, and Hefner had effectively retired from the company years ago. Ensconced in his mansions, surrounded by servants and sycophants, traveling in closed limousines or in his private plane, Hefner knew as much about what went on in the United States as Patty Hearst on the lam with the SLA.

"There was no leadership, no strategy, no people to carry it out, no corporate structure at all—just a circle of people trying to get Hefner's attention and favor, and they changed every six months. When I arrived in 1970, I wrote endless memos saying that despite new highs in circulation, the company was in terrible trouble. I got A for prescience and Z for effectiveness. By 1972 it was clear that something had to be done. Times were changing. *Penthouse* was coming on strong. Research showed that our hold on readers was lessening. Hefner was only a part-time participant. You could sit with him all night about the purpose of the magazine and the need to meet *Penthouse* head-on. But it all got misted over. Nothing was done."

Perhaps Lownes could turn things around. If anyone could, it was Lownes. But the rot was far advanced, and unless corporate thinking changed—and it might even be too late for that—the company's financial plight could well be terminal. "I'm sorry it didn't work out," Gutwillig ended, "and I hate to see what's happening."

Several weeks after Gutwillig's visit to New York Arthur Kretchmer kicked his suitcase resentfully down the corridor from his office on the tenth floor of the Playboy Building. Another one of those damn trips to New York. An advertising crisis. All right, so some of the covers had been too raunchy of late. Advertising director Howard Lederer was hopping mad about them. Maybe just a bit too mad. Promising advertisers *Playboy* would swear off raunch alto-gether was not necessary, not yet.

He did not see a company in crisis, not completely. "I went to put out several specific fires of which advertising was only one. Calming a nervous internal situation was just as important to me. I was not nervous in a big sense about the future of the magazine. If I was nervous that day, it was about being an editor out front where he didn't belong. But I thought to myself, 'I can sell this maga-zine . . .' "

Out on East Walton Street, Kretchmer flung his bag into one of the Checker taxis that wait outside the Drake and leaned back for the long ride to O'Hare. The cab nosed through lunchtime Michigan Avenue traffic, across the West Side and toward the highway. He had dressed carefully—more carefully than he usually did for his New York trips: dark suit, dark tie, lemon-yellow shirt, polished black shoes instead of boots. There were even stays in his shirt collar. He remembered, wryly, the time he had gone to some New York meet-ing and had dressed with equal care, even forcing his mop of black hair into a stylish bowl. And someone had pointed to the missing stays in his collar. Those fuckers on Madison Avenue. Maybe he should have stayed on as assistant manager of the Bleecker Street Cinema. He'd seen a lot of movies and learned about pictures. How they move. How they stand still.

Kretchmer squeezed his long legs uncomfortably in the narrow American Airlines Whisperjet aisle and began to shuffle through the papers he would need for his presentation to media directors of major agencies. He was just as glad that the earnings figures weren't out yet. They wouldn't make his job any easier—and keeping advertising and sex in the book without doing violence to either was no picnic. *Playboy* would change. He and Hefner had agreed on that during a meeting in the awful weeks that followed Bobbie Arnstein's sentencing. And he had the blueprints for the first face-lift in his briefcase.

He spent the next week holed up at Playboy's suite at the Drake on Park Avenue discussing his plans with small groups of media directors. There would be less raunch and more service features, a better blend of old and new. At the end of the week, Kretchmer summed it up for *New York Times* advertising writer Phil Dough-erty: "*Playboy* will be sexual. Sex is one of its favorite topics. But it will be more aware of the line separating sensuality and vulgarity. In the latter half of this year, it was slipping across that line too often, and . . . that's not necessary for the health of this magazine."

In his piece, Dougherty also pointed to the continuing circulation slide. In September, he noted, Playboy had announced a 10 percent reduction of the base rate, beginning in January 1976, from 6 million to 5.4 million.

Most of the media people who met with Kretchmer were impressed by his presentation. Madison Avenue had gotten to like *Playboy* over the years and was distressed when the magazine began to follow *Penthouse* and the others. It didn't get them any new ads, one media director explained, but it lost them quite a few—people they had trouble persuading to buy space in the first place.

But if Kretchmer had encouraged some advertisers, many remained unconvinced, especially agencies with accounts like liquor and tobacco that had begun to move toward *Penthouse*. "*Playboy* has lost a lot of pizzazz," a balding media director of one such agency mused on a bright November afternoon. "They'll have a tough time reestablishing that magazine as an advertising medium. It started taking itself too seriously. It is no longer a fun book, no longer different. *Penthouse* takes readers a step beyond titillation. And there's something else. I've never seen a magazine cut circulation guarantees and resurrect the sales momentum it had as number one. That's an advertising weakness. I think it's ominous—I really do. I hope I'll be proven wrong."

He struck a match and fussed with his pipe. "There was a time when we saw visible retail response to *Playboy*. But today *Playboy* has lost even that. There's been an erosion of advertising representatives. They always thought they could just take orders over the phone and not bother making personal calls. They had the *Time* syndrome. We're number one—you have to buy us. In the last two or three years, they simply stopped hustling for calls—and they stopped making good media rationale. A good agency listens to a rep when he explains why his book can solve marketing problems. Ten years ago, *Playboy* did that. It was a hot book ten years ago. But I haven't seen that lately, and most of their sales force is here. Look at how much direct mail has dropped out. They can smell death and defeat.

"*Playboy* ought to do more market research. Something is wrong. They've changed their philosophy about what appeals to the American male eye. They aren't as risqué as the others. We're examining *Playboy* a lot more closely than we were a year or two ago. And we're as much concerned with the lost excitement as the lost leadership role. It is harder now to tell clients they ought to be in *Playboy*."

He is unimpressed with *Playboy*'s decision to forsake raunch and return to the life-style concept; unimpressed, too, with Kretchmer's trip to promise reform and a new look.

"I think going back is the worst thing to do. It's an admission that they can't compete. Circulation will drop to four million."

Playboy finally released its annual report for fiscal 1975 in the week before Thanksgiving. Results were unrelievedly bleak. PEI lost another $700,000 in the fourth quarter and was able to eke out a bare $1 million profit only because of the strong showing in the first quarter. It was the lowest net since 1963, when sales had totaled $23.8 million. In contrast, sales in 1975 amounted to $197.7 million, the second highest ever. About the only good news in the report was that the entertainment group had halved 1974 losses—to $2.3 million.

But cutting losses was no longer enough to halt the decline. *Oui* lost $2.2 million, hotels $3.8 million—too much for Lownes's London earnings to pull the "Leisure Division" into the black. Most ominous, *Playboy* magazine, the anchor of financial stability and long-time guarantor of profitability, had started to slip. Sales were still over $86 million, but the magazine's pretax earnings plummeted to $8.4 million from $21.9 million two years earlier.

Perhaps the critics were right: Playboy had reached the end of the road at twenty-one. There was talk of the magazine's falling back into the special-interest ghetto, back to *Esquire*'s circulation of under a million.

But for all the thick gloom that enveloped the Playboy Building that November, and the deep pessimism many felt about the company's future and viability, a silver stripe had already been pasted on. PEI sales were picking up even as the report was distributed. Results for the first quarter of the new fiscal year showed that for the first time in nine months, the company had turned a profit: sales of $48.7 million netted $899,000.

More importantly, perhaps, Hefner, however reluctantly, was moving more forcefully back into the management and planning of corporate affairs. He will admit that for many years before the financial squalls struck his company, he had not been much involved—or, at any rate, not involved regularly enough to provide needed stability and direction. Many people who worked for him in the late sixties and seventies felt that Hefner came in and out of corporate affairs like the Cheshire cat—his smile lingered long after he was gone. And, they say, it was an attitude that bred disarray.

"Let's see if I can give you a frame of reference," Hefner mused in response to those charges. "I've been operating as chairman of the board for more than ten years. Other people have been running the company for a long time and have made the day-to-day decisions. Major decisions in terms of deciding, okay, the next place this ship will go is this particular island, yes, I'll make that decision. But getting there is largely up to the captain and the crew."

Hefner says his life has gone through three stages. In the fifties, he was deeply enmeshed in all the detail of running his company.

After he bought the Chicago mansion, he worked from home and gave up total immersion.

"I went through the first transition then. It was difficult. It meant delegating authority so I could stop being involved in day-to-day detail. But little by little, I let go of various things."

Hefner stopped reading all the copy in the fifties, then, later, approving content for every issue, and, finally, no longer edited "all the subcaptions and subtitles and titles for the pictures." Beginning in the early sixties, he never went to his office. Day-to-day kind of presidential duties were left to Preuss, "who acted as the president of the company for many years without the title, and if it had worked out, would eventually have become the president in title."

Hefner paused, groping for words. "You know, you get together a bunch of guys. Whether on the form sheet or not, they seem to be the best equipped for the job. You are not apt to look too closely at the bits and pieces, and at the individuals, if they start doing a thing and the end result is better than that thing has ever been done before. When the end result begins to change, however . . ."

A lot of mistakes can be buried under a $20 million profit—mistakes that emerge all the more sharply when the protective cushion of money wears too thin.

"The amount of years given over trying to correct the problem where jobs had just outgrown some of the guys was enormous. We've never been quick to terminate a key executive in either editorial or the other areas because they weren't cutting it. If there has ever been a failing, it has probably been the other way."

In the hard days, Hefner was often accused of turning a hard heart on men who had stayed the course with him. The charges still hurt.

"I'm too loyal. There are things more important to me than being a good businessman. Obviously, one has to find some kind of balance. You have loyalties to the business and to other investors, and you have personal loyalties. It's a complicated kind of thing."

Whatever the reasons for his hesitation—whether they were disinterest, as some charge and Hefner admits up to a point, or unresolved personal loyalties to old hands and new friends—a point came where loyalty stopped, emotions were suppressed, and tribute paid to the needs of corporate and personal survival. And Hefner has a healthy respect for the requirements and needs of "survival" in Holmby Hills.

Who went. Who stayed. How to bring in the managerial pros. Hefner never doubted his business; neither its present soundness nor its future potential. And he made the decision to clean house during the agonizing weeks surrounding the Arnstein suicide. For a man unaccustomed to pain and deprivation, and with a "Christmas-morning view of life," that took guts; so did the decision to move deliberately, with care, caution and his own view of compassion.

Whatever the mitigating circumstances, and there seem to have been plenty, the finger of blame had to point squarely at Robert Preuss, the man who shouldered the responsibility without title or full authority over the company. From the time of his first demotion early in 1975, it was clear that Preuss could not long survive. But Hefner let his old roommate down gently, and with kindness, as he saw it. Preuss was demoted gradually; he quit the company he had served for twenty years in June 1976. Hefner was careful to insist that Preuss had not been fired, and Preuss seemed to have accepted his fate without visible bitterness (what he said in private may have been something else). But no matter how gently Hefner treated him (and Preuss left Playboy wealthy), or how great his failings as a corporate executive—and he admits that Playboy's explosive growth overwhelmed him as much as it did everyone else—Preuss was the fall guy. If he had been given too much responsibility earlier on, he was now assigned too much blame.

It had happened gradually. As Hefner let go the pieces, Preuss picked them up, one by one. "Hefner was so involved with writing the philosophy that he was not accessible to anyone for making decisions," Rosenzweig says, and he should know. He had front-row seats as Hefner's long-time executive assistant. "Hef looked to Preuss for running the company, and Preuss developed a huge span of control. I guess Peter Drucker would say one should not have any more than eight or nine people reporting to you. Preuss had thirty. That's an impossible situation. But the reason he did was because Hefner looked to him to keep the lid on."

Hefner announced Preuss's second demotion—to vice-president, Corporate Projects—in the first-quarter report the company issued for fiscal 1976. At the same time, he dismantled the makeshift office of the president and promoted Rosenzweig to executive vice-president in charge of the flagship Publications Division. Kretchmer and Koff went back to their editorial duties. However rickety, the organization had done what Hefner wanted from it—buy him time in which to think and act.

Marginal improvements continued in the second quarter, with British gambling again plugging the fiscal dikes. But what brightened Playboy's fortune the most was U.S. Attorney Samuel Skinner's announcement on December 29, 1975: He dropped the drug charges against Hefner for lack of evidence.

In the spring Lownes finally found a buyer for the plane, and this time Hefner agreed to sell. The price of $4 million exceeded book value. Advertising began to show new vigor, thanks to a reduction in ad rates. The third-quarter report showed a profit, thus replacing three losing quarters with three profitable ones, but earnings were still slim. Playboy's fiscal recovery was as yet anything but robust.

At his fiftieth birthday party on April 9, 1976, Hefner said he was looking for a president and chief operating officer to run day-to-day operations. The announcement triggered reports that Hefner was stepping down. He issued a patient disclaimer: "This is a newly created position. And while I've been looking for quite some time for a president who would take over the operations of the company, he will report directly to me. I'm not stepping down."

Many in the company thought it eyewash. "Hefner will never pick a president," one said flatly. "He'll never let go." He was wrong.

But the shy bloom of a turn in Playboy's fortune did not change many minds. Bad publicity continued to haunt the company. On April 13, 1976, the *Wall Street Journal* put "Playboy's Slide" on the front page.

"Hotel Losses, Decline in Circulation Weakens Hugh Hefner's Empire," the second head said. Not exactly designed to brace your average executive's morning cup of coffee. Neither was the article that followed just what the doctor ordered.

Lownes's decision to take the Playboy name off the hotels was "quite an admission for an outfit that a few years ago was sure it was going to conquer the world." The earnings slide was continuing, and so were other corporate woes. Yet "eating humble pie was never Playboy's style . . . and it isn't now." Hefner told the *Journal* he saw brighter days ahead. Finance chief Lewis explained, "We know what our problems are, and are taking steps to solve them. We are confident we will succeed."

The *Journal*'s reporters were not convinced. They had talked to a dozen people intimately acquainted with Playboy operations and concluded that "although these observers don't rule out a temporary rebound, they believe that Playboy's days of booming growth have ended. They believe that the company sooner or later must sever its string of money-losing hotels, key clubs and other entertainment operations and perhaps even fold *Oui* magazine." Worse still, *Playboy* was "getting a little frayed by competition" and unless something was done, the circulation slide would continue. "Playboy Enterprises is like a man who's getting a transfusion while he's bleeding from a dozen wounds," the *Wall Street Journal* quoted a security analyst as saying. "For years the transfusion—*Playboy* magazine's profits—has kept him alive but now that's diminishing too. Without radical surgery, the life of the body is in danger."

The authors conceded the impact of competition on the magazine and of higher fuel cost on the hotels, but put most of the blame on management. "Its executive suite has had a revolving door; seven of 14 corporate officers listed in the 1975 annual report were new, and there have been additional executive changes since." Despite Hefner's announcement that he was looking for a new president outside the company, "Playboy still endures its reputation for poor management, disdainful of outside expertise and heedless of the risks involved in its ventures." And they quoted a former top Playboy official who struck a familiar theme: "It starts at the top with Hefner. He's in, he's out, he's a bottleneck. You never know what he's going to do next. Decisions at Playboy often aren't based on normal business considerations. Hefner or another top guy will get excited about something and they'll plunge ahead without even taking out a pencil. If you don't go along, you're put down as a negativist who can't be trusted."

Next the *Journal* proceeded to cite chapter and verse on the corporate position, but unlike earlier accounts, this one focused on a five-year decline rather than the year-to-year losses. Hotels had lost $14.4 million. Occupancy rate for all four of them—Lake Geneva, the Towers, the Jamaica resort and Great Gorge—had dipped below 60 percent in fiscal 1975; some were below 50 percent. Great Gorge alone had lost $6 million since it opened. The interest rate on the $14.3 million hotel debt was three points above the going prime rate. Fixed costs swallowed 25 percent of revenues, double the industry average.

Lewis conceded that the company could not even realize the book value from a sale. A hotel man told the *Journal* he'd ask for $25 million and take $20 million for the complex that had cost $33.5 million to complete. The company still had potential liabilities of $4 million from the Miami Plaza deal, should the new owner default on his mortgage payment. Overall film losses totaled $6.2 million. Records had lost $5.8 million since the start. Even the banks were balking again. The *Journal* reported that in 1975 The First National Bank of Chicago had yanked two lines of credit totaling $6.5 million after looking over the operating losses and reading about the drug probe. Even after Skinner's exonerating statement, the credit was not restored. Efforts in 1975 to go private again by purchasing the outstanding shares at bargain-basement prices had failed because the company could not raise the needed cash. The IRS was auditing deductions Playboy had taken on the mansions and the plane, and the litigation might take years to resolve. Nor did the *Journal* hold out much hope for the success of cost-cutting efforts. "Sceptics doubt that all this will restore Playboy to its imperial grandeur."

Among those who read the story with special interest was a top executive at the Knight-Ridder newspaper chain headquartered in

Miami. Derick January Daniels, forty-seven years old, headed the thirty-two-paper chain's news service and was on the nine-man governing body that managed the papers. One day that spring he received a call from Allan J. Cox, a Chicago executive recruiter. Would he be interested in a job as president and chief operating officer of Playboy Enterprises, Inc.? Not really, Daniels said. He had risen quickly through the Knight-Ridder organization, moving in 1970 from executive editor of the *Detroit Free Press* into management. His future with the organization was both promising and secure. He already earned around $120,000 a year.

But Cox pressed him to reconsider. Would he at least go to California to see Hefner? Daniels agreed and flew out the first week of July. The two men hit it off at once. "The reaction was almost chemical," Daniels remembered over dinner in his Playboy Towers suite in the spring of 1978 (he was awaiting completion of a lavish lakefront penthouse). "Somehow I knew maybe thirty minutes after we started talking that we talked the same language, had the same feel, were philosophically compatible, and liked each other a lot at an almost gut-level kind of way people do like each other."

The formal photographs published after Daniels accepted the job do not make the attraction seem natural. They show a forbidding, coldly handsome man saved from startling good looks by craggy features and brooding eyes, impeccably turned out in boldly cut vested pinstripes; clearly someone who could stride into Playboy's offices and make the ruthless decisions the hard realities dictated. But the pictures are deceiving. So are the the first interviews he gave. Once he smiles and begins to talk, with a slight drawl and an intonation in his voice reminiscent of David Brinkley, a charming and roguish rebel emerges, the very antithesis of the New York corporate manager. Instead, he seems shrewd very much the same way Hefner is; intuitive, quick, breezily liberal, tough-minded without a macho veneer, self-confident enough for a sentimental side to show without embarrassment, warm, relaxed, yet with none of the practiced professionalism that marks salesmen and public relations executives.

Also, Daniels appears almost as much by sex possessed as Hefner himself. "I think of sex more than of anything else," he says candidly, "but I don't think that makes me so unusual. Most men do." It is, of course, speculative to assume that Hefner and Daniels saw something of themselves in each other, a shared delight and appreciation of nubility, and a recognition of two lions on the field. But then maybe it is not so speculative.

Back from Holmby Hills, Daniels dug into the company and its background. "I talked to people who had worked there, knew its problems, its political makeup, to people in a position to know its real financial condition. Obviously, this was a company with a lot of problems due to overexpansion; a company where the man who founded it and had run it for so long recognized the need for a change. The reason I finally decided to do it was that it struck me as a company in a classic turnaround situation with much sinew and muscle there that needed shaping and tuning and some redirection, but that had more success in its future than in its past if it was done well."

There was another, more personal reason for Daniels' decision, and one that sounds more valid than his professional concern or the $250,000 and heavy corporate perks that went into the five-year contract he and Hefner hashed out that summer: Daniels was bored in Miami, bored with the corporate gloss of Knight-Ridder, the ivory-tower atmosphere he attributes to top-level newspaper management. "They only talk about the Common Market and pat each other on the back," he grouses. "I thought I was very happy where I was," Daniels explains. "But as I look back on it, I recognized that I was really bored to death, that I was running in place. I was doing things I had done last year and last week and yesterday, over and over and over again. It was a kind of maintenance function. Playboy, with all its problems and opportunities, is like a big hunk of clay, amenable to being molded."

Daniels feels that journalism has become a respectable profession, and he doesn't think it should be. The willingness to take risks, he found, to be scratchy or crunchy, "to step on toes that should be stepped on," had been diminished. "You get a little too careful, you get interchangeable managers and editors who are moved around and worry about what corporate headquarters think of them, and they wind up being just a little too cautious, and I don't think journalism ought to be cautious. It ought to be the hair shirt, and make people uncomfortable a lot. It ought to comfort the afflicted and afflict the comfortable. And, in most instances, it has gotten away from that. But it needs irreverence and suspicion. People ought to shake a little when they see you coming."

Finally, Daniels liked Playboy's swinging and rebellious side. He was itchy with being the corporate rebel, the unconventional executive, divorced, fond of women, living with a girl younger than his oldest son. On September 8, 1976, Playboy announced Daniels' appointment as president as of October 4. And two days before taking over, Daniels rebelled one more time and married twenty-two-year-old M. J. Taylor, with whom he had been living. To all and sundry, they announced that she would continue to be known as M. J. Taylor.

The publicity that accompanied the announcement was equally

divided between the sober and the frivolous. Daniels' first interview appeared in the business pages of *The New York Times* and went heavily into his Georgetown background, his schooling at St. Albans, a posh Washington prep school, and his family background (Grandfather Josephus Daniels had been Wilson's Secretary of the Navy; Uncle Jonathan, FDR's press secretary; and the family still owned the *Raleigh News-Observer*), his newspaper career (at the *Free Press,* he helped his paper win a Pulitzer prize for coverage of the 1967 Detroit riots), and his business acumen. His second interview, in the home-town *Washington Star,* dubbed him "The Prince of Playboys" and focused on a big bash given for him at the New York Playboy Club. In December, Daniels threw an even gaudier party for himself and M. J. at the Coconut Grove in Miami, to which he wore a gold lamé jump suit, and ended up on the cover of *Miami* magazine. The party featured a lot of nudity and bunnies serving drinks.

Hefner had opted for change but in substance, not style. And he had deliberately decided not to go the route of an Eastern money manager, which Wall Street and his financial critics surely would have preferred. Even the in-house model, finance chief Don Lewis, didn't last. A year after Daniels took over, Lewis was on the way out. But the new president did not trail fire and brimstone. He held back and spent the first six months in rigorous on-the-job training for the many businesses Playboy practiced, and which he did not know well or at all.

Daniels' judgment of PEI as a company in a classic turnaround situation was quickly vindicated. Corporate performance in 1976 was far from great, but the rot had been halted and the chaos had subsided. Arab petrodollars were flowing across Playboy's British gaming tables, and Lownes told stories of Arabs dropping "a hundred thousand quid a night" without folding a single tent. The British casino operation netted $6 million, enough to cover hotel losses of $5.7 million, and, added to higher earnings from domestic clubs, to turn the division's 1975 loss of $584,000 into a $3.5 million profit. But the rest was a cost-cutting and holding operation. On virtually unchanged sales of $197.8 million, net profits doubled to $2 million, still anemic by historic standards. *Playboy* magazine sales were off $8 million; pretax earnings down to $3.8 million (compared to 1975's recession-plagued $8.4 million). Entertainment Group losses were pared to $2.7 million, while *Oui* turned a $2 million loss into a $200,000 profit on unchanged revenues.

Oui's spectacular rebound had to be chalked up on Nat Lehrman's ledger. He had added the publisher's hat to his editor's cap the previous year and deserved full credit. He also got his reward. The publishing end had been long Playboy's weak sister. Hefner was never happy with Spectorsky's performance in that role, and after his death, neither Preuss nor Rosenzweig had the time or the talent to give publishing the attention it deserved. Now Kretchmer suggested that Hefner stop looking outside for a *Playboy* publisher and give Lehrman the job. Hefner agreed, and Lehrman was named *Playboy*'s associate publisher and a senior vice-president.

On November 16, 1976, when Hefner and Daniels took the stage together for the first time at the annual meeting, they had more good news to report: first-quarter 1977 results showed a strong rebound, with both sales and profits the highest for any quarter in the company's history: $57 million and $3.7 million, respectively. Gambling continued as the corporation's strong right arm. Long-lagging key sales, which had fallen off drastically, began to show new strength. *Playboy*'s advertising, under the direction of Henry Marks, brought in from Dow-Jones to replace the retired Howard Lederer, perked up visibly. The entertainment division was paring losses and curtailing activities, part of Hefner's grand strategy to keep Playboy's oar in the TV business so the company would be in a position to profit from the coming revolution in home entertainment (at least Hefner remains convinced there will be one): videodiscs, expanded cable and pay TV. Foreign editions, including newly licensed versions in Mexico and Brazil, had a combined circulation of 1.5 million, with half that total coming from Japan. A new Playboy Club was opening in Tokyo, another in Dallas, franchise operations both.

At the turn of 1977, barely four months into his new job, Daniels made his first moves. Rosenzweig was out as head of the publishing division and was replaced by Nat Lehrman, promoted to group executive in charge of both *Playboy* and *Oui*. Rosenzweig said he had structured himself a new job, that of Playboy spokesman to the business community. As usual, he was enthusiastic and confident. The years of management-by-crisis were over. Playboy could at last start planning for the long haul. "Many of our problems have been solved," he mused in January 1977, "and we're ready to move ahead to the next threshold." He talked grandly of Playboy's "various communities," of Washington, New York and Los Angeles, of the power of the bunny logo from Tokyo to Brazil to Europe. Six months later, he was settled in Los Angeles, first to manage another crisis that followed the departure of Harvey Markowitz as entertainment division head, then to become West Coast division manager, where, Daniels says, he is doing a good job.

Slowly, cautiously, Daniels brought in his own people. First he hired Lee Templeton from Knight-Ridder to head up new business ventures, foreign operations, and product licensing. Next he took Mort Pesky from the *Philadelphia News* as editorial director for new publications, and named James Horton to head that division. Around midyear, Don Lewis was eased out as chief financial officer and replaced by Marvin Huston, who had financial experience both on newspapers and in manufacturing companies. Daniels also instituted zero-based budgeting, which he calls "organized common sense," and put every division on notice that it would have to annually justify its continued existence. It was a clear harbinger of more personnel changes to come.

In March 1977, Daniels and Lownes decided to close down the Jamaica resort, Playboy's first. The political situation on the island had deteriorated to the point where Ocho Rios could no longer make a go of it. At the same time, more promising ventures beckoned in the United States. With legalization of casino gambling in Atlantic City, Playboy moved quickly to capitalize on Lownes's squeaky-clean decade as London gambling impresario. Lownes testified before various state and federal bodies looking into the writing of gambling regulations. Plans were drawn up for first a $50 million—and then a $75 million—hotel-casino on the Boardwalk. The facility was to be built with other people's money, under Playboy management. By the spring of 1978, Playboy had invested $4 million in the project, but expected to take its money out when other financing had been found. In May 1978, a Playboy-managed casino opened in the Bahamas.

By late summer 1977, Daniels was ready to cut fat where it bulged and to add muscle where it was needed. He had put division heads on notice to justify every job and every position. Jobs that couldn't be costed out were to be eliminated. The firings began in August, pretty much across the board from secretary to vice-president. Then, in September, the ax fell on 69 employees in one day. Among those who left were Lee Gottlieb, the public relations vice-president who had been with the company since 1961, and Richard Koff, Playboy's assistant publisher and business manager. Kretchmer had to let fiction editor Robie Macauley and senior editor Bob Shea go. The company's top-ranking black, vice-president Howard Bond, was dismissed (without the opposition this time that marked Tony Jackson's firing two years earlier); so was a fourth vice-president. All told, 100 people were let go, roughly 10 percent of the 745 headquarters employees.

There is a story, perhaps apocryphal, that made the rounds after the shakeup: At the end of their last day on the job, Gottlieb and two other victims took the elevator down to the lobby of the Playboy Building. When it reached the ground floor, Gottlieb cracked, "Last one out, turn off the bunny beacon."

Well, not quite. A couple of months later, Daniels chaired his second annual meeting, this one in Los Angeles, and could point to a startlingly improved financial performance. Sales rose more than $25 million to a record $223.4 million. Net earnings doubled to $4.1 million (and would have been considerably higher except for a losing fourth quarter, due, Daniels explained, to various write-offs). Once again, gambling led the pack with net earnings of $10 million. Key sales were up, too, to $6.2 million.

But though the bunny beacon atop the Playboy Building had not been dimmed; it did not shine much brighter, either—at least, the numbers did not indicate that basic problems had been resolved. If anything, the gap between profitable and unprofitable activities widened. Sure, casino earnings were up, but so were hotel and record losses. Together they accounted for $12.5 million, and both were records. *Oui* lost another $1 million. *Playboy*'s sales rose, but earnings fell to $2.5 million. Unsold newsstand copies alone cost the company $1 million a month. True, advertising was showing real strength. Marks was building a hustling sales force that had shucked the number-one syndrome. But, to get higher sales, Marks had cut the base rate 17 percent, from 5.4 million to 4.5 million, and had slashed costs to advertisers. Circulation continued slipping, averaging 4.9 million in the first six months of 1977, compared to 5.5 million the previous half. The IRS slapped Playboy with a $7.7 million assessment for 1970–72 and was looking into more recent corporate write-offs. PEI promised to fight the judgment, but it added to the uncertainty. At best, though, results were still mixed and inconclusive. *Forbes,* for example, conceded that Playboy had made something of a rebound and become more businesslike, but proclaimed that "at middle age, the bunny clearly ain't what he used to be."

The years of a surging growth which management couldn't handle were certainly over. But as Daniels' hand firmed on the tiller, improvements did look solid and steady. First-half sales and earnings for fiscal 1978 ran well ahead of 1977, despite a December dip in the casino. PEI was getting out of some unprofitable businesses. Nearly half a dozen clubs had been closed, the movie theaters sold off, movie and TV production reduced to a holding operation. Most important, though, Daniels finally pulled the plug on the music-publishing and record businesses. Cumulative six-year losses approached $12 million with fiscal 1977 losses alone of $4.1 million.

A couple of days after Easter, Daniels sprawled in one of the leather armchairs in his suite, sipping coffee and puffing Benson & Hedges Gold, his tie loose, the dark velour vest open, while a jeans-clad M. J. hunkered on the couch.

Daniels mused, "Sure, it's an immense challenge to professionalize the company, build stability, the people, the procedures, the systems, the planning, the solid foundation blocks that can forever support a company that is selling dreams. It grew so fast, I don't think it was ever professional. It grew out of the genius of one guy, the founder, who let loose a lot of free spirits chasing ideas, often brilliant ones. When success came, Playboy didn't learn early enough that it was becoming a great big company and that it had to develop the foundations of a great big company. It is still evolving from entrepreneurship into a professional company. Part of the challenge is to do that without losing the flavor and the spirit which the entrepreneurial company has. It's an energy factor that tends to go out of over-managed companies. You have to maintain a willingness to live with people who have spectacular gifts and the defects that go along with those talents. My challenge is to put together people who have spectacular gifts, perhaps with defects, but so as to have the gifts of one overlap the shortcomings of another. If you do that, the potential of the whole rising is much greater than bringing in a lot of safe people out of the middle. There is some danger in it, but the potential is greater than looking only for the corporate types."

Daniels is building for the long haul, not the short gain. *Oui*'s renewed loss doesn't bother him. He feels that the magazine has the potential and that locating it in California was the right move. *Playboy*'s low profitability? No sweat. He has people working on cutting down returns, and he is bullish on Lehrman and Marks. Circulation and advertising will continue to go up. Atlantic City? It'll be profitable, even if the Arab petrodollars that made London so successful don't follow the bunny to America. Playboy products are being upgraded, and he is phasing out the schlocky kitsch sold in places like the Great Gorge gift shop. Instead the focus will be on stylish cigarette lighters, sunglasses, scarves, and fancy leather goods. The new Publications Division is looking at proposals others bring in. Some it will help launch with an option to buy if they prosper. A food and wine magazine—*The International Review of Food and Wine*— is in the works, done by professionals in New York. Playboy is the lender, with an option to buy. Failure would be someone else's failure, Daniels explains, and that is easier to swallow than your own. "It's very tough to kill your own baby at the right time." Still, in the summer of 1978, *Playboy* pondered a dummy for a show business magazine it would bankroll—a magazine that would give stars the *People* treatment.

Daniels is even upbeat about the hotels. He has brought in new management. "The big turnaround is in Great Gorge. It has the greatest potential for improvement. We're tracking it month by month. It is going to be much better this year—not profitable, but better. We have put effort and attention into it, better management, sales, controls, and service. Great Gorge is a nice place to go. Inaccessibility is not a fatal defect. It was never well marketed. It is now. People are willing to go and find it."

Suddenly Daniels sounds familiar. Ever since Arnold Morton left in 1972, management has said the hotels were about to turn around —and they never have. Gambling, of course, is the hope for Great Gorge. Should New Jersey ever legalize casinos for the whole state, the resort would become a bonanza. Meanwhile it remains dicey. So does the company. Gambling is risky; the whole leisure business is, too. Another recession, another oil embargo, the pressure of higher costs on the magazines. Still, Daniels and Hefner think conservatively on economic and business matters, and that conservatism is being adapted to the realities of the late seventies and eighties. No more financing projects out of pocket, more emphasis on product and ideas, less on real estate. "We sell the sizzle, not the steak," Hefner says, and he has a point—if he can hold his executives and himself to it. With Daniels holding the leash, he just might, too.

Hefner certainly has no qualms or doubt. He rarely has. Dreams and reality, the dream merchant thinks, "are much closer than they were. More people can afford the dreams. We have new opportunities. We're going international. The stock is underpriced. Better times are ahead. It's going to be wild."

12

Saving the Dream

WHEN Arthur Kretchmer succeeded Auguste Comte Spectorsky as editor of *Playboy,* he was haunted by his mentor's ghost; he could not bring himself to move into Spec's northwest corner office with its splendid view of Lake Michigan and dark oak-paneled walls. The ghost lingered. Even business manager Robert Preuss could not convince the young editor to take the office to which he was entitled, and which Preuss felt corporate decorum demanded he take.

Six years later, Kretchmer succumbed to the lure of symbols and moved. There is booze on his windowsill now, and not hidden shyly in a cabinet. The Fleischmann's gin is gone, replaced by better brands. A very good stereo system plays rock and Haydn Symphonies. He wears a tie under unshaven chin these days and pokes a *New York Times* article about unshaven chic among men important enough not to have to shave across his desk. He wears a hat in the picture and is quoted as saying that going unshaven does not require the statement wearing a beard makes. Does he believe that? Of course not. But you have to say something.

The internal battling that marked Spectorsky's last years and the succession has faded. Even before he died, Spectorsky, a man of the 1930s, had, as Kretchmer puts it, "lost to the sixties as a style," and, judging from the memos and letters he wrote in his last year, even enjoyed losing that way. The difference in style and time, Kretchmer believes, "is more to the point than left or right. We were journalistic, rude, direct, heavy hitters. We weren't programmatic. Get the government from the left, from the right—if there's a bullshit factory, burn it down."

Pondering the years of his editorship, the bright promise at the beginning and the time of drift, Kretchmer wondered about his early years. "What happened was that I reacted against the hortatory, cause-related essay Spectorsky, Fisher, Goode, and I had brought to the magazine. They helped make *Playboy* abstract by discussing abstract ideas—things like the future of leisure, which was dumb, and future shock, which was great. A mood of saving the world began to permeate the magazine. For a little while, we were messianic, indulging in a self-conscious kind of public-spiritedness, which embarrassed me some. There are things I wish I hadn't published. Our nonfiction was becoming pompous between 1968 and 1971. A guy in Washington got us cause-related, important pieces under big by-lines—senators and people like that. Some of the writing was not significant, but we saw those articles as little medals we gave ourselves.

"The magazine needed to get down to the way people really talked, to become more genuinely topical. We dropped a lot of abstract material, and as a result lost some conceptual leadership. The believing stuff slowed down. Pieces became more routine, more concrete, more journalistic. It was a proper correction for what had gone too far in the past, and we did have some terrific stories, but the magazine was not articulating a position of its own. We stopped being a thoughtful magazine. Between 1972 and 1974, we got too generalized.

"If you pull together the tables of content for those years, there was a lot of extraordinary writing that will last a long time; but much of it was aimless and random, a kind of ongoing eccentricity. Will the writer get an interesting story, as opposed to will it be interesting to the reader? We indulged the writer and did not entertain the reader. *Playboy* can't repeat Cronkite or *Time* or *Newsweek,* so it had to find a space to grow into. We had to have an angle. We had to stretch more. We tried to do it in the context of our enlightened position. But that role got harder to play. Take the December 1974 issue. It was a good, impressive magazine, but it didn't have a definable character. We were too high-and-mighty. We went overboard. That year we weren't figuring out who we could be."

In short, Kretchmer had inherited a magazine with an identity crisis; a crisis that took some years to emerge and define, and one that does not seem fully resolved yet. For Robert Gutwillig, reflecting from his hilltop Los Angeles home (lit swimming pool, orange trees in the yard, a spectacular view through the canyon to the city below) a couple of years after leaving *Playboy,* the problem lay in faulty editorial perception:

"Most of the editors are young and a little embarrassed about

working for *Playboy.* They reflect their interests and their tastes, and
these do not have a lot of relevance to the people who still read the
magazine. The content is too intelligent and intellectual, not full of
the zest for life and the instructional material this audience wants.
This is not the *New Yorker* or *Rolling Stone* audience. *Playboy* isn't
dealing with leaders of government, academe, or the arts, but with
a cross-section of pretty average Americans. *Playboy*'s politics are
total boredom for them. The magazine was miles to the left of its
constituency. Sure, it always took a respectable position on civil-
liberty issues, but that made it respectable, not popular, and the
country has moved beyond the respectable cover."

Gutwillig's points are valid. Kretchmer may have opposed "trendiness," as he contends, but he was "buffeted by the unconscious
currents running through our society" and for the first couple of
years of his editorship, the magazine became a little precious.
Streaked under the layers of pictorials and cartoons were bits and
pieces of radical chic weaving together the war, civil rights, and that
righteous brand of antiestablishment rhetoric that flowered in the
late sixties and still bloomed through Nixon's first term and into
Watergate.

In November 1972, Garry Wills wrote a piece titled "Imprisonment Chic" that best exemplified the mood. He had taken part in a
celebrity protest on Capitol Hill with arrests all but prearranged with
Washington police. The polite shuffle between establishment and
antiestablishment establishment—the list of those arrested was star-
studded—had its comic moments. Wills touched on them, but he was
too outraged by the policy he opposed to exploit the inherent ridicule
the way Tom Wolfe had in his *New York Magazine* article on radical
chic. Without the leavening of humor, the impact was numbing.
Wills presented a formal and ritualized protest movement that could
be choreographed like a ballet. *Playboy* was made to look like a chic
little stage on which to perform the dance. Outrage began to sound
shrill; perhaps there had been too much of it.

But the waning Vietnam War and the Watergate scandal did lend
themselves so splendidly to moralizing, so for a time *Playboy* moral-
ized, often disdainfully, as Jane Fonda and her new husband Tom
Hayden did in an interview. Fonda hates *Playboy*'s sexism, but, like
Germaine Greer, she lusted for its reach. So she and Hayden flayed
American attitudes on Vietnam and Watergate, deplored mid-
America's failure to fully understand the significance of either, and
were contemptuous of those who thought the tragedy of Vietnam
was over. It was a revealing glimpse into the thinking of the aging
New Left, but the moralizing tone was oppressive.

As *Playboy* careered into its time of financial trouble and corporate turmoil, Kretchmer grew increasingly uneasy and unhappy with his editorial mix. He was missing the connections. Pieces he wanted to work didn't; the whole magazine failed to jell.

After a staff meeting with Hefner at the Chicago mansion in December 1974, Kretchmer stayed behind to talk about his troubles. The editor-publisher, then immersed in troubles of his own—the Arnstein case, the drug probe, the resignation of his outside directors —listened attentively. Kretchmer remembers the scene vividly:

"We were in his living quarters. Hefner was shaving to go out. He was the only man I ever saw shave without using water. He just put cream on his face and started. Maybe I was impressed because it always takes me twenty minutes and he was so efficient. He got out of his pajamas and opened his closet. There must have been two hundred suits in it and eighty pairs of socks in his drawers. He has a good tailor. That's when it hit me: My God, he's a rich man. It took me by surprise. Because of our working relationship, it never occurs to me that he's actually wealthy.

"While he was buttoning his shirt, I told him I feel like I have been preserving the magazine's past and that we should be making leaps and bounds in terms of what the magazine is, that we need a conceptual change. And Hefner said he couldn't agree more. We are still in that process of changing."

But Kretchmer was uncertain about what to do first. He knew that *Playboy* had to adapt more quickly to change in general and to the changed climate in which it operated. "It was late. We needed a think tank. If we had an idea, we should go ahead and do it. If it works, fine; if not, junk it. Have our dress rehearsals in public. It would give us new vitality."

The *Playboy* editor was reacting to several things: the recession, the energy crisis, changing life-styles, different perceptions of national drift, and finally, to the challenge of the competition. For five years, *Playboy* had simply refused to acknowledge the newcomers or their staying power. Hefner argued that the "imitators" were not in *Playboy*'s league and should not be taken seriously. His editors rarely bothered looking at *Penthouse* and at the others. "We felt that whatever we did, somebody would imitate it in six weeks," Kretchmer says. "And we made the mistake of judging *Penthouse* on its literary quality."

There was another mistake: *Oui* magazine. For a couple of years, Hefner believed his newest offspring would stop *Penthouse,* and PEI executives were slow to admit that *Oui* took most circulation away from *Playboy,* not from the others.

Originally, *Oui* had been created to stop a deal between *Penthouse*'s Bob Guccione and a French skin merchant named Daniel Filipacchi, the proprietor of a French *Playboy* ripoff titled *Lui*. Filipacchi was determined to crack the U.S. market—and ready to sell out to the highest bidder. In the ensuing negotiations, Gutwillig outbid Guccione. *Oui* was born in a deal that gave Filipacchi a 50 percent royalty for *Lui* material used in *Oui*. Despite the high cost, Gutwillig figured it was worth it because he could use the new publication to hold *Playboy* rack space in the market-share war with *Penthouse,* and because he was looking for a licensee to do a French *Playboy*. And Filipacchi fitted that bill.

What Gutwillig had not anticipated, however, was the fracturing of the skin-book market. *Oui*'s road to survival has been rocky, at best, but it started off briskly and surely encouraged even more imitators to start up. "What I didn't understand was that bad money would drive out the good," Gutwillig says ruefully, "and that magazine loyalties would break down so completely." No matter how cruddy the product, it made money, and by the mid-seventies, *Playboy*'s quality—and the magazine still had a good deal of it—became a drag on a marketplace full of racier imitators. Neither radical chic not straight journalism was much of an answer.

Guccione had tagged the problem in the very first ad he ever ran for *Penthouse* in the United States back in 1969. "We give our readers the pictures without the lectures," Guccione wrote. "The pinups without the hangups. Writers yes, philosophizers no."

By 1974–75 that issue had become acute. While editorial content floundered, *Playboy* moved inexorably toward greater sexual explicitness. Kicking and screaming, literally, *Playboy* was dragged into the raunch war; dragged so slowly and so unwillingly that Hefner and his editors still do not see the surge for what it was, and put *Playboy*'s entry into the fray at least a year behind the facts.

The difficulty, clearly, was one of timing. *Playboy* lagged behind the others. Beaver shots were soon a commonplace. Girls on the cover licked stamps and cigars with fake abandon, but it was already tame, too tame. *Penthouse* pets looked wicked and touched their bodies in wild and wonderful ways that were loaded with guilt and sin and deep, dark pleasures. Other imitators, from *Gallery* to *Genesis,* breathed harder, and when Larry Flynt put *Hustler* on the market, the last fences came crashing down. As the race for the most daring grew fiercer, *Playboy* was forced to play catch-up ball—and never quite made it. Hefner's heart was not in the raunch war, and while his editors did their raunchy duty, they did not hide their distaste.

But as the months wore on, *Playboy*'s troubles grew. The magazine became raunchier and raunchier, for all of Kretchmer's insistence that "heating up" the book was more osmosis than design.

"Pubic hair and crotch shots appeared in *Playboy* long before we felt the heat from *Penthouse*. There was a gradual movement in the magazine to let that happen. What Guccione did was take away our ability to move at our own pace."

In March 1975, Hefner complicated matters. He held a meeting to take a critical look at Playmates. The girls, he decreed, were too pinuppy, too abstract, too unbelievable. "He never said, 'Show cunt shots,' but our photographers didn't know how else to interpret what he said than to be more explicit, and to do that, the girl had to lie down," Kretchmer explains, and he insists that the results of that decree did not show up until the July 1975 issue. That claim is open to debate and interpretation, but there is no doubt that the spread on Playmate Lynn Schiller was an extended orgasm displayed on yards and yards of pink satin sheets with the cloth pressed into service, on occasion, as a limp dildo. The setting, however, is ornate and antique and as classy as anything *Playboy* ever put together. A delicate, two-handled bone china cup filled with cream touches Miss Schiller's thighs while she licks the cream off a silver-painted finger; pale tea roses in a silver vase; a silver hairbrush; gold-plate-embossed screens; kerosene lamps atop china bowls; glass swans; oval mirrors; thick strands of pearls; a fruit bowl; rich fabrics. Opulence literally beyond avarice. Art Paul considers the layout one of his favorites.

The accessories had enough class to pull Miss Schiller up along with them. But on the cover she is made to stand alone, nude, dressed in a plastic raincoat that shows all, her face pinched into a "come-hither" coo, her eyes all-inviting with a fifty-buck yes. And there had been similar covers. April's, for example. It featured blonde Cindi Wood in a white negligee, swathed in pearls, a pink rose embedded on green leaves pinned to her waist, a pearl ring the size of a martini onion on her finger, and what looks like a beer bottle placed firmly against her twat. Closer inspection reveals it to be an expensive bottle of champagne. The visual mix-up—and it was more widespread than Kretchmer would admit—says a lot about *Playboy*'s state of mind.

Most of 1975, in fact, was mired in an often-vulgar gutter. Covers grew hornier, inside picture spreads more explicit. In October, Kretchmer gambled on a lesbian cover, but wrapped his gamble in perhaps the most tasteful photographic layout *Playboy* has ever run. "Sappho," the cover line proclaimed, "stunning portraits of women in love." They were that. Kretchmer had developed the feature from New York photographer J. Fred Smith's picture book about lesbians. Kretchmer also selected a suggestive cover of two women touching and holding each other. Inside, little verses accompanied each picture. Most were by "anonymous" but one was by Ezra Pound:

Thy soul
Grown delicate with satieties
Atthis
Oh Atthis,
I long for thy lips
I long for thy narrow breasts,
Thou restless, ungathered.

The layout had the hard Weimar style that was so much the hallmark of *Playboy*'s fashion photography then. Some pictures were raw and shocking. A shot of two women kissing is like the flick of a wet towel. The pictorial flow has a balletlike choreography to it. Skin tones are painted on like Marcel Marceau's pantomime mask, compositions within each picture laid out with the care of a Géricault. Hands, wineglasses, arms, legs, touching fingers. The effect is electrifying, by far the most erotic spread ever to appear in the magazine. Yearning, longing, desire, fulfillment. *Playboy* has never done it as passionately—before or since. It was Eros triumphant, and Sexus marched offstage.

Yet that cover and the story inside tore it. All the class and style didn't help, or the fact that the previous issue of the magazine was alive with kicking sluts and faked orgasms. The dam didn't burst for that. But lesbianism was too much. *Time* even used the spread to kick off a clucking piece titled "Skin Trouble" which predicted that skin magazines had bumped up against the final frontier and that the "sultans of skin" had lost the war. Advertisers were furious and told *Playboy* so. Ad director Lederer wilted. He sent letters to the major agencies apologizing for the cover and promising reform. Kretchmer prepared for his journey to New York to make a less-cringing peace with Madison Avenue than Lederer wanted—and to battle his ad chief for caving in too quickly. Lederer won the first round, but six months later, he was out. Kretchmer fights rough in the clinches, and though he didn't bring Lederer down by himself, he helped.

But even while Kretchmer explained the "new" *Playboy* to the media directors in the magazine's Drake suite, the "old" *Playboy* hit the stands with as-yet-unmatched vulgarity. November's cover was the pits. Her name was Patricia Margot McClain, a baby-faced blonde with pixieish, wicked eyes. She sat in a movie-house seat, a bag of popcorn on a slim thigh. Her legs were spread wide. Spiked heels almost came together on the floor. She wore green bikini panties with white polka dots and white trim. Her brown skirt was pulled above the crotch, her brown blouse wide open to reveal what looked like a transparent brown body suit (either that, or Miss McClain was tanned and taut all over). Three fingers of her right hand were stuck inside the panties, and she is clearly masturbating to the film on an invisible screen. Even the densest reader could not miss the cover line's implication: "More Sex in Cinema."

"That magazine sold very well," Hefner mused, "and I hate that cover. The reason I hate that cover is because it looks like a cheap girlie magazine. It didn't have another dimension—an aesthetically pleasing dimension."

"I see every cover from the beginning," Kretchmer explains, "from the very first transparency. The first shots looked all right but when I saw the final copy with the type already on the picture I asked myself are we really going to publish this? It is very raw. Holy shit, this is raw, it's too raw. And then I signed it anyway, figuring it would be all right. It wasn't."

If Sappho had outraged the New York advertising community, the November cover made up Hefner's mind. *Playboy* not only had to bail out of the raunch war, as Kretchmer had promised the ad men, but needed to return to "basics." He called together his magazine staff, fifty people in all, with this blunt message: We cannot go down this road. We will not compete. We have to stress service and the availability of alternate life-styles. We must explore new directions and give the reader more information and get it to him in new ways. Kretchmer rose to defend his lesbian cover, arguing that it was an exercise in sensuality, not vulgarity, and an affirmation that *Playboy* would not abandon sex or turn asexual. Hefner agreed. He would not give up "the ladies." But there was more to *Playboy* than sex. There always had been. He would not chase *Penthouse* and *Hustler* any further.

Playboy didn't. On the other hand, it didn't retreat much, either. Women still touch themselves fondly on their privates, wear garter belts and long boots. Some issues are raunchier than others, though covers have grown noticeably more attractive—beginning with December 1975. A film director writing a script for redemption could not have orchestrated the flow with greater panache. After the slut of November, celestial trumpets blew in December. Playmate Lillian Muller floats on clouds, while blowing soap bubbles through a rabbit head and the bubbles bounce down some Milky Way to the sun. Muller's nude body is innocent bliss.

How are they picked, these American love Goddesses, successors to Marilyn Monroe, and more distantly to Betty Grable and Rita Hayworth? The method borders on the cold-blooded and smoothly professional, though it has at times some of the cottage industry touches that mark the book-publishing business. There is, first of all, the slush pile that accumulates in the Chicago offices of the photography editor—there have been only three in *Playboy*'s history—Vincent Tajari, Mark Kauffman, and the current occupant of that throne, Gary Cole, the first to rise from the ranks rather than be brought in from the outside. Somewhere around 400 unsolicited pictures of a bewildering cross-section of American beauties, or not such beauties, arrive every month, sent in by boyfriends and husbands, mothers and aunts, and by girls who catch a first flush of their own looks in someone else's snapshots. Like book publishers, photography boss Cole has slush-pile "lookers" who sort and file, and mostly reject. Lightning does strike the slush pile, but not often enough for Cole to remember any spectacular beauty to emerge from it. A much more likely source of viable pictures is the free-lance photographer who had some contacts with *Playboy* or thought he could make one. The lensmen literally comb the country looking for girls who might fit *Playboy*'s bill.

Cole insists that the *Playboy* approach is low-key. Photographers will approach girls and tell them, "I think you are very pretty, and if you are interested in trying out for a Playmate, call me," and then they will slip them their cards. More often than not, girls are flattered, even if in the end they are not chosen. Nor do the photographers pick only on single girls. If the woman is part of a couple, the photographer first approaches the man, tells him who he is, and that he thinks his date or wife or girlfriend is very pretty. "We don't push too hard," Cole adds.

If Cole or any of his associates are struck by a girl's picture, they will invite the model to Chicago or to California (and sometimes to places like Miami, where photographers with long *Playboy* experience live and work and are trusted) for additional shooting sessions and "to give us an idea of how she photographs." Standards remain strict. On an average, one out of a hundred girls is considered interesting enough to pursue further. Candidates who make it as far as Chicago or Los Angeles are put through one- or two-day shooting sessions in front of a 35 millimeter camera. Test results are then circulated among Cole, two other photography editors, two staff photographers, executive art director Tom Staebler (though Art Paul remains in overall charge, his graphic responsibilities now include the whole corporation, with the *Playboy* nitty-gritty left to Staebler), Kretchmer, and managing editor Wax. The committee then votes on candidates, and the winner's pictures are taken to Hefner in Los Angeles for the final decision. Cole says that years of experience have given him antennae sensitive to Hefner's likes and dislikes so that "I know what Hefner will go with."

Once a centerfold subject is agreed upon, the really hard work begins—exhausting shooting sessions that can take three to four weeks to complete. Girls selected make good enough money—$10,-

000 for the whole works—but hardly in the Cheryl Tiegs or Las Vegas league. But then, few are professionals. In the last year, Cole said in 1978, only two girls had professional modeling experience; the rest were still found walking up and down the avenue—or had responded to ads *Playboy* photographers will place in campus newspapers or that of other organizations with a large pool of hopefully nubile lens fodder.

But the *Playboy* girl has changed over the years, too. "In the mid-sixties, the first thing we'd go for was the body. Now it is the face, teeth, complexion, hair, and whether she's healthy-looking. Then we inspect the figure. If the figure is not so good, then we have a problem, but the body without a face is past."

Part of the thrust for quality is dictated by advances in color photography and by the broader scope of the spread. In the past, the whole feature was the color centerfold garnished by a few black-and-white shots that could be made to disguise flaws. Now the chosen girl must survive seven pages of color pictures in addition to the centerfold and black-and-white stills. There is no room left to hide imperfections.

"We do more face shots to see how they look. We look for character and expression. Some women are more animated than others. We do run girls with only one expression to them, but they have to be awfully pretty."

Copy is assigned by senior editors on the magazine to junior staffers and handled like any house-written stories. "Hopefully," Cole says, "the writer will sit down with the girl in person and base his text on a personal interview. The stories are true; the quotes real and not made up. We try not to put words in their mouth. In the past, some girls were unhappy with the quotes, so now the writer will read his quotes back. Hefner is sensitive to the women and wants them to be happy with the stories and the pictures." But Cole will admit that a reasonably skilled interviewer can get most girls to say pretty much what he wants to hear.

Clearly, Playmates have won mythical stature in the American pantheon. To be a Playmate is to be somebody in the American Dream. And women try who have no dreams left. Sometimes, even a man who has seen as many nudes as Cole is touched by "the amazing range" of those who pin their sense of self on a snapshot. "They range from very pleasant and pretty to those who waited too long, who are too old or too fat. We do get dogs. Our standards are not the only standard. Some women should know they are not candidates. Some know they won't make it, but want to say that they tried, that they got as far as coming in for an interview. They become mythologized."

Others are so frightened by the experience of being actually photographed, and in the nude, yet, that they cannot stand up. Cole remembers one girl who had to be photographed on her knees and lying down because she was too terrified to stand up.

Even Hefner—teacher, guru, apostle—cannot drain the holy terror of sex from some members of the Playboy generation.

Reform of the editorial package Hefner and Kretchmer had agreed upon in December 1974 proved harder to implement. Even as they talked, the recession and the oil embargo had changed the American landscape, and *Playboy* had not been able to develop an effective editorial approach to the new realities. Recession and economic woes were problems beyond *Playboy*'s ken—something its editors may have read about but did not really comprehend. And as unemployment lunged toward 10 percent in the spring of 1975, *Playboy* continued to insist that it sold fantasy, a commodity, it said, much in demand in harsh times. Kretchmer expounded that theme in several interviews but sounded uncomfortable doing it.

The trouble was that *Playboy*'s dreams had worked so well for so long because they were attainable—attainable from the beginning. Yes, a $57 suede jacket, offered in the men's shop guide to the first issue was expensive, but not out of reach. The spicy chicken dish it featured could be made at no great expense. By the mid-seventies most of the artifacts of the good life featured in *Playboy* were affordable, a point Hefner never tires of making. Now, suddenly, these things seemed tantalizingly out of reach.

Editorial content reflected the confusion. Kretchmer tried to face the bitterness of the new economics, but failed to come to grips or to terms with it. His writers attempted to make it funny or scary or to patronize the men who handled the problems. The articles didn't work. Too often they were askew, off base, overstated. They no longer measured the temper of the times, or at best, measured it badly.

An article on the collapse of the Franklin National Bank was scarier than the facts—bad as they were—warranted, and the piece lacked the hard professional competence *Playboy* had shown in other areas. An interview with Treasury Secretary William Simon lunged over the head of the readership and too often became an ideological battle between interviewer Peter J. Ognibene, a regular contributor to *The New Republic* and a certified member of the left-liberal establishment (in 1976 he published a devastating book on Senator Henry Jackson that helped kill his presidential bid) and the conservative Treasury Secretary. Golson's argument that Simon had sent him a thank-you letter for allowing him to express his opinions so fully did not make the printed product any less a battlefield, or less abstruse.

A March 1975 piece titled "Who's Afraid of Hard Times?" explained away hard times as simply the result of bungling government and bungling economists. If good ideas just got to those in power, author William F. Rickenbacker opined, the stage would be set for the "next great economic miracle." If government were to remove its feet "from the country's neck, it will rise up and start running very nicely." *Playboy* had been that simplistic in the past, of course, but not often enough to make it a habit. Such embarrassments in *Playboy*'s journalism—and Golson, among others, is careful to make the distinction between the magazine's journalism and its entertainment side—stick out.

Kretchmer admits to slackness and confusion. Writing lost its sting. It became sloppier. Captions, heads and subheads wilted. "*Playboy* was getting aimless again and appeared weak-willed or too flaccid in the way it was doing things. Even the language was bad again. The cover lines were kind of low-key and hip and turned a phrase rather than stating what the issue was about."

That spring, Jim Goode returned to *Playboy*. He became, as Kretchmer put it, "available," and was hired as a New York–based executive editor. When he left Playboy in 1970, he had indeed managed to start *Earth* and to run it for sixteen months before his capital ran out and he had to close it down. Two days later, Guccione hashed out a deal with him in Los Angeles and made him executive editor of *Penthouse*. There he proceeded to do pretty much what he had at *Playboy* in the sixties: stir things up, add bite and content to a magazine that had little of either, assign provocative ideas, and hire name writers to put them down on paper.

"I think he proved his power when he went to *Penthouse*," Kretchmer says. "Proved that he could see through a situation and to give some substance to a very tawdry and totally useless magazine."

And why had Kretchmer hired Goode the second time? To get him out of *Penthouse* and cut the opposition down to size?

"You the Clayton antitrust man on the floor?" Kretchmer growled, spooning vanilla ice cream out of a paper cup. We were sitting in one of Playboy's bare New York offices, and I wondered whether the ice cream would drop on Kretchmer's big-city clothes: blue blazer, knife-crease gray slacks, dark tie.

"I hired him because he had something I wanted then. As a defensive move, it was too late in 1975. If I had hired him a year earlier, that would have made some sense. But at that point, the fucking magazine [*Penthouse*] was too big—there was no way to stop its growth. I guess there was a time when it would have been an advantage to take him away, but there was more to it than that. Jim came back with a brusque aggressiveness, and he helped me. The whole redesign of the front of *Playboy*—something I had wanted to do for years—was helped along tremendously by Jim coming back with the *Penthouse* experience and saying it could look like this. Now, we didn't want it to look the way Jim wanted it to look, but on the other hand, what he suggested was a big step from where we were. He was just a nice thing to throw into the mix. He made us think about the essence of what we were doing. He is great at that —brilliant, in fact."

Playboy welcomed Goode back with a bash at the Rainbow Grill atop Rockefeller Center to which the maverick editor wore a gabardine suit and high-collared white shirt and tie, a uniform he generally disdains. *Playboy* had sent telegrams to every major publisher and agent in New York, and, docilely, they came and submitted to a door check—outré for Gotham but de rigueur for *Playboy*. Conversation was bitchy and standard, but the turnout said something for Goode's —and the magazine's—pulling power, despite the recession.

Goode's second tour was uneasy and lasted only six months. He conducted business out of his St. Luke's Place apartment, felt cut off from Chicago, and disliked his isolation and lack of power. A clash with the rising Golson, then an assistant managing editor, was inevitable. (In 1978, an icy-voiced Golson said of Goode's hiring, "I believe it was a mistake, and I told Arthur so at the time. I do not see Jim Goode's influence as being a critical one.") Most important, there was the pull of the West Coast. Goode loves California and thinks Los Angeles the cultural capital of the United States. When *Playgirl* offered him the editorship, he jumped.

A day or two before he left for the Coast in November 1975, Goode agreed to talk in his apartment, located in a graceful brownstone with a white stoop and a few trees on the sidewalk. The floor-through street-level apartment has fluted french windows and high stuccoed ceilings. A curlicued sofa stands desolately in a beautiful room crammed with crates and wrapping paper. Packers stride purposefully through the confusion. Goode, in jeans and Western boots, smokes a thoughtful cigarette and supervises. People move in and out. The phone bleats constantly. Goode is polite but distracted, and conversation is difficult. But when he focuses on someone, his eyes cut through the skin.

Hefner is a dinosaur, *Playboy* a stranded whale. Party jokes, for God's sake. What can a University of Colorado freshman do with the titters of the fifties? And if you don't win him for an audience, you don't have one for long. Readers turn over constantly and must be replenished from below, from the pool of the young. Print must reflect the McLuhanite revolution, become film played on the tube of the mind. Look how long *Playboy* stuck grimly to jazz and ignored rock, only because Hefner was an aficionado. When the magazine began to cover the rock scene, it was too late.

"What you do if you're Henry Luce or Hugh Hefner is discover a product that quite by chance has a strong social meaning. Unlike other businesses, the proprietor of a magazine believes that because the public responds to his product, he represents the state of the art, that once you've perfected the basics, that's enough. Luce froze at the controls, and Hefner froze, too. They do it out of fear of losing what they have. It's a kind of insurance mentality. At *Playboy*, they're still not willing to change basics—not even now. Yet if a publisher has confidence in his managers and in his own ability to find good managers and administrators, the sky is the limit. I believe the real potential of *Playboy* was 18 million—look at *Reader's Digest* and *TV Guide*.

"But to do that you need a happy, uninhibited magazine. Still *Playboy*, but *Playboy* without fear. The whole magazine business has changed in the last five years. Layout, feel, and look of a magazine is a film. It is no longer conscious or cerebral. Nonfiction is drama. Watergate was a movie. High drama has moved from theater to print. When I was at *Penthouse*, I commissioned fifteen pieces on the CIA. The reason was entertainment. I'd like to see Kissinger in jail, but the stories about him are entertaining. ˙'s the same thing as *Three Days of the Condor*. That's why Nader failed. He lost the ability to dramatize the struggle. Nader is just like Hefner. He dramatized a demand, froze into a position and never came out. What Hefner doesn't realize is that he has the last public-opinion forum left in the United States. TV has no opinions. The newspapers don't. You have only two policy-making publications left anywhere: *Playboy* and *Penthouse*."

Was Kretchmer sorry to see Goode go a second time? His answer is opaque: "Jim was so unhappy in this new relationship with *Playboy*, being in New York and not really on the staff and not listened to or responded to in the way he wished to be, and wanting so much to live on the Coast that I was not unhappy. . . ."

Clearly, however, Goode had played the battering ram to Kretchmer's scalpel once again, but this time there was no Spectorsky to fight—only Kretchmer and Golson—and this time they were the status quo. Out at the mansion in Los Angeles, Goode watched in astonishment as Hefner and his editors argued the pros and cons of the December 1975 cover. "You didn't need to think about it," he said disgustedly. "It was a natural."

Assigning credit for who did what on a magazine without having been on it is dumb business at best. But it is, nevertheless, hard to escape the impression that Goode had some impact on the magazine in the few short months he was on it a second time, an impact that went beyond finding "only" one piece (Mark Vonnegut's "Lunatic Express"). If nothing else he irritated the magazine's staff.

"I think he got us to think about our social conscience a little," Golson concedes. "But the examples of that conscience Jim seemed concerned with looked like examples out of the 1960s and not the seventies."

Moreover, coincidental or not, after Goode left, having helped to put the March 1976 issue to bed, some of the aimlessness of earlier years began to fade. The good journalism—and at its nadir *Playboy* always had its share of interesting and provocative articles such as Robert Sherrill's pinpointing of bible thumpers in politics—stuck out less and became more smoothly integrated into the package. Change did not come all at once and everywhere in the publication, but there was enough to be noticeable. Golson, who took over interviews after Fisher left, gave those with Jerry Brown, Nelson Rockefeller (actually a "profile" with an interview folded inside), Jimmy Hoffa, Jimmy Carter, Daniel Patrick Moynihan and Andrew Young a new and sharper bite. The space for diverse opinions was still there, but the form became looser, less insistently linear, and not so adamant about scoring important points. Intellectually, *Playboy* began to relax a little, to look for the vivid difference more than for the quickly sensational. Knowingly or not, Kretchmer became aware that he had a bully pulpit and began to use it with new vigor. In an article that impressed even William F. Buckley, Jr., not always a fan of *Playboy*'s liberal politics, *Playboy* attacked the IRS and the Social Security system. Hefner suggested that a "casebook" section be added to Forum where specific legal cases involving drug or sex convictions were discussed and given journalistic, legal, and financial support, with money coming from the Playboy Foundation. A new strain of muckraking entered the magazine that added an occasional *Rolling Stone* flavor.

Robert Scheer, who did several major interviews and articles, helped give that flavor spice. There was, first of all, the sheer incongruity of *Ramparts* in *Playboy,* and of the Bronx socialist out of Berkeley baiting the likes of Rockefeller, Jerry Brown, and Jimmy Carter. And Scheer added new dimensions.

"When Scheer did Rockefeller, nobody had ever done Rockefeller like that," Kretchmer says. "He got to a side of the man nobody ever saw before. And Scheer and Rockefeller was such a wonderful notion."

He is right. Scheer is an antagonist in a way the more disciplined Fisher and the writers he employed never were. He confronts his subject, nags, attacks, probes, moves quickly in the verbal clinches. He disdains objectivity as a cover without slipping on the banana peel of the "new journalism." The interview form, no matter how loose Golson has allowed it to become (and it is not that loose), made that difficult anyway. And Scheer's portraits are etched as sharply as Tom Wolfe's at his vitriolic best.

Governor Brown emerged from Scheer's typewriter crucified by his own words. The ambivalences and contradictions in the man stood out. The masks covering his face and mind fell one by one and were revealed as stage props rather than the changing but real moods of one man. And in an article Scheer wrote to go with the interview, he put his own views on the line: Brown was an attractive chameleon whom the American people would trust at their peril.

Not all interviews stood out, of course—not even the serious ones. A conversation with Abbie Hoffman, living underground, was 1960s nostalgia and an exercise in Hoffman's self-pity. Who gives a damn? Who will—unless Hoffman or his underground friends pull off an Aldo Moro–style kidnapping? Yet the probing look at Sara Jane Moore the month after Hoffman was a stark piece of work. President Ford's second would-be assassin emerged as the complete victim; a woman seized by the times in which she lived and by the half-awakened fluttering of her spirit, and shaken into a jellied frenzy. Truly a woman scorned, a woman alone, a human being torn bleeding from her moorings. The interview deserved more attention than it received, but *Playboy* lacks the instinct for publicizing its journalism. Promotion is still seen in terms of Hefner and bunnies.

The Carter interview drove that point home. Kretchmer and Golson knew they were sitting on a keg of dynamite, worried that it would explode too soon, and desperate to have the corporation exploit the publicity they knew would accrue. "Golson and I begged Koff (the Assistant Publisher) to print an extra million copies of that issue," Kretchmer says. Koff refused. Others weren't much more helpful. The consensus was to sell out the issue. One senior executive told an enraged Golson, "Believe me young fellow, that interview won't sell one extra copy."

Perhaps corporate insouciance was best symbolized by a little scene I witnessed on Friday, September 16, 1976. Jody Powell called Golson from a phone booth in Atlanta. The clock ticked past six o'clock. The Playboy operator pulled the plug, leaving Powell with a dead receiver in Atlanta and Golson with a silent phone in his office. Golson marched anxiously into Kretchmer's office where the editor and I were talking. Couldn't Golson get Powell back? In a corner phone booth? Well, they had better try, Powell had sounded awful mad. Neither man wasted a moment's wrath on the Playboy phone operator.

The dynamite exploded on Monday, September 20, when Golson and Scheer broke the story on the Today Show. The press went wild. It had finally found something to enliven a somnulent campaign. The outcry seems to have bewildered Playboy, but failed to convince executives to change their mind on the print run. As press comment on the interview continued, Playboy felt pushed into an editorial defensiveness. The "us" and "them" syndrome—so long an integral part of the publication—resurfaced. Many at *Playboy* felt they were being victimized again, and unfairly at that. Even Golson's self-assured Ivy charm was ruffled. He is still sore that the press pilloried *Playboy*—and Carter for just talking to *Playboy*.

Yet neither he nor Kretchmer nor anyone else realized, or at least is willing to admit, how much the interview did for the magazine. The uproar that followed publication gave Playboy the relevance it had lost. In a matter of weeks the episode erased U.S. Attorney Jim Thompson's March 1975 judgment that he wasn't sure that what *Playboy* stood for was all that relevant or that any prosecution of Hefner would mean that much. Clearly, *Playboy* had become relevant again, and prosecution of Hefner did mean something to the millions who made the magazine a target of new rage. The idea of a presidential candidate talking about sex in *Playboy* six weeks before an election was simply too much.

Golson argues persuasively that without this confluence there would not have been an uproar. An unmemorable interview, a recycled campaign speech would have passed unnoticed; so would a "hotter" content voiced at some other time. Back in 1971, George McGovern had expounded some of his most radical ideas in *Playboy*, but the interview ran a year before the convention, and McGovern had not talked about sex.

The fact that Scheer and Golson had drawn a first-rate interview out of Carter never emerged fully, except perhaps in retrospect, by showing that *Playboy* could be both respectable and politically influential. The reality of that influence shimmered through the editorial commentary on the interview. Though most pundits focused on Carter, it was quickly apparent that the magazine was, if anything, more of an issue than what Carter had said in it. Columnist George Will speared the problem neatly: Carter could not appeal to *Playboy*'s readers—the avowed intent of the interview was to persuade the audience that Carter was not a prude—"without offending many nonreaders. . . . The problem is less with what he said than where he said it."

President Ford said much the same thing: "I don't think the

President of the United States ought to have an interview in a magazine featuring photographs of unclad women."

It was a view shared by Texas preachers and habitués of peep shows. The real majority may have come to terms with its own sexuality and that of its children; but lust among its leaders, especially in the heat of a campaign, remained taboo, a fact Carter himself noted ruefully in his last debate with Ford. Notables from Albert Schweitzer to Governor Brown had done *Playboy* interviews, he said. "But they weren't running for president. . . . I would not have given that interview had I to do it over."

With *Playboy* a campaign issue, Golson suggested an Op-Ed page piece in *The New York Times* in which he defended the substance of the interview and *Playboy*'s role as a legitimate journalistic forum. He does not stress the public relations triumph he scored for *Playboy* in writing and placing it in so prestigious a corner (though he is surely too bright not to have known it) but emphasizes that he wrote it because "I had a feeling that I had been a partial cause for a national hysterical reaction and an election was too important to be decided by hysteria."

It did not stop the hysteria, of course. The Republicans were not about to let go of so good a campaign issue. Hefner watched the GOP attacks with mounting unease. Finally, a week before the election, he issued a statement attacking Ford for tarring Carter "through guilt by association, as though granting an interview to *Playboy* were equivalent to posing naked in the center of the magazine." Of course, in many people's minds, it was.

Though a new confidence had been seeping through the magazine for some months, the Carter interview pinpointed an intellectual turnaround. The circulation slide began to bottom out; there were even signs of a revival, however faint. A more viable balance between raunch and seriousness was found. Some of the double-dome quality that had appeared so naggingly in 1974–75 began to ebb. Nudeless covers took the figleaf off faces. Service features began to disentangle from mammaries, and were actually of some use. New features were added, the look of the magazine redesigned.

"What do you want to know about aesthetics for? It's not an aesthetic magazine. It's a skin book."

Kretchmer burrowed into the chair behind his Stendig desk—a slab of blond wood on top of metal legs—and stared at the afternoon sun hitting tinted windows. Spring 1978. Clearly, Spectorsky's ghosts were gone from the office, and Kretchmer was enjoying the status.

"There is a care, a kind of compulsive delicacy. No, that's the wrong word. But an artisticness, a graphicness about the magazine.

It is edited visually. Hefner is predominantly a visual editor. He could have saved *Life* magazine. He understands the visual components of magazines better than anyone I have ever met in this business. Hefner and Art Paul evolved a clear and careful visual style. The magazine is visually paced. And pacing is the favorite word about this magazine. It has an internal rhythm, which I don't think the reader recognizes. But subconsciously he does grasp the enhancing value. We orchestrate the magazine so its features complement each other rather than jar each other.

"You'll never find a pictorial followed by a second pictorial or a second set of photographs. It is usually followed by art work or cartoons, or text pages and art work, or text and cartoons. Constant use of photography creates a cacophony, a visual disturbance. If you vary the sequences, you get greater visual harmony. Sometimes we change positions in the magazine, move things backwards or forwards depending on whether it interferes with that visual harmony. Sometimes we take important pieces and put them in less important slots because we think their visual nature would disturb the reader.

"When they started the magazine, Hefner and Paul brought in a vast array of other visual styles—and this at a time when the *Saturday Evening Post* style dominated magazine art work—like surrealism and expressionism and much less naturalism than had been used in the immediate past. So *Playboy* became a touchstone for many new trends in art, and its symbolic approach became the style others used. That daring, that absolute willingness to plunge into the avantgarde, into very unorthodox styles, that still goes on. . . .

"We refuse to insert ads in the main editorial sections because that would disturb the flow of the magazine. The flow is primary. We try to have a parallel content flow and to maximize the impact of important stories, textually on the one side and visually on the other. My favorite line about the magazine comes from Truffaut. Truffaut said that movies are like the circus. You can't follow the high-wire act with the lion tamers. Once you have people on the edge of their seats, you must make them laugh. Bring on the clowns, then the bareback riders, and when they're completely relaxed, bring in the lions. I have that very much in mind when I schedule the magazine. We try to pace the most intense moments and put in the most amount of variety in the magazine.

"The one obsession of this magazine has been the incessant need to be varied—internally varied—all the time. You don't run five pieces on the war in Vietnam in a row, or five pieces on fashion. You touch every base. You do a light piece. You do a heavy piece. You do a girl pictorial. You do something else. You do a travel piece one month and a piece on the environment some other month. Redundancy is our biggest single enemy. We don't like there to be two cartoons in the same issue that might have a joke about going to the movies, for example. We've yanked things because two artists will have drawn in a similar style, used the same colors, or drawn the same subject. If that happens, one piece comes right out. We don't want repetition. Monotony is the hallmark of *Penthouse,* and variety is the hallmark of *Playboy.* I mean, if I had to sum it up in one expression, the magazine is obsessed with being different all the time."

Yet Kretchmer insists that the thirst for difference does not conflict with the magazine's patience. "It is not jump cuts because it is so easy to do jump cuts in magazines. This magazine is linear: heads, subheads, captions. Explanatory things. The Playbill to explain it. This is not"—Kretchmer begins to snap his fingers loudly in a percussive rhythm—"I can't do this in words. This magazine is not a crazed Godard movie. Spec and Hef used to say, 'Tell them what they're going to read, tell them what they are reading while they are reading it, and sum it up for them. Tell them what they read. Help them along.' The best single entity I personally put in the magazine was a drug package we ran in 1972. I took it to Hefner—it was the first time I had dealt with him very closely on an editorial thing, one on one—and his whole instinct was: 'Are you confusing the reader? Are you going too quickly? Where are the captions, the subheads? Where is the material that will let the reader get through this easily without any puzzlement.' Hefner likes captions and clues. The whole notion of saying short story by, nonfiction by, investigative report by, is part of that, to give the reader information. It is not a contest.

"*Esquire* was a magazine that had a contest with its readership: 'Hey, reader, are you hip enough to figure out what we are doing?' There is some noxiousness there, a sardonic aspect that we try to avoid at almost all costs. Sometimes we are too simplistic; sometimes we explain too much. But we would much rather err on that side than cause confusion or move too quickly. In that sense, the magazine is old-fashioned. It doesn't have television instincts. It doesn't want to go too fast. It wants to be varied without shocking the eye. It wants to have impact, but it doesn't want to explode. I don't want it to be *People.* We will die if we become *People* magazine. *People* comes along and everybody says, 'Hey, this is the wave of the future. Do this, do this, do this.' " Kretchmer snaps his fingers again, but it is an angry noise this time, like a beetle hitting a screen on a summer night.

"I hate *People,* " he says. "*People* is 'Look at everybody out there who has the money you don't have and lives a life you don't lead.' Camus said—are you ready to get all heavy here?—Camus said that comparison is the bane of life, and *People* is the thing Camus was most afraid of. *People* is a magazine that comes out every week to make people envious."

Doesn't *Playboy* make people envious?

"We are a source book for the possibilities of life, not an envy book. We don't rub the reader's face in somebody else's success all the time. The peopleization of things is the trivialization of ideas. The one thing you can say about us is when we go into a topic, when we do Anita Bryant, when we do intelligence, when we do water, when we do Plato's Retreat when we do whales, I mean we are looking to do it. We are looking to deliver the whole shot in a popular magazine. We are looking to be reliable. We think that the reader who goes to *Playboy* magazine expects us to be reasonably informative. We don't just fuck around. When we do profiles, the writer gets to the guy. You don't do profiles without some intimacy.

"We're intellectually curious, and against antiestablishment central thinking. We like counterthinking, right and left. We did Milton Friedman. For a time we were Murray Rothbard. There is a libertarian streak to the magazine. To tell you that I was born of socialist grandparents is not to tell you that the magazine has an orthodoxy. It doesn't, particularly. But it doesn't like to be bullshitted or conned. If there is one thing you can rely on, it is that no matter who is in the White House or what is the mood of the country's intellectual and political establishment, you will be conned in some way. *Playboy* reflects the idea that people in power are not my friends, that they are more of a problem for me than the bogeyman I grew up with. *Playboy*—and I think people in their twenties and thirties—feel there is an antiauthority mood in this country.

"You know what the movie *M.A.S.H.* was all about? It's about fuck sergeants. You know, stop taking orders from people who don't know any more than you do. I think we reflect something kids and young adults have. Look, when the drug shit came down, if we had printed T-shirts that said 'I'm for Hef,' young guys all over the country would have worn them, as a symbol against the DEA. That's the mood we reflect and stand for and where we lead."

Under Kretchmer, *Playboy* will reflect that mood on occasion, and display a careless willingness to offend and oppose those in power, to have writers say—or draw from interview subjects—outrageous things, and spin them out at length. But the controversy is no longer engendered in the Peck's Bad Boy that Hefner founded in the fifties or in the radical publication of the late sixties, but in a solid twenty-five-year-old establishment publication whose role as opinion molder is no longer questioned or doubted. In fact, as George Will noted in a scathing column about the interview with UN Ambassador Andrew Young ("his act . . . is diplomatic vaudeville"), *Playboy* "is becoming the preferred place for a peculiar kind of political musing."

The word "musing" is apt. Few publications have the space or leisure to allow it at quite such length. And the longer that volatile men like Young—not all that used to musing—muse, the more likely they are to say something outrageous. Young did. Almost as an aside, he called Nixon and Ford racists "who had no understanding of the problems of colored people," and sure enough *Playboy* emblazoned the headlines again.

New York's Democratic Senator Pat Moynihan, who is used to musing, mused his way through a *Playboy* interview without a slip, and without winning any attention. That's a pity because nowhere else has Moynihan mused quite at such length, or with as much grace and subtlety. It is as splendid a look at one of the more interesting social and political minds around the United States in the last quarter of the twentieth century as one is likely to find. And, moreover, its owner hardly ranks as one of *Playboy*'s—or Kretchmer's—favorite people.

Larry Schiller's predeath interview with condemned murderer Gary Gilmore was an abhorrent exercise in the worst prurience of which this society is capable—the prurience of death. Yet nowhere else were Gilmore's mind, thought, and feelings explored with more skill, detachment, and empathy than in *Playboy*.

Finally, there was *Playboy*'s interview with Anita Bryant published in May 1978. No other interview captured quite as many contradictions, or made the point of *Playboy*'s endless diversity as well. Interviewer Ken Kelley, a blond kid with a blond moustache who had tracked Abbie Hoffman for *Playboy* two years earlier, somehow got inside Bryant. Not because he was smart or intuitive or because of any shared empathy. He had none of that. But she responded to something in him—his naïveté, perhaps—or his own vulnerability that matched hers.

Whatever the reason, Bryant bared her mind and soul in a cunning mixture of ignorance and street smarts. Kelley was earnest. He asked the "tough" questions of which *Playboy* is so proud. He nailed her "contradictions." But he could not handle the slippery ease with which Bryant glided off the ropes to leave him flailing at air while she mused about her life and her crusade. Bryant emerged as a troubled, honest, and bewildered woman—and as deadly as a striking cobra. She must have persuaded as many people of the justness of her cause, and of the evils of homosexuality, as she dissuaded and frightened. And much of her impact is due to the room *Playboy* gives her ruminations about God, love, sex, childhood, ambitions, and fears.

The intimate look at Anita Bryant makes up for all the awful pop trivia that spiked *Playboy*'s interview pages over the years, from Tiny Tim to Elton John, the price editors from Fisher to Golson had to pay for the serious journalism in the magazine. It does not, however, compensate for such aberrations as Kretchmer's decision to publish in June 1977 what is probably the worst, most vicious, and cheapest article ever to disgrace *Playboy*'s pages—Thomas Gordon Plate's "The Many Dr. Strangeloves." An attack on Henry Kissinger, it blasted all the "foreign" Dr. Strangeloves, who, together with their foreign accents, have contributed so much to America's misfortunes. The list is catholic and ranges from political scientist Dr. Strausz-Hupe and scientist George Kistiakowsky to Zbigniew Brzezinski. The man most notable for his absence: Dr. Wernher von Braun. But then Plate argues that Jewish refugee Kissinger is the original Dr. Strangelove, not the Aryan Nazi von Braun. Kretchmer took the flak —and there seems to have been quite a bit of it, *Playboy* is not often quite as jingoist, and rarely anti-Semitic, and this piece was both— without flinching; neither apologizing nor justifying.

Even at twenty-five, *Playboy* can still dish up the best and the worst of it, maturity and stupidity. Boy and man, *Playboy* has straddled many fences. "Hugh Hefner is America," Michelle Urry says, and she is close. Not all of America, but a large and significant slice. Seen whole and in perspective, *Playboy* has genuinely touched the lives of millions.

Hefner married religion and sex—serious moral concerns—with unbridled hedonism. He taught millions how to handle their new affluence without slipping their traditional moorings. He has eased the pain of living with ambivalence, ambiguity, and contradiction. *Playboy* has not been able to reconcile the conflicting pressures of change that have wrenched the nation. But it has argued, and often with effect, that it is possible to live side by side with the irreconcilable. That good taste and vulgarity are not incompatible, that good literature is enjoyable, that trash is often fun. *Playboy* has been shallow and deep, earnest and frivolous. Many of its concerns are humane and loving (Hefner is fond of the word "loving" and uses it as a friend and not as a sometime acquaintance); some are silly, and some dangerous.

Playboy has defined political territory that offered a home base to an amorphous amalgamation of Americans, ranging from the champions of a consumer society and its worst excesses to the graduates of the counterculture, eager to infuse a new sense of moral urgency into the American spirit. Much of its political journalism has been seminal; and future historians, putting together the strands of American political thought, will not be able to ignore it. At its sappiest—

and God knows no one can hold a candle to *Playboy* when it comes to playing the political sap—the pieces say something worth knowing about a national mood or feeling. The voice may be inchoate, but its struggle to be heard is worthy of attention.

Playboy is a hard magazine for intellectuals to handle. They rarely resist the temptation to make fun of its pretensions. Being clever at Hefner's expense is a favorite sport. Yet it is too easy and too empty. Making fun of 20 million people doesn't mean much, and is at best a senseless form of elitism. Dismissal of *Playboy* as just a slickly packaged pornographic magazine, as George Will has done, is no better. Of course it has a distasteful and vulgar side, but it is only one side and not the most significant. If *Playboy* has little influence on the New York scene, as the *Village Voice*'s Jack Newfield (though Newfield thinks Kretchmer the best editor he ever dealt with) among many others contend, it does have enormous reach at home and abroad. A small example: author Joseph Heller told his *Playboy* interviewer in 1975 that he was fond of Jarlsberg cheese. A few months later, Heller visited Norway, where his academic hosts served him Jarlsberg cheese. They had read *Playboy* to keep up with what was going on in the United States. After publication of *The Best and the Brightest,* David Halberstam became a minor celebrity on Nantucket, where he has a summer home. But only after his *Playboy* interview did he become truly famous on the island.

Yet, in many ways, *Playboy* remains a maddening publication. There are issues so loaded with bilge as to make *Playboy*'s most ardent defender despair. The lavish display of consumer goods is often sickening. Efforts to reconcile ecology and the good life reek of hypocrisy. The legal tedium that accompanies defense of drug or sex offenders can be deadening. Some of the causes it espouses contradict its liberal core. Urging motorists to break the 55-mile-an-hour speed limit is, to be charitable, irresponsible—especially for editors who are genuinely committed to environmental concerns.

When the chips are finally down, *Playboy*'s stand on women's rights and woman's dignity is untenable. Listening to Hefner rant against militant feminists—not in the late sixties, but in 1977— reveals a sudden and ugly Dr. Hyde. He does not understand what has happened to women and society, and he does not want to learn. The cloak of his liberalism falls as easily as his pajamas. And somehow all the money his foundation has given to women's causes, the women writers he has published and furthered, and the careers open to women in his corporation don't make up for his hard-line stand, for his failure to grasp the deeper reality of feminist outrage.

For Hefner, women remain the objects of men's pleasure. Sex is an imperative. Eros may be struggling for a place in *Playboy*'s pages, but hasn't found it yet, though in all fairness Kretchmer is trying to make one.

Good sex remains the Holy Grail. Unless you are wholly under-sexed, you cannot come away from *Playboy* without feeling, "Shouldn't I be having sex now?" The pressures of sexual conformity are huge. Options exist only in the variety of sexual experience, not in its narrowing, or, God forbid, in chastity or partial abstinence— no matter what Hefner and Lehrman say to the contrary. There is never any "counterthinking" in matters of sex; no argument for the joy of fidelity, or the closeness between man and woman without penetration and orgasm. Tenderness is noticeable chiefly in its ab-sence, despite Hefner's vigorous espousal of "romanticism." What he really means is the Saturday triple feature at Loew's Orpheum around 1941.

Given all that, however, and the occasional trendiness, the fre-quent vulgarity, the magazine's continuing ignorance of economics and foreign affairs, the know-it-all tenor of so much of *Playboy*'s prose, no intelligent reader can do without it and pretend to any serious understanding about the United States. Some issues are must reading. *Playboy* is a mirror of the culture: good, bad, or indifferent.

Agree with it or not, moreover, Playboy remains one of the few bully pulpits left in a nation increasingly fractious and fragile, grow-ingly unsure and uncertain of what it is and where it is headed. The forum *Playboy* offers is a cultural and political asset. On it, Hefner has become a genuine folk hero. His inarticulateness, his stargazing, his celebrity collecting, his eccentricities, his public vulnerability, even his messianic streak, make him endearing. For many young Americans, "Hef" and his life-style are the stuff dreams are made of, much the same way the films of the 1930s were for the young Hefner. Basically, Hef is seen as a good guy, a regular guy, even a friend by the millions who follow his life. He remains an endlessly fascinating parlor game. In a way, he has become part of the American myth, the basic contradiction.

He can be a gentle and courteous man with the good manners born of genuine kindness more than of breeding. He cares about his fellow man, and he often puts his money where his mouth is. He takes risks. He has survived. He has influenced the culture, and chances are that he will continue to influence it. He has already made the needed preparations for the transition so that Christie Hefner can one day take over and run the company. Christie seems ready. After several years of working for the corporation, she says she is willing to make it a career. If she does, her rule of the empire may prove the ultimate irony: The most tarred and feathered symbol of male chauvinism will hand the keys of power to a confidently liberated woman of whom he is so fiercely proud that he nearly bursts when he talks of her. Hefner the father is one of the nicer sides of the man. This woman is no object, no thing, somebody to be stuffed in a secretarial pool. He fears only that in starting a woman's magazine, as Christie had wanted to, she will limit herself too much and not grow enough.

Hefner need have no fears. At twenty-five, his daughter has a steely mind, an awesome amount of self-assurance and determination, the custom of power, an inbred sense of authority, and the will to command. She is so bright and so quick and so articulate that her mind almost hides her startling good looks (which do intrude periodically on conversation). If Derick Daniels can make Playboy prosper over the next decade, Christie Hefner may emerge as the most powerful woman in America, mistress of a vast communications empire, molder of public opinion and shaper of life-styles. And she will hold this power over millions of men.

A List of Sources

Chapter 1

Conti, Lou. "Frisco—Gateway to Sin." *Men,* March, 1952, p. 4.

Dubois, Larry. *"Playboy* Interview: Hugh M. Hefner." *Playboy,* Vol. 21, January, 1974, p. 63.

Friedman, Bruce Jay. "True Adventures of a Man's Pulp Editor." *Rolling Stone,* October, 1975, p. 45.

Kogon, Eugen. "A Thousand Ways to Kill a Man." *Men,* June, 1952, p. 25.

"Marilyn Monroe." *Playboy,* Vol. 1, December, 1953, p. 17.

"Table of Content." *Men,* March, 1952, p. 4.

Untitled Editorial Statement. *Playboy,* Vol. 1, December, 1953.

Chapter 2

Brady, Frank. *Hefner.* First edition. New York: Macmillan, 1974, p. 112.

Crosby, John. "It's Like This with TV." *Playboy,* Vol. 5, June, 1957, p. 23.

Feather, Leonard. "Rock 'n Roll." *Playboy,* Vol. 5, June, 1957, p. 19.

Gold, Herbert, Boal, Sam, and Clad, Noel. "The Beat Mystique." *Playboy,* Vol. 5, February, 1958, p. 21.

Ginzburg, Ralph. "Cult of the Aged Leader." *Playboy,* Vol. 6, August, 1959, p. 59.

Sobran, M. J. "The Sage and Serious Doctrine of Hugh Hefner." *National Review,* Vol. XXVI, No. 5, February 1, 1974, p. 133.

"The Contaminators. A Statement by the Editors of *Playboy." Playboy,* Vol. 6, October, 1959, p. 38.

"What Is a Playboy?" *Playboy,* Vol. 3, April, 1956.

Chapter 3

Birmingham, Frederic. "Spring House Party." *Playboy,* Vol. 5, No. 5, May, 1958, p. 31.

"Playbill." *Playboy,* Vol. 6, June, 1957, p. 3.

Rutherford, Blake. "Ivy in Action." *Playboy,* Vol. 4, July, 1957, p. 20.

Rutherford, Blake. "Formal Forecast: The Return to Black." *Playboy,* Vol. 5, January, 1958, p. 60.

Rutherford, Blake. "Fashion Afoot." *Playboy,* Vol. 6, March, 1959, p. 39.

Chapter 4

Lukas, J. Anthony. "The 'Alternative Life-Style' of Playboys and Playmates." *The New York Times Magazine,* June 11, 1972, p. 7.

Mailer, Norman. *The Presidential Papers.* Second impression. New York: G. P. Putnam's Sons, 1963.

"*Playboy* Holds Key to Night Club Success." *Business Week,* June 25, 1966, pp. 89–90.

"*Playboy* on the Town in London." *Playboy,* Vol. 13, December, 1966, p. 148.

"The World's Most Beautiful Walkout." *VIP, The Playboy Club Magazine,* Fall, 1975, No. 47, p. 8.

Chapter 5

"An Infinite Number of Monkeys." *The Christian Century,* August 28, 1963, p. 1062.

Cox, Harvey. "*Playboy's* Doctrine of the Male." *Christianity and Crisis, a Christian Journal of Opinion,* May, 1961, pp. 56–60.

DeMott, Benjamin. "The Anatomy of *Playboy.*" *Commentary,* August, 1962, pp. 111–119.

Evans, J. Claude. "The *Playboy* Philosophy." *The Catholic World,* October, 1964, pp. 42–48.

Fiedler, Leslie. "The Literati of the Four Letter Word." *Playboy,* Vol. 6, June, 1961, p. 85.

Hefner, Hugh M. "The *Playboy* Philosophy." *Playboy,* Vol. 9, December, 1962.

Hefner, Hugh M. "The *Playboy* Philosophy, Part IV, Installment 21." Chicago: HMH Publishing Co., 1964–65, p. 183.

"Hemingway Speaks His Mind." *Playboy,* Vol. 8, January, 1961, p. 55.

Kazin, Alfred. "The Love Cult." *Playboy,* Vol. 9, March, 1962, p. 62.

Miller, Henry. "I Defy You." *Playboy,* Vol. 9, January, 1962, p. 102.

Peterson, Theodore. "*Playboy* and the Preachers." *Columbia Journalism Review,* Spring, 1966, p. 32.

"*Playboy* Panel: Sex and Censorship in Literature and the Arts." *Playboy,* Vol. 8, July, 1961, p. 27.

"*Playboy* Panel: The Womanization of America." *Playboy,* Vol. 9, June, 1962, p. 43.

"*Playboy* Panel: Religion and the New Morality." *Playboy,* Vol. 14, June, 1967, p. 55.

Spectorsky, A. C. "*Playboy* and Its Readers." *Commentary,* January, 1963, pp. 71–72.

"The Pursuit of Hedonism." *Time,* Vol. 89, No. 9, March 3, 1967, pp. 76–82.

Chapter 6

"Playboy Mansion West." *Playboy,* Vol. 22, January, 1975, p. 94.

Chapter 7

Galbraith, John Kenneth. "Resolving Our Vietnam Problem." *Playboy,* Vol. 14, December, 1967, p. 139.

Harrington, Alan. "A Novelist's Personal Experience." *Playboy,* Vol. 10, November, 1963, p. 84.

Hentoff, Nat. "Through the Racial Looking Glass." *Playboy,* Vol. 9, July, 1962, p. 64.

Huxley, Aldous. "A Philosopher's Visionary Prediction." *Playboy,* Vol. 10, November, 1963, p. 84.

Masters, R. E. L. "Sex, Ecstacy and the Psychedelic Drugs." *Playboy,* Vol. 14, November, 1967, p. 94.

"*Playboy* Interview: Miles Davis." *Playboy,* Vol. 9, September, 1962, p. 57.

"*Playboy* Interview: Martin Luther King." *Playboy,* Vol. 12, January, 1965, p. 65.

"*Playboy* Interview: Timothy Leary." *Playboy,* Vol. 13, September, 1966, p. 93.

"*Playboy* Interview: Malcolm X." *Playboy,* Vol. 10, May, 1963, p. 53.

"*Playboy* Interview: George McGovern." *Playboy,* Vol. 18, August, 1971, p. 55.

"*Playboy* Interview: Jawaharlal Nehru." *Playboy,* Vol. 10, October, 1963, p. 51.

"*Playboy* Interview: George Lincoln Rockwell." *Playboy,* Vol. 13, April, 1966, p. 71.

"*Playboy* Interview: Bertrand Russell." *Playboy,* Vol. 10, March, 1963, p. 41.

"*Playboy* Interview: Ayn Rand." *Playboy,* Vol. 11, March, 1964, p. 35.

"*Playboy* Interview: Frank Sinatra." *Playboy,* Vol. 10, February, 1963, p. 35.

"*Playboy* Interview: Norman Thomas." *Playboy,* Vol. 13, November, 1966, p. 71.

"*Playboy* Interview: Arnold Toynbee." *Playboy,* Vol. 14, April, 1967, p. 57.

"*Playboy* Panel: Business Ethics and Morality—Discussion." *Playboy,* Vol. 9, November, 1962, p. 47.

Wakefield, Dan. "The Prodigal Powers of Pot." *Playboy,* Vol. 9, August, 1962, p. 51.

Wakefield, Dan. "A Reporter's Objective View." *Playboy,* Vol. 10, November, 1963, p. 84.

Chapter 9

Haveman, Ernest. "The Sex Institute." *Playboy,* Vol. 12, September, 1965, p. 139.

Hefner, Hugh M. *The Playboy Philosophy, Part I, Installment 1.* Chicago: HMH Publishing Co., 1962, p. 4.

Hefner, Hugh M. *The Playboy Philosophy, Part I, Installment 7.* Chicago: HMH Publishing Co., 1963, p. 47.

Hunt, Merton. "Sexual Behavior in the 1970's." *Playboy,* Vol. 20, October, 1973, p. 84.

Mano, D. Keith. "Tom Swift Is Alive and Well and Making Dildos." *Playboy,* Vol. 25, March, 1978, p. 132.

May, Rollo. *Love and Will.* New York: W. W. Norton, 1969.

Moore, Pamela. "Love in the Dark." *Playboy,* Vol. 4, February, 1957, p. 55.

"*Playboy* Interview: Dr. Mary Calderone." *Playboy,* Vol. 17, April, 1970, p. 63.

"*Playboy* Interview: Masters and Johnson." *Playboy,* Vol. 15, May, 1968, p. 67.

"Playboy Panel: New Sexual Life Styles." *Playboy,* Vol. 20, September, 1973, p. 73.

"Playbill." *Playboy,* Vol. 4, February, 1957, pp. 3–4.

Pomeroy, Wardell B. "What Is Normal?" *Playboy,* Vol. 12, March, 1965, p. 97.

Chapter 10

Braudy, Susan. "The Article I Wrote That *Playboy* Wouldn't Print." *Glamour,* May, 1971, p. 202.

Friedan, Betty. *It Changed My Life.* New York: Random House, 1976, p. 157.

Hunt, Morton M. "Up Against the Wall, Male Chauvinist Pig!" *Playboy,* Vol. 17, May, 1970, p. 94.

"Playboy Interview: Germaine Greer." *Playboy,* Vol. 19, January, 1972, p. 61.

Reply to Reader's Letter. *Playboy,* Vol. 17, April, 1970, p. 60.

Steinem, Gloria. "What *Playboy* Doesn't Know About Women Could Fill a Book." *McCalls,* Vol. XCVIII, No. 1, October, 1970, p. 76.

Chapter 11

"Big Problems for *Playboy*'s Empire." *Business Week,* April, 13, 1974, p. 74.

Cappo, Joe. "Hefner's Hutch Not Without Its Woes." *Chicago Daily News,* September, 10, 1974, p. 28.

Dougherty, Philip H. "Advertising." *The New York Times,* October 31, 1975.

Farrell, William E. "Hefner Sees Bright Future for *Playboy* Empire Despite Critics." *The New York Times,* March 11, 1974, p. 42.

Greene, Bob. "Column." *Chicago Sun-Times,* December, 17, 1974.

Klein, Frederick, and Laing, Jonathan. *"Playboy*'s Slide." *The Wall Street Journal,* April 13, 1976, p. 1.

Nelson, Bryce. *"Playboy* Faces Naked Truth on Revenues." *Los Angeles Times,* April 8, 1975, p. 1.

Phillips, Richard, and O'Brien, John. *"Playboy* Mansion Guests Suspected." *The Chicago Tribune,* December 8, 1974, p. 1.

"Playboy Puts a Glint in the Admen's Eyes." *Business Week,* June 28, 1969, p. 142.

Rhodes, Richard. "A Very Expensive High." *Playboy,* Vol. 22, January, 1975, p. 131.

Smith, Lee. *"Playboy* After Hefner." *Dun's Review,* Vol. 103, No. 2, February, 1974, p. 45.

Chapter 12

Golson, G. Barry. "When Carter and *Playboy* Spoke in Plains." *The New York Times,* September 30, 1976.

Pound, Ezra. "Atthis." *Playboy,* Vol. 22, October, 1975.

Will, George F. "That Lusty Nonsense." *Washington Post,* September 30, 1976, p. A27.

Index

Spectorsky, Auguste Comte, 37–41, 43,
44, 45, 48, 50, 51, 52, 58, 61, 64, 88,
89, 93, 95, 100, 101–2, 105, 117, 118,
119, 121, 122, 123, 124, 125, 126, 129,
131, 136, 147, 148, 161, 168, 169,
170–71, 172, 173, 174, 175–82, 184–
88, 189–91, 192–93, 194, 252, 270,
281, 286, 287, 299, 303, 305; *Exurba-
nites, The,* 37, 38, 170, 171
Spock, Benjamin, 160, 208
Staebler, Tom, 294
Steinbeck, John, 50
Steinem, Gloria, 76–78, 226, 227, 233,
239–41
Stevenson, Adlai, 43
Strage, Mark, 44–45
Stroup, R. Keith, 263, 266
Stuart, Mary Ann, 242, 246
Swados, Harvey, 46
Swank, 8, 38

Tajari, Vincent J., 45, 293–94
Talese, Gay, 198, 217
Tannenbaum, Marc, 109, 113
Taylor, M. J., 279, 280, 283
Templeton, Lee, 281
Terkel, Studs, 188
Thomas, Norman, 53, 141, 157, 159
Thompson, James, 265, 266, 302
Time, 29, 49, 66, 102, 103, 178, 243,
287, 292
Tiny Tim, 308
Titter, 7
Todd, Richard, 188
Toffler, Alvin, 147–49, 152–53
Tompkins, Calvin, 117
Toynbee, Arnold, 52, 157–58
Trelease, Julia, 229, 230, 244–45
Trillin, Calvin, 188
Trilling, Lionel, 39, 89
Troobnik, Eugene, 168
Truffaut, François, 304
Trumbo, Dalton, 188

Trump, 250
Tynan, Kenneth, 159, 187, 188

U.S. Supreme Court, 220, 221
Urey, Harold C., 53
Urry, Michelle, 242, 245–47, 308

Van Gelder, Lindsay, 227
Vietnam war, 153, 156–65, 172, 175,
183, 186, 188, 240, 288
Viorst, Milton, 163
VIP, 84
von Braun, Wernher, 308
Vonnegut, Kurt, 190
Vonnegut, Mark, 300

Wakefield, Dan, 143–44
Wallace, George, 138, 140
Wallace, Lois, 226
Wallace, Mike, 152
Wall Street Journal, 276–77
Warhol, Andy, 226
Watergate, 288
Wax, Sheldon, 89, 100, 169, 183, 187,
191–92, 193, 235–36, 294
Welch, Robert, 213
Welles, Orson, 152
Wicker, Tom, 162, 183–84, 188
Wilder, Billy, 151
Will, George, 302, 306–07, 309
Wills, Garry, 112, 288
Winters, Jonathan, 29, 91
Wirtz, Arthur, 71, 72
WITCH, 227
Wodehouse, P. G., 50, 57–58, 180
Wolfe, Tom, 48, 288, 301
Women's liberation movement, 225–47
Wylie, Philip, 50

Young, Andrew, 300, 306–07

Zilbergeld, Bernie, 218